McGRAW-HILL SERIES IN HISTORY

RALPH E. TURNER, *Consulting Editor*

The World in Crisis

POLITICAL AND SOCIAL MOVEMENTS IN THE TWENTIETH CENTURY

MCGRAW-HILL SERIES IN HISTORY

RALPH E. TURNER, *Consulting Editor*

THE WORLD IN CRISIS

Political and Social Movements
in the Twentieth Century

J. SALWYN SCHAPIRO

Professor of History, Emeritus
The City College of New York

FIRST EDITION

McGRAW-HILL BOOK COMPANY, INC.

NEW YORK   TORONTO   LONDON · 1950

THE WORLD IN CRISIS

Preface

The modern world broke in two as a result of the First World War and the Russian Revolution of 1917. This division became complete with the Second World War and its aftermath. One part, the West, has continued to maintain the libertarian principles inherited from the nineteenth century, whereas the other part, the East, has rejected them by establishing a new order based on totalitarian dictatorship. Soviet Russia has vowed to destroy democracy and to establish totalitarianism everywhere, as evidenced by the cold war that she has launched against the Western democracies. This division in the mid-twentieth century is both wide and deep, and every attempt to bring about "one world" has thus far failed. As a consequence, fear of a third world war, more devastating than the two previous ones, is prevalent. That is the world in crisis.

World wars and world revolutions have precipitated this crisis by accelerating tendencies already in existence. What were these tendencies? How were they accelerated? This book endeavors to answer these questions by analyzing the political, social, and economic movements that arose during the first half of the twentieth century. Into the analyses of these movements is woven background historical material, explaining how they came into being, how they have operated, what problems they have created, and what has been done to solve these problems. Events are woven meaningfully into this pattern, rather than told as narrative history. The book further endeavors to explain how and why democracy ceased to be purely political and sought to apply its egalitarian principles to the social and economic order; how and why nationalism, by upholding the sovereign political state, was out of harmony with the international economic order; how

v

and why colonial imperialism was doomed with the rise of political consciousness in the Orient; and how and why the economic
system, based on laissez-faire capitalism, could not meet the
rising demand for security. The chapter on totalitarianism, in
both its Fascist and Communist forms, analyzes the background
and ideological basis of this new movement; and the succeeding
chapters, dealing with Germany and Russia, explain how totalitarianism inspired these states to challenge the existing world
order by precipitating conflicts on a world-wide scale. The chapter on the United States of America deals with the emergence of
that nation as the greatest power in the world, and as the leading
champion of democracy against totalitarian dictatorship. Finally,
the book takes up the great problem confronting the world today, world peace, and the many efforts to solve it.

The purpose of the author in writing this book was to enable
those who are interested in the problems of our day to obtain an
historic perspective and an understanding of events that are now
shaping the future of mankind. The book endeavors to give
some direction to those who have been overwhelmed with confusion by the rapid succession of critical events. Briefly, it aims to
orient the reader in giving intelligible answers to the questions:
Where are we? How did we get here? Where are we going?

In his preparation the author has had the assistance of his wife,
Kathrine. She has been more than an assistant; to some extent
she has been his collaborator, who participated in the planning,
in the organization, and in the final preparation of this book. In
all gratitude, the author hereby acknowledges his debt to Kathrine Kerestesy Schapiro.

J. SALWYN SCHAPIRO

New York, N.Y.
August, 1950

Contents

vii

Contents

Chapter 1. What the Twentieth Century Inherited from the Nineteenth

We are now at the meridian of the twentieth century. It is already clearly evident that the twentieth is not just another century in history, but a new era in civilization like its predecessors, the thirteenth and the eighteenth centuries. What characterizes a new era of civilization is a distinctive attitude of mind toward life and life's problems that makes itself felt in almost every form of human activity. As there was once an eighteenth-century mind, there is now a twentieth-century mind that penetrates every corner of the world in varying degree, in Asia and in Africa as well as in Europe and in the Americas. More than any previous period the twentieth is the century of "one world." China and Egypt are living in the twentieth century along with France and the United States. There was no "one world" even in the cosmopolitan era of the eighteenth century. Japan and India were not in the eighteenth century along with France and England. As a consequence, the world war of the French Revolution and Napoleon had practically no effect upon Japan and India. How different was the case of the Second World War! Its outcome directly affected every part of the world, even the fate of the individual inhabitants. The personal fortune and future status of the Chinese peasant, of the Manchester cotton spinner, of the Sorbonne professor, of the New York businessman, and of the Brazilian coffee planter were in the balance, to be tipped by the side that won.

This new era was created by the almost miraculous advance of science and its offspring technology. If a mechanism can be dematerialized into a symbol, then it can be said that the radio and airplane became the symbols of the newly born one world. Time and space, which had divided and separated regions, were annihilated by these inventions. The earth became a whispering gallery, and a man's voice could be heard 'round the world. Its vast stretches were telescoped into "neighborhoods," with London about eleven hours distance from New York. The unity of mankind, "humanity," had for long been a concept entertained by philosophic thinkers. But it was the hard facts of modern industry and the cold abstractions of modern science that caused "humanity" to pass from a concept held by the enlightened few to a universally recognized reality of twentieth-century life. Isolation of any nation now meant isolation from humanity itself. A nation could not, any more than could a man, live unto itself alone and die unto itself alone. Men the world over now sought ways and means to organize their work and their institutions in accordance with the demands of the new time. Especially was this true in the field of international relations, long the field of stubborn national sovereignties, jealously guarding their independence. The two world wars of the twentieth century dramatized in a fearful manner the fact that the price of national isolation was impoverishment and ruin of the strong as well as of the weak, of the victors as well as of the vanquished. The need for a peaceful, harmonious one world became imperative if civilization was to survive.

It was "only yesterday" that man began to live in the new environment created by the Industrial Revolution. Until the beginning of the twentieth century, only Western Europe and the United States lived in the machine age; the rest of mankind continued in the agricultural and handicraft, and even in the primitive, stage. The twentieth century witnessed the growth of an industrial economy that encompassed the entire world and tied all lands together, the most backward with the most advanced. The economies of agricultural Spain and Italy grew to depend on those of industrialized Britain and Germany. When oil was discovered in Saudi Arabia, its pastoral inhabitants felt the impact of the more advanced industrial nations. As in the political, so in the economic sphere a need arose for an integrated one world.

History teaches that a great era does not suddenly appear like an unknown comet in the skies. All events in history are part of a "chain of being" in human development; hence in every era are to be found the residues of the past and the germ of the future. The twentieth century, so different from all previous periods of history, had its roots deep in the nineteenth century. And from these roots it sprouted and flowered.

What was the heritage that the twentieth century received from the nineteenth? First and foremost was the system of constitutional government and civil liberties, the fundamental tenets in all liberal systems of government, anywhere and any time. During the first half of the nineteenth century, the liberal state was greatly attenuated by the high property qualification for the franchise, which gave political control to the middle classes. Civil liberties for all and government by the wealthy few was the rule in liberal Britain, France, and America. A democratic movement began that advocated the establishment of manhood suffrage. It achieved its earliest triumph in America, where it was established in all the states, except in the South, by the middle of the nineteenth century. In Great Britain, the Reform Bills of 1832, 1867, and 1884 established virtual manhood suffrage. After many trials and tribulations, democracy at last came to France with the establishment of the Third Republic in 1875. All the other nations in Europe, except Russia, accepted the liberal state on a more or less democratic basis, more in Scandinavia and less in Germany.

Despite the great progress of democracy during the nineteenth century, it did not by any means achieve its goal. Even in those states enjoying manhood suffrage the promise of democracy had not been fulfilled because women remained without the vote. And in America many men, the Negroes in the South, were disfranchised. In some of the European nations, such as Spain, Portugal, and the Balkan states, the right to vote was limited by property and educational qualifications. One nation, Russia, continued to be an absolute monarchy by divine right, reinforced by the Cossack savagery of the Romanov dynasty. Another, Bismarckian Germany, had, in form, a liberal constitution but was, in fact, a semiautocracy. The powers of the national legislature, the *Reichstag,* elected by manhood suffrage, were so circumscribed that it functioned as a fifth wheel to the government coach. In the vast stretches of Asia democracy was all but unknown. Japan, during the seventies and eighties, established the outlines of a democratic state, but they remained only outlines. Nearly all of Asia and of Africa were divided into colonies of the European powers, and little if any self-government was permitted. All the Latin-American nations were military dictatorships in fact, though they had liberal constitutions.

The twentieth century did indeed receive a heritage of self-government from the nineteenth. And this heritage was to be greatly enlarged by the progress of democracy in many lands. But in tsarist Russia and Bismarckian Germany the twentieth century also inherited the greatest enemies of democracy in modern times. Of the two Germany was a far greater menace than was Russia. The Russian autocracy was inefficient and corrupt; moreover, it was constantly threatened by a revolutionary upheaval. At the beginning of the twentieth century, tsarism had its hands full in maintaining its existence without becoming, as in 1848, the "policeman of Europe." Not so Germany, who was able, strong, and confident of popular support of the semiautocratic system of government established by Bismarck. She was ready at all times to come to the support of reaction anywhere in Europe. Furthermore, the Germans were inspired by a racial egotism, which, given favorable circumstances, would drive them headlong on a career of conquest to dominate the Continent.

Nationalism, like democracy, constituted another part of the liberal pattern inherited from the nineteenth century. The rights of nations were advocated by liberals as the collective equivalent of the rights of man. Self-determination for a national group was regarded as the counterpart of self-government within the group. Nationalism and democracy became inseparable during the nineteenth century; the former, like the latter, made notable progress in many parts of the world. Divided peoples, such as the Germans and Italians, were unified. Subject peoples were liberated and became nations, as in the cases of the Greeks, the Belgians, the Latin Americans, the Serbs, the Rumanians, the Bulgarians, and the Montenegrins. Another type of nationalism came with the creation of the Dual Monarchy of Austria-Hungary. A partnership of two nations, the Empire of Austria and the Kingdom of Hungary, was devised by the *Ausgleich* of 1867 which granted self-government to each in domestic matters but united the two for common purposes, such as the army, navy, foreign affairs, and tariff. In the case of this Dual Monarchy, nationalism triumphed through division not through unification.

The New World, too, witnessed triumphs of nationalism. It might be asserted that the United States was "unified" by the Civil War, which settled once for all the problem of the right of a state to secede from the Federal union. The American nation was now definitely an "indestructible union" in which the states, though "indestructible," were definitely subordinate to the central government. Nationalism was recognized astonishingly enough within its very antithesis, the colonial empire, by the British North America Act of 1867. Britain initiated a new policy in relation to her colonies by establishing Canada as a Dominion; this status gave Canada almost complete power of self-government in domestic matters.

A remarkable triumph of nationalism occurred in Japan, the first truly sovereign, national state in Asia. During the short period from 1868 to 1889 a backward, feudal, hermit people was transformed into a nation on the latest Western pattern. A strong central government was established as well as uniform, national systems of law, administration, finance, and education, all on Western models. A national army and navy appeared, and aroused intensely nationalistic sentiments among the Japanese people. Before long Japanese nationalism became the object of admiration among the colonial peoples of Asia.

For all these great advances of nationalism, the problem of self-determination for many peoples remained unsolved at the end of the nineteenth century. Central and Eastern Europe, from Finland to Albania, constituted three immense cemeteries of nations: the Russian, the Hapsburg, and the Ottoman empires, wherein lay many subject peoples. Though buried for centuries, these people were not dead; they lay in a comatose condition awaiting resurrection. Nor was the problem of nationalism solved fully in Western Europe. There existed national minorities, notably the Poles and Alsatians in Germany and the Irish in Britain, who demanded autonomy and even separation. Most of Asia and nearly all of Africa continued under European rule or tutelage. However, nationalist movements appeared in these continents, notably in China, India, and Egypt, striving to eliminate every vestige of foreign control.

Religious freedom was another heritage of the twentieth from the nineteenth century. During the first half of the nineteenth century there existed two patterns of religious freedom: one, toleration, the great example of which was the English Toleration Act of 1689; and the other of equality, inaugurated by the American constitution. By religious toleration, as a system, is meant that an established church exists, recognized and supported by the state as the official faith of the nation, but freedom of worship is granted to nonmembers. By religious equality is meant that religion is a private matter of a man's conscience, not a state matter of national policy; church and state are separated and whatever support a church receives is purely voluntary.

It was the English, rather than the American, religious system that made most headway during the nineteenth century. At the beginning of the century, England maintained the established Anglican church, with toleration for the Protestant dissenters, known as "Nonconformists." Catholics, Jews, and freethinkers were allowed to worship but under heavy penalties in law and custom. Gradually toleration was extended during the nineteenth century to all believers and nonbelievers. France, by the Concordat of 1801, established a religious system similar to that of England. Catholicism was the state religion, with toleration for all other faiths. The Concordat became the prevailing model throughout Western Europe.

But the problem of religious freedom was not solved during the nineteenth century. There continued to exist large areas in the world where religious discrimination, and even persecution, was open and widespread. Russia maintained an established church, the Orthodox, with scant toleration for those who did not belong to it. Dissenters, Protestants, Roman Catholics, all suffered legal disabilities; and Jews were savagely persecuted. In Spain, Portugal, and Latin America, the Roman Catholic church was the established church; non-Catholics were permitted to worship but under severe restrictions. In India two great religious groups, Hindu and Moslem, lived in separate and mutually hostile communities. In Moslem countries, especially in Turkey, there existed a system which might be described as toleration through isolation. The various groups of non-Moslems lived in special communities where they were permitted to practice their faith—at the price of discrimination and sometimes of massacre. Even in tolerant Western Europe, religious problems continued to plague the nations. At best toleration was only a halfway house to complete religious free-

dom. The established churches did in a measure use the coercive power of the state to advance their faith and their interests.
As a consequence, hostility to the establishment became widespread in both Catholic and Protestant countries. An especially
irritating religious problem existed in Italy. A "cold war" was
waged between the pope and the Italian government because
the former refused to recognize the Italian government with its
capital in Rome, the ancient city of the popes. The twentieth
century was to solve the religious problem in many lands by
the only method that had proved successful, the American
method of separation of church and state.

Another heritage of the twentieth century from the nineteenth was imperialism. Briefly, imperialism means the rule
imposed on one people by another. In modern times imperialism has generally been associated with "colonies," backward
regions conquered and annexed by European powers and ruled
by their governments. Colonial imperialism has flourished since
the discovery of the New World, which resulted in the creation of the colonial empires of Britain, France, Spain, Portugal,
and the Netherlands. During the eighteenth and early nineteenth centuries, colonial imperialism suffered serious setbacks
through war and revolution. France lost Canada and India;
Britain, the Thirteen Colonies; and Spain and Portugal, their
colonies in the New World. Furthermore the Industrial Revolution discredited the economic restrictions imposed by mercantilism, and encouraged free and unrestricted trade between
countries, irrespective of what flag floated over them.

A great change, however, took place after 1870. The discovery
of central Africa and the opening up of eastern Asia created
new sources of raw materials, new hosts of prospective customers, new territories to conquer and to annex. A wave of
imperialism again swept the Western World, which reached out
for these advantages. France created a colonial empire far larger
than the one she had lost in the eighteenth century. Britain

added vast lands to her already great world empire. Germany and Italy made their debut as colonial powers by acquiring territories in Africa. Japan, barely out of isolation, reached out for lands on the Asiatic mainland. Russia again resumed her glacierlike drive to the Pacific and Indian oceans by reaching out for Manchuria and Turkestan. Most surprising of all was that America, born as a protest against imperialism, herself joined the imperialist drive by acquiring the Philippines and Puerto Rico.

Rivalries arose between the imperialist powers over the share of each in the colonial booty. Especially bitter were the rivalries between the old and the new imperialist powers. At the end of the nineteenth century, the new imperialism of Germany, Italy, and Japan was too weak to challenge the old imperialism of Britain and France. Colonial conflicts became an evil heritage of the twentieth century, when the new imperialist powers became sufficiently strong to throw down the gage of battle to their rivals.

Economically, the twentieth century inherited new tensions and new rivalries from the nineteenth. Britain, hampered by the momentum of an early start, was confronted by Germany, who took advantage of the latest scientific knowledge and technological inventions. Nature had played favorites by giving coal to some countries and not to others. Italy and Spain lacking sufficient coal were seriously checked in their industrial development, and became discontented with their economic lot. Far more serious, however, was the sudden appearance of new industrial giants, America, Germany, and Japan, whose economic power constituted a threat to the prosperity of the old, industrialized nations.

It was the new economy that brought into focus a new class conflict, that between the *bourgeoisie* and the working class. The old class conflict between the aristocrats and the *bourgeoisie* that had raged in Western Europe during the first part of the nineteenth century had ended in the triumph of the latter. Owing to high property qualifications for voting, the working class had no essential part in the pattern of bourgeois liberalism that flourished in Western Europe during the period 1815–1870. After 1870, however, notable changes appeared on the political scene. The workers ceased to be second-class citizens as a result of being enfranchised. With the vote came the emancipation of the trade-unions; the workers now had an economic, as well as a political, weapon with which to fight their class enemies.

The first battle was over education. Inequality in education has been the striking aspect of every social order dominated by class privilege. From the period of the Renaissance until nearly the end of the nineteenth century the propertied classes in Europe were almost entirely identical with the educated classes. This condition became even more striking during the brilliant periods of modern European culture: the Renaissance in Italy, the age of Elizabeth in England, and the age of Louis XIV in France, when the upper classes were superbly educated, refined, and sophisticated and the masses were illiterate, uncouth, and superstitious. The highly civilized and the semibarbaric then lived side by side in the same land. Regarded as a class privilege, education became an adornment of those who could pay for it. Except in the professional schools the systems and methods of education then in vogue prepared students, not for work, but for the refinements of leisure.

The advance of modern industry gave a powerful stimulus to popular education. Concentration of population in cities and of workers in factories made necessary a knowledge of reading and writing in order to facilitate rapid and easy communication, so essential under industrial conditions. An illiterate man, living in a city and working in a factory, would encounter insurmountable difficulties in his daily life. And with manhood suffrage came the need of educating the new voters for good citizenship. Today a man cannot be an intelligent citizen any more than he can be an efficient worker without the ability to read and to write. After 1870, England and France established free elementary schools and compulsory education laws. In Germany and in America elementary education became almost universal. Japan established a national system of public schools; by the end of the nineteenth century illiteracy had virtually disappeared in these countries. Though education laws were passed in Italy, they were not carried out, and large numbers of Italians remained illiterate. By the end of the nineteenth century, illiteracy had virtually disappeared in Scandinavia, Belgium, the Netherlands, and Switzerland.

Popular education, however, was a spotted heritage of the twentieth century from the nineteenth. In Western Europe there were areas of illiteracy: in Spain, Portugal, and Italy; and in America, in the Southern states. In Eastern Europe the masses of people received little or no schooling. In China, India, and Latin America the overwhelming majority of the people was illiterate. Moreover, there were no provisions anywhere, except in America, for free secondary and higher education.

It became inevitable that once the workers had become enfranchised and literate they would form political parties to further their interests. Had not the bourgeois used their political power to advance their economic interests? Could not the workers do the same by using similar methods? To answer this need, socialism made its appearance early in the nineteenth century, largely as a philosophic movement. After 1870 socialism became a militant workers movement with the organization of socialist parties in almost every country. Though world-wide in extent the socialist movement was strongest in Western Europe, where the rigid class system, a heritage from feudalism, convinced the workers that they could improve their individual lot only by improving their class as a whole. It was weak in America, where the loose class system and the great natural resources made possible an expansive capitalism unequaled in history. As a consequence, the American worker felt that his status as a wage earner was temporary; either he or his children would rise into the ranks of the property owners by taking advantage of the economic opportunities that beckoned from all sides. So why establish socialism, the aim of which was to make everyone a wage earner for all time.

Socialism in Europe had another, a revolutionary, aspect. It became heir to the tradition of *social* revolution through popular uprisings, inaugurated by the French Revolution. Again, on some "famous night," capitalism would be abolished, as was feudalism on the night of August 4, 1789. And a socialist Reign of Terror would suppress without mercy all those who would oppose the revolutionary government to be established by the proletariat. This time it would be the capitalist, despoiled of his property, who would mount the guillotine.

Socialism, both in its constitutional and revolutionary aspects, became a legacy bequeathed by the nineteenth to the twentieth century. To which would the laboring masses turn once socialism was accepted by them as the only solution of the problem of poverty? The progress of democracy during the nineteenth century augured well for the advance of constitutional socialism, which promised to solve the problems of the workers by the ordered liberties of democratic government. However, social revolution had a fascination for the radical-minded thinkers in Europe. It was to be applied in an unexpected way in a land far removed from the life and thought of Western Europe, namely, Russia.

The diplomatic heritage of the twentieth from the nineteenth century was a system of international relations based upon the balance of power. Let it be clearly understood that the balance of power was a European principle that aimed to maintain the *status quo* of the nations divided into three ranks: the great powers, the middle-sized powers, and the small powers. Any attempt of a great power to dominate Europe by aggrandizing itself at the expense of the other powers would be met by a coalition of European states to resist the aggressor. Though no general war took place in Europe from 1815 to 1914 the balance of power failed to preserve peace. Wars, civil and national, took place during every decade of this "century of peace."

As long as the principle of national sovereignty, the basis of the balance of power, was maintained, the building even of the framework of one world was well-nigh impossible. It became clear to the more farseeing that unless this principle was repudiated and a world organization with power to preserve peace was established new world wars would break out that would be far more widespread and devastating than those in the past. With the rapid advance of scientific methods of destruction humanity would face the issue of one world or none.

Despite many disappointments, optimism reigned when the twentieth century opened. Many saw the unfolding of the future in terms of the progress of the preceding century. Democratic government, national self-determination, religious toleration, and freedom of thought had made definite gains that were assured—or seemed to be so. Hopeful philosophers, like John Stuart Mill, had been convinced that in time liberal principles would encompass the entire world. And the fact that no general war had taken place for almost a century created a hopeful mood. No one, not even the most circumspect, could visualize the appearance of new forces, far more uncompromising in their hostility to peace and democracy than had ever been the absolute monarchs and privileged aristocrats of the past. These new forces, communism and fascism, were to burst forth and shatter the hopes for a peaceful, united, and free world.

Chapter 2. Capitalism and the Transition from a Liberal to a Planned Economy

ECONOMIC CONTRASTS BETWEEN THE TWENTIETH AND NINETEENTH CENTURIES

The twentieth century witnessed extraordinary changes in the capitalist system of production, distribution, and exchange. These changes were most marked where capitalism was most advanced, but they were felt even in those countries where industrialism had made little progress. As a consequence, economic methods, policies, and theories in the twentieth century stood in striking contrast with those of the nineteenth. At the root of this transformation, and to no small degree creating it, were the great discoveries in the fields of science and of technology. Little did the creators of new industrial techniques, or the discoverers of new sources of power, or the scientists who made new products in their laboratories realize the great role that they were playing.

Entirely new patterns of industrial organization and relationship arose in those countries where the new industrialism was most advanced, namely, in the United States and in Western Europe. Striking was the contrast between the fairly small factory, or mill, of the nineteenth century and the giant plant, or works, of the twentieth. The former was owned and managed by one or several individuals, or by a small group of stockholders, and employed at most a few hundred workers. But the industrial giant of the twentieth century, employing hundreds of thousands of workers, operates not only a huge plant that produces its particular product but various other plants carefully integrated to produce the materials required and the various parts needed in the manufacturing process. Often it is associated with other plants, in some cases reaching beyond national boundaries, to form pools, trusts, or cartels. The plant is administered not by the owners, *i.e.,* the stockholders, who now number hundreds of thousands, but by a new managerial class consisting of a hierarchy of officials resembling that of a government exercising tremendous powers.

As with capital, so with labor. Ineffective and powerless in the face of the industrial giant of the twentieth century became the small trade or craft union of the nineteenth century, comprising, generally, skilled manual workers in specialized trades, such as carpentering, plumbing, engineering, and tailoring. Since it had few members and a small treasury, its power was limited. In case of a strike the conflict was localized and concerned only the factory where the strikers were employed. In the place of the craft union rose the industrial union of the twentieth century, comprising all the workers, skilled and unskilled, manual and white collar, employed in the entire industry throughout the nation. An industrial union is managed by a hierarchy of labor officials, controlling a huge treasury and employing legal, economic, and political experts. In its hands lies the power to paralyze an industry, even the economy of a nation, by calling a general strike.

To cope with the many problems created by these new developments, the twentieth century witnessed a striking change in the attitude of governments toward economic activity. No longer could a government stand by inactively, as in the nineteenth century, and let nature take its course. Governments became supervisors, regulators, and active participants in economic activities. They also assumed responsibility for the welfare of the workers and the consumers. To protect consumers, laws were passed regulating the quality and the prices of essential

commodities and public services, such as the rates charged by
companies operating railways, telegraphs, telephones, gas works,
and electric power. In some countries, regulation has been super-
seded by government ownership of public utilities. To protect
workers against underpayment by unscrupulous employers, laws
were passed establishing minimum wages and maximum working hours and abolishing child labor. To protect workers against
injuries at work, laws were passed establishing standards of
safety and health. To protect workers against the hazards of insecurity in the industrial world, compulsory social insurance
laws were passed to provide subsistence during periods of sickness, disability, unemployment, and old age. To protect honest
businessmen from unscrupulous competitors and monopolies,
and stockholders from dishonest manipulators, and to ensure
the stability of the economy as a whole, business and financial
practices were to be carefully supervised and regulated.

The contrast between the economic system in the twentieth
century and that in the nineteenth is indeed striking. But that is
not the whole story. Where freedom of enterprise still exists,
it is not at all that envisaged by the great apologists of capitalism
in the nineteenth century. Ricardo and Gladstone would not
recognize the England of the Labor government with its great
advances in nationalization and social reform. And for that
matter neither would Jefferson and Jackson recognize the
America of the New Deal with its tight regulation of business
and its radical labor policies.

The collapse of an economic system, once almost universally
regarded as the most beneficial, the most enlightened, and the
most progressive of all economic systems, is indeed startling.
Was capitalism doomed to complete destruction, as its opponents, the socialists, insistently declared? Or did it contain
within itself the seeds of its own regeneration? What were the
evils of capitalism unforeseen by its upholders in the past? Were
capitalist principles universal, or were they applicable only to

those countries and at those times where and when conditions were favorable? It is important to examine in the cold light of experience the ideas and policies that the protagonists of capitalism had advocated in the rosy dawn of its advent in the early nineteenth century.

RISE OF LIBERAL CAPITALISM

Economic liberalism, or liberal capitalism, or just "capitalism," as the economic system has been called, had a life principle without which it could not function, indeed could not exist. This life principle was "freedom of trade in a free market," anywhere, anyhow, in goods, in services, in labor, and in money. Modify this principle and liberal capitalism sickens; destroy it and it dies. The greater the freedom, the greater the trade; and the greater the trade, the greater the profits, the fees, and the wages. The individual must be free to produce in order to buy and sell: free from regulations by governments, friendly or unfriendly; free from coercion by monopolistic combinations whether of capital or of labor. Logically and necessarily, the free market involved freedom of contract: between buyer and seller, between employer and employee, between landlord and tenant. *Laissez faire,* or "hands off," became the slogan of liberal capitalism wherever and whenever it appeared.

This life principle of liberal capitalism—"freedom of trade in a free market"—was of the very essence of planlessness in the most important aspect of material existence, namely, in that of production. Obviously, such planlessness would lead to anarchy of production with chaos as the inevitable outcome. Every system must have elements of stability in order to function at all, and there seemed to be none in liberal capitalism. Nevertheless, asserted its famous apologists, the classical economists **Adam Smith, David Ricardo, Thomas Robert Malthus,** and

John Stuart Mill, there was planning, invisible and intangible, yet operating surely and faultlessly, in regard to all transactions in the free market. Nature herself did the planning and what could be more desirable than nature's simple yet perfect plan? Natural law, universal, inevitable, and harmonious, asserted the classical economists, operated in the economic as in the physical world by regulating economic life through the price system, a kind of economic compass that always pointed toward the right direction in the maze of the myriad transactions in the free market. The index of prices constituted an automatic, elastic, and infallible indication of the constant shifts of the free market in the buying and selling of every commodity.

Curiously enough the price system under liberal capitalism functioned as a mechanism both for competition and for co-operation between capitalists. The changing index of prices enabled a producer to calculate the extent of his ability to lower prices in order to triumph over his competitors. At the same time it enabled all the competitors to estimate the amount of the product, the size of the investment, and the number of laborers each needed to enter the market with hope of success. By establishing a basis for economic relationship between all producers the price system brought about their cooperation in order to maintain the free market.

Economic transactions, under liberal capitalism, were not, however, entirely according to the "obvious and simple system of natural liberty." There was one "artificial" regulator, the gold standard, that stabilized the currency. Gold was a precious metal that varied little in value, and was therefore universally recognized and accepted. Early in the nineteenth century, Britain adopted the gold standard, and her example was later followed by almost every other nation. The monetary unit of the national currency in every nation, the pound sterling, the dollar, the franc, equaled a definite weight of gold. But the prestige of the British pound sterling was such that it became a universal currency in relation to which all other currencies were valued. Gold stabilized international trade by creating a universally recognized standard of adjusting payments between nations. By providing an international means of payment the "golden international" gave assurance that each nation had the means to meet its foreign obligations.

Liberal capitalism found its pioneer in England. During the second half of the eighteenth century, England was the only country that had something approaching a free market. Within its natural boundaries there were no internal tariffs to hinder the transit of goods from one district to another. Feudal dues and services were virtually nonexistent, and serfdom had entirely disappeared. Mercantilism persisted but in a decayed form; its restrictions were honored more in the breach than in the observance. Quite otherwise was the situation elsewhere in Europe. Tariffs, both high and complicated, existed between the various provinces in united France and in united Spain, and between the various states in divided Germany and in divided Italy. Feudalism and mercantilism were still powerful forces in these nations. Despite the advantages that Britain then possessed in having a plentiful supply of capital, of labor, and of natural resources in coal and iron, it is doubtful whether she would have made much progress industrially were it not for the free internal market which gave her the opportunity to utilize these advantages to the very fullest.

As the pioneer of the free market, England sought to enlarge its area from the national to the international sphere. The relics of mercantilism, especially the Navigation Laws restricting shipping, were gradually abolished early in the nineteenth century. In the forties of the same century, Britain dealt a death blow to the very heart of mercantilism, the tariff system, by repealing the Corn Laws, which restricted the importation of foodstuffs. Free trade with all the world was the new British policy. In principle, it was based on the division of labor, fundamental in the capitalist system of production. In production, each worker did only a part, often very small, in making an article. In industry each factory made one product, and only one product. So in commerce, argued the free traders, each nation should concentrate on those products that geographical situation, skill of inhabitants, and national traditions enabled it to produce the cheapest. France should, therefore, concentrate among other products on silks; England, on cottons; the United States, on tobacco and raw cotton; and Russia, on wheat and lumber. If all nations did this and then exchanged their products freely in a system of multilateral trade, all the world would benefit from a large market and from low prices.

A free world market became the gospel of the classical economists and of their disciples in politics, John Bright and Richard Cobden, leaders in what was called the Manchester School. Economic policies in conformity with natural law could lead only to beneficent results. Was not the harmony and universality of nature the very model of beneficence to all mankind? Once "nature's simple plan" was applied to economic life, poverty would be abolished by the greatest possible output at the cheapest possible prices, freely bought and freely sold in a free world market. War, too, would be abolished by the elimination of tariffs, a species of "cold wars" which encouraged national rivalries, thereby heightening national antipathies which inevitably led to aggression and war. There was something unique in the *Weltanschauung* of the British free traders. For once men dealing with the hardest of hard facts in human relations, business, dreamed dreams and saw visions of universal happiness not in a far-off imaginary utopia, but in the matter-of-fact world here and now.

What followed the adoption of free trade was something unprecedented in man's history, a genuine world economy. To a considerable degree there existed an unrestricted movement across national boundaries of raw materials, foodstuffs, manufactures, labor in the form of immigration, and capital in the form of foreign investment. During the period 1850–1880, the golden age of liberal capitalism, Britain rose to dizzy heights of prosperity. On this small island pivoted the economic life of the world. Britain became the workshop, the forge, the shipper, the banker, the insurance broker, and the commission merchant of the world. In commerce Britain was something unique in history, an international trading concern with doors wide open to all trade from and to anywhere. Her exports were in the main cheap manufactures and coal, her one great natural resource; and her imports were chiefly foods and raw materials. In the seventies Britain became the first industrialized nation in history in that a majority of her people lived from commerce and industry, not from agriculture and the handicrafts. Britain produced primarily for the world, not for the domestic market; hence, cheapness of production was all-essential to her in order to win out against competitors in the world market. She achieved this advantage by the extensive use of machinery and by long hours and low wages of labor. It was in Britain that a new ruling class, the capitalists, first appeared, whose wealth was far greater and whose power was far broader than that of the old, landed aristocracy. Their prosperity was regarded as being synonymous with national prosperity, and their interests with those of the community. Profits were regarded as the measuring rod of the general welfare. When profits were high, the laborer had more work and higher wages; the farmer, better prices; the landlord, higher rents; and the shopkeepers, more and better business. When profits were low, poverty, destitution, bankruptcy, and unemployment stalked through the land.

It became almost a universal belief that capitalism could take root only where a free market was established and would advance only as this market was extended. Britain took the lead, and other nations followed readily. The first and all-essential step was to establish a free national market. In the new nation

that now arose, the United States, a free-trade area was created
that grew ever larger as new states entered the Union. The desire to abolish the tariffs of the Thirteen States had not been
least among the causes for the adoption of the American Federal
Constitution. In France the French Revolution established a
free, national market by abolishing all internal tariffs, by suppressing feudalism, and by dissolving the mercantilist guilds and
corporations. Almost two generations before it was unified politically Germany had been unified economically. Feudalism
was abolished during the first decade of the nineteenth century.
During the third decade, the famous Zollverein was created to
establish a free-trade area in nearly all the German states. In
1871, united Germany put the political seal on the free-trade
area of the Zollverein. As steps toward political unification
were taken in Italy, the free-trade area became ever larger. It
became nation-wide when, in 1870, Italy became a fully united
nation.

Central and Eastern Europe lagged behind Western Europe
in the movement for a free market. Not until 1848 was feudalism abolished in the Hapsburg dominions; and not until 1867,
with the establishment of the Dual Monarchy, was a nation-
wide free-trade area realized. The emancipation of the serfs in
the sixties created a favorable terrain in Russia for the introduction of capitalism, which soon followed. There now existed a
plentiful supply of free, mobile labor without which the capitalist system of production could not function. This was equally
true of the South in the United States, where industrialization
became possible only after the abolition of slavery. Nothing even
remotely resembling a free market then existed in Asia and
Africa. The export of British capital to India, which became
noticeable about the middle of the nineteenth century, marked
the beginning of capitalism in that ancient land.

The resounding success of liberal capitalism in Britain inspired other nations to adopt its principles. For once practical

business policies vindicated abstract economic theories, and the vindication was in the tangible form of hard cash, and plenty of it. Toward 1870 the various nations began revising their tariff policies in the direction of *international* free trade. France took the lead in the famous Cobden treaty with England (1859) that drastically reduced the duties on English imports. Prussia, in 1862, entered into a tariff treaty with France on the model of the Cobden treaty. Prussia's move in the direction of free trade brought all its fellow members in the Zollverein into line. The United States, almost from its very inception, had adopted a high tariff policy. But, as industry advanced, the principles of liberal capitalism became widespread. A movement for tariff reform began, which resulted in the adoption of the tariff of 1857, the lowest since the "tariff of abominations," enacted in 1828. An economic world order was emerging that inevitably would be followed by a political world order. Mankind seemed destined to be united by the strongest bonds of economic well-being, which promised not only prosperity but universal harmony and peace. This was the Manchester dream of a new world order.

For a time the dream was realized. Liberal capitalism, with its drive for "free trade in a free market," went on from triumph to triumph bringing prosperity to the nations that had adopted it. The products of the entire nation came freely to every local market, and the products of each nation circulated with greater freedom than ever before throughout the world. There existed not only a free movement of goods but also a free movement of labor through unrestricted immigration and a free movement of capital through foreign investments. A genuine world economy had actually appeared for the first time in history as a result of the web of economic relations created by the international division of labor. The great advance of technology created an abundance of manufactures, food, and raw materials. Greater production was followed by a rise in the living standards of the middle and working classes. And the possibility of ever greater production held out prospects of still greater prosperity for individuals, classes, and nations.

THE NEW INDUSTRIAL REVOLUTION

Liberal capitalism was, however, destined to be destroyed by the very technique that had created it—the machine process. Once installed, the machine gave an impetus to production that increased with accelerating speed. Ever greater necessities became the mother of ever greater inventions. So marked was the improvement of the machine process that, toward the end of the nineteenth century, a new Industrial Revolution began, introducing economic changes as great as those introduced at the end of the eighteenth century by the old Industrial Revolution.

The new Industrial Revolution originated in Germany and in America. Germany contributed the application of science, notably chemistry, to industry. America contributed a new technology, called "mass production," or the organization of workers, machines, and materials in one productive whole on the "assembly line." Nature now had a rival in the production of raw materials, the laboratory, from which came oil, rubber, dyes, and new synthetic materials, such as rayon, and plastics. From the laboratory also came new methods of producing manufactured articles better and cheaper. Abundant production now became possible with a minimum of human labor.

The machine itself underwent a revolution. No longer was the machine, as formerly, a more efficient tool, driven by steam power and operated by a worker to produce more goods than he could with a hand tool. It became more complicated, more refined, more rapid, more powerful, and, most important of all, automatic, operating almost without human aid. The prime function of the machine has been to abolish human labor in order to liberate man from backbreaking toil that has been his lot since his very appearance. Today the heaviest tasks of lifting, pulling, pushing, carrying, and hammering are largely done by automatic machinery. As a consequence, the number of manual workers, skilled and unskilled, relative to the population of an industrialized nation has actually declined.

A new source of power, oil, greatly accelerated the progress of the new Industrial Revolution. It was first discovered in Pennsylvania about the middle of the nineteenth century but it was not refined for industrial use until much later. As the invention of the steam engine had made coal vitally important for the progress of the old Industrial Revolution, the invention of the internal-combustion engine made oil vitally important for the progress of the new Industrial Revolution. From crude oil was derived gasoline. Without gasoline the new means of transportation, the automobile and airplane, would have been impossible. Without oil the new Diesel engine in land and water transportation could not be operated. Oil became as vital a necessity in the twentieth century as coal had been in the nineteenth. Without a plentiful supply of oil a nation could make but little progress in the economic world of today.

A new form of power, electricity, came into prominent use during the new Industrial Revolution. Its substitution for steam marked the advent of a new power age. Electricity was "power devoid of bulk," available in any quantity where and when wanted, easy to control and to regulate, and operating machines with speed, steadiness, and smoothness. Electric power was received through wires from a plant situated almost any distance away, which generated power either from coal or from hydroelectric stations created by the damming of rapid streams. It gave freedom of movement to the factory, which now could be built in places most advantageous to the supply of raw materials and of labor.

As a result of technological progress, in agriculture as well as in industry, the production of goods and of food became so prodigious as to seem miraculous. It was best seen in America where the machine was omnipresent in industry, agriculture, and even in commerce. Production increased enormously despite the reduction in the number of manual laborers and in the hours of labor. Food production especially increased despite the rapid decline in the rural population. It is estimated that only about one-quarter of the population of America now produces all the food, both for domestic consumption and for export.

The extraordinary production that came with the new Industrial Revolution was dramatically shown in the rapid recovery of Europe after the two world wars. Within a decade after the end of the First World War, the belligerent countries of Europe had a substantially higher level of prosperity than in 1913.[1] By 1949, only four years after the end of the Second World War, Britain and France had exceeded their industrial production of 1939. By contrast, it had taken Germany almost a century to recover from the effects of the Thirty Years' War in the seventeenth century.

The new Industrial Revolution spread rapidly in all directions and in all ways. Its impact was felt in distant lands where industry had never before penetrated. The vital need of oil for the new forms of transportation, the automobile and the airplane, was the chief cause. Though the production of this new source of power increased phenomenally, many nations faced the problem of obtaining a sufficient supply. Oil was found only in a few places of the world, chiefly the United States, the Middle East, the Soviet Union, and Venezuela. Great industrial nations like Britain, Germany, and France produced none at all. Hence they had to make every effort to assure a supply by controlling places, governments, and corporations that were in possession of this precious liquid, so essential in peace and war. In reaching out for oil, the industrial nations of the West went

[1] Arthur Salter, *Recovery* (1932), 29.

into such remote places as Iran, Iraq, and Saudi Arabia, the primitive peoples of which beheld the magic and wonders arising from the new technology.

The new industrialism, however, did not remain only in the places of its origin, Germany and the United States. It spread to all parts of the world though in varying degrees: to backward Russia, the Near East, the Far East, India, South America, and even to primitive Africa. When industry was introduced into a backward country by European and American capitalists, it was of the twentieth-, not the nineteenth-century, type. The textile factories built in India, China, and Japan were of the latest model, with automatic looms run by electric power. The railways, such as the Trans-Siberian, the Baghdad, and the Cape-to-Cairo spanned an entire continent. However, most people in these lands continued to live by agriculture and the handicrafts as they had done for centuries. But all around them they felt the tremendous impact of the sudden leap from a primitive economy to the scientific industrialism of the twentieth century. The consequences were to be fateful in shaping world history.

CONSOLIDATION OF INDUSTRY

As the new Industrial Revolution progressed, the economic structure erected by liberal capitalism was being undermined. New and aggravating problems appeared, unforeseen by the classical economists who had been convinced that their principles were eternally true and that their policies would unfailingly solve whatever problems arose under modern industrialism. Toward the end of the nineteenth century new and unexpected economic problems appeared in the countries that were fairly well industrialized. These problems became more acute during the first half of the twentieth century, and created a sharp reaction against liberal capitalism. Nation after nation repudiated its principles and flouted its policies. Not only liberal capitalism but freedom of enterprise in any form was repudiated when communism triumphed in Russia and when fascism triumphed in Italy and in Germany.

What were these new economic problems? First and foremost was the consolidation of many industries into monopolies or semimonopolies that threatened to nullify the principle and practice of freedom of enterprise. This movement spread in many industrialized countries, often despite severe laws passed against them in an effort to preserve freedom of trade in a ·free market.

During the period 1815–1870, personally owned and personally managed businesses were the rule, whether they were single proprietorships, partnerships, or corporations. The capital assets of a corporation were generally not much greater than that of a partnership or of a single proprietor. Many individuals took advantage of the opportunities to go into business, as the amount of capital required was not excessive, the cost of production was calculable, credit was easily obtainable, and the market was fairly discernible.

After 1870, a change took place in the evolution of capitalism. Great consolidations of capital, or Big Business, began to displace the adventurous entrepreneur. These consolidations, known as "trusts" in America and as "cartels" in Europe, generally consisted of a number of concerns that entered into an agreement to "discipline production" by establishing unified control of the market for their products by limiting or eliminating competition among them. Consolidated industry became inevitable as a result of conditions created by the technology of the new Industrial Revolution. Business now needed large amounts of capital to finance the huge, specialized plants housing complicated machinery and scientific laboratories and employing thousands of workers and many highly trained scientists and administrators. Only large corporations could raise the necessary capital; the small ones were either eliminated or absorbed in the consolidation. The economies effected by large-scale production acted as a great stimulant to consolidation. Lower costs of production resulted in higher profits, and, moreover, enabled the consolidated industry to compete successfully in the world market.

Consolidations soon dominated entire industries. They regulated production and prices, assigned sales territory to each unit in the combination, and apportioned profits. They flouted competitive liberal capitalism, with its blind price mechanism, by their efforts to free business from the control of the market and to subject the market itself to the conscious will of businessmen. Prices were fixed not by the "higgling of the market," as under free competition, but by the decision of those who controlled the consolidation. In a competitive industry profit or loss was the lot of the competitors. But in a trust, or cartel, with its monopolistic or semimonopolistic control of the product, profits, high or low, were assured to each unit over a long period.

What greatly accelerated the movement for consolidation was "finance capitalism." So large was the amount of capital needed that it was beyond the means of even wealthy corporations. A new agent entered into the picture, the investment banker. Large issues of corporate stocks and bonds were underwritten by financial houses, such as J. P. Morgan of New York, Baring Brothers of London, and the Dresdener Bank of Berlin, that sold securities in any amount to anyone, anywhere. Not infrequently did the bonds of a corporation exceed in value those of some nations. From floating securities the bankers came to exercise great control over corporate industry. They became almost partners in the enterprise, and were members of its board of directors. In order to consolidate an industry, the bankers used the devices of the "holding company" and "interlocking directorates" by means of which various firms were in effect united. Finance capitalism, or the fusion of two great masses of capital, bank and industry, was a striking characteristic of business enterprise in the twentieth century.

The trend toward consolidation became so marked during the first half of the twentieth century that it was regarded as the central law of the evolution of capitalism. Where consolidation was possible, competition became impossible. At first consolidation took place only in those industries that required large amounts of capital, such as public utilities, mining, shipping, and the manufacture of automobiles. Later, it made inroads in many other fields, and even appeared in the retail trades when mail-order houses and chain stores made their appearance. These changes in economic life were bringing to a close the era of competitive capitalism.[2]

Consolidation of industry became most prominent in the lands where the new Industrial Revolution had its origin, America and Germany. In America during the sixties of the nineteenth century, there had been only two industrial combinations, and these were small. By the thirties of the twentieth century so great had been the advance of consolidation that the four largest firms in the iron and steel industry did about two-thirds of the business; the five largest in petroleum refining, three-fifths; and the four largest in meat packing, half.[3] It was estimated that, in 1948, 455 corporations controlled 51 per cent of American business assets.[4] In Germany, where liberal capitalism was not strongly rooted, consolidation had full and free sway. The heavy industries, such as coal, iron, steel, electric power, and shipping, were in 1914 virtual monopolies. Japan, like Germany, plunged into consolidation almost from the beginning of her industrial development. A small group of great capitalists, the Zaibatsu, in which four families were prominent, dominated the economic life of Japan. It was estimated that

[2] A. R. Burns, *The Decline of Competition* (1936), Introduction.
[3] S. H. Slichter, *The American Economy* (1948), 16.
[4] Chester Bowles, *New Leader,* June 5, 1948, 5; see p. 355.

more than half of all investments in joint stock companies were controlled by the Big Four.[5] Consolidation was slower in England, the classic land of competition. However, in the twentieth century, industry in England showed marked tendencies toward consolidation, especially in chemicals, iron, civil aviation, and steel.[6]

Consolidation proved to be so profitable that it jumped national boundaries and entered the international field. International cartels were generally limited to bulky, heavy products, such as rubber, metals, sugar, and chemicals. Those who controlled these combinations parceled out trading areas among members, fixed prices, and regulated the supply for each area. They circumvented tariffs by agreements on prices for each nation. These agreements established in many instances international private control of production, investment, trade, and prices. Most famous of the international cartels was the I. G. Farben industries of Germany, the most powerful combination in the world. It dealt in chemicals and allied products, and controlled hundreds of enterprises all over the world through a system of closely interlocking agreements.

An unexpected outcome of consolidation was the changed status of business and of property. The owner of an enterprise was now divorced from its management by the combination, as, at one time, the artisan had been divorced from his tool by machinery. The need for large amounts of capital dissipated ownership, which became hazy and intangible. What has been called the "folklore of capitalism" was the belief that the "owners" of a large business enterprise were the thousands of stockholders, most of them small and constantly changing. The stockholders generally knew little and cared less about the business

[5] G. C. Allen, The "Concentration of Economic Control in Japan," *Economic Journal*, Vol. 47 (June, 1937), 271–286.

[6] Herman Levy, *Monopolies, Cartels and Trusts in British Industry* (1927); A. F. Lucas, *Industrial Reconstruction and the Control of Competition* (1937).

that they "owned"; what concerned them almost entirely were the dividends. In reality they constituted a *rentier* class of passive recipients of income, not active participants in a business enterprise. The sole function of the many listless stockholders was to sign automatically "proxy" slips empowering the managers to do whatever they had already decided to do.[7] Those who really controlled, the "management," constituted a body of officials and an inner block of privileged stockholders who exercised their power through all sorts of devices, legal and otherwise. Often the management was self-perpetuating and constituted a closed group resembling the "guilds and corporations" in the mercantilist past.[8] Another example of the "folklore" of capitalism was that, in America, a corporation was legally a "person," entitled to all the constitutional guarantees of individual rights. Hence, any attempt by the government to control its operations was denounced as a violation of the individual's freedom of enterprise, and any attempt to tax its great profits as confiscation.

Consolidation was a blow at liberal capitalism delivered by the capitalists themselves. They forced to the wall the very entrepreneurs that had created freedom of enterprise and had been its stoutest defenders. In Germany the cartels were accepted, and even encouraged, by the government on the ground that consolidation was a necessity for German capitalists in meeting British competition in the world market. In America, where private enterprise was almost an article of faith, popular opposition to the trusts became widespread. An era of "trust busting" began that culminated in the famous Sherman anti-trust law of 1890. In the face of economic development the law availed little.

What was to be done? Here were great aggregations of eco-

[7] For the best study of this phase of capitalism, see A. A. Berle and G. C. Means, *The Modern Corporation and Private Property* (1933).

[8] *Quarterly Journal of Economics,* May, 1938, 371, 378, 381.

nomic power controlled by irresponsible groups whose policies affected the lives of millions, even the destiny of the nation itself. In the twentieth century, the democracies became alert to the abuses arising from economic despotism as they had in the nineteenth century to those arising from political despotism. Movements looking to the control of capitalism—and even to its abolition—became prominent in the nineteenth and twentieth centuries. Socialist parties appeared, in Western Europe especially, and became the recognized opposition not only to the parties in power but also to the capitalist economic order.

MALDISTRIBUTION OF WEALTH

What about the distribution of the vast wealth produced by the new Industrial Revolution? All classes benefited, though not equally, from the progress of industry, receiving ever larger shares as production increased. Profits of capital rose rapidly and greatly and so did wages—real wages—of labor, though not as rapidly and not as greatly. The poor were getting less poor, and the rich, richer. There were two indubitable, incontrovertible facts that faced economic thinkers during the twentieth century. One was that the increased prosperity of the nation came—and only could come—from increased production. And the other was that consumption did not keep pace with production, even in times of prosperity, owing to the maldistribution of wealth that denied sufficient purchasing power to the masses of people. This situation became clearly evident in the two most industrialized countries, Britain and America. During the first decade of the twentieth century it was estimated that about half of the income earned in the United Kingdom went to about 12 per cent of the population. Fully 88 per cent of the population were classified as "poor," earning just enough to keep body and soul together. Many in the large cities were even below the poverty line, and lived in constant want.[9] During the same period in America, which had the highest standard of living in the world, about 2 per cent of the population received about 12 per cent of the income.[10] In 1936, over 87 per cent of all families in the United States had an income of less than $2,500 a year, then considered necessary to maintain a family in decent comfort.[11] Far worse was the distribution of income in less industrialized lands, where production did not come up to the levels of Britain and America.

The contradiction of poverty in the midst of plenty excited widespread comment. It led to the conclusion that there must be something wrong with an economic system in which abundance produced want. There could be no valid reason for widespread poverty in the surplus economy of modern industry, as there had been in the deficit economy before the Industrial Revolution of the eighteenth century. Never was nature so prodigal in her gifts of food and raw materials. Never was science so inventive in devising machines that both increased and speeded up production. Never was man so skilled in utilizing both nature and science. And never before were governments as well organized to direct the forces of nature and the skill of man into productive channels. What was wrong? Could it be that liberal capitalism provided no method, no plan, not even an idea of a better, a juster system of distributing the wealth produced?

The contradiction between vast production and underconsumption became tragic in times of business depression. Recurring periods of prosperity and depression have been aspects of economic life since the Industrial Revolution. Depressions

[9] L. G. Chiozza, *Money, Riches and Poverty* (1912), 42.

[10] For a study of the distribution of wealth in America, see Wesley C. Mitchell (ed.), *Income in the United States—Its Amount and Distribution, 1909–18*, 2 vols. (1921–1922).

[11] C. E. Ayres, *The Divine Right of Capital* (1946), 62.

in the early days of the nineteenth century had been mild and short; hence they were slighted by the classical economists who were convinced that a recession in business was a temporary aberration and not a too important dislocation of the economic system. Economic laws would soon right matters and all would be well again. As the century advanced, what is now called the "business cycle" became a recurrent phenomenon that lasted for periods varying from three to seven years. The "business cycle" has been described as a "revival, expansion, recession, and contraction" of business. In plain English it was "boom and bust." A depression was not an aberration but a recurrent period of hard times that brought widespread misery. Businessmen were ruined; workers were unemployed; stockholders were wiped out; and banks were closed. There is no final, definite explanation of the "business cycle." The following explanation is generally accepted.[12] The advance of industry results in the growth of population and in a rising standard of living. An increased demand for goods of all kinds then arises, and a "boom" begins. In their eagerness to take full advantage of the rising prosperity producers manufacture beyond the power of the consumers to buy their products. Overproduction results because supply exceeds demand. Then a "bust" begins. Prices fall in the frantic desire of the producers to get rid of their stock; they sell below a reasonable profit, and even at a loss. Production is cut, and factories are closed. Profits are squeezed more and more as the decline goes on. The less efficient businessmen are ruined. Unemployment becomes widespread. Low prices, low wages, low interest rates, all combine then to tempt those who had survived and those who had been shrewd enough to foresee the calamity to venture forth into new enterprises. Costs of doing business are low. Outlays for wages and raw materials are at rock bottom. Bargains again tempt buyers and speculators.

[12] For the leading works on the business cycle, see W. C. Mitchell, *Business Cycles* (1927), and J. A. Schumpeter, *Business Cycles* (1939).

Once more a "boom" begins, and the cycle of "boom and bust" is complete.

The first serious depressions took place in 1847 and in 1857, chiefly in Britain, France, and America. More serious was the depression of 1873, which lasted six years and affected Western Europe and America. By far the greatest of all depressions was the one that began in 1929 and lasted almost ten years, though its most acute stage was in the first three years. The Great Depression was a veritable economic earthquake that reverberated throughout the world, bringing untold suffering to millions, even to those in backward countries. The causes of the business cycle may be obscure, but its results have been only too plain: instability, insecurity, and widespread discontent.

INROADS OF PROTECTION ON THE
FREE MARKET

Economic relations, like all others, have their contradictions. Inadvertently a nation striving for a definite objective will adopt policies that in time will defeat it. Britain certainly did all in her power to establish the "perfect market" of freedom of trade throughout the world. And, as we have seen, success attended her bold pioneering efforts. By the middle of the nineteenth century she reached a height of economic well-being, hitherto unattained by any nation in modern times.

Then followed something unique in economic history, the export of capital in large quantities. The British merchants, manufacturers, and bankers made so much money that they could not invest all of it in home industries. And they beheld in the industrially backward countries of Europe and of the New World opportunities to invest their surplus capital very profitably. By extending loans or exporting capital goods Britain began the economic fertilization of these lands.[13] The British reasoned—and for a time correctly—that the industrial development of a country would raise its standard of living and thus enable its inhabitants to buy more manufactures from and to sell more food and raw materials to Britain. Capital left Britain in the shape of machinery and came back in the shape of food and raw material. Free trade in capital went hand in hand with free trade in goods on the theory that wherever the foreigner borrowed he also bought. And thus the increased wealth of the debtor would be shared by the creditor.

The outcome of Britain's policy of exporting capital was unforeseen. It aimed to create more and better customers, but it resulted in creating more and stronger competitors. As the eldest daughter of capitalism, Britain complacently assumed that being so far ahead in the industrial race she would always stay ahead. But the dynamic nature of capitalism and the inexorable advance of science and technology introduced new methods of production and of business organization, and created new markets and new commodities. Chemistry applied to industry, mass production, new sources of power in oil, gas, and rapid streams, all combined to make new industrial athletes of hitherto backward nations who now entered the world markets. That old industrial athlete, Britain, found herself seriously handicapped. Old machinery, a heritage of the old Industrial Revolution, could not be scrapped except at great cost, and it became a hindrance to Britain in the now strenuous competition for world markets.

What followed after 1870 was a series of staggering blows

[13] L. H. Jenks, *The Migration of British Capital* (1927). In 1875, it was estimated that Britain's total foreign and imperial investments amounted to about £1,200,000,000; in 1913, to about £4,000,000,000, about half being in the British Empire. About one-quarter of England's national wealth lay outside of the nation. See G. D. H. Cole, *British Trade and Industry* (1932), 109.

at the free international market created by liberal capitalism.
The new industries, established in other lands, insisted that
they could not compete on equal terms with those long established in Britain. A demand for high tariffs to protect home industry soon made itself felt. In America, after the Civil War,
there no longer existed the necessity of appeasing the free traders of the South. A high tariff law was enacted in 1864, even
while the conflict was raging. Thereafter the tariff policy of
America became increasingly higher, and it culminated in the
very high McKinley tariff of 1890. Germany followed suit with
the famous Bismarck tariff of 1879 that reversed the free-trade
tendencies of the Zollverein by laying heavy duties on both agricultural and industrial products. France repudiated the Cobden treaty by a series of tariff laws, of which the highest was
that of 1892. Italy in 1887 and Russia in 1891 also adopted high
protective tariffs.

But the increase of production made imperative some degree
of freedom of trade. The great world market which had come
into existence could not be squeezed within the narrow confines
of a national economy. No nation, not even continental America,
could for long be contained within its home market. Accordingly, the nations adopted various devices designed to
modify, and even to circumvent, the very restrictive tariffs that
they had adopted. A common device was the "most favored nation" clause in commercial treaties, according to which one nation agreed to give another the best terms that it had given to
every other nation. Another device was the reciprocal trade
agreement, whereby the signatories agreed to a mutual reduction of duties on certain articles. Germany adopted the system
of "free ports," whereby certain great seaports were given the
right to import goods free of duty, provided these goods were
designed, not for home, but for foreign consumption. France
adopted the scheme of "assimilated tariffs," whereby goods
from her colonies were imported free of duty. A similar policy

was followed by the United States in relation to the Philippines and Puerto Rico.

When the twentieth century opened, it became noticeable that liberal capitalism had passed its meridian. However, its fundamental principles were still generally accepted, and its policies were generally followed. Freedom of enterprise continued for the businessman; freedom of occupation for the worker and professional man; and freedom of choice for the consumer. As the twentieth century advanced, liberal capitalism, however, began entering the shadow of its night. What gave the system the *coup de grâce* was the two world wars and the depression between them.

DECLINE OF LIBERAL CAPITALISM; THE FIRST WORLD WAR

Future historians will judge the two world wars not only as world conflicts but even more as constituting a world revolution. These wars resulted in disrupting the bonds that had tied nation to nation, system to system, and class to class, and set in motion new forces driving to create a new world order. Mechanized warfare in the field and total war behind the lines first appeared during the First World War. Production of munitions, of food, and of supplies generally were all essential to victory. And the battles of production in the munitions plants, in the factories, and on the farms became as important as the struggles of the armies on the field of battle. In order to speed up production, industry and agriculture were organized by the government to aid in the war effort. The government allocated raw materials, took over railways and shipping, regulated the output of farms and factories, controlled imports and exports, and, in some countries, fixed profits, prices, and wages. In these ways the state made economy the servant of war, and, for a time, ended the free play of the market. Never before 1914 had there been so much government intervention in economic life. All the principles and practices of liberal capitalism went by the board. After the war many of the government controls were removed, but a new situation had been created that could not be removed. The forces that had been undermining liberal capitalism—concentration of industry, trade barriers, business depressions—all were accelerated and accentuated when peace came. War economy had demanded standardized production; and high war profits had enabled the large concerns to become larger and more efficient in order to produce the vast quantities of goods required by the war. Gigantic industrial enterprises emerged, especially in America and in Germany, that continued to produce after the war the standardized products now in great demand. Some of these enterprises were not satisfied with being "horizontal" by controlling one industry; they became "vertical" by controlling two or more industries.

After the First World War came the Great Depression of 1929. Its chief cause lay in the disruption by the world conflict of the economic equilibrium that had been established in the world. As a consequence, currencies were depreciated, foreign investments were liquidated, international trade was restricted by higher tariffs and quotas, and foreign borrowings were greatly increased. The Depression brought unemployment on a vast scale, and many workers despaired of improving their lot or even of maintaining it; consequently they turned to communism as the only way out of their difficulty. Many ruined shopkeepers, professional men, and white-collar workers, long the staunch supporters of liberal capitalism, turned to fascism as their way of economic salvation. Some economists considered the debacle not a depression in terms of the "business cycle" but the collapse of the capitalist order itself.[14] There was a

[14] Frank Knight, "Social Science and the Political Trend," *University of Toronto Quarterly*, Vol. 3 (July, 1934), 441.

general conviction that the industrial system, now so vast, so complicated, and so vital to the welfare of everyone, was likely to bring universal ruin if left uncontrolled and undirected by the government. For the "first time in industrial history the powers of government were extensively invoked to stem the tide of depression and to stimulate recovery." [15] Industrialists, bankers, farmers, and workers all now turned to the government to subsidize business, to support the banks, to raise prices and wages, to stimulate employment through public works, and to establish social security.

Liberal capitalism was now universally discredited. Socialist parties in Britain, France, and Germany for the first time in history rose to the seats of power. They put through drastic social reforms, all based on government intervention in economic matters.[16] *Laissez faire* in America, rock-ribbed for so many years, vanished into history with the election of Franklin D. Roosevelt in 1932, and his re-election for three more terms. President Roosevelt, supported by the Congress, put through the famous New Deal, a number of radical measures of economic and social reform. The government intervened in economic matters by regulating the output and prices of agricultural products, and brought an ever-tightening control over many public utilities. Banks and stock exchanges likewise fell under government control. New laws established compulsory social insurance, minimum wages, and maximum hours for workers. Collective bargaining, whenever demanded by the workers, was made legally compulsory. These and similar radical measures put America on the high road of a planned economy in which the hazards of economic life were mitigated by an all-embracing system of securities established by the government.

Another outcome of the war was the collapse of the gold

[15] Harold G. Moulton, *Controlling Factors in Economic Development* (1949), 86.

[16] See p. 99.

standard. Owing to the necessity of purchasing foreign supplies for war purposes, England, France, and Germany were compelled to pay in gold for much of their imports. They produced little goods for export, and that little was seriously hampered in delivery by enemy action. Monetary uncertainty followed the war; and it was increased by the Great Depression, which severely curtailed foreign trade. The pound, mark, and franc sank in value as their gold backing became weaker. The gold standard was losing the power to adjust the balance of trade between nations, and monetary instability spread throughout the world. In order to stop the drain on its gold reserve, England abandoned the gold standard in 1931. France followed suit in 1936. Italy and Germany, having little gold, ignored the gold standard by resorting to barter. Even America, with the greatest of all gold reserves, seriously weakened the gold standard in 1933 by reducing the gold content of the dollar 40 per cent. The collapse of this one stable "regulator" of international commerce was a great blow to liberal capitalism, even to the capitalist system itself. Faith in the invisible and intangible economic laws as natural stabilizers and regulators of economic life had long since vanished. And now came the crumbling of the faith in its one visible and tangible regulator, the gold standard.

What undermined the capitalist system itself was the partial collapse of credit. The first blow was struck by Soviet Russia, when it repudiated its debts, foreign and domestic. Credit suffered another blow when the Allies refused to pay their huge war debts to America, a sum even greater than the foreign debts repudiated by Soviet Russia. Another great credit repudiation took place when Nazi Germany refused to pay its foreign debts and confiscated foreign investments in German commerce and industry. Confidence in the future of the capitalist system was considerably shaken with the loss of faith in the gold standard and in the credit structure.

The erosion of the free market of liberal capitalism through protective tariffs spread rapidly and widely after the First World War. With the collapse of Austria-Hungary went the great free-trade area of Central Europe. The states that emerged from its ruins exhibited their spirit of new-found independence by adopting the policy of economic nationalism. They erected high tariffs in the vain hope of becoming industrially self-sufficient. This was likewise true of the new states in Eastern Europe carved from the Russian Empire. Wherever nationalism spread, so did high tariffs, even in Asia. During the twenties and thirties, India and China adopted tariff policies which imposed rates as high and on as many articles as possible.

What about the tariff situation in the old capitalist countries Britain, France, and America? Britain now found herself a free-trade island in a protectionist ocean. She was even flooded with foreign manufactures that competed successfully with home products kept out of foreign markets by the high tariff walls. This was exasperating as well as unprofitable. It became only too evident that the former "industrial athlete" was losing out in the race with younger competitors. It was a notable event in history when Britain in 1931 abandoned her historic free-trade policy and adopted a protective tariff system. France limited imports, and America reached an all time high in her tariff policy with the enactment of the Hawley-Smoot tariff law of 1930.

High tariffs were not the only means of restricting foreign trade. New forms of limiting "free trade in a free market" appeared during the postwar era that went even farther than protective tariffs. One was the quota system, initiated by France in 1931, which was widely imitated. By a "quota" was meant that the total volume of an imported article was fixed irrespective of the duty on it. Another form of restriction was by the method of exchange control through the manipulation of the currency by government action. The currency of a nation would be devalued in order to increase exports and decrease imports. Far more comprehensive restrictions were imposed when foreign trade became a government monopoly, according to which the government bought all the imports and sold all the exports. Government monopoly of foreign trade was complete in the totalitarian dictatorships: Soviet Russia, Fascist Italy, and Nazi Germany. But, to a limited extent, democratic nations, especially Britain, resorted to the same practice.

Restrictions on the free movement of goods were accompanied by restrictions on the free movement of peoples. Under the regime of liberal capitalism during the nineteenth century, both had been fairly free. A tendency to restrict immigration became marked during the first half of the twentieth century, especially after the First World War. Severe immigration laws and quotas were adopted by the countries in the New World, notably by the United States, which effectively kept out immigrants from Europe and Asia. These restrictions created serious hardships for Germany, Italy, and Japan, which had few or no colonies. They raised the cry of *Lebensraum,* demanding colonies as outlets for their surplus population.

An economic world now appeared characterized by severe restrictions on international trade. The science and technology of the new Industrial Revolution had made imperative that each nation have access to the natural resources of the entire world. For example, in order to manufacture the best quality of steel, the most basic of all industries, a nation had to have the nickel of Canada, the chrome of Turkey, and the manganese of Russia. Again, in order to maintain high food production, a nation had to have the necessary fertilizer: the potash of Alsace, once German now French. The vast production of specialized products by great industries had to have an outlet in foreign markets. No nation, no matter how great its natural resources and how large its domestic market, was entirely self-sufficient. It must import or suffer serious, if not fatal, handicaps to its prosperity. And foreign trade being a two-way affair, a nation had to export in order to import. A conflict now appeared between an economic world that was international and a political world that was national. Some new method, some new political invention, must be devised to resolve this conflict; otherwise capitalism would sicken and die behind the very tariff walls designed to protect its health and to promote its well-being.

Highly industrialized nations, like Britain and America, felt this conflict acutely. How could they dispose of the ever-mounting mass of goods piled up behind their tariff walls? Britain sought to find a new outlet in the famous system of "imperial preference." In 1932, at the Ottawa conference, Britain, the Dominions, and India established freer trade among themselves by means of mutual and reciprocal tariff reductions on certain articles. America, too, made a step toward freer trade. In 1934, Congress passed a law approving the policy of reciprocal trade agreements, advocated by Secretary of State Cordell Hull. According to the Hull treaties, America would agree on reciprocal reduction of tariffs and other trade barriers with those foreign nations willing to accept such a treaty. The law gave the President power to lower tariffs to a maximum of 50 per cent in negotiating a trade agreement. These efforts to restore liberal capitalism achieved only moderate success.

A totally unexpected outcome of the First World War was the extinction of capitalism in Russia. When the Bolshevists came into power in November, 1917, they confiscated all productive property almost at one blow. A series of decrees destroyed capitalism, root and branch in all its forms, throughout the vast lands of Russia. A highly centralized system of planned economy was set up in which economics and politics were made one and indivisible. All economic life was planned to the minutest degree through government ownership and regulation of industry, agriculture, finance, and commerce.

Communist Russia became the spearhead of a world revolutionary movement against capitalism. It enlisted the enthusiastic support of millions who turned toward Russia in the hope of economic salvation. Many others, who detested the "dictatorship of the proletariat" with its suppression of democratic liberties, looked with friendly eyes on the "great experiment" in Eastern Europe. For the first time in history, a great state appeared that was dedicated to the destruction of capitalism and that extended powerful aid to revolutionary movements in every land.

Fear of communism seized hold of the propertied classes everywhere in Europe. In order to protect themselves against the onslaught of the communists, they supported the fascist parties as the strongest enemies of communism. This powerful backing was chiefly responsible for the triumph of Mussolini in Italy and of Hitler in Germany.[17] Once in the seat of power, however, the Fascists proved to be anything but friends and protectors of historic capitalism. The new economic system set up in Fascist Italy and in Nazi Germany, though giving lip service to the principle of private property and to the methods of capitalist production, smothered both in a web of governmental control so rigid, so minute, and so comprehensive that it was impossible to say where capitalism ended and nationalization began. Like Soviet Russia, the fascist states established foreign trade as a government monopoly; they regulated exports and imports not only by tariffs but even more by all sorts of restrictions with the object of attaining complete self-sufficiency, known as "autarchy." In order to satisfy their need for certain foreign goods, all three totalitarian states actually resorted to the primitive system of barter, and "swapped" goods instead of importing

[17] See pp. 111, 234, 235, 269.

and exporting them. Free enterprise in a free market became a mockery in Italy and Germany and a crime in Russia.

FALL OF LIBERAL CAPITALISM; THE SECOND WORLD WAR

Capitalism was at a low ebb in Europe when the Second World War broke out in 1939. This conflict was more mechanized in the field and more total behind the lines than had been the First World War. As a consequence, the controls imposed by the governments on private industry were wider and more drastic. Never was production so great! America outdid every other country, and even herself, in the production of goods. Profits were high; wages were high; and unemployment had vanished.

The war was the most devastating conflict in modern history. All the belligerent nations in Europe were in a state bordering on collapse, so great was the destruction of cities, industrial equipment, and of morale. Europe, "like the shell of a once great house, now burned out, bullet-ridden, sacked and gutted, groaned and listed as it settled on the debris of its foundations."[18] Many now despaired of the revival of the Continent that had given modern civilization to mankind.

Western Europe found itself in a new economic relation to the rest of the world. Before 1939 it had dominated the economic life of the world through its preeminence in commerce, industry, and finance. Its chief function was to process raw materials imported from abroad into manufactures, which were then exported. So lucrative was this activity that Western Europe attained a high standard of living. Its imports of cheap food and raw materials were more than balanced by exports of manufactures and by income from foreign investments and shipping.

[18] J. C. Roucek, *Contemporary Europe* (1947), 38.

Western Europe controlled about one-half of the world's international trade, about two-thirds of the world's tonnage, and most of its foreign investments. But the war disrupted the system that had functioned so long and so smoothly. Much of Europe's merchant marine was at the bottom of the sea. Most of its foreign investments were liquidated. International trade was twisted out of shape because Eastern Europe and the Far East, great centers of food and raw materials, had been devastated. Revolutions, following the war in these regions, cut the few economic ties that remained. Britain and Germany, the chief pillars of European economy, were dealt the hardest blows. Britain's losses were staggering; her assets sank to the vanishing point and her liabilities mounted sky high. Once the world's largest creditor Britain became the world's largest debtor. And Germany, truncated and impoverished, ceased to dominate the economic life of the Continent.

Was Western Europe done for? The problem of reconstruction was the problem of survival itself. Unless it was solved, social revolution, stark and foreboding, threatened to sweep from country to country. But Western Europe could not re-create its old economy; that was gone never to return. Could it create a new economy, which would enable this center of modern civilization to maintain its cultural heritage and to participate greatly in the life of the world? The natural resources of Western Europe were many and various; its population was large and efficient; and its technical knowledge, superabundant. These advantages could be utilized to bring about recovery, provided (1) the various countries in the region entered into new economic relations and (2) a new economy was established within each country.

A bold idea was proposed in responsible quarters, namely, to create a Zollverein for all Western Europe. This highly productive region consisted of separate national sovereignties, each with its own tariff. French iron and steel were protected against the competition of that of Belgium; Belgian dairy products against those of the Netherlands; British cottons against those of Italy. In this way the production of Western Europe was divided into uneconomical units, which prevented the best use of its resources. If the various states in this region united economically by removing the barriers to the free movement of goods, persons, and capital, a large free-trade area would come into existence that would create a mass market for 250,000,000 consumers with a high standard of living. So revolutionary a scheme could not, however, be adopted all at once; centuries of separate economies had built up powerful vested interests in each country that opposed the scheme. However, significant beginnings were made to establish a common economy for Western Europe. In 1947, Belgium, the Netherlands, and Luxemburg entered into a collective agreement to reduce gradually the tariff barriers between them, with the aim of establishing a common economic system for all three nations. "Benelux," the collective name for the three nations, took an historic step in the direction of a united Western Europe. Another advance was made in 1948 when the Western Union was established. This was a union of Britain, France, and the Benelux nations, who agreed to coordinate their policies in commerce, industry, and finance with the aim of creating a freer trade area.[19]

A far more important plan for the integration of Western Europe was proposed by France in 1950. This plan envisaged the pooling of the entire French and German production of coal and steel. Once established, this powerful production merger would be open to all other countries who desired to participate in it. In supreme control of the pool would be a joint authority, chosen on the basis of equality by the governments of the member nations. The flow of coal and steel between member nations would be exempted from all tariffs. The output of this pool would be offered to the whole world without discrimination

[19] See p. 403.

or exclusion, as a contribution to the improvement of living standards. Economic integration of the kind proposed would be the first decisive step to end the age-old opposition between France and Germany. War between them, according to the proposal, would become "not only unthinkable but in actual fact impossible."

After the war, the movement for freer world trade, initiated by America through the Hull treaties, received a great impetus. An imbalance of international trade had arisen because of the heavy restrictions on imports imposed by many nations in order to safeguard their gold reserves. To ameliorate this situation, a convention, representing 54 nations, met in Havana in 1948 and adopted a charter establishing economic agreements that were both comprehensive and extensive. Soviet Russia refused to attend; of her satellite states only Czechoslovakia signed the charter. The object of the Havana charter was not to reestablish the liberal capitalism of the nineteenth century but to reduce or eliminate the barriers to world trading which had arisen after the First World War. It aimed to establish equality in trade by forbidding quotas, either import or export; discriminatory taxes, regulations, and insurance rates affecting imports; and restrictions on the transit of foreign goods across the territory of a nation. Tariffs were permitted, but according to the principle of the most favored nation clause; preferential rates could be imposed only by special permission. Export subsidies were to be restricted. All the signatories agreed to devise plans to promote trade by mutually lowering tariffs. Unfortunately, however, the Havana charter was riddled with "escape clauses" that permitted barriers to continue under certain circumstances. Nevertheless, instead of the old method of seeking national prosperity by means of protective tariffs, quotas, controls, and other restrictions a new method was now envisaged, that of freer world trade through multilateral agreements. The Havana charter was ratified by only a few of the nations that had initiated it.

ECONOMIC PLANNING

Far more important were the changes in economic policy made within each country. These changes, known as "economic planning," constituted a decisive departure from the policies of liberal capitalism. In general, economic planning envisages a central agency, the government, directing the economy of the nation toward general welfare. Economists now study the extent of production and that of demand. They now know how and why changes in the volume of demand are brought about. Of great importance in these changes are the policies of the government in taxing and spending and in the contraction or expansion of bank credit. The government, therefore, holds a strategic position in directing the nation's economy. And only the government has the supreme authority and the coercive power necessary to carry out national policies. Individual capitalists and corporations have always planned their activities but they have done so primarily in their own, not in the public, interest. The government alone is fitted to carry out the objectives of national economic planning: maximum production, conservation of natural resources, full and stable employment, and social security. Economic planning has been well defined as "a process of purposeful action to attain ends which are conceived in the interests of the entire nation by means of coordinated policies which involve all groups of the people and which are applied on a national scale." [20]

The objectives of economic planning were to be carried out in Europe in the following ways, all or in part, depending upon circumstances:

1. Key industries, such as coal, iron, steel, electricity, gas, transport, and communication, were to be nationalized.

[20] Lewis L. Lorwin, *Time for Planning* (1945), 5–6.

2. There was to be government control of credit either through the nationalization or the complete regulation of banks.

3. There was to be government control and regulation of prices, wages, food production, and the output of raw materials and basic manufactures. No longer would there be reliance on the "invisible hand" that, according to liberal capitalism, guided the self-interest of capitalists toward the general good. Now the visible hand of the government was to compel capitalists to adopt policies primarily in the public interest. In effect, economic planning repudiated the price system as the sole regulator of economic life.

4. The government was to do all in its power to encourage high production in order to avoid depressions. When capital investments began to fall and production to slow down, the government was to advance money to businessmen to aid them in maintaining and expanding their enterprise.

5. The government was to make every effort to maintain full employment. The great failures of liberal capitalism had resulted in unemployment, great or small, depending on business conditions, and the nonutilization of the full capacity of industry to produce. Even in times of prosperity there existed unemployment and insufficient production. "The twentieth century is coming to regard as the greatest sin against nature and the greatest crime against society the unuse or abuse of natural and human resources—idle land, idle machines, idle men." [21] Unemployment is chiefly responsible for underconsumption, thereby creating an inadequate outlet for investment at home; hence "surplus" capital and goods are exported. Only the government can assure full employment and full production, as it did during the Second World War. How can it do so in time of peace? Only by encouraging full capacity of production. In periods of serious unemployment, especially in times of depression, the government was to embark on a policy of "compen-

[21] *Ibid.*, 257.

satory spending," by which is meant that it was to make up the deficiency of private business by building public works of all kinds. Labor on public projects would give employment to many who otherwise would be obliged to seek public relief.

6. The government was also to create an integrated system of social security, which would maintain to some degree the purchasing power of the workers, in case of personal adversity and in periods of business depression.

It is important to keep in mind that planning under a democracy differs sharply from that under a totalitarian dictatorship. Under the former some industries are nationalized; others are regulated; and still others—by far the largest sector of the national economy—continue under free, private enterprise. This is not the situation in a totalitarian dictatorship, such as Soviet Russia, where the government operates and regulates the entire economic life of the nation.

The issue of economic planning has aroused many heated controversies in the democracies. Could it be reconciled with self-government and with civil liberty? Would not a "statist" economy unloose abuses as great as, and even greater than, those under liberal capitalism? The opponents of economic planning have argued that democracy and liberal capitalism are indivisible, being the political and economic counterparts of individual freedom. They were born together; they grew up together; and they will die together. Opponents of planning are convinced that any departure from liberal capitalism, whether through communism, fascism, socialism, or even the New Deal, are steps—short or long—on the road to serfdom.

How is the average propertyless citizen, argue the champions of planning, to be protected against the great aggregations of capital under corporate control? How is he to have the security against poverty, unemployment, and destitution that the wealthy man has through the ownership of property? How are the depressions, so characteristic of capitalism, to be avoided? These liberals of the twentieth century, the economic planners, stoutly maintain that their system of reform alone can assure stability with progress; can bring security to both labor and capital in good times and in bad; and can moderate, and perhaps even abolish, the panics and depressions of the business cycle.

What of the danger to democratic liberties in a system of government regimentation, even if limited? The answer of the economic planners, whether socialist or nonsocialist, is that, if popular government and civil liberties are strictly observed, abuses would be remedied by reform, as have been other abuses in a democracy. Because of its very nature democracy secretes its own antidote to whatever ill may arise in the body politic. The state lives in a glass house in full view of the citizens; hence, its efforts, successes, and failures can be judged by the nation. What the people can give, the people can take away. Above and beyond all, the extension of government control over economic life should be gradual; and when an enterprise is nationalized, full compensation should be paid. If these conditions are strictly observed the new will be easily and peacefully absorbed with the old. Only when, as in Soviet Russia, there is a revolutionary seizure of power and a sudden transition is made from private to public ownership through wholesale confiscation of property is there the likelihood of dictatorship and the subversion of democratic liberties.

Only the government could undertake the task of economic planning. And, after the war, only the government could provide the necessary resources without which the devastated countries, especially Western Europe, could not be rehabilitated. Britain and France became the leaders in the movement to establish economic planning, thereby repudiating liberal capitalism. The elections of 1945 in both countries put into power parties whose programs called for radical ventures in the new field of "limited" capitalism, visualized by economic planning, in contrast to the "absolute" capitalism of *laissez faire*. The British Labor party, committed to socialism, swept into power by a large majority. In France, an overwhelming victory was won by a combination of the parties of the left: Communists, Socialists, and the newly formed Mouvement Républicain Populaire (MRP).

The Labor party promptly proposed to carry out its program of planned economy. At the head of this program was to be an integrated national system of social services. During the war there had been full employment at high wages, the result of the greatest possible production and the greatest possible demand for labor. After the war the idea became prevalent that industry be planned in times of peace, as in times of war, in order to promote general well-being. Must a nation go to war in order to have prosperity? And could not prosperity be equitably shared through social legislation that would guarantee security and well-being to the workers? When peace came, a war against poverty began that was waged with great vigor and was attended with considerable success. It resulted in a radical transformation of the status of the working class. The famous National Insurance and National Health Service Acts, passed in 1946, are described elsewhere.[22] In 1947, laws were passed designed to carry out some of the principles of economic planning. One law revolutionized land tenure by giving to a government body the power to direct land development.[23] Another gave power to an agricultural commission to control and regulate food production, to fix prices, to assure markets, and to remove inefficient farmers. Cash subsidies were given to farmers to make up for the low prices at which food was to be sold. The desperate plight of Britain caused the government to adopt "directive" policies, unprecedented in the history of the nation in peacetime. Parliament, in 1947, passed a law giving the government power to

[22] See pp. 101–102.
[23] See p. 99.

conscript every person, every piece of property, and every penny in the United Kingdom. Under this system of "labor direction," all men and women, capable of labor, could be directed to work in those industries where they were most needed. Wages and profits were put under government control. To carry out this law Sir Stafford Cripps was given almost dictatorial power over the economic life of the nation.

France took similar, though not so radical, steps in the direction of a planned economy, or *dirigisme*. The social reform laws of 1930 and 1936 were extended, though moderately.[24] A commission, headed by Jean Monnet, was created to devise a four-year plan of economic reconstruction. It was given full authority to reorganize the following key industries: coal, power, steel, cement, transport, and agricultural machinery. The other Western democracies, notably Scandinavia, also witnessed the triumph of socialist or semisocialist parties, who likewise embarked upon similar plans. Soviet Russia, repudiating capitalism altogether, established a complete system of economic planning. And the satellite states emulated her as best they could. Economic planning in one form or another became the order of the day.

PROGRESS OF NATIONALIZATION

Prominent on the agenda of the triumphant left was nationalization, the economic mortal sin of liberal capitalism. Curiously enough the pioneers of nationalization were the semiautocratic governments of the German and Japanese empires and the autocratic government of tsarist Russia. These countries had nationalized their railway systems before 1914, but their motives for this radical move were chiefly military, not economic. For the same reason America had nationalized the Panama Canal. Before

[24] See p. 99.

1914, nationalization had made some headway in the democracies. France had nationalized telegraphs, telephones, and some of the railways; England, telegraphs and telephones; and Italy, railways, telegraphs, and telephones.

After the First World War the movement for government ownership took a great spurt. It had the support of the socialists and the trade-unions, now numerous and influential. Britain nationalized electric power and radio communication, and Canada, some of her railways. France, during 1936–1937, when Léon Blum headed the Popular Front ministry, nationalized all the railways and munitions plants. In Japan full nationalization was not adopted. However, there existed a close partnership between the government and the leading capitalists, whose activities were controlled and directed by public officials.

After the Second World War, nationalization, swift and widespread, became the order of the day in Western Europe. Radical, even revolutionary, measures were adopted with but little opposition. The capitalists had neither sufficient funds nor the inclination to undertake the gigantic task of renovating the economic machine that lay in ruins all about them. Moreover, the capitalists in the countries that had been occupied by the Germans were generally discredited; many had collaborated with the Germans or were suspected of having done so. Hostility to capitalists was deep and widespread; the property of many, convicted of having been collaborators, was confiscated by the restored governments. Largely for this reason, resistance to nationalization was popularly regarded as a confession of hostility to national interests. In this way, patriotism, curiously enough, came to the aid of socialism.

Britain, under Labor party rule, took the lead in the movement for nationalization. It was quite astonishing to behold the land that had given birth to liberal capitalism become the chief protagonist of its complete opposite, socialism. During 1945–1948, with amazing rapidity and with only half-hearted opposi-

tion, Parliament passed laws nationalizing the Bank of England
with its vast power over credit; it also nationalized coal mines,
overseas air lines, railways, and inland road and water transport.
However, despite this rapid extension of nationalization, about
80 per cent of Britain's economy continued under private enterprise. France nationalized civil aviation, the Bank of France,
the Renault automobile works, many of the insurance companies, the coal mines, gas, and electricity. Italy retained the
nationalization of banks and of the iron, steel, and armament
industries that had been inaugurated by Mussolini.

In order to avoid the evils of economic regimentation by a
bureaucracy, the device of a "public corporation" was adopted in
both Britain and France. A nationalized industry became an
autonomous "public corporation" and administrative agency
responsible to the government, not to the stockholders. The industry was run by a board of directors, appointed by the government; the members represented in general the state, the public,
and the employees. The managers of a public corporation operated much in the same manner as did those of a private enterprise. They planned and organized production, bought and sold,
"hired and fired," all with the object of making the nationalized
enterprise self-sustaining and even profitable. Strict adherence
to business methods was the guiding rule.

Backward Turkey and Latin America also adopted nationalization, but for different reasons. For centuries the capitalists of
Turkey had been chiefly Armenians, Greeks, and Jews. During
the First World War, the Armenians were massacred. After the
war, when Turkey fell under the rule of Mustafa Kemal, the
Greeks were driven out of Turkey. And after the Second World
War the few non-Turkish capitalists that remained, chiefly Jews,
were driven out of business by confiscatory taxes. As a consequence, an economic vacuum was created, as there did not exist
a Turkish middle class to undertake private enterprise. This vac-

uum was filled by the government, which, in a short time, took over railways, banks, shipping, foreign trade, and many industrial enterprises. Only Soviet Russia now has a greater degree of government ownership than does Turkey.

The situation in Latin America was somewhat different. There the capitalistic enterprises, especially the large ones, were owned by absentee foreigners, chiefly Europeans and Americans. The leading officials of these enterprises were also foreigners, resident in the country, and their policies were in the interest chiefly of the absentee owners. Nationalist resentment among Latin Americans at foreign economic control led to the adoption of the radical policy of government ownership. The method, adopted to force out the foreign capitalists, was expropriation, either through purchase or through near-confiscation. In 1927, Mexico took over the oil wells owned by American capitalists, paying insufficient compensation, and put them under some form of public ownership. Argentina, in 1948, bought out the British- and French-owned railways, which were then nationalized.

At the opposite ends of the movement for a planned economy were Soviet Russia and America. From the day they came into power, in November, 1917, the Communists set about to create a completely planned economy through the adoption of the various Five Year plans. They succeeded in doing so by using the swift and ruthless methods of totalitarian dictatorship. But the economic system in Soviet Russia served neither as a model nor as an inspiration to other lands. In the first place, it was established at the complete sacrifice of human freedom in all spheres of life, political, economic, social, religious, and cultural. In the second place, it failed to promote prosperity, even a modicum of well-being, among the masses of people, whose standard of living has been far lower than that in any nation of Western Europe.

At the other extreme of the movement for a planned economy

stood America. There free, private enterprise continued almost unabated, in contrast with Europe which was committed to planning through various degrees of public control of the national economy. America succeeded in establishing the highest standard of living not only in the world but in all history. Not having been invaded she escaped the chaos and destruction visited on the other belligerents during the Second World War. There was no shortage of capital in America as in Europe. On the contrary it existed in superabundance, and American investors were only too willing to put their money into private enterprise.

However, even in America, planned economy has had its beginnings. It began when *laissez faire* was repudiated by the New Deal policies of social reform and regulation of agriculture and industry.[25] America took one notable step of nationalization with the creation of the Tennessee Valley Authority (TVA). In 1933 a law established government ownership and operation of the power development stations at Muscle Shoals, Alabama. By using the device of "public corporation" a government board was constituted to which was given authority to develop agriculture and industry in the Tennessee Valley; to control the flood waters of the rivers in the region; to build dams, power stations, and hydroelectric plants; and to manufacture nitrogen products. The TVA conducted its affairs much in the manner of a great private corporation, but its responsibility was to the government of the United States, which appointed the board of directors and the leading officials.

Though America remained committed in the main to private enterprise, the world in general repudiated *laissez faire,* the fundamental principle of liberal capitalism. It was weighed and found wanting in satisfying man's most essential need, that of security. With the abandonment of *laissez faire* came a steadying of the production of goods and a wider distribution of wealth,

[25] See p. 99.

characteristic of a managed, planned economy. That spelled security for the great masses of workers. Does it also spell progress, which, in economic matters, means ever greater production? The test will come in the semisocialist democracies of Western Europe that have gone far on the road toward the goal of a collectivist economy.

Chapter 3. Progress of Political Democracy

THE THREE REVOLUTIONS

The history of democracy is short. As a system of government and a way of life and thought it is distinctively modern. The ancient Greek and Roman republics were not democracies; they contained not even the seeds of democratic growth. The citizens of Periclean Athens, whether rich or poor, constituted a political caste comprising no more than about ten per cent of the population. A citizen was one whose parents were both citizens. The ninety per cent were slaves and foreigners, who continued in this inferior status from generation to generation. Only in rare instances, such as for notable services to the state, was a noncitizen made a citizen. A similar situation existed in the Roman republic of Cicero. In medieval times the self-governing communes of Western Europe made no notable advance over this ancient political pattern.

The first great and definite advance toward democracy was made by the English Revolution of 1688. It was the pioneer revolution of modern times in that it destroyed an old political system and established a new one, the framework of which has continued to exist down to the present. Two great principles emerged from the Revolution of 1688: (1) the Bill of Rights which guaranteed the "liberty of the subject," traditional in the common law; and (2) the supremacy of Parliament in the government of the nation. The machinery of democracy now existed, but it was predicated on inequality. In theory, Parliament represented the "people," but it was chosen by a very limited electorate and was controlled by a privileged aristocracy. However, equality before the law of all "subjects" was clearly established and became the accepted practice in England. No such equality then existed anywhere else in the world.

From its very beginning to the present, equality has been acknowledged as the fundamental spiritual principle of democracy. Without the liberty of the individual to develop his powers, unhindered by the restrictions of law and of custom, the quest for equality would be futile. Hence liberty and equality have been the Siamese twins of the history of democracy; the health and vigor of one mean the health and vigor of the other. So great has been the passion for equality among men that, as de Tocqueville observed, people would prefer equality in slavery to inequality in a system of aristocratic privilege. But equality does not mean that all men are equally endowed with ability, with moral insight, or with personal attractiveness. Nature itself has stamped differences in individuals by giving each person a distinctive appearance. Equality means that society and government should not for reasons of race, class, faith, nationality, or occupation declare some permanently superior by favoring them with privileges and others permanently inferior by burdening them with discriminations. Expansion of equality became the acid test of the progress of democracy.

A whole century had elapsed after the Revolution of 1688 before another decisive step had been taken toward democracy. This step was the American Revolution, which now looms large as a world event of supreme importance in the progress of mankind. The American Revolution proclaimed the doctrine that "all men are endowed by their Creator with certain inalienable Rights, that among these are Life, Liberty and the pursuit of Happiness." This new egalitarian doctrine was incorporated in the American Constitution, which improved on its English model (1) by expanding the Bill of Rights to include freedom of speech, of the press, and of assembly; (2) by forbidding Congress to establish a national church; and (3) by establishing a republican form of government. These notable advances became a beacon light in the onward march of nations toward democracy.

In all its essentials, however, the American Revolution was a political one. It made no changes in the social and economic structure of society. Before long, however, America's libertarian ideal was broadened by Jeffersonian democracy, the adherents of which sought to apply the principle of equality to a far greater extent than had the fathers of the constitution. Could not this principle be applied to the social and economic order? Jeffersonian ideals became the driving force of the radical movements in America, from the democracy of Andrew Jackson to the New Deal of Franklin D. Roosevelt.

Far more radical than the American Revolution was the French Revolution. The French Declaration of the Rights of Man improved on the American Bill of Rights by adding equality to freedom. It proclaimed that all men "are born and remain free and equal in rights," and that law, to be valid anywhere, had to be the expression of the "general will" of all citizens. These doctrines pointed the way to universal suffrage. By contrast the American Constitution had recognized slavery and the right of the states to maintain property qualifications for voting, limitations that had precluded both legal and political equality for all men.

Even more significant was the fact that the French Revolution was a social as well as a political revolution. It changed the social order that had existed in the nation from almost Roman times, swiftly and drastically. During the decade 1789–1799, government, property, education, law, religion, and even geography were revolutionized. Wholesale confiscations of property completely shattered the class structure of France. The very status of property, with all its ramifications, was radically altered. The French Revolution became the inspiration of social revolutionists everywhere down to the present day.

DEMOCRACY IN THE WEST, 1900-1939

The three revolutions served as the prelude to the sweep of democracy during the nineteenth century. The fundamental spiritual principle of equality achieved a great success when a new equality, that before the ballot box, was gained. "Democracy" in its historical meaning is a political term used to express the advance of equality through government action. No system of government can be classified as democratic unless it has two essential features: (1) that majority rule is exercised by a legislature, freely elected by universal suffrage, in which every citizen counts for one, and only for one; and (2) that all citizens are protected against despotic acts of the government by constitutional guarantees of civil liberties. Whether the government is in form republican, as in the United States, or monarchical as in Britain, does not essentially affect the democratic pattern. What a democratic government does to advance equality is, however, another matter. At one time it concerned itself chiefly with advancing equality in the political, religious, and cultural fields. In our day it concerns itself chiefly with advancing equality in the social and economic fields.

During the nineteenth century, many nations had been won for democracy. Most of the nations of Europe, the United States, and the British Dominions had established governments based more or less on democratic principles. However, when the twentieth century opened, it became only too evident that democracy was suffering from a political "lag." Where constitutional governments existed, the absolute rule of the kings had been abolished, but popular rule was neither complete nor unchallenged. In many instances it encountered serious limitations in the form of property qualifications for voting, in nonrepresentative upper chambers, and in constitutional monarchs whose influence remained though their power had gone. One great nation, Russia, continued to be an absolute monarchy by divine right; and another great nation, Germany, was a semiautocracy. Though it provided for manhood suffrage and for civil liberties, the constitution of the German Empire contained so many "catches" that real power rested in the hands of ruling groups, the Junkers and the capitalists, who were openly hostile to democratic government. The problem of the twentieth century was to fulfill the promise of democracy by making popular rule direct, unmistakable and complete in all lands, and by applying its principle of equality to the social and economic order.

How fared the democratic world of the twentieth century? Progress was both rapid and decisive; whatever gains were made were, by and large, maintained in those countries where democratic principles had taken deep root. In general, it may be said that democracy advanced along three main lines: (1) the completion of political, religious, and educational equality in countries already democratic; (2) the establishment of constitutional governments in nondemocratic countries; and (3) the extension of the principle of equality to social and economic life. So notable has been progress along these lines that the twentieth century has been well called the "century of the common man."

The first and vital steps to be taken in order to realize these objectives was the extension of the franchise. Universal equal suffrage has been accepted as fundamental in the progress of a nation toward full democracy. Without it, reaction always looms as a threat to the gains already made. America, France, and Britain had set the pattern of a democratic suffrage, and nations that had property qualifications for voting hastened to catch up with the democratic procession. Serbia in 1903, Russia in 1906, Austria in 1907, Sweden in 1909, Italy in 1912, and Japan in 1925 established manhood suffrage. The new European nations that emerged from the First World War all accepted this reform. The old distrust and fear of the common man as a revolutionist, so prevalent during the nineteenth century, had disappeared. Timid conservatives as well as bold radicals discovered that manhood suffrage was the preventive of, not the incitement to, revolution.

But another suffrage movement came to the fore during the first half of the twentieth century, namely, that of woman suffrage, which became as live an issue as manhood suffrage had been during the nineteenth century. Women insistently asserted that they were "people"; hence there was neither reason nor justice in keeping them outside the constitution as "passive" citizens. The movement to enfranchise women did not lead to violent conflicts as had the movement for manhood suffrage. And the explanation lies partly in the fact that women, because of physical limitations, could not engage in revolutionary upheavals. In the main, however, the precedent of manhood suffrage played the determining role. Once all men had the vote, it constituted a precedent that could be disregarded only by deliberately relegating half of the human race to the humiliating position of permanent inequality. And men, even those skeptical of woman's political capacity, were loathe to do this.

The woman suffrage movement, handicapped by ancient traditions and strong prejudices, was slow in getting started. But once it gained the ear of the public, its progress became fairly rapid in almost all the democratic lands. Before the First World War, Norway had the distinction of being the only nation that had enfranchised women.[1] After the war, woman suffrage made rapid progress. In 1918, Britain became the pioneer among the great nations by giving votes to women. The United States soon followed by adopting a constitutional amendment in 1920. The Weimar constitution (1919) of the first German Republic provided for equal suffrage for men and

[1] Norway was anticipated in this reform by Wyoming in 1890, New Zealand in 1893, and South Australia in 1894.

women. Nearly all the small nations in Western and in Central Europe adopted this reform. Women were "enfranchised" by Soviet Russia, but their vote, like that of men, meant little.[2]

Once established, political equality of men and women quickly became an accepted truism. This equality in the sphere of the state, the most powerful of all institutions, was bound to have repercussions in the other aspects of life in the modern world. Other equalities followed: in law, in education, in the professions, and in industry. The progress of women in these fields has been striking during the short period of their emancipation.

Another violation of democracy that prevailed at the beginning of the twentieth century lay in the undemocratic nature of the bicameral system of legislation. Generally, the upper house was so chosen and so organized as to constitute a check on the popularly elected lower house. In Britain, the House of Lords, being largely hereditary, was plainly organized on an aristocratic basis. In the United States and in France, the senates were chosen indirectly—in the former by the legislatures of the states and in the latter by local electoral colleges—and with the avowed intention of making them function as conservative bodies. In Italy, members of the Senate were appointed for life by the king. In the German Empire, the members of the *Bundesrat,* as the upper house was called, represented the ruling princes in the various states and were appointed and dismissed by them at will.

During the twentieth century, undemocratic upper houses, like other relics of political privilege, either withered away or were put under direct popular control. Britain, by the Parliament Act of 1911, virtually eliminated the House of Lords as a legislative body. The most that it could now do was to delay bills for two years; later, in 1949, the period was reduced to one year. An amendment to the American Constitution, adopted in 1913, established direct, popular election of Senators. The

[2] See p. 224.

strong Senate of the Third French Republic was succeeded by the weak Council of the Fourth French Republic, to which was given only advisory power. The all-dominant *Bundesrat* of the German Empire was succeeded by the weak *Reichsrat* of the German Republic. In turn the latter was succeeded by the even weaker *Bundesrat* of the German Federal Republic. The largely appointed Senate of the Kingdom of Italy was succeeded by the largely elected Senate of the Republic of Italy. Upper houses were altogether abolished by Finland in 1919 and by Turkey in 1925.

In many countries the substitution of a republic for monarchy was deemed as essential to democracy as was the supremacy of a popularly elected legislature. The great outstanding example of a democratic republic was the United States. When the Latin-American nations came into existence, they emulated this example by becoming republics. But the republic was only a form that merely veiled the arbitrary rule of military dictators. France was the only great nation in Europe that, in 1875, definitely established a republic. So little had republicanism progressed in Europe that, at the beginning of the twentieth century, out of twenty-one states only two were republics: France and Switzerland.

During the first half of the twentieth century, republicanism made rapid headway. With the defeat of the four empires, monarchy received a mortal blow. Revolutions that overthrew the ruling dynasties took place in Germany, Russia, Austria-Hungary, and Turkey. Nearly all the succession states that emerged from the ruins of these empires became democratic republics fashioned along the latest pattern. Europe was now almost all republican. Out of some twenty-six states in 1950 only eight were monarchies: Britain, the Netherlands, Belgium, Luxemburg, Greece, Norway, Sweden, and Denmark. In all these states the crown existed merely as a symbol of national unity, but democracy was accepted as an unchallenged reality.

Monarchical Europe of a thousand years had, in the short period of half a century, become republican Europe.

DEMOCRACY IN THE EAST

Most extraordinary has been the course of democracy in Asia. From time immemorial, inequality throughout the Orient had been maintained as an all-embracing system of life and as a cherished, even as a sacred, ideal. It was the entrance of Europeans on the Asiatic scene that made possible the beginnings of the modern ways of life and thought among the Asiatic peoples.

As a consequence of the expansion of Europe during the eighteenth and nineteenth centuries practically all Asia had fallen under European control and influence. The problem of establishing democracy was consequently twofold: one, to overthrow the native despots; and, the other, to oust the European overlords. Revolutionary groups appeared in the various countries that fought both for self-government against absolutism and for nationalism against imperialism. The struggle to establish nationalism and democracy, hitherto confined to the West, became world-wide during the twentieth century.

As in Europe during the nineteenth century, leadership of the democratic movements fell to the intellectuals, nearly all of whom were the products of Western education and training. Either they had studied in the schools of Europe and America or they had imbibed Western ideas in the native schools established by Christian missionaries. Though resentful of European intervention, the Asiatic democrats, nevertheless, aimed to establish a new order in which would be combined the best features of their native culture with what was best in Western civilization. They clearly realized that the ancient ways of their native land, if persisted in, would lead only to decay, ruin, and enslavement.

In all Asia, Japan was the only truly independent, sovereign nation. Therefore it behooved the Japanese to set the pace of freedom for all other Asiatic peoples. Quite the contrary proved to be the case. Japan became as dictatorial and as imperialistic as the worst of the European powers, sometimes even more so. During the famous era of reform, from 1868 to 1889, she adopted a complete set of Western institutions: a constitution establishing parliamentary government and guaranteeing civil liberties; a unified national administration; a national army and navy; a Western code of law; compulsory elementary education; and mechanized industry. But these liberal reforms were often nullified in their application by the strict maintenance of ancient beliefs and traditions that inculcated subservient obedience to those who ruled the nation.

Of all the nations in the West Japan chose the German Empire as her political model. The constitution of Japan, like that of Germany, was made into a façade behind which operated the real powers that ruled the nation. These were the old, landed aristocrats, the new industrial capitalists, called the Zaibatsu, and the army, who, as in Germany, combined to thwart the popular will. By making use of certain "catches," deliberately put into the constitution, and by keeping under their influence the emperor, revered as a god by the people, these powerful groups were able to control the government in their own interests.

As in Germany, the military exerted a great influence in the conduct of affairs in Japan. This influence grew stronger and stronger as the nation emerged victorious from a succession of wars: with China (1894–1895); with Russia (1904–1905); and with Germany in the First World War. The first and most difficult problem of democracy in Japan was to destroy militarism. And only defeat in war held out this prospect. Defeat would discredit the system under which militarism flourished and would eliminate the influence of the powerful classes that operated it. In all instances a nation, afflicted with militarism, develops an overweening pride in its own prowess coupled with an overwhelming contempt for that of other nations. This was true of the France of Louis XIV and of Napoleon I and of the Germany of William II and of Hitler; it was equally true of the Japan of the Mikados. On December 7, 1941, Japan recklessly plunged into a war with America by her sneak attack on Pearl Harbor. Blinded by success and corrupted by power, the ruling classes were confident that Japan would win this war as surely as she had won the wars in the past.

Victory had not brought democracy to Japan, but defeat did. Her defeat in the Second World War was so complete and overwhelming that she was reduced from a great to an insignificant power. Japan lost everything that she had gained in fifty years of aggression; her territory was reduced to the homeland, and her military power was shattered. An American army occupied Japan, and its chief, General Douglas Mac-Arthur, was given supreme authority during the period of occupation. Through his initiative a constitutional convention was elected to establish a new regime for the nation. In 1947 a constitution was adopted which established a democratic government by giving supreme authority to a national legislature, elected by universal suffrage, including women, and by establishing individual liberty through a bill of rights. The emperor was retained, but his powers were abolished. From being in theory a theocracy, in form a constitutional monarchy, and in fact a military oligarchy, Japan became a democracy, at least to the extent of adopting a thoroughly democratic constitution.

Democracy in Japan did not limit itself to political reform. In order to advance democratic principles in society, a body

blow was struck at the wealthy classes by drastic social and economic reform. The Zaibatsu group of capitalists were deprived
of ownership and control of the great consolidations of commerce, industry, and finance. Efforts were made to pulverize
these consolidations in order to encourage competition, but these
efforts were not entirely successful.

Far more successful was the destruction of the landed aristocracy, which, for so many centuries, had controlled the life of
the nation. Agrarian reform was supremely important in Japan,
where, before the war, about half the population of 80,000,000
lived from tilling the soil. Drastic measures were necessary because the great majority of the peasants were tenants and laborers, in almost feudal bondage on large estates. Furthermore,
there were "too many people on too little land"; only 16 per
cent of the surface of Japan is arable. A law, passed in 1945,
called for the elimination of "economic bondage which has
enslaved the Japanese farmer for centuries of feudal oppression." It required the compulsory sale of large estates to the
government, which, in turn, was to sell the land, in small lots
and on easy terms, to the peasants. The application of this law
was to be made gradually in order not to disrupt the economy
of the nation.

This agrarian law, in effect, abolished economic feudalism
that had persisted despite the Westernization of Japan. By liberating vast masses of people from a serflike condition and by
establishing peasant proprietorship, democracy in Japan at last
had a favorable soil in which to grow. The democratic constitution could now count on widespread popular support.

By contrast with that in Japan the democratic movement on
the Asiatic mainland struggled chiefly against external foes,
the Western imperialists. For this reason democracy was inex-
tricably bound up with nationalism, and the latter came first.
The supporters of democracy and nationalism were convinced

that the primal step must be to free their country from foreign rule; and not until nationalism triumphed would democracy have full opportunity to develop.

The democratic nationalist movement on the continent of Asia centered in China and in India. Two great leaders appeared in these countries: the Chinese, Sun Yat-sen, and the Indian, Mohandas Gandhi, both of whom gained world-wide renown. Though Western in education they yet became uncompromising champions of their native land against European domination. However, neither resented Western civilization, and neither was chauvinistic in his nationalism.

Sun Yat-sen was a kind of Chinese Mazzini, who preached democratic nationalism with almost religious fervor. His famous "Three Principles of the People" were: the people's nationalism, or the freeing of China from foreign control; the people's sovereignty, or the establishment of a democratic republic; and the people's livelihood, or social and economic reforms. These Three Principles became the clarion call of young China.

Gandhi was a saint turned statesman. He was deeply convinced that war was the root of all evil, and he opposed violence in any and every form. How then was India to free herself from Britain's autocratic rule? Gandhi's answer was "noncooperation," namely, that Indians should refuse to obey the laws, refuse to take office, refuse to pay taxes, and refuse to enter the army. This wholesale boycotting of British rule would bring about its breakdown, and the result would be a free India. Gandhi was a democrat on the most approved Western pattern. His championship of the principle of equality extended even to a criticism of India's hallowed caste system. He denounced in unmeasured terms the treatment of the pariahs, or outcasts, and demanded the immediate abolition of this iniquitous practice.

The story of democracy in China is a tragic one. A revolutionary movement appeared toward the end of the nineteenth century headed by Sun Yat-sen. It spread rapidly, and in 1912 the Manchu dynasty was overthrown and a Republic was proclaimed. But it proved easier to overthrow the old order than to establish a new one. China was now a republic without republicans, other than a handful of Westernized intellectuals. The majority of the vast population was sunk in poverty, ignorance, and superstition with but one thought in mind: how to live from one day to the next. Death had no terrors for them; life did. The story of the Chinese Republic is a long and harrowing one, from its very birth to this very day. First, it had to fight the war lords, military adventurers who sought to divide China into various regions ruled by them. No sooner were the war lords suppressed than Japan entered on her aggressive policy toward China by demanding concessions and by seizing territory. Even before the outbreak of the Second World War in 1939, China had become the battleground of savage warfare between her armies and those of Japan. Bad as the situation was for the Republic it was made even worse by an incipient civil war between well-organized Communist forces and the Nationalist government, headed by Chiang Kai-shek. If China managed to escape the devil of Japanese imperialism, she was likely to fall into the sea of totalitarian dictatorship.

With the defeat of Japan, China emerged "victorious" from the Second World War. Japanese control, with all its ramifications, was completely eliminated. At last, after a desperate struggle lasting a decade, the way seemed clear for the establishment of a united, democratic China. But this was not to be. During the war all the Chinese parties had united to defend the country against the Japanese invaders. No sooner, however, was the war over than a desperate struggle broke out between the Nationalist government and the Communists. For four years civil war raged in China. In 1949 the Communists scored a resounding victory over the Nationalist government. The rule of Chiang

Kai-shek was overthrown, and a Communist government was established headed by Mao Tse-tung.

At first the democratic movement in India faced greater obstacles than in China. Unlike the latter, in theory at least an independent nation, the former was a dependency of Britain. Hence, the Indians could not mobilize popular resentment against Western imperialism as freely as could the Chinese. Furthermore, India was deeply divided by religion and by caste. About 60 per cent of the people adhered to the Hindu faith; about 20 per cent to Islam; and the remainder to other faiths. Bitter hatred and contempt existed between the followers of the different faiths, especially between the Hindus and the Moslems. Equally serious—perhaps more so—was the caste system, according to which all Hindus were divided by unbridgeable barriers into four main groups, or castes: priests, soldiers, merchants, and laborers, in each of which membership was hereditary. Outside of the caste system were millions of "outcasts," or pariahs, marked from birth as permanent inferiors and relegated to the most menial occupations. Democracy, if it means anything, means the recognition by state and society of the worth and dignity of every individual. The caste and outcast system, ordained by the Hindu faith, was a complete negation of the very essence of the democratic ideal. From the outset it was evident that democracy would lag far behind nationalism in the movement for Indian freedom.

As in China, the nationalist movement was led by the educated youth. Young India, inspired by the teachings of Gandhi, roused the masses against the British authorities by means of demonstrations, strikes, boycotts, riots, and even assassination of officials. Repression merely served to increase the ardor of the nationalists. The struggle between British imperialism and Indian nationalism was carried on in a continuously exacerbated form. Any move by the British to make concessions was immediately followed by greater outbursts of Indian discontent.

Freedom for India was an unexpected result of the Second World War. Because of her great economic difficulties, Britain was compelled to decrease her imperial commitments. Especially urgent was this necessity in the case of India, where popular discontent with British rule made the maintenance of armies and of officials both costly and provocative. In 1947 the British government announced its determination to leave India, who was then to decide freely on her political future. As described elsewhere,[3] two new states arose in this ancient land, the Union of India and Pakistan, each of which accepted Dominion status.

Nationalism having been achieved, the way was now open for the establishment of democracy. What kind of democratic order would the ancient, caste-ridden land of India establish, now that she was freed from imperial bondage? In 1950 the Union of India adopted a constitution which compares favorably with the most democratic constitutions of the postwar era. A comprehensive, detailed bill of rights did away with many ancient evils. It established equality of all citizens before the law, irrespective of religion, race, caste, or sex. Discrimination against any citizen was forbidden in public places, such as hotels, restaurants, theaters, and highways. "Untouchability" was declared abolished; and 60,000,000 outcasts were recognized as being civilly and politically equal to other Indians. Provision was made for civil liberties, for universal suffrage, social security, free, secular public schools, equal pay for equal work as between men and women, and the right of minority races to maintain their own schools and language.

The system of government, established by the constitution, was a federal republic. Executive power was to be exercised by a president, chosen by an electoral college consisting of the members of both houses of parliament and the members of the legislature of the states, and by a cabinet, appointed by the president and responsible to the lower house. Parliament was to

[3] See pp. 155–156.

consist of a Council of the States, chosen by the states, and a House of the People, elected by universal, equal suffrage. Money bills were the prerogative of the House of the People; the Council had to accept such measures within 30 days. A joint session of both houses was to decide on the fate of any other bill over which they disagreed.

Democracy in Asia made further important gains in another part of the continent, namely, Turkey, long the mighty citadel of autocratic power in the Near East. The revolution of 1908 overthrew the sultan as an absolute monarch and established Turkey as a constitutional monarchy. But that was only a beginning. The real transformation of Turkey into a modern state on the Western model did not take place until after the First World War. In 1923 the sultan was deposed and a republic was established. A constitution was adopted, which provided for a single-chamber parliament to be elected by manhood suffrage. Executive power was to be exercised by a president and by a cabinet responsible to parliament. For the first time in the history of Turkey all citizens were made equal before the law, irrespective of race or faith.

The first president was Mustafa Kemal, one of the extraordinary men of the twentieth century. He became virtually a dictator and used his power to introduce drastic, even revolutionary, reforms. He separated church and state; abolished polygamy; introduced Western codes of law; reconstituted the educational system; and reformed the administration. After the death of Kemal, in 1938, the one-party dictatorship established by the latter was continued by his successor, President Ismet Inönü.

New elections for the National Assembly took place in 1950 and roused world-wide interest. Opposition parties were permitted, and voting was free. As a consequence the ruling People's party was defeated by the opposition Democratic party that now assumed power. After 27 years of dictatorship, Turkey experimented with free elections and emerged as a democratic nation.

Only during the twentieth century did democracy make its appearance in the Orient. Its progress was notable despite the many handicaps of ancient ways and of European imperialism. Most notable of all was the progress of women. For countless centuries the inferiority of women to men was not merely a prejudice but an article of faith. Manhood suffrage was sufficiently revolutionary, but woman suffrage was well-nigh inconceivable. And yet Turkey enfranchised women in 1934 and the postwar constitutions of Japan, the Union of India, and Syria adopted woman suffrage. It is well to remember, however, that Asiatic democracy is more of a promise than a performance. The widespread revolutionary disturbances following the Second World War have created an even greater instability than that in Europe. Then there has been the ever-present threat of Soviet Russia who has sought in all manner of ways to take advantage of the situation in order to destroy the newly created democratic order. Democracy has been undergoing far more serious trials in Asia than it ever did in Europe or in America.

RELIGIOUS EQUALITY

Equality before the law and before the ballot box came with the triumphal march of democracy. What about equality in religion? Was the movement to free men from political oppression to be followed by a parallel movement in the sphere of religion? The answer is emphatically "yes." As already described, religious toleration had made considerable progress during the nineteenth century.[4] But religious equality, a system that made religion a private matter through separation of church and state, existed only in America. In other Christian countries

[4] See pp. 6–8.

religion was a public matter, in that it was officially recognized by the system of established churches that gave special privileges to the national church but permitted nonconformists to practice their faith, with few restrictions in some countries and with many in others.

During the twentieth century, France became the pioneer of religious equality in Europe. The famous law of 1905, which separated church and state in France, became the inspiration of those Europeans who sought to secularize government and politics. After the First World War there were three notable instances of separation, all of them inspired by different motives. In the constitution of 1920, Czechoslovakia, inspired by the American ideal of religious equality, decreed separation of church and state. In the constitution of 1922, Soviet Russia decreed separation out of hatred of religion in general and of the Orthodox church in particular. Most surprising was Turkey, which separated church and state in 1922, not because of hostility to Islam but because of nationalism. The Turks became convinced that the new secular bond of nationalism would prove stronger than the old religious bond, in uniting the nation against foreign aggression. Separation of church and state in Turkey, the leading Moslem state, set a precedent, which was followed by Syria in 1949.

The progress of religious equality in Latin America was slow and halting. As the population was almost entirely Catholic, the church was regarded as the one stabilizing influence among the Latin Americans, whose instability, political and otherwise, had become notorious. However, strong anticlerical movements developed that made considerable headway during the twentieth century. Church and state were separated in Uruguay, Mexico, Ecuador, Brazil, Cuba, Panama, Chile, and Colombia. Nevertheless, so deep and widespread was the Catholic faith that the church was given privileges in these countries, especially in educational matters.

Religious equality has by no means succeeded in becoming universal. Established churches continue to be maintained throughout Western Europe, except in France, Wales, and the German Federal Republic. As religious toleration was widely practiced, separation of church and state ceased to be the burning issue in Europe that it had been during the nineteenth century. It was relegated to the rear by the new and burning issue of economic equality.

EDUCATIONAL EQUALITY

The movement for religious equality progressed slowly and, at times, suffered serious setbacks. Not so the movement for educational equality, which can boast of sure and steady gains from generation to generation. Often these gains came with surprising speed because of the vital need of knowledge and enlightenment by the enfranchised masses. The "social role of education in a democratic society is at once to secure equal liberty and equal opportunity to differing individuals and groups and to enable the citizens to understand, appraise, and redirect forces, men, and events as these tend to strengthen or to weaken their liberties." [5]

Education was especially important for the progress of the workers. Literacy was the primal requirement for effective organization to advance their economic and political interests; the magic of the written word, reaching millions almost simultaneously, enabled them to mobilize quickly for economic or political action. But literacy constituted only the first installment of the workers' education program. A demand soon arose for free secondary and higher education, in order to develop an elite of labor administrators who would be in a position to exercise power in the state.

[5] *Report of the President's Commission on Higher Education,* Dec. 15, 1947.

The twentieth century marked a phenomenal advance of popular education on all levels. At the beginning of the century, secondary and higher education in Europe was almost a monopoly of the well to do. High schools, colleges, and universities were public but not free. Only in America did the children of the poor have opportunities for higher education: in the free public high schools and in the free state universities and city colleges.

After the First World War, demands arose in Europe for free secondary and higher education. "All the fathers," as a slogan had it, "had fought in the same trenches; therefore their children should sit on the same benches." Free, public secondary education was widely extended. The requirements to enter colleges and universities were liberalized, and many free scholarships were established. Students of humble origin now appeared in the exclusive seats of learning, such as Oxford, the Sorbonne, and Berlin University. Soviet Russia abolished illiteracy by establishing free, compulsory, elementary schools; in addition, opportunities were given to many to enter the secondary and higher institutions of learning.

After the Second World War, a new spurt was given to popular education. New education laws in Britain and in France raised the school-leaving age and established free secondary education for all. In nearly all the countries of Europe many flocked to the universities, where they crowded the classrooms and lecture halls. The governments did all in their power to encourage students by giving subsidies to old universities and by establishing new educational institutions. Most remarkable was the educational progress of America, where free higher education reached an all-time high.[6]

With the rapid growth of popular education, a great change took place in its objectives, and consequently in methods and in

[6] See p. 361.

content. Hitherto, the main objectives of education had been either to produce an intellectual elite or to adorn the rich with cultural plumage. But now that the masses were crowding into the institutions of higher learning, many of them from the lower strata of society, the objective of higher education, and for that matter of all education, necessarily changed. The new objective was to prepare the rising generation of all classes for life: to be more intelligent citizens, to be trained for better occupations, and to enjoy more fully the cultural heritage of mankind. As a future citizen, the student was to be trained to know the problems of his nation and of the world and to participate in the efforts to solve them. As a future worker, he was to be trained to fill a place in the many-sided economic life of our day; without such training he would be cut off from the more attractive and more remunerative pursuits. However, the liberal arts were not to be neglected; they, and they alone, could enrich a man's life by giving him a sense of higher values through the study of literature, art, music, and the natural and social sciences. Higher education for the many would, it was believed, abolish the "cultural lag," namely, the difference between the rapid pace of technology and the slow pace of social and moral enlightenment.

The social importance of higher education for the masses was felt in the movement for adult education, which became as prominent in the twentieth century as the movement for universal schooling had been in the nineteenth. Education was no longer limited to the young; it became a continuous life process. To attract adults colleges and universities organized extramural courses, and trade-unions established workers' education centers, notably in Britain and America. Men and women from all walks of life flocked to the adult education classes seeking light on the problems that confronted them as individuals and as citizens. A class in an adult education center became a vital discussion group that sought knowledge with the object of using it to solve the great problems that confronted mankind after the two world wars.

DEMOCRACY AFTER THE SECOND WORLD WAR

The defeat of the fascist powers, the all-out enemies of democracy in any form, was followed by a resurgence of the democratic faith. This was made evident by the extension of popular rule in all manner of ways, notably in France, Italy, and Germany. The Fourth French Republic that appeared in 1946 adopted a constitution that boldly proclaimed the abolition of all man-made inequalities. France, it asserted, "is a republic—indivisible, secular, democratic, and social." Equality was the keynote of the constitution: equal rights as between men and women; equal opportunities for all in education on all levels; and equal security for all against the economic hazards of life. Along with the traditional Rights of Man it proclaimed the right to work, the right of labor to organize and to strike, the right to social assistance, and the right to elementary education. Supreme power of making laws was given to a National Assembly elected by universal suffrage. A second chamber, elected indirectly, was given merely advisory power. The president, chosen by a joint session of both houses, was given only nominal power. The cabinet, nominated by the president, was made responsible to the National Assembly.

In Italy, the dream of Mazzini was realized with the establishment of a democratic republic. So deep was popular resentment against King Victor Emanuel III, because of his support of Mussolini, that a referendum held in 1947 ousted the house of Savoy in favor of a republic. The new constitution, adopted by a popularly elected convention, declared that "Italy is a democratic Republic founded on labor." A bicameral par-

liament, the Chamber and the Senate, was established, both to
be elected by universal suffrage. The president was to be chosen
by a joint session of both houses, and his power was to be
nominal. The members of the cabinet were to be nominated
by the president and to be responsible to both houses of parliament. Because of fascist experience the constitution contains a
long, detailed, specific bill of rights. Along with the traditional
rights it proclaims the right to work and the right to social
security. Very emphatically the constitution proclaims the principle of equality before the law without distinction of sex, race,
language, religion, or political opinion.

Germany, like Italy, broke a path to democracy. In 1949, at
Bonn, a convention, elected in western Germany, adopted a
constitution for a new state, the German Federal Republic. It
created a federal union of eleven *Laender,* or states, with the
powers of government distributed between the states and the
central government. A bicameral national legislature was established: the *Bundestag* elected by universal suffrage in the nation, and the *Bundesrat,* representing the states, chosen by the
state governments. The president, having only nominal power,
was to be elected by a convention consisting of the members of
the *Bundestag* and an equal number of delegates from the
state legislatures. The prime minister, or chancellor, was to
be chosen by the *Bundestag,* and was given the power to designate his fellow ministers. The principle of ministerial responsibility, according to which a cabinet remains in office only as long
as its policies are supported by the lower house, was not fully
accepted. Only when the chancellor himself asks for a vote of confidence can this principle be applied by the *Bundestag.* As in the
case of the Italian constitution, and for the same reason, the
German constitution contains a long, detailed, specific bill of
rights. In addition to the traditional civil liberties it proclaims the
right "to form associations to safeguard and improve economic
conditions." Discrimination is forbidden against anyone because

of sex, descent, race, language, homeland and origin, faith, or political opinion. The constitution outlaws parties that aim to impair or to abolish the democratic order established by the Republic.

This resurgence of democracy was made notable by the adoption of woman suffrage in countries that had never before accepted this reform. What better way of showing faith in democracy than by enfranchising half the population! More voters would give added power to the nations liberated from fascist dictatorship. Women were given the vote for the first time in France and in Italy, when these nations adopted their new constitutions. In 1949, Belgium likewise adopted this reform. Women had been enfranchised in Germany under the Weimar Republic, but their vote, like that of men, became a mockery under the Nazi dictatorship. But the German Federal Republic reaffirmed its faith in democracy by the establishment of universal suffrage as the fundamental basis of the new republic. As already noted, women were also enfranchised in Japan, India, Turkey, and Syria.

A dramatic step toward the realization of world democracy was taken when civil rights entered the international field. For the first time in history, governments, representing most of the world, reached an agreement on what constituted civil rights and accepted freedoms. In 1948, the General Assembly of the United Nations adopted a Universal Declaration of Human Rights. The vote in the General Assembly was unanimous; Soviet Russia and her satellites abstained from voting.

The Declaration was to serve as "a common standard of achievement for all peoples and all nations, to the end that every individual and every organ of society, keeping this Declaration constantly in mind, shall strive by teaching and education to promote respect for these rights and freedoms . . . and to secure their universal and effective recognition and observance." It asserted the faith of the members of the United Nations in fundamental human rights, in the dignity and worth of the human person, and in the equal rights of all without distinction as to race, sex, language, or religion. The Declaration reaffirmed the traditional civil rights, such as equality before the law, civil liberty, and freedom of religion, of assembly, of association, of speech, and of the press. It went beyond these rights by including social, cultural, and economic rights, such as the right to work, to social security, to an adequate standard of living, to education, to rest and leisure, to form trade-unions, and to equal pay for equal work. It conceives man as born not only with certain inalienable rights but also with certain inalienable claims on society which must not be denied.

In still another respect did the Declaration have a wider reach than had the previous declarations of human rights: the English Bill of Rights, the American Declaration of Independence and Bill of Rights, and the French Declaration of the Rights of Man. Each of these was the product of a distinctive national outlook, whereas the Universal Declaration was international in character and scope. Hence a new factor was introduced in the age-old struggle for human freedom in that the nations accepted an international responsibility. Hitherto the authority to recognize or to deny civil rights had been vested exclusively in the nation. But now the Declaration asserted the new principle of the responsibility of the United Nations for the maintenance of civil rights by all its members. What still remained was to implement the Declaration by devising ways and means to enforce it.

In the same year the General Assembly adopted another striking document, the Genocide Convention. Genocide was defined by the Convention as acts that aim "to destroy, in whole or in part, a national, ethnical, racial, or religious group as such." It declared genocide a "crime under international law," and those guilty, whether rulers, public officials, or private individuals, were to be punished by tribunals within the nation where the crime had been committed or by international tribunals to be organized to deal with this crime. The Convention was adopted as a result of the mass extermination of Jews by the Germans, a new and fearful form of inhumanity which the United Nations resolved to outlaw. Both the Universal Declaration of Human Rights and the Genocide Convention exist, as yet, only on paper. Nevertheless, they are important as expressions of organized world opinion, which the future may see translated into action.

Democratic progress during the first half of the twentieth century achieved a high watermark. And the trial by battle with its fascist enemies, Germany, Italy, and Japan, resulted in their crushing defeat. However, fascism was not entirely extirpated in Europe; it persisted in Spain and Portugal. South America, the classic land of military dictatorship, had for a time made notable progress in establishing democratic rule. But after the war democracy suffered a distinct setback in a number of the Latin-American states. Military coups overthrew democratic or semidemocratic governments in Bolivia, Nicaragua, Ecuador, Costa Rica, Paraguay, Peru, Venezuela, and Colombia. The most significant of these overturns took place in Argentina. In 1946, Juan Domingo Perón, who openly favored fascist policies, became president as a result of a free election. Repression of democratic liberties followed, which turned Argentina into a semifascist state.

A far more serious threat to democracy came from Soviet Russia. What totalitarian dictatorship lost in its fascist form it gained in its communist form. And even more! Soviet Russia emerged from the war greatly strengthened and more determined than ever to destroy democracy in any and every part of the world. And her many successes created fear in every democratic land. Communist Russia became the successor of Nazi Germany as the world enemy of democracy.

Chapter 4. Progress of Social Democracy

PROMISE OF THE INDUSTRIAL REVOLUTION

The progress of democracy in the political, religious, and educational fields was notable, even extraordinary. Far more so was the progress of democracy in the economic field, which took place almost entirely during the first half of the twentieth century. In the nineteenth century, even the most advanced thinkers had little understanding of the economic limitations on human freedom; they did not realize that the full enjoyment of civil rights and of political equality depended on the possession of property or of unusual ability. By separating politics from economics, they failed to recognize the political relevance of economic power. What did it profit a man to have a vote and freedom of speech if he was unemployed and destitute! It was then widely believed that if a man was poor he alone, not the economic system, was responsible. Either he lacked the capacity to take advantage of the many opportunities to acquire wealth offered by free enterprise or he lacked character, being a lazy person or a drunkard, and hence was morally unfit to cope with life's problems. Or he was the victim of hard luck, such as suffering from an incurable disease, or was incapacitated by an accident, or was impoverished as a consequence of a business depression. If the unfortunate was not himself responsible, then his parents were; they had no moral right to bring him into an already overcrowded world. This Malthusian apology for poverty was widely held; even so enlightened a thinker as John Stuart Mill favored laws that would prohibit marriage of those without a prospect of giving a "desirable existence" to their future offspring. One and all—or nearly all—the progressive think-

89

ers of the nineteenth century stubbornly upheld the policy
of *laissez faire,* which, they were convinced, was the only road
to universal prosperity. Yet all about them were the underpaid,
overworked, miserably housed millions, a flat denial of the promise of *laissez faire.*

In the deficit economy prior to the Industrial Revolution,
poverty had not been considered a problem to be solved but a
fate to be endured. Because of the scarcity of food, shelter, and
clothing, the needs of everyone could not then be satisfied,
and as a consequence the poor had accepted their misery and
the rich their good fortune as part of the order of the universe.
Equality in a deficit economy would result only in making everyone equally poor. "The poor ye have always with ye" was a
maxim hallowed by religion, respected by custom, and enforced
by law.

Poverty did become a "problem" capable of solution in the
surplus economy introduced by the Industrial Revolution. That
great economic change created a horn of plenty from which
poured great quantities of goods of all sorts. Wealth increased
rapidly, but poverty continued to exist. To be poor in a poor
country was considered natural, but to be poor in a rich country was felt to be unjust, unbearable, and not to be tolerated.
The problem of production was solved, or at least was on the
way to being solved, as wealth increased by leaps and bounds
with every advance of agriculture and industry. Production now
reached such magnitude that "freedom from want" became a
distinct possibility if the productive capacity of an industrialized
nation was fully utilized. What was needed was a just system
of distribution in order that mankind might free itself once and
for all of the scandal of physical want for which there was no
economic or moral justification. Poverty amidst plenty was a
denial of the promise of democracy.

What was to be done? Many widely differing answers were
given to this question, all the way from moderate reform to vio-

lent revolution. There was one matter on which all progressives were agreed, namely, that *laissez faire* must go. The new democracy of the twentieth century proclaimed in all lands that the government would have to assume responsibility for the economic welfare of the citizens by becoming the over-all agency of social and economic reform. Laws were to be passed with the object of narrowing the gulf between rich and poor by raising the standard of living of the masses through social insurance, higher wages, and shorter hours. "The 'right to work' and the right to a 'living wage' are just as valid as the rights of person or of property. That is to say, they are integral conditions of a good social order." [1] During the first half of the twentieth century the political theory of democracy was expanded into a social theory, according to which it behooved the state to secure social rights, as, at one time, it had secured political rights. This new view implied that the state was to be given power to mitigate, and eventually to abolish, the injustices that arise from great inequality in economic life. Democracy in the twentieth century meant individual liberty plus economic security.

There began a war on poverty that was waged with increasing intensity as the years wore on. *Laissez faire* was repudiated by the liberal parties in Europe, notably by the Liberals in Britain and by the Radical Socialists in France who in the beginning of the twentieth century embarked on a program of social reform. They received the support of the powerful socialist parties that had appeared in almost every country in Western Europe. First on the agenda of the social reformers was security legislation for the workers, and with good reason. Of all classes the workers had least to fall back upon in case of an emergency. The capitalist had securities, savings from profits, credit at the banks, and wealthy relatives and friends. The member of a profession, too, had security; his knowledge, experience, and reputation stood him in good stead at all times, good and bad. So did

[1] L. H. Hobhouse, *Liberalism* (1911), 159.

the farmer, who had land, tools, and a home; he could always depend on having food and shelter. But the unskilled industrial laborer, the factory "hand," had nothing: no savings, as his wages were seldom more than sufficient to enable him to live; no credit, except to a limited extent at the food stores; no opulent relatives or friends; and no knowledge and experience of consequence. Sickness, unemployment, and old age decreased the laborer's income and increased his expenses. At all times he was exposed to the uncertain working of capitalist economy with its shifting markets, technological changes, and periodic depressions. On the back of the worker fell the full weight of the business cycle. When business showed signs of slowing down, the capitalist would begin to retrench by discharging employees and by reducing the wages of those still employed. When business showed an upturn, unemployed laborers would be happy to get jobs even at low wages. Of all the industrial ills that afflicted the worker the worst was unemployment, the very acme of insecurity. The unemployed could be described as a form of surplus population, now in one locality, now in another; now in one season, now in another; now in one industry, now in another. Unemployment existed in good times as well as in bad, and it rose to tragic heights during periods of depression. Being a conspicuous waste of labor power, unemployment harmed not only the workers but industry and the community as well. In the opinion of social reformers it was a problem of industry, not an act of God, an economic disease to be cured, not a passing misfortune to be alleviated by charity.

RISE OF THE SOCIALIST MOVEMENT

The socialist movement became prominent during the first half of the twentieth century. Its primary aim was to solve the age-old problem of poverty with its attendant evils. Socialism proposed to abolish the capitalist social order, based on competition in economic life and on class inequality in society, and to establish a new social order in which the production of wealth would be by cooperative instead of by competitive methods and its distribution would be according to the principles of economic equality. In the classless society, as envisioned by socialists, all economic enterprises would be owned and operated by the state, and all persons would be required to work at wages fixed by the government according to the position held and the worker's ability. Private ownership of productive property, such as factories and mines, would be banned, but personal property, such as clothes and furniture, would be permitted. By this system, called "socialism" or the Cooperative Commonwealth, socialists hoped to inaugurate the golden age of a happy humanity free from the cares and worries that have come with the economic insecurities of capitalism.

Socialism had its birth in Western Europe during the first half of the nineteenth century. A group of thinkers appeared, known as the "Utopian socialists," of whom the most prominent were two Frenchmen, Claude Henri, Comte de Saint-Simon, and Charles Fourier, and the Briton, Robert Owen. The Utopian socialists severely criticized the methods of competitive capitalism as wasteful, unjust, and inhumane because they were based on the exploitation of man by man. They advocated a harmonious economy in which the production of goods would be by a cooperative association and the wealth produced would be distributed by the members according to the principle "from each according to his capacity and to each according to his needs."

During the middle of the nineteenth century a new and sharp turn was given to the socialist movement by the German thinker, Karl Marx. What became known as "Marxism" was far more militant in character than Utopian socialism. Unlike the latter it advocated revolutionary methods by emphasizing the class struggle between capital and labor. So great was the appeal of

Marxism to many European workers that it swept Utopian socialism aside and became the recognized creed of the socialist masses in nearly every country of Europe.[2]

Socialism took definite shape as an international working-class movement with the organization in London, in 1865, of the First International. It consisted of all sorts of revolutionists, some representing radical organizations and others self-chosen, who aimed at world revolution. Marx succeeded in dominating the assembly, which adopted his views. Because of internal dissension, the First International went out of existence in 1873. However, the idea of a world socialist organization persisted, and in 1889 the Second International was formed in Paris. Unlike its predecessor the Second International was a world federation of national socialist parties, and it rigidly excluded all those who favored revolutionary action. It aimed to establish socialism solely by the democratic method of organizing a socialist party in each nation and appealing to all citizens for support. Only when socialists succeeded in winning a majority in parliament would laws be passed looking to the final establishment of the Cooperative Commonwealth. This policy of gradualness was in complete harmony with democratic principles and methods.

The Second International grew rapidly. In 1914 it included the socialist parties of 27 nations, with a membership of about 12,000,000. Socialist parties succeeded in becoming a factor to be reckoned with in the politics of almost every European country. They became the rallying point of discontented workers and of those who sympathized with them. Socialist parties played a decisive role in the parliaments of Germany, France, Italy, and Britain. The largest socialist party in the world, prior to 1914, was the German Social Democratic party, which in the elections of 1912 polled about 4,250,000 votes and elected 110 members to the *Reichstag*. The French Socialist party rose to great importance during the Dreyfus Affair. In 1899, for the first

[2] For a fuller description of Marxism, see pp. 208–217.

time in history, a Socialist, Alexandre Millerand, became a minister, in the cabinet formed to review the Dreyfus case. In the French elections of 1914 the Socialist party polled about 1,500,000 votes and elected 102 members to the Chamber of Deputies. The Italian Socialist party won the support not only of the workers but of those who despaired of any reform from the other parties. In the elections of 1913 the Italian Socialist parties polled about 1,000,000 votes. Socialism in Britain was slower to get under way. The British Labor party, organized at the beginning of the twentieth century, succeeded in becoming an important factor in politics as a result of the elections of 1905, when it polled about 323,000 votes and won 29 seats in Parliament.[3] Even in America where socialism had little attraction for the workers, the Socialist party polled almost a million votes in the presidential election of 1912. Socialist parties appeared in Latin America, but their influence was small, owing to the constant flouting of parliamentary government by military dictators.

The socialist party in every land became the mouthpiece of the discontented workers. In every way and on every occasion it championed the cause of labor by demanding radical changes in the capitalist economy. The minimum demands of the socialists included drastic social reforms that would give security and a higher standard of living to the workers as the first necessary step in the direction of the Cooperative Commonwealth. Discontent, as expressed by large and militant political parties, was not to be trifled with. An embittered working class discontented with its lot constituted a standing threat to the existence of the social order. Farsighted statesmen, even conservative ones like Waldeck-Rousseau in France and Winston Churchill in Britain, saw in social reform the best method of maintaining stability along with progress. Revolution might become the alternative to reform.

[3] See p. 101.

SOCIAL REFORM BEFORE THE FIRST
WORLD WAR

To socialism belongs the chief credit for the comprehensive social reforms of the first half of the twentieth century. Curiously
enough this latest phase of democracy had been initiated by the
least democratic nation in Western Europe, the German Empire.
As early as the eighties of the nineteenth century, laws were enacted in that country establishing compulsory sickness and invalidity insurance, which gave benefits to those workers who
suffered from illness, temporary or permanent; workmen's compensation for disability caused by industrial accidents; and old-
age pensions to workers who reached the retirement age. Why
did semiautocratic Germany march in advance of the democracies in these great reforms? Several explanations may be given
for this anomaly. Once united, Germany made rapid economic
progress, almost a leaping advance from an agrarian to a Big
Business economy. Therefore, *laissez faire,* characteristic of the
era of competitive capitalism, did not become deeply rooted
among the Germans, as it had among the British, the French,
and the Americans. State intervention in economic matters, long
traditional in Germany, became relatively easier to accept in
the new era of consolidated industry. But there are other explanations. Bismarck, who was chiefly responsible for the passage of the social laws, was motivated, in part at least, by his
desire to weaken the faith of the German workers in socialism
and to strengthen their faith in the newly founded nation that
was willing to show solicitude for their welfare. Military motives, too, played an important part in the adoption of these
ultraradical reforms by an ultraconservative government. German policies, domestic as well as foreign, were always geared
to military objectives. One aim of the Bismarckian reforms was

to protect the German workers against the devastating effects of laissez-faire capitalism in order to make them physically effective as soldiers and devotedly loyal as citizens of the empire.

Not until the twentieth century did Britain, France, and America take up social reform. The explanation for this belatedness of the democratic nations lies chiefly in the fact that competitive capitalism with a minimum of state intervention had flourished among them for over a century. *Laissez faire* became a national tradition, which acted as a serious obstacle to reforms that could come only through state intervention in economic matters. A cherished theory proved to be a greater obstacle than an evil fact.

Before the advent of democracy a belief had prevailed among the wealthy that their security lay in keeping the masses ignorant and poor. Being ignorant the masses would neither know nor understand why they were poor; and being poor they would lack the necessary means to mobilize the strength of numbers in a struggle with the upper classes. But democracy came and made the people sovereign. It became evident even during the nineteenth century that the masses would not be content for long to remain "miserable and sovereign." Demands arose for the extension of democracy to the economic field through government intervention in the relations between capital and labor. This demand was backed up by powerful labor and socialist parties.

Britain was the first of the great democratic nations to repudiate *laissez faire*. When the Liberals came into power in 1906, they promptly inaugurated a program of social reform. For almost a decade, the Liberal ministry put through social security laws, such as old-age pensions, workmen's compensation, insurance against sickness, disability, and unemployment. Britain's distinctive contribution to social reform was unemployment insurance. France lagged behind Britain. Before the First World War, France had adopted only two important social reforms: workmen's compensation and old-age pensions. Austria-Hungary, Scandinavia, the Netherlands, Belgium, and Switzerland adopted social reforms modeled more or less on those of Germany. America continued unabated her traditional individualism in economic matters. In America, where *laissez faire* was more deeply rooted than elsewhere, it was upheld by government, by business, and even by organized labor itself.[4]

SOCIAL REFORM AFTER THE FIRST WORLD WAR

After the First World War, social reform made extraordinary progress in all democratic lands. The war had been fought "to make the world safe for democracy," and democracy had come to mean social reform. What made social reform urgently necessary was the economic dislocation following the war, which deepened into the Great Depression of 1929. An almost total breakdown of the industrial system confronted Europe and America. Millions were thrown out of work for long periods, and the whip of unemployment goaded many to seek desperate remedies. Democracy now met the greatest crisis in its history. The totalitarian dictatorships, Communist Russia, Nazi Germany, and Fascist Italy, promised economic security for all classes. They established stringent control and regulation of all economic life with the prime objective of abolishing depressions. Many ruined businessmen and unemployed workers now turned either to fascism or to communism as ways of economic salvation. To survive, democracy had to present comprehensive plans for economic well-being under the regime of political freedom. Social reform now passed from the stage of remedial emergency to that of an integrated social program, comprehensive in scope and generous in benefits.

[4] See p. 342.

In 1930 France enacted a comprehensive social insurance law, providing for financial benefits in the events of sickness, invalidity, maternity, old age, and death. Later, in 1936, the Popular Front ministry, headed by Léon Blum, put through laws limiting the work week to 40 hours and granting paid vacations to workers. The law establishing paid vacations constitutes France's distinctive contribution to social reform. Britain revised her prewar social legislation by making it more comprehensive and by granting more generous payments. Germany, under the Weimar Republic, extended the social reforms of the German Empire by adopting insurance against unemployment and a national 8-hour workday. Switzerland, the Scandinavian states, the Netherlands, and Belgium extended their existing systems of social reform. The new nations that emerged in Central Europe fell under the rule of socialist or semisocialist parties that hastened to put through radical social measures. Even backward countries, like those in Latin America, in the Balkans, and in the Middle East, adopted some forms of social security.

America, a newcomer in the field of social security, made rapid strides to catch up with Western Europe. During the New Deal era of Franklin D. Roosevelt, who became President in 1932, many radical social reform measures were adopted. The Federal government established systems of old-age pensions and of unemployment insurance. Liberal workmen's compensation laws were passed by many of the states; in some of the states such laws had been enacted even before the advent of the New Deal. America made an innovation in the field of social reform when Congress, in 1938, passed a national wages and hours law, establishing a minimum wage and maximum hours of work for almost all employees engaged in interstate commerce.

The New Deal constituted a drastic repudiation of America's tradition of *laissez faire*. The social reform laws were put through Congress with little opposition and were accepted by virtually the entire nation. Even the Republicans, in opposition to the

Democratic administration, accepted much of the New Deal, though they denounced its ideas and methods. To signalize the advent of a new era in American history, President Roosevelt, in a notable message to Congress, recommended the adoption of an economic bill of rights. As the Bill of Rights guaranteed the civil and political rights of the individual citizen, this new bill of rights, according to the President, would guarantee his social and economic rights, such as the right of the worker to earn a satisfactory livelihood; of the farmer to sell his products at satisfactory prices; and of all citizens to adequate medical care and to protection from economic hazards due to old age, sickness, accident, and unemployment.

Social reform as a policy now ceased to be an issue in the public life of democratic nations. What still divided political parties was the question of the extent of the coverage and the amount of the benefits. Almost every wage earner could now demand as a right that the government protect him against economic misfortunes for which he was not responsible. This right is something new in the annals of "the most numerous and the most poor."

SOCIAL REFORM AFTER THE SECOND WORLD WAR

The Second World War was followed by world-wide ruin, discontent, and dislocation. Social reform was everywhere now regarded essential in the plans for national recovery and economic stabilization. And social reform had to be generous in benefits, expanded in scope, and unified in application to be effective in postwar reconstruction. A guarantee of an assured higher standard of life for the workers would encourage them to strive in every way to increase production, all-essential to recovery. In order to achieve this objective, social reform was integrated with economic planning and expanded to such an extent that a new political concept came to the fore, known as the "welfare state." The prime duty of a government, asserted its champions, was so to allocate the national income as to provide a minimum of economic well-being for everyone able and willing to work.

Britain led the way in the establishment of the welfare state. The Labor party, socialist in aim, democratic in principle, and with faith in the "inevitability of gradualness" emerged victorious from the elections of 1945. For the first time the Laborites controlled Parliament by a large majority, and hence were free to carry out their program of social reform and nationalization. Their victory constituted as great an event in the history of modern Britain as did that of the Whigs in 1832. As after the Reform Bill of 1832 great reforms followed, primarily in the interest of the middle class, so the Labor victory of 1945 was followed by great reforms, primarily in the interest of the working class. Under the Labor Ministry headed by Prime Minister Clement Attlee, Britain set the most rapid pace and reached the most advanced stage of social reform in history. In 1946 two extraordinary laws, the National Insurance Act and the National Health Service Act, established unified systems of social security superseding all previous legislation in these fields. Inspired by the famous Beveridge Plan (after its author, Sir William Beveridge) the National Insurance Act had a twofold aim: (1) to establish a national minimum of subsistence below which no one would be permitted to fall and (2) to give security to all persons against the hazards of life "from the cradle to the grave." Those employed by others, the self-employed, and the nonemployed were all required to be insured. The insured made a single contribution to which were added contributions by employers and by the state. The benefits from this fund were numerous and various: allowances for sickness, disability, maternity, and unemployment; old-age pensions and death benefits; and allowances to widows and to orphaned children.

The National Health Insurance Act marked a high peak in the progress of socialized medicine. It was grounded on the principle that it was the duty of the government to provide health service for all, as, for long, it had been its duty to provide education for all. Medical services were made available to every one "from duke to dustman." Those unwilling to patronize the public health services could obtain private treatment at their own expense. The law created a complete system of health services, physical and mental, general and special: treatment by doctors and dentists, medicines, appliances, nursing, and hospitalization. Doctors were to be paid by the government. All medical services, of whatever kind, were made free to the patients. The cost was borne chiefly by the government through general taxation, supplemented by contributions from the funds created by the system of national insurance. No longer need the poor look to private charity, which was on the way to being abolished. Both "Lady Bountiful" and "Little Orphan Annie" vanished from the new Britain of the mid-twentieth century.

Would the welfare state with its drastic social reforms and nationalized industries [5] be maintained in Britain? The answer came in the elections of 1950. During the campaign the Conservative party stated officially that, if victorious, it would make no essential changes in the reforms already enacted, but would oppose further nationalization, as advocated by the Labor party. The British elections excited world-wide interest because of the issue of socialism, now clearly before the electorate. The outcome disappointed both parties; neither gained a decisive victory. Out of 625 seats the Laborites won 316; the Conservatives, 297; the Liberals, 9; and independents, 3. All the Communist candidates were defeated. Of the popular vote, the Laborites received over 46 per cent and the Conservatives over 43 per cent.

[5] See pp. 56ff.

The Labor ministry, headed by Prime Minister Attlee, continued in office, but its precarious majority forbade further nationalization. In harmony with the British tradition of gradual reform the welfare state was safe, though its advance was slowed down.

The radical reforms passed by the Labor party made Britain the great exemplar of the welfare state. The other nations followed her lead but not her pace, as postwar economic conditions put serious limits on government expenditures. But everywhere, economic security was now accepted as a new civil right, not, as formerly, merely as a means to tide over a passing crisis. The constitutions of the Fourth French Republic, of the Italian Republic, and of the German Federal Republic all proclaimed economic security as one of man's fundamental rights. Even in the backward Orient were these new rights proclaimed, notably in the post-Second World War constitutions of Japan and of the Union of India.

Social reform proved highly successful in accomplishing its aims, namely to protect the workers against extreme exploitation by employers and against the insecurities of the industrial system. It did not touch the fundamental problem of bringing about a juster distribution of the national income, now recognized as another facet of democracy. True, laws were enacted laying heavy taxes on large incomes and raising the standard of living of the workers by establishing minimum wages and maximum hours of work. But these laws merely touched the problem of wealth distribution. Wealth, and very great wealth, continued to be the privilege of comparatively few, and poverty, even grinding poverty, continued to be the lot of millions of the "underprivileged." A fair test of social progress, at any time and under any political system, is improvement in the status of the lowest class. Today, the workers constitute the lowest class, being the most numerous unpropertied element in a social order in which the man of property is considered the

very epitome of success. Some of the workers have managed to
become men of property, especially in America, but the great
majority have remained, and are likely to remain, wage earners. How could their standard of living be made progressively
higher?

Could the state undertake to distribute the national wealth
without regard to property rights? Obviously, "no." Was a
juster distribution of wealth possible under capitalism? The
answer was "yes." But how? The very nature of the industrial
system itself showed the way. Immense quantities of goods had
to find an outlet; otherwise production would slow down and
finally end in a depression. It became obvious that high wages
would create a demand for more goods, which in turn would
stimulate production. Capitalists would thereby gain the advantage by selling more goods, thereby reaping greater profits.
Instead of beggaring the workers through low wages they
would find more and better customers through the increased
purchasing power that would come with higher wages. Henry
Ford, the famous automobile manufacturer, initiated what was
a novel policy in his day, by voluntarily raising wages in his
automobile works and by producing a cheap, serviceable car.
High wages and low prices proved to be profitable for Henry
Ford because the large output found a large market in the
higher standard of life of the masses of people.

PROGRESS OF TRADE-UNIONISM

However, few capitalists followed Ford's example. Their shortsighted view inclined them to see greater possibilities for profit
in high prices and low wages. To attain a higher standard of
living by getting a larger share of the national income, the
workers perforce had to fight for it themselves. And their most
powerful weapon in the many conflicts that took place be-

tween capital and labor was the trade-union. No more striking evidence of labor's progress can be shown than a comparison between the status of the industrial worker of the first half of the twentieth century with that in the first half of the nineteenth. And the institution that made possible this advance was the trade-union, an institution created by and for the industrial workers. During the first half of the nineteenth century the trade-union was under the ban of both law and public opinion. Its effective weapon, the strike, was banned as seditious; and its life principle, collective bargaining, was condemned as being in restraint of trade, and hence antisocial. Their organizations having been thus outlawed, the workers could not fight effectively against both employers and the government.

A great change came with the enfranchisement of the workers. The trade-unions were emancipated almost on the morrow of the establishment of manhood suffrage: in America, for the most part, during the Jacksonian period in the thirties of the nineteenth century; in England in 1871 and 1875; in France in 1884; and in Germany in 1890. By the twentieth century trade-unions were legal in Western and Central Europe, in the United States, and in the British Dominions. They continued to suffer legal restrictions in those countries that were backward industrially and politically, such as Russia and most of the Latin-American states. In order to unify the labor movement and give it general direction, the trade-unions formed powerful national federations, such as the British Trades Union Congress, the French General Confederation of Labor (CGT), the German General Federation of Labor, the Italian General Confederation of Labor, and the American Federation of Labor (AFL).

Freed legally, recognized by the employers, and accepted by public opinion, the trade-unions now enjoyed a normal existence as legitimate institutions. In order to get a larger share of the national income, they concentrated their efforts in two directions: toward obtaining a living wage and a shorter workday. The power of the trade-unions proved the decisive factor in causing real, or purchasing power, of wages to rise markedly during the last quarter of the nineteenth century: over 100 per cent in the United States from 1865 to 1890; 47 per cent in Britain from 1870 to 1900; and about 30 per cent in France and in Germany from 1870 to 1900. During this period, hours of labor were reduced from about 60 hours a week in Britain and in the United States to about 54.[6] It is well to note, however, that increased production, due to technological progress, made possible the success of trade-unions in obtaining for the workers a higher standard of living with fewer hours of work. They now shared, along with the capitalists, in the benefits of increased production.

Once a higher standard of living was gained by the working class, any threat to lower it was bound to rouse resistance, even to the point of revolution. During the first decade of the twentieth century a decline in real wages began in the highly industrialized nations: Britain, Germany, and America. Prices increased more rapidly than did money wages; this sent tremors of discontent reverberating throughout the world of organized labor. The trade-unions, now powerful, militant, and respectable, were roused to action. Strikes became frequent, but whether the workers won or lost they failed to advance their standard of living or even to maintain it.[7]

What aggravated this situation was the hostile attitude of the government toward trade-unions. When serious industrial conflicts arose during the first decade of the twentieth century, notably in Britain, America, and France, government intervention favored the employers. In 1901, as a consequence of a railway strike in Wales, a judicial decision in the famous Taff Vale case

[6] H. U. Faulkner, *American Economic History* (1935), 574–575; and W. Bowden, M. Karpovich, and A. P. Usher, *An Economic History of Europe since 1870* (1937), 545.

[7] Faulkner, *op. cit.,* 689; Bowden *et al., op. cit.,* 545.

declared that the union by striking caused losses to the railway company; hence the latter was entitled to damages for its loss of business. The strike was broken, and the union treasury was depleted.

A similar situation arose in America. A strike of the hatters in Danbury, Connecticut, resulted in the equally famous Danbury Hat case (1908). The court held that the members of the union were financially responsible for the company's loss of business, occasioned by the boycott of its hats that had been instituted by the union. The strike collapsed, and the strikers had to pay heavy damages.

Far more dramatic was the great labor struggle in France. In 1910 a general strike took place on the railways tying up the whole country. The situation became serious, and Premier Aristide Briand broke the strike by resorting to a novel method. He called the strikers to the colors as reservists, and then commanded them to operate the railways. They obeyed, as defiance to military orders would have entailed severe punishment.

The reverses suffered by labor in these famous conflicts, and in many others less notable, created a mood of bitter resentment among trade-unionists. They were convinced that action in the industrial field alone was inadequate to advance, and even to maintain, their living standard. Political action was now considered necessary in order to supplement industrial action, with the aim of using the government to shift the balance of economic power in favor of labor. According to the trade-unionists, democracy must broaden its scope by taking into account the demands and the driving power of organized labor in order to advance "the greatest happiness of the greatest number."

Political parties devoted to the cause of labor democracy came to the fore. Britain became the pioneer of this new form of political activity when the trade-unions organized the Labor party at the beginning of the twentieth century. In 1905 it scored an initial success by electing 29 members to Parliament. Though

small, the Labor party was sufficiently influential to persuade
Parliament to nullify the Taff Vale decision by passing a law
(1906) which exempted trade-unions from damage suits in
connection with strikes. Organized labor in France had shunned
politics. The CGT had espoused syndicalism, a semianarchist
creed, according to which the trade-unions sought to employ
"direct" action to gain favorable conditions of employment and
even to abolish capitalism altogether. By "direct" action was
meant continuous industrial conflict through strikes and sabotage, by contrast with political action, or legislation to ameliorate the condition of labor. But the collapse of the railway strike
of 1910, as a result of government action, caused the French
workers to rally to the support of the Socialist party in order
to gain influence in the government. As a consequence of labor
support, the Socialist party rapidly became one of the leading
parties in the Chamber. The story of organized labor in Italy
was similar to that in France. Most striking was the advance of
socialist trade-unionism in Germany. Unlike the situation in
Britain, where the trade-unions formed the Labor party, those
in Germany were formed by the Social Democratic party.
Throughout the period of the German Empire, the trade-unions
constituted the solid core of this party. Largely because of this
support, the *Reichstag* elections of 1912 resulted in making the
Social Democrats the leading party in Germany.

Because of favorable economic conditions, class consciousness
among the workers in America was far weaker than in Europe.
Trade-unionism grew, but it did not develop socialist tendencies
as marked as those in Europe. Although organized labor in
America persistently refused to form a socialist party, it did have
a political policy, which was to reward the friends of labor and
to punish its enemies. Generally, American trade-unionists supported candidates of any party favorable to labor and opposed
those hostile to it. This policy bore fruit in 1914, when Congress,
acceding to the demands of organized labor, passed the Clay-

ton Act, according to which a trade-union, unlike a business corporation, could not be sued on the charge of being in restraint
of trade. This law protected the trade-union against prosecu-
tion as a monopoly, by exempting it from the Sherman Anti-
trust Act.

NEW IMPORTANCE OF TRADE-UNIONISM

The trade-unions emerged from the First World War more
powerful than ever before. Their patriotic cooperation in the
Allied countries had played no small part in bringing victory
to the cause of the Allies. After the war, the trade-unions gained
so markedly in numbers, in power, and in prestige that a new
attitude of labor toward society became discernible. No longer
was the worker content to work for wages only and to remain
in a subordinate position in the hierarchical order of industry,
a "depersonalized hand" to be compensated well or ill by those
above him. His growing strength gave him a feeling of importance, as being a vital element in the preservation of the
social order. And the trade-unions, clearly and definitely, measured his new power and importance. Though representing a
minority of the wage earners, these bodies could and did speak
for the working class as a whole. Having the cohesiveness of
organization and the strategic advantage of being concentrated
in the fundamental industries, the trade-unions came to be considered the spokesmen of the working class. Any advance in the
living standard of the organized workers would, in time, be
reflected in that of the unorganized.

Never before had the power of the trade-unions been so
great. Politically, it was felt in the rise to power of the socialist
parties in Western Europe; and socially, in the enactment of
radical social legislation. Even greater was the influence of the
trade-unions in the economic field because of a significant shift

in their unit of organization. This shift was from the craft union consisting of skilled workers in a specialized field, such as carpenters or plumbers, to the industrial union consisting of all the workers in one entire industry: skilled, unskilled, manual, clerical, and executive, all the way from factory "hand" to manager. Good examples of industrial unionism were the British National Union of Mineworkers and the United Steel Workers of America. Generally this type of organization prevailed in highly concentrated, monopolistic industries, such as coal, iron, steel, railways, shipping, telegraphs, and telephones. In general, the change to industrial unionism in Britain came as a result of merging many small, craft unions into one large union consisting of all workers in an industry. From 1900 to 1939, trade-union membership in Britain tripled, but the number of unions had declined by one-third.[8] Industrial unionism in America came, generally, with the advance of the mass-production industries, such as automobiles, rubber, and electrical equipment. Unskilled and semiskilled workers, who predominated in these industries, had been neglected by the craft unions of the American Federation of Labor. With the advent, in 1938, of the Congress of Industrial Organizations (CIO), these workers were rapidly enrolled in gigantic industrial unions.

Concentrated labor now confronted concentrated capital. At the conference table, the bargaining power of an industrial union equaled, and sometimes surpassed, that of a combination of employers. A general strike in a key industry, such as coal, steel, or railways, would paralyze not only that industry but would also create a great emergency involving the economic life of the entire nation. Such a strike could not be regarded as a "private fight" between workers and employers, as had been the localized strikes during the nineteenth century. The govern-

---

[8] In 1900, there were 1,323 registered trade-unions; by 1947 the number had declined to 730, though the total membership had increased. *Trade Unions in Britain,* British Information Services, December, 1949.

ment perforce had to intervene in a strike that created a national emergency by using its influence to compel both parties to settle their differences peacefully. Toward this end industrial machinery was created by governments with the object of promoting mediation and arbitration in industrial disputes.

The menace of the general strike became greater with the growth of communism in the trade-unions. Some of the most powerful ones fell under the control of Communists, who set the pace of aggressive trade-union action by their militant championship of the workers' demands. In some European countries, notably France, the Communists controlled the trade-unions in the key industries, and they openly avowed their aim to use general strikes as a means of creating a "revolutionary situation." Even more effective than a general strike in a key industry would be a general strike of all organized labor in the nation, called by the national federation of trade-unions. In order to compete with the Communists, the noncommunist trade-unions often stepped up their demands on capital and resorted to general strikes. The CGT called general strikes of all labor in France in 1920, 1934, and 1938, but they proved ineffective. In 1926, the Trades Union Congress called a general strike of all labor in Britain, but it collapsed within a week. Though it had no communist aims, this revolutionary kind of strike, novel in Britain, created widespread fear. In 1927, a Conservative Parliament passed a new trade-union act that, among other restrictions, forbade the calling of a general strike. The most tragic result of a general strike took place in Italy. In 1920, a general strike of all labor was called with the object of bringing about a social revolution. The workers seized factories, ousted the managers, and proclaimed their revolutionary aims. Although the strike failed, it created so much fear that many Italians turned to fascism. Two years later, Mussolini came to power largely because of the widespread fear of communism roused by the general strike. Confronted with the power of labor to create national emergencies, and even to threaten social revolution, something had to be done to avert such calamities.

Efforts were made in democratic countries to mollify the trade-unions. In some instances labor was placed on an equal footing with capital by governments eager to preserve industrial peace. An outstanding example of this new policy was the "Whitley councils" in Britain, so-called after their founder, J. H. Whitley. These were legally created bodies, representing labor and capital, that could be established in any trade that so desired. A Whitley council was given the power to consider "matters affecting the progress and well-being of the trade from the point of view of all those engaged in it."

The Weimar constitution of the German Republic made a notable advance in the movement to promote industrial peace. It contained provisions for the establishment of industrial councils in each trade, representing capital and labor, and for a national industrial council to coordinate their activities. Laws were passed creating these councils that, for a time, functioned successfully. So influential were the trade-unions in the German Republic that a law was passed that made collective bargaining a national policy by giving the government power to extend any trade-union agreement throughout the entire industry.

Industrial councils, similar to those in Britain and in Germany, were also established in France. Trade-unionism scored a great triumph with the advent in 1936 of the Popular Front ministry, headed by the Socialist Léon Blum and supported in the Chamber of Deputies by a bloc of Socialists, Communists, and Radical Socialists. One law made collective bargaining compulsory between the national federation of trade-unions, the CGT, and the national federation of employers. Another law gave the government power to transform an agreement between a trade-union and an employer in one enterprise into a code for the entire industry.

Trade-unionism in America achieved unprecedented triumphs

during the interwar period. The CIO, organized apart from and in opposition to the AFL, manifested a spirit of militancy far greater than that of its rival. Some of its unions fell under the control of the Communists, who endeavored to set a revolutionary pace to organized labor in America. The successes of the CIO in winning labor battles spurred on the conservative AFL to make more radical demands.

Both federations continued the traditional policy of American labor by refusing to organize a third political party. Nevertheless, they were active politically, and played a notable part in the four presidential elections from 1932 to 1944. The extraordinary success of the Democratic candidate, Franklin D. Roosevelt, was to no small degree due to the almost solid support that he received from the organized workers. And their reward came with the passage in 1935 of the National Labor Relations Act, the most complete and the most far-reaching trade-union law in the history of America up to that time. It was heavily weighted on the side of labor in every provision. Among other provisions of the law, popularly known as the Wagner act, an employer was compelled to recognize and to bargain with the trade-union that represented a majority of his employees. He was forbidden in any way to discourage the formation of a trade-union by his employees, or to discriminate against or discharge an employee because of union activity. The Wagner act gave labor a decided advantage over capital.

TRADE-UNIONISM AFTER THE SECOND WORLD WAR

Trade-unionism now had a new status in Western Europe and in America. Hitherto its fundamental principle, collective bargaining, had been recognized as legal; now it was enforced by the coercive power of the government. What the First World

War had done to give prestige and power to the trade-unions the Second World War greatly intensified. Their patriotic support of the democratic governments, in keeping up the production of war materiel, proved vital in the terrific struggle against fascism. Consequently, the trade-unions came to regard themselves as the saviors of democracy, and their interests as being paramount in the nation. Their demands became excessive; their methods, arbitrary; and their aim, the monopolistic control of the labor supply. Like other vested interests they desired power without responsibility.

The postwar problem in respect to labor was to devise ways and means to curb the irresponsible power of labor. It had different aspects in Britain, on the Continent, and in America. In that classic land of trade-unionism, Britain, the Labor ministry of Clement Attlee, mindful of the political power of organized labor, put through a law repealing the trade-union act of 1927. Again, British labor became free of curbs on its activities. And yet, the victorious sweep of labor in the elections of 1945 brought responsibilities to that party. Ever since the English Revolution in the seventeenth century, a national tradition had been established that no power could be exercised in the land by any one person or by any group of persons without responsibility. On coming to power, the Labor party, almost insensibly, accepted this national tradition and acted accordingly. This was forcefully illustrated in 1949, when shipping was tied up by a "wildcat" strike of the dockers. As national recovery was seriously endangered by this strike, the government acted promptly and decisively. Parliament declared a state of national emergency. The ministry took drastic action against the strikers, including the use of troops to load and to unload ships. The strike collapsed.

Quite different was the story in the democratic nations on the Continent, where the Communists had succeeded in winning over many workers. As a consequence, these nations came to regard trade-unions as enemies of the state. In France and Italy the Communist-controlled labor federations determined to use their power to overthrow the democratic governments and to establish a totalitarian dictatorship. Under Communist direction these labor bodies called general strikes, organized systems of sabotage, and even prepared for insurrection. Great resentment followed, and a reaction against communism took place within the ranks of organized labor itself. In both France and Italy many trade-unions seceded from the national federation and formed rival national bodies in opposition to the Communists. These noncommunist federations, some socialist, others Catholic in tendency, strongly supported the French and Italian governments in their struggle against communism.

Also different was the story of labor in America after the war. A violent reaction took place against the Wagner act, which had given the trade-unions great power with little responsibility. As a consequence, serious abuses developed: the trade-unions often became arbitrary; their demands, unreasonable; and their practices, antisocial. Public opinion was aroused against them, especially against some of their leaders, such as John L. Lewis, leader of the miners, and James C. Petrillo, leader of the musicians, both of whom had become notorious because of their dictatorial methods. In 1947, Congress passed the Taft-Hartley law, which aimed to do away with trade-union abuses. The right of collective bargaining and other protective measures of the Wagner act were kept, but bargaining power was equalized as between employers and employees. The trade-unions could now be charged with unfair labor practices; only employers could be so charged under the Wagner act. The Taft-Hartley law forbade secondary boycotts, or refusal by workers, not on strike, to handle the goods of a firm against which a strike had been declared; jurisdictional strikes, or the refusal to work by one trade-union in dispute with another as to which had the right to the job; "featherbedding," or the creation by workers of useless jobs; and the closed shop, or the monopolistic control by a trade union of "hiring and firing." Important provisions of the law aimed to advance industrial peace through methods of mediation and arbitration. In order to make use of these methods, no strike or lockout could take place without notice of 60 days; and, in case of a vital industry in which a shutdown would create a national emergency, a strike was forbidden by means of a court injunction for a period of 80 days. The Taft-Hartley law aroused the bitter opposition of the trade-unions, and it became an issue in the presidential election of 1948.

The advance of organized labor in Western Europe and in America kept pace with the industrialization of these regions. In Latin America and in Asia the advance of organized labor was retarded, chiefly because industrialization was slow and haphazard. The economic dislocation and the rapidly rising cost of living in Latin America, following the First World War, stimulated the formation of trade-unions that championed the workers' demand for higher wages. The governments, being generally dictatorial, opposed the trade-unions. However, the latter were permitted to develop, largely because of the strong nationalist sentiment against alien capitalists, who, in many cases, controlled the industrial enterprises.

Mexico was the center of Latin-American trade-unionism. The Revolution of 1917, for the first time, granted employees the full right to form trade-unions and to strike. A powerful national organization of labor, the CROM, appeared, which directed the policies of Mexican labor. The CROM, from the outset, was radical politically and cooperated with the revolutionary movement in the country. Shortly before the Second World War it fell under Communist control, which caused divisions in its ranks.

The most highly industrialized Latin-American state was Argentina. Trade-unionism was introduced there by immigrants from Spain and Italy, who were largely syndicalist in sentiment. Despite repression by the government, trade-unionism managed to survive and even to grow. As in Mexico, Communists became influential in Argentina's labor movement, which was not least among the causes for the election of the dictatorial Perón as president in 1946. Under the semifascist regime of Perón the trade-unions underwent a transformation similar to that in Italy under Mussolini. They were placed under the full control and direction of the government, which forbade strikes and, at the same time, sought to alleviate the condition of the workers by compelling the employers to raise wages.

Trade-unionism in Asia, like that in Latin America, made little progress because of industrial backwardness. In the most industrialized nation of Asia, Japan, the trade-unions were weakest because of the hostility of the government. The imperial regime regarded them as revolutionary organizations, and, though permitted by law to exist, the trade-unions were unable to function because of severe governmental restrictions on their activities. Emancipation came with the defeat of Japan in the Second World War. When the country was placed under the control of the American army of occupation, trade-unions were freely encouraged as potent forces of democracy that America aimed to spread among the Japanese people.

China and India exhibited similarities in the development of trade-unionism. In both countries it was an expression of nationalism as well as that of the desire of the workers to raise their standard of living. Trade-unions appeared in China and in India during the twentieth century, chiefly in the industrial centers, where foreign capitalists constituted an important element among the large employers of labor. Strikes were a common occurrence during the interwar period; often they were revolutionary in character. Nationalists, Socialists, and Communists, each in turn, strove to get control of organized labor. In China, after the Second World War, the Communists be-

came dominant in the unions, a fact which contributed not a
little to the triumph of the Communists over the Nationalist
government. In India an All-Indian Trades-union Congress was
formed, in 1920, representing all organized workers. The Congress became the scene of a struggle for mastery between Nationalists, Socialists, and Communists. This struggle resulted,
after the Second World War, in a threefold division of the Indian labor movement.

The future of trade-unionism in Latin America and in Asia is
bound up with the future of democracy in these regions. Organized labor constitutes an effective opposition to the rule of
a dictator because it has the power to create economic chaos
by means of strikes and sabotage. Not even an all-powerful dictator can function in a country in which economic life is at a
standstill. Because of the concentration of a large number of
workers in modern industry it is easier to organize a trade-
union and harder to suppress it than any other form of opposition to a despotic government. Chiefly for this reason trade-
unionism in Latin America and in Asia has been regarded as
the advance guard of democracy.

Trade-unionism, as the name implies, began modestly by
organizing the workers in a single trade. As industry spread,
so did trade-unionism, and the local bodies expanded into
national federations. After the First World War the movement
for an international federation of trade-unions took definite
shape. Two world federations of labor appeared, one communist
and the other noncommunist. Neither, however, attracted much
support, and they consequently ended in failure.

The first powerful world federation of labor appeared with
the organization, in 1945, of the World Federation of Trade
Unions (WFTU). It enrolled not only the socialist trade-unions
of Western Europe but also the communist trade unions of
Soviet Russia and the radical trade-unions of the American
CIO. Before long this powerful organization fell under Com-

munist control; it constantly supported the foreign policies of Soviet Russia and denounced those of the Western democracies. Especially did the WFTU show bitter opposition to the Marshall Plan and to the North Atlantic Pact.

Widespread dissatisfaction arose among the noncommunist trade-unions affiliated with the WFTU. The British and American members seceded, as did the noncommunist French and Italian members. In 1949 a great convention met in London with the aim of forming an international organization of "free and democratic trade-union movements throughout the world." It created a new labor body, the International Confederation of Free Trade Unions (ICFTU), representing about 48,000,000 organized workers. It issued a manifesto condemning all forms of totalitarian dictatorship, whether in Communist Russia or in Fascist Spain. Economic and political democracy were declared to be inseparable, and the ICFTU pledged itself "to achieve a world in which men can be both free and secure and in which the peoples of all nations may live in peace with each other." It reaffirmed labor's right to strike and demanded full employment, international agreements on maximum hours of work, annual wages, social security, and an end to racial and religious discrimination. In the international field the ICFTU favored a universal system of atomic energy control; the unification of Western Europe, including Germany; the Marshall Plan; regional defense agreements; the abolition of the veto in the United Nations Security Council; and technical assistance to undeveloped countries.

Two rival world federations now appealed for the support of the workers. The WFTU received the allegiance of the Communist trade-unions in Eastern Europe, in France and Italy, and in the Far East. The ICFTU received the allegiance chiefly of the British trade-unions, of the non-Communist trade-unions in France and Italy, and of both the CIO and the AFL in America. These rival labor internationals reflected in the world of labor the great conflict between Soviet Russia and the Western democracies known as the "cold war."

PROGRESS OF ECONOMIC EQUALITY

Social reform and trade-unionism have been the driving forces behind the new democracy of the twentieth century. There is a striking historical parallel between the transformation that took place in the political and social scene during the first half of the twentieth century and that during the first half of the nineteenth. In the latter period the shift of power was from the landed aristocrats to the industrial capitalists. In the twentieth century the shift of power was from the capitalists, organized in great business combinations, to the workers, organized in great labor combinations. In both instances the change was made by gradual reforms in some lands and by violent upheavals in other lands. The political and economic gains achieved by the middle class during the nineteenth century are well known. What have been the political and economic gains of the working class resulting from the social democracy of the twentieth century?

These gains have been both definite and considerable, despite the serious setback to progress caused by the two world wars. The workers, organized economically in trade-unions and politically in socialist parties, have become so powerful that no retrogression is possible in democratically governed countries. The repeal of the social reform laws is almost inconceivable. These laws, affecting the workers in both private and public enterprises, now give security to millions who hitherto had suffered most from the hazards of economic life under capitalism.

The new democracy of the twentieth century has been chiefly concerned with economic equality, or the narrowing of the gap between the rich and the poor. Did the vastly increased production of the new Industrial Revolution result in raising the living standard of the masses? Did the workers receive a larger share of the national income? The answer to both questions is an unequivocal "yes." Real wages in Britain from 1914 to 1938 rose 11 per cent, and from 1938 to 1947, 20 per cent; in Germany from 1914 to 1935 36 per cent.[9] The most striking advance was in the United States where from 1939 to 1947 real wages of factory workers rose 58 per cent.[10] The standard work week in Britain and in the United States in 1950 was about 40 hours; in some cases more, and in some even less. A great ideal of union labor during the nineteenth century, the eight-hour day, has been surpassed in actual practice. The poor were getting, if not rich, at least decidedly less poor.

What about the rich? The two world wars resulted in a social transformation in Europe that shook the very foundations of the class system. This transformation was brought about by the severe curtailment, even by the elimination, of extreme wealth. Much property was lost by those who had suffered from the vast destruction inflicted by acts of war; they were not, and could not be, sufficiently compensated by the governments. After the First World War, many lost their wealth as a result of confiscations on a colossal scale: (1) of all private productive property in Soviet Russia and (2) of property belonging to Jews in Nazi Germany. After the Second World War, the property of those convicted of collaboration with the Germans was confiscated, in many instances, by the restored governments in Western Europe. The property of Jews confiscated in Germany and in the occupied countries was not fully restored. When the nations in east central Europe fell under Communist control, the property of aristocrats and of capitalists, as in Soviet Russia,

[9] E. L. Bogart, *Economic History of Europe, 1760–1939* (1942), 672, 684; and *United States News*, Sept. 24, 1948.

[10] See *United States News*, Aug. 15, 1947.

was confiscated wholesale. In these ways large sections of the wealthy classes in nearly every part of Europe disappeared.

Another aspect of this social transformation made great headway in democratic lands where property rights were respected. In addition to the losses of property suffered by the rich as a result of the war, exceedingly high taxes were levied on them by socialist governments. Redistribution of income by means of the taxing power became the deliberate policy of these governments. Economic equality was thus advanced on the one hand by leveling down the living standard of the rich through taxation and on the other hand by leveling up the living standard of the poor by making a significant transfer of purchasing power to the wage earners.

Britain became the outstanding exemplar of this process. For long the land of wealthy landowners and capitalists, severe taxation in Britain virtually shattered the class structure that had survived so many assaults in the past. The government took in taxes about 40 per cent of the national income. Especially severe was the income tax that, in some instances, was almost confiscatory in character. The government, in its egalitarian tax policy, took much of the income of those in the higher brackets. Thus the rich in Britain were a vanishing class.[11] The wealthy classes suffered less in France, where taxation, as formerly, continued to be lenient toward the well to do. Italy emerged from the war impoverished to the point of ruin; almost everyone, except a few black-market speculators, faced poverty in some form. The acme of economic ruin was Germany, where wealthy aristocrats and capitalists and prosperous bourgeoisie were reduced to beggary.

[11] In 1939, about 7,000 persons in Britain had net incomes, after taxes, of the equivalent of $24,000 or more; in 1949, only 70 persons. In 1939, about 12,000 persons had incomes, after taxes, of $16,000 to $24,000; in 1949, only 3,430 persons. See *United States News,* July 30, 1948, and Aug. 12, 1949.

America presented a totally different picture. Not having been a theater of war, America did not suffer from the destruction of property caused by military action or from confiscation resulting from either enemy or revolutionary action. On the contrary, the economic machine expanded to an unprecedented degree, and peace found America the lone prosperous nation in an impoverished world. Profits and wages were at an all-time high; unemployment was virtually nonexistent. Despite the tremendous national debt, and despite the heavy taxation that continued after the war, all classes enjoyed a degree of prosperity unprecedented in human history. The rich became more numerous; and the poor, in the sense of absolute want, virtually ceased to exist. In America the approach to economic equality was through plenty, as in Europe it was through want.

Can these social and economic gains be maintained? The history of the first half of the twentieth century has shown conclusively that social progress can be made safely and securely without violating the fundamental principles of democracy. No longer does democracy tolerate, as in the nineteenth century, gross inequalities of income and ever-present economic insecurity. In the new era of the welfare state social democracy has been creating a new synthesis in which political liberty is reconciled with economic security. The state must become stronger by adopting an ideal of common welfare or it will be made all powerful through the new despotism of totalitarian dictatorship. Above and beyond all, democracy must not disown its great heritage of "a government of the people, by the people, and for the people." Chiefly through this heritage has it extended wide the dignity of the individual: from men of property to all men; from all men to all women; from the orthodox to the heretic; from favored national and ethnic groups to all groups. This has been democracy's chief claim to glory. By no means has it achieved perfection in human relations. What it

has achieved, and very definitely, has been a marked improvement in human relations; in some places, more, and in others,
less. Self-government is the only efficient, peaceful method of
correcting inequalities in the social and economic order. The
only alternative is despotism, whatever its appeal and whatever
its form.

Chapter 5. Nationalism: Past, Present, and Future

WHAT IS A NATION?

The central fact of modern history is the existence of the sovereign, national state as the unit of political organization. Every people has either succeeded in establishing itself as a sovereign, national state or is striving, definitely and passionately, to do so. Nationalism has been the supreme political emotion that has dominated political thought and action in the modern world. So pervasive and so universal has this emotion been that many are led to believe that nationalism is a natural phenomenon, the product of natural laws applicable at all times, in all places, and to all peoples.

Students of history are convinced that nationalism is an historic, not a natural, phenomenon. It has arisen as an outcome of political, social, and economic conditions at a certain stage of historical development. Patriotism, or the loyalty of individuals to the community, has always existed. It is as old as history, and perhaps even older. But the nature of patriotism has varied with the nature of the community. In the ancient city-states of Rome and of Greece, and in the medieval communes and manors, the community was local; membership in it was greatly limited by racial, class, and religious restrictions. As modern times approached, the community began to expand and to undergo profound changes. What was the nature of the expanded community? Who were its members? What was the tie that bound them? The community became the nation, large or small, consisting of urban and rural areas within a definite frontier; the members were all the inhabitants; and the tie which bound them, first and foremost, was political. These new answers spelled nationalism.

As nationalism has taken many forms and expressions, it is well-nigh impossible to define it exactly. Almost every definition will suggest exceptions, more or less pertinent. In history, not in a dictionary, must be sought the essential elements which constitute a nation, at least a highly developed, historically recognizable nation. In the first place it is an independent, sovereign entity, being a law unto itself. A nation is the sole judge of its actions toward its citizens and toward all other nations. The people are bound to the nation by the indispensable tie of citizenship. Unlike any previous political tie, citizenship is an act of free, personal choice, made by an individual, and can be shifted from one state to another. A citizen, say of Sweden, can become a citizen of France or of the United States through the simple process of naturalization. All citizens owe supreme allegiance to their nation whatever their class, faith, racial origin, or local association. The supreme power of the nation is exercised by the central authority, whether in a highly centralized state like France or in a federal union like the United States.

From sovereignty arises another essential characteristic of a nation: equality of all nations before international law. Not that all are considered equal in power and in influence, but equal in dignity and in honor. The claims of a nation, be it a great or a minor power, are given equal consideration in everything respecting its independence and sovereignty. Any infringement on the rights of little Denmark is, according to international law, as grave a matter as against Great Britain. Such, at least, is the theory.

A nation, being a collective personality, has perforce developed distinctive patterns of behavior and characteristic attitudes of mind as a consequence of its history, its language, and its literature. Of these the national language is perhaps the clearest expression of the nation as a cultural entity. Language has almost magic power in creating unity, whether in a fairly homogeneous nation like France or in one of many and diverse origins like the United States. So closely related is language to nationality that a subjected people will cling desperately to its language despite all efforts by the rulers to obliterate it, as was notably the case of the Poles during the period of partition, when they were under the rule of Russia, of Prussia, and of Austria. Once liberated and recognized as a nation, a people will revive even its long forgotten, historic language, as in the revival of Gaelic in Ireland and of Hebrew in Israel.

Never before in history has a principle proved so cohesive and so persistent as has the principle of nationality. History furnishes many examples of the extraordinary strength of the national spirit. When partitioned in the eighteenth century, Poland was a feudal state having little if any national characteristics. The spirit of nationalism caught the imagination of the Polish people *after* their state had disappeared. And Polish nationalism grew and persisted despite division and persecution. Finally, after the First World War, a national rebirth took place, when Poland was united after having been divided for 125 years. Another striking illustration concerns Ireland. After the English conquest, during the twelfth century, the Irish kept up a continuous resistance, in one form or another; their national spirit was born and grew under the heels of the conqueror. Finally, in 1949, after almost eight centuries of alien rule, southern Ireland became an independent nation, as the Republic of Ireland. Still another striking illustration concerns the Jews. The Jewish state of ancient times had disappeared into the Roman Empire, and the people were scattered all over the world. During the twentieth century a nationalist movement known as Zionism made great headway among Jews everywhere. Zionism scored a resounding success when, in 1948, after almost two thousand years, the Jewish state was restored in the part of Palestine now called Israel. The emergence into nationhood of

these long subjected peoples gave to the world a dramatic vindication of the principle of nationality.

HOW NATIONS CAME INTO EXISTENCE

The nation is distinctively a modern political phenomenon. The
thrill of spontaneous identification, felt by millions, with a
common fatherland, irrespective of their class, faith, or origin,
was unknown in ancient and medieval times. When and how
did the nations appear? All now in existence appeared at different times and in different ways. England and France "just
grow'd" by slowly developing bonds of union among their
people in the course of centuries. The United States and the nations of Latin America were "born" as a result of colonial
revolutions against the mother country. Germany and Italy
became nations through the process of unification, by uniting
different states inhabited by the same people. Some nations
appeared as a result of separating from other nations, as when
Belgium separated from the Netherlands; Norway, from
Sweden; Iceland, from Denmark; and Burma, from the British
Empire. Some, like the nations in east central Europe, achieved
their independence as a result of the breakup of the German,
Russian, Austro-Hungarian, and Ottoman empires. The latest
method of becoming a nation was by way of the mandate system, established by the treaty of Versailles, according to which
certain backward regions were temporarily assigned as trusteeships to various powers. In the course of time Iraq, Israel, Syria,
and Lebanon ceased to be mandatories of Britain and of France
and were recognized as independent states.

As important as the manner has been the period in history
when a people became a nation. The first definitely independent
sovereign states appeared in the seventeenth century with a
united England, a united France, and a united Spain. Powerful,

centralized governments were established by absolute monarchs in these countries on the ruins of feudalism: the Tudors in England; the Bourbons in France; and the Hapsburgs in Spain. These rulers united their subjects into a common obedience to a common authority, thereby laying the foundation of the independent, sovereign state. They were greatly aided in their effort by two important events: the Protestant Reformation and the Commercial Revolution. The former disrupted the Roman Catholic church and gave each ruler the power to determine the faith of his subjects, thereby augmenting his power and uniting his people. By means of the mercantilist system, resulting from the Commercial Revolution, the nation was organized as an economic unit through the central government that regulated commerce and industry. There were now religious and economic, in addition to political, ties that bound a people together into a national whole.

By the eighteenth century a number of independent, sovereign states had appeared in Europe. Of these the most national was Britain, being far more unified than any other state in Europe, chiefly because the centralizing influence of her kings came earlier and was more effective than elsewhere. The government in Britain was centralized; the administration and law, unified; the economy, integrated; and the language and culture, fairly uniform. Furthermore, in Britain alone were the people represented in Parliament, the authority of which was supreme in the government. The national flag and the national anthem, popular symbols of nationalism, made their first appearance in Britain; the "Union Jack" in 1707 and "Rule Britannia" in 1740. France and Spain, by contrast, lagged behind Britain in their national development. Though centralized, they were not unified. The supreme authority of the king was recognized, yet there existed within France and Spain great diversities of law, of administration, of language, and of fiscal policy in the internal tariffs among the various provinces. Whatever national spirit inspired the French and Spanish peoples was expressed in loyalty to the ruling dynasty. In time of war, the people fought for their "king," not for their "country."

THE BALANCE OF POWER

The independent, sovereign state, as a political entity, was then a distinctively European phenomenon. Depending on the time and on the historical conditions of their appearance, the European states were unequal in size and importance. Some were large, like France, England, and Spain; some middle-sized, like Portugal and the Netherlands; and some small, like the Italian and Scandinavian states. As no common European authority was created to guarantee the independence and the integrity of each state, the field became wide open for ambitious rulers to increase their territory and prestige by aggression against their neighbors, large and small. To prevent such aggression, an international *modus vivendi* was devised, known as the "balance of power." It was the first attempt to create peaceful relations among the European states. In essence the balance of power meant that an equilibrium would be established, according to which all existing states would be guaranteed security. How? By an *understanding* that all the states would combine to defeat any nation that had disturbed the equilibrium by embarking on a career of conquest. The balance of power would be restored by the defeat of the aggressor. It was then believed that fear of disturbing the balance of power would effectively deter would-be aggressors, and thereby maintain the peace of Europe. "One sword holds another in its sheath."

Thus the balance of power was brought into play whenever an ambitious ruler embarked on a career of conquest: against

Charles V in the sixteenth century; against Louis XIV in the seventeenth and eighteenth centuries; and against Napoleon in the nineteenth century. History, however, records only too plainly and too painfully the many failures of the balance of power to maintain peace and security in Europe. The defeat of one aggressor did not discourage the next one. And the chief reason lay in the fact that the balance of power provided no means of checking an aggressive monarch *before* he attacked his neighbors. A general war to vindicate the doctrine was a method like that, as told in the fanciful tale of Charles Lamb, used by the ancient Chinese to get roast pork. A house was burned down in order to roast a pig that had been placed inside. Europe failed to provide a regular and efficient method for roasting a pig without burning down a house.

After the Napoleonic Wars it became evident that the balance of power had to be put on a more stable basis to ensure peace among the nations. Hence there appeared, more definitely than before, what came to be called the "Great Power" system. Britain, France, Prussia (later, Germany), Austria (later, Austria-Hungary), Italy, and Russia organized the "Concert of Europe" to maintain peace on the Continent. Because of the military might of the Great Powers, it became the practice for all the other European powers to dance to whatever tune the Concert played. And frequently disharmony arose among the Great Powers themselves because of their conflicting interests and rival ambitions.

During the nineteenth century the balance of power doctrine appeared to have been vindicated. This "century of peace," from 1815 to 1914, witnessed no general war such as had devastated Europe during the Napoleonic Wars. Did it witness a general peace? A glance at the record shows that during every decade of this "century of peace" war was going on somewhere. No fewer than thirteen wars were waged in Europe itself, not counting the wars fought by European powers in Asia, in Africa, and in the Americas. One war, the Crimean, was almost a general European conflict in which the big powers were involved, either as belligerents or as malevolent neutrals.[1] History shows only too plainly that Europe always has been getting ready for a war, fighting a war, or recovering from a war.

Despite undeniable historic evidence that the balance of power failed to preserve general peace, Europe clung to it desperately. No alternative seemed possible. Ancient and deeply rooted jealousies, rivalries, and antipathies, with each nation fiercely clinging to its sovereignty, prevented even tentative efforts to formulate plans for a European union, which alone could preserve peace. However, the long period without a general war, which followed the Napoleonic Wars, created a mood of optimistic fatalism, which persisted until the beginning of the twentieth century. Quarrels and even localized wars would go on, but the peace of the world was assured. What gave this assurance was Britain's unwavering support of the balance of power. For long she had realized that the domination of the Continent by any one power was for her a matter of life or death. Should such a situation arise the whole force of a united Continent would be thrown against her one vital defense, the English Channel, which then might be breached. Whenever the balance of power was disturbed, Britain mobilized coalitions of European states against the aggressor, and supported them with money, armies, and fleets. During the nineteenth century the British navy constituted a powerful deterrent to any nation ambitious to dominate the Continent. Should, however, a nation arise to challenge British sea power the situation would be fraught with danger to the peace of the world. In the twentieth century such a nation did arise. It was Germany.

[1] J. Salwyn Schapiro, "That Great Illusion: the Balance of Power," *The Social Studies,* Vol. 33 (December, 1942).

LIBERAL NATIONALISM

It was the intense nationalism of the European peoples that kept them divided and belligerent. Unlike the states in America, the states in Europe could not or would not yield one bit of their sovereignty to establish a supreme common authority. As a consequence, nationalism proved to be the stumbling block to peace. Despite this shortcoming, many were deeply convinced that nationalism was the force that held out the promise of contributing greatly and permanently to the progress of human freedom.

At the end of the eighteenth century, nationalism experienced a new birth as a result of the American and French revolutions. These movements created the sovereign *national* state of democracy. The American nation was actually born, free and independent, before the eyes of an astonished world. For the first time in history a constitutional convention created a new nation by uniting thirteen separate states. And the new nation was a democratic republic! According to the Founding Fathers, the only legitimate basis of government was the consent of the people; hence the powers of the new Republic would be used to protect the freedom of the citizens and to promote the general welfare of the nation. Hitherto, government generally had been a repressive force, used by irresponsible monarchs to bolster their power and to protect the interests of the privileged classes. The sovereign people now took the place of the sovereign king.

France was "reborn" during the French Revolution. The French were profoundly influenced by the American example, which became their inspiration during the first years of the Revolution. As a result of the reforms made by the Constituent Assembly from 1789 to 1791, France became a nation, "one and indivisible." These reforms established uniform systems of law, of administration, of weights and measures, and created a common fiscal policy for the nation by abolishing the internal tariffs. Citizenship was established in France, as in America, on the basis of equality. France was reborn free in that the new government, established by the constitution of 1791, was pledged to protect the Rights of Man. Like America, France adopted the popular symbols of a democratic nation: the national birthday, the national flag, and the national anthem. These symbols were to appear wherever and whenever a free nation appeared in the world.

The American and French revolutions proclaimed the ideals and laid down the pattern of "liberal nationalism" that flourished during the nineteenth century. In its very essence liberal nationalism constituted the integration of democracy with nationalism, on the theory that the right of a people to choose its rulers rested on the same foundation as the right of a people to "self-determination," or freedom from foreign rule. Liberal nationalism had as its great prophets, the Italian, Joseph Mazzini, and the Hungarian, Louis Kossuth, who preached its doctrines with patriotic fervor and thrilling eloquence. The nation, they asserted, was the chief vehicle of modern progress; hence it was in the interest of all mankind for every people to achieve nationhood, free from the arbitrary rule of foreign despots and therefore free to make its special contribution to progress. A political vision enraptured the liberal nationalist, who beheld a vision of free individuals moving freely in society, each striving to realize his special talents for the benefit of both himself and the community, and of free nations moving freely in the world, each striving to develop its own unique culture in order to contribute to the sum total of modern civilization. Democracy and nationalism became the Siamese twins of modern political life.

Liberal nationalism was not preached in a vacuum. It became

influential because the new social and economic conditions, established by the Industrial Revolution, gave nationalism power and reach. Capitalism in Western Europe created needs that only nationalism could satisfy. The factories, the railways, the telegraphs, and the telephones were so many veins and arteries that bound the nation into a living whole. A united nation under capitalism could succeed in creating a large and diversified domestic market for the goods produced by its factories and fields. And the domestic market could be protected by tariffs only through acts of the nation. Extensive foreign markets could be opened up by favorable treaties, backed by the influence of a powerful nation That trade followed the flag became an axiom. The middle class, or *bourgeoisie,* was always in the forefront of national movements, and its influence could clearly be seen in the upsurge of nationalism in Western Europe during the nineteenth century. And this influence was generally on the side of liberalism, which aimed to destroy absolutism in government, feudalism in society, and mercantilism in commerce and industry.

Europe was the seedbed of nationalism. There it sprouted most luxuriantly, and from there the seeds were wafted throughout the world. As already described, nationalism achieved great triumphs during the nineteenth century, in Europe and the New World, but these triumphs unfortunately were not always those of liberalism. After the failure of liberal nationalism in the Revolution of 1848, a reaction set in, not against nationalism but against liberalism. In Germany the failure of the Frankfort Assembly to unite the country caused many German nationalists to look to forces and to favor methods other than those of liberalism to realize their dream of a united country. An anti-liberal nationalism now came to the front, supported by reactionary Prussia, that proposed to unite Germany by using the Bismarckian "blood and iron" method of aggressive war. A similar, though not so extreme, reaction took place in Italy. The failure, in 1848, of the republicans Mazzini and Garibaldi to establish a united Italian republic led to a reaction in favor of monarchy. Cavour now proposed to unite Italy, as a liberal kingdom, under the aegis of the Savoy dynasty.

This break with liberal nationalism created widespread uneasiness. In the case of Germany, Bismarck had succeeded in performing an operation on the Siamese twins, nationalism and democracy, by establishing the German Empire on a nondemocratic basis. Bismarckian Germany became the political model for Japan when she passed from a feudal to a national state. German political methods and systems were assiduously emulated by the Japanese nationalists, who especially admired the dominant role of the army in the government of Germany. Because of the great influence of Germany in Europe and of Japan in Asia, nationalism began to assume a sinister aspect that confounded and dismayed those who clung to the traditions of its liberal origin.

INTEGRAL NATIONALISM

As the power of Germany and Japan grew, nationalism underwent a transformation. During the two decades before the First World War it entered on a new stage, that of "integral" nationalism, which was widely espoused by influential writers and powerful classes. Like its liberal predecessor, integral nationalism proclaimed the nation as the chief vehicle of human progress. But it repudiated the liberal nationalist idea that every people, becoming a nation, had something valuable to contribute to civilization, provided it was free to do so. The integral nationalists divided peoples into superior and inferior catagories; only the superior peoples—their own, especially—had the right to be free and independent. They alone had a "mission" and therefore the right, even the duty, to increase their power by conquering "inferior" peoples and reducing them to their rule. Integral nationalism has been defined as "the exclusive pursuit of national policies, the absolute maintenance of national integrity and the steady increase of national power, for a nation declines when it loses military might."

Integral nationalism easily passed over into racialism and imperialism, the very opposites of liberal nationalism. Germany came forward as the leading defender of racialism, which became a veritable passion in that land. Germans were obsessed with the notion that they were a "master race" destined to rule the "inferior" races of mankind. Teutonic racialism influenced even stoutly liberal Britain. A new school of British historians arose, notably Edward Augustus Freeman, Richard Henry Green, and Bishop William Stubbs, who gave an "Anglo-Saxon" interpretation of English history. According to these historians it was the conquest of Britain by the Teutonic Anglo-Saxons that was the determining factor in England's subsequent greatness. Their influence was widespread, and the English became acutely conscious that they were "Anglo-Saxons," something that they had hardly been aware of earlier in their history.

Logically and inevitably the predatory character of integral nationalism led to imperialism. A great revival of imperialism began toward the end of the nineteenth century that deeply influenced both the old nations, like Britain and France, and the new nations, like Germany and Italy.[2] With the exaltation of the "superior" race or nation went a contempt for the "lesser breeds," or the "inferior" peoples. In Britain the new imperialism was benevolently described as the "white man's burden"; in Germany it was frankly and brutally described as the natural role of the superior Teuton; in Italy as the "sacred egoism" of the Italians, heirs of the ancient Romans; in France as the method of spreading the superior culture of the French; and

[2] See p. 172.

in Japan as the preordained destiny of a god-descended people to be "lord of the Far East." Even American nationalism, consistently liberal from the very beginning, now turned toward imperialism. A school arose that preached America's "manifest destiny" to ascend the "glory crowned heights" of national power by conquering territory in the Caribbean and in the Pacific.

The teaching of history popularized integral nationalism. In schools and colleges, books and teachers of history emphasized the uniqueness and greatness of the fatherland and stressed its rivalries and struggles with other nations. Ancient enmities were revived and even exaggerated, and generations grew up embittered and bellicose. Especially was this true of the French and the Germans, who came to regard themselves as hereditary enemies, destined to war upon each other until one or the other was annihilated. The greatness of the British Empire was stressed in British school histories, influenced largely by the famous work of Sir John R. Seely, *Expansion of England*. The role of the empire in promoting Britain's greatness, and the welfare of mankind generally, was stressed as never before.

Imperialism influenced policies inside as well as outside the nation. Internal imperialism sought "to conquer" the many national minorities that existed in the east central European states by forcible methods of assimilation. In Germany discriminatory laws were passed against the Poles, designed to suppress their language and to uproot them from their homes. In the Russian Empire where the dominant group, the Great Russians, constituted a bare majority of the population, the minority groups, especially the Poles, the Finns, the Baltic groups, and the Jews, were subjected to a policy of ruthless Russification. In polyglot Austria-Hungary, those who did not belong to the ruling groups, the German Austrians and the Magyar Hungarians, were made to suffer various disabilities. In the European part of the Ottoman Empire the Turks, a small portion of the population, sought to assimilate the non-Moslem groups. Integral nationalism recognized the "principle of nationality" only as it applied to dominant peoples.

After 1870 the Industrial Revolution made progress in east central Europe. Its advance was slow but by the twentieth century industrialization was well under way in this region. The result, as regards nationalism, was just the opposite of what had taken place earlier in Western Europe. Instead of binding peoples together it split them apart. The Provençal and Breton had been only too happy to become more "French"; the Tuscan and Sicilian, more "Italian"; and the Prussian and Bavarian more "German," when the new economy bound them more tightly into a unified nation. Not so the Czechs, the Rumanians, and the Yugoslavs in the Dual Monarchy, or the non-Russians in the Russian Empire, or the non-Germans in Germany, who bitterly resented the prospect of being assimilated. A nationalism of resentment made rapid progress among these minority peoples who feared the assimilative powers of modern industry and who struggled desperately to throw off the political ties that bound them to these empires. They aimed to create their own national economy in their own national state. This nationalism of resentment among the subject peoples in east central Europe had a far sharper edge than had the liberal nationalism in Western Europe.

Still another aspect of nationalism characterized these subjected peoples. Freedom to them came to mean freedom from despotic, *alien* governments, rather than freedom of the individual within the nation, as preached by the liberal nationalists of 1848. The nationalists in east central Europe stressed the uniqueness and superiority of the cultural heritage of their particular group, in opposition to the culture of their rulers and even to that of the nations of Western Europe.[3] Their national-

[3] On this point, see the interesting discussion in Hans Kohn, *The Twentieth Century* (1949), 19–31.

ism often became self-centered, intolerant, chauvinistic, and
sometimes even racial. Once freed, the subjected nationalities
promptly took the road to integral nationalism. This they did
most markedly after the First World War.

NATIONALISM AFTER THE FIRST WORLD WAR

Nationalism was the political cause of the First World War.
The unfulfilled promise of self-determination for all peoples
had created widespread resentment among the subjected minorities everywhere in Europe. East central Europe was seething
with nationalist movements that threatened to destroy the empires of that region and to involve Europe—perhaps the whole
world—in a general war. Especially critical was the situation
in Austria-Hungary where the subjected minorities, aided by
their kinsmen in neighboring states, made ready to tear apart
the ramshackle empire of the Hapsburgs.

Equally ominous was German nationalism. Divorced from
democracy, it quickly turned into an imperialism of the most
strident and the most embittered kind. Where and how could
Germany's imperial designs be carried out? Not overseas, where
her expansion had been effectively checked by the combined
opposition of Britain and France. Only in Europe could Germany hope to expand, and only by the method of conquering
her neighbors. No nation, however strong, felt safe from a
German attack; it soon became obvious that Germany would
be satisfied with nothing less than the complete mastery of the
Continent. On the accession of Wilhelm II, in 1888, Germany
began throwing her great weight around in the diplomatic ring,
to the terror of her neighbors. The strength of Germany combined with the weakness of Austria-Hungary created crisis after
crisis, which led straight to the First World War.

The conflict was touched off by Austria-Hungary. A struggle arose between the latter and Serbia that highlighted the great problem of liberating the subjected peoples in east central Europe. As the war progressed, nationalism became the all-absorbing issue; five of President Woodrow Wilson's Fourteen Points dealt with this issue. The national minorities in the Hapsburg dominions proved more of a liability than an asset to that government in the conduct of the war. Desertions and mutinies were common. Toward the end of the war, when the defeat of the Central Powers seemed certain, there took place an almost spontaneous disruption of Austria-Hungary. The various national minorities revolted and set up independent states. That centuries-old monarchy suddenly passed into history.

The peace treaties following the First World War recognized the principle of nationality far more than had any preceding peace conference after a general war. The dissolution of the Russian, German, Hapsburg, and Ottoman empires made possible the application of this principle on a far larger scale than ever before in history. Nine new or partly new nations arose from the ashes of the dead empires. All of them strenuously asserted their independence and their sovereignty, and sought to get as much territory as they could, whether their claims were valid or not.

Eager as were the peacemakers to apply the principle of nationality they found it impossible to do so. To put one nationality into one state in the ethnological crazy quilt that is east central Europe went beyond the wit of man. National, religious, racial, and linguistic groups in that region were hopelessly intermingled; parts of one group often spilled over into another. There were Bulgarians in Greece, and Greeks in Bulgaria; Rumanians in Yugoslavia, and Yugoslavs in Rumania; Czechs in German Austria and German Austrians (Sudeten) in Czechoslovakia. National "enclaves" existed entirely surrounded by an "alien" majority. The best that the treaty makers could do was the best that they did. Whenever they considered a region inhabited by a majority nationality, such as the Poles in Poland, they established that nationality into a state. But not one of the succession states, or the new states that emerged from the disrupted empires, was uninational; neither did all the members of a national group live in one state. What was self-determination for one meant alien rule for another. To protect minority groups the Conference adopted a principle, novel in history, namely, the protection of national minorities by international treaties. In the treaties with Poland, Rumania, Yugoslavia, Czechoslovakia, and Greece "minorities of race, minorities of language, or minorities of religion" were given full and equal rights as citizens. In addition they were given special privileges, such as using their national language in the courts and schools of their districts and receiving subventions for their educational and charitable institutions. In some of these treaties the Jews were, for the first time, recognized as a "national" minority. Jewish nationalism, known as "Zionism," received a great impetus when Britain issued the Balfour Declaration, which urged the establishment in Palestine of a national home for the Jewish people.

It was widely believed that satisfying the national aspirations of the peoples in east central Europe would bring peace and contentment to that turbulent region. Instead, it brought widespread discontent, which, as before 1914, became a menace to world peace. Hardly one of the new states was satisfied with its boundaries, and most of them promptly set about trying to annex territories at the expense of neighbors. Greece plotted to seize part of Albania; Poland and Hungary, parts of Czechoslovakia; Bulgaria, part of Yugoslavia; and Yugoslavia, part of Greece. The treaties in regard to minorities were deeply resented as a violation of the sovereignty of the states that had signed them. As a consequence, they were honored more in the breach than in the observance. By using all sorts of subterfuges these treaties were violated both directly and indirectly; the authority of the League of Nations, to which had been entrusted the power of supervision, was flouted. The minority groups soon discovered that their "liberation" merely meant a change of persecutors. The most flagrant violator of these treaties was Poland, who severely persecuted her minorities, especially the Jews. Deep resentment was aroused against the Poles, especially as they themselves had been the victims of persecution during the partition of Poland. Only too often in the history of nationalism has the oppressed turned oppressor when fortune changed. During the struggle for freedom, an oppressed people would proclaim liberal and democratic ideals; once freed, it would promptly violate them.

Another evil result of the treaty of Versailles was the "balkanization" of Europe, or the creation of new, small nations. At the very time when economics was in the process of welding the world together, politics broke Europe into more national pieces. There were now some twenty-eight sovereign national states in Europe, of which ten were new or partly new: Finland, Esthonia, Latvia, Lithuania, Poland, Czechoslovakia, Hungary, Austria, Yugoslavia, and Iceland. The application of the principle of nationality in the twentieth century, unlike that in the nineteenth, proved to be less of a creative and more of a destructive force. The great error of the Congress of Vienna in 1815 had been its failure to recognize the principle of nationality. The great error of the Conference of Paris in 1919 was its failure to organize the liberated nations into regional federations, with a common tariff policy and with a common system of defense. Because of this failure each new nation became jealous of its sovereignty, of its rights, of its honor. And the smaller the nation, the more intense was its nationalism. All adopted high protective tariffs, which strangled their economy. They wasted their substance on military establishments, which made them weaker, not stronger. As a consequence, the liberated nations, small, weak, poor, and internally divided, could offer little re-

sistence to a *Drang nach Osten* by a revived Germany or to a
Drang nach Westen by a revived Russia.

The older nations no longer exercised great influence, as they
had before 1914. Soviet Russia was too deeply concerned with
stabilizing her revolution to bother much with problems of diplomacy. Moreover, she was deliberately isolated by other European powers, who, at first, refused to recognize the Soviet
government. Germany, shorn of her military power, ceased to be
the terror of the Continent. Italy fell to the rank of a second-rate
power. Britain was seriously weakened, and could no longer
assert herself vigorously as a great power. France emerged from
the war victorious but terrified. More than once during the conflict had she looked into the face of national death; well did she
know what fate was in store for her in case of a German victory.
Her industrial regions had been laid waste. Almost a generation
had perished on the battlefield. The postwar spirit of France was
so low and hopeless that, come what may, she was minded to
avoid another war at any cost, by yielding anything, even national honor.

European economy was disrupted by the war. Destruction of
factories, dislocation of commerce and industry, and the drying
up of credit resulted in business failures that eventually led to
the Great Depression of 1929. Two great centers of international
trade, Britain and Germany, were knocked out, with serious
consequences to the trade of the European nations, and to that
of the world generally. Before the war, a balanced economy had
come into existence in Europe. Most of the exports from the
Western nations, chiefly manufactures and capital goods, went
to the Eastern nations in exchange for foods and raw materials.
And Germany, the largest exporter and importer on the Continent, was its economic heart. On the recovery of Germany
chiefly depended the recovery of Europe.

Victorious Britain was in the same economic position as was

defeated Germany. Her recovery depended likewise on that of the Continent; therefore she became interested in putting Germany, her prewar competitor and great customer, on her economic feet. During the interwar period, Britain aided Germany by substantial investments in industry, by generous loans, and by advocating a generous policy in regard to reparations, all aimed to revive German economy, and thereby that of the Continent.

Two new world economic centers appeared after the war, America and Japan. As a consequence of the war effort, America developed a tremendous industry and merchant marine. Foreign commerce and foreign investment now became great factors in American economy. American goods and enterprise displaced those of Britain and of Germany in many lands, especially in those of South America. Japan also took advantage of the war to advance her foreign trade. Japanese goods displaced those of Europe, especially in China, India, and the East Indies. As a result of the First World War, Japan became an economic power to be reckoned with. Her industry, commerce, and merchant marine were now important factors in world economy, and were all-important in the economy of the Far East.

RACIALISM AND NATIONALISM

The interwar period witnessed the appearance, not only of new nations, but also of a new type of nationalism known as "fascism." In one sense fascism resembled integral nationalism in that it sought to make a strong nation stronger through war and conquest. In another sense it differed from all hitherto known types of nationalism in that it repudiated the idea of assimilating conquered peoples to their conquerors. Basic in fascism was the idea of racialism, according to which the people of a nation constituted a biologic unit, a "race," distinct, separate, and different from all other races.[4] Assimilation of various peoples into one national unit was a tenet of liberal nationalism, which Germany was first to repudiate. When, in 1933, the German fascists, called "Nazis," came into power, they promptly organized the country as a racial state. Nazi Germany became the model for all the other fascist states, who emulated her racial as well as her aggressive policies. In order to attain racial homogeneity, these states inaugurated a policy of substituting population. A minority racial group would be removed from a region, and its place would be taken by settlers of the same race as the dominant majority in the country. The methods followed by the fascist governments varied all the way from inducements to settle in the new home to downright expulsion, and even to extermination where the Jews were concerned.

Fascism intensified the evils of nationalism by fully and completely organizing the state as a predatory power. Once a state became fascist, it promptly turned to conquest in every direction. Nazi Germany flouted the principle of nationality by conquering the small states in east central Europe and reducing them to the position of satellites, completely dominated by her. Fascist Italy conquered and annexed Ethiopia and Albania. Driven on by the lust for power, the fascist powers planned to conquer the world and to subject all peoples to their rule.

The first application of the fascist method of substituting population was in the case of south Tirol.[5] By an agreement between Mussolini and Hitler, in 1939, about 75,000 German-speaking

[4] For a more complete description of fascism, see pp. 237–239.

[5] A precedent for removing minorities had been set in 1923 by the agreement between Greece and Turkey concerning their minorities. According to this agreement, the Moslems in Greece and the Greeks in Turkey were forced to leave their homes. About a million Greeks, whose ancestors had lived in Asia Minor since ancient times, were uprooted and driven into Greece. Fewer Moslems left Greece for Turkey. The many refugees from Turkey crowded into Greece where they suffered severe hardships.

inhabitants of this region were induced, often under pressure, to migrate to Germany. Their places were taken by Italian settlers sent by their government.

German minorities existed in nearly all the states in Eastern Europe. Centuries ago they had come or had been sent as settlers, and they continued to live in separate communities, clinging to their language and customs. When Hitler came into power, he evinced great concern for these "lost" Germans as racial "comrades." To a large degree these German minorities, stirred by racialism, rallied to the side of Nazi Germany. Racial Fifth Columns, notably the Sudeten Germans in Czechoslovakia, threatened the integrity of the nation of which they were citizens.

Racial nationalism put through a policy of substituting population on a scale that horrified the world. As a result of the treaty of Munich (1938), Czechoslovakia was compelled to cede to Germany the Sudeten region, inhabited by about 3,600,-000 people, chiefly Germans. The Czechs in the region fled or were driven out. When, in 1939, Poland was partitioned by Germany, many Poles were killed or sent as slaves into Germany. Virtually all the Jews who had not fled were exterminated. Their places were taken by about half a million "lost" Germans, who had lived in Poland, in the Baltic states, and in Russia.

Soviet Russia, while abjuring racialism, followed its policy of substituting population. When, in 1940, the Baltic states were conquered, about 200,000 inhabitants were deported to the interior of Russia. Since then the entire region has been undergoing a substitution of population; the natives being sent out and Russians being sent in. After the defeat of Finland by Russia, in 1940, about 400,000 Finns fled from Karelia, the part ceded by Finland to Russia; their places were taken by Slavs sent by Soviet Russia. During the Second World War, two autonomous regions in Soviet Russia, the Volga German Republic, inhabited by Germans, and the Crimean Autonomous

Republic, inhabited by Tatars, were abolished. Their many inhabitants were deported, and their places taken by Russians.[6]

Mankind was horrified by the new method of attaining unity and homogeneity through the substitution of population. Never before had so many people wandered over the face of the earth, dispossessed, unwanted, harassed, deprived of the security once given to them by political ties. Never before had so many people been killed or driven out for no reason except that they belonged to political, economic, religious, or ethnic groups other than those of the majority in their native land. The dream of nationalism in the rosy dawn of the nineteenth century became a fearful nightmare in the shadows of the twentieth.

The evil that fascism did lived after it. With Germany's defeat in the Second World War, a racial policy was applied against the Germans by those who had suffered at their hands. The hatred felt for them by the liberated nations in east central Europe passed all bounds. Czechoslovakia confiscated the property of about 3,000,000 Sudeten Germans and drove them penniless across the border into Germany. The German inhabitants of Poland, of Rumania, and of Yugoslavia were driven out under even worse conditions. When East Prussia was partitioned between Poland and Russia, about 3,000,000 Germans disappeared from the region; some were killed, many fled, and many others were deported to Soviet Russia. Virtually no Germans were left in Eastern Europe; their places were taken by Poles and Russians.

As a consequence of the transfers of population, the character of east central Europe has been profoundly changed. The reconstituted nations were more "homogeneous," it is true, but more distracted, more embittered, and even more helpless than before the war. Destruction is a "solution" of the problem of

[6] For the best studies of population substitution, see J. B. Schechtman, *European Population Transfers, 1939–1945* (1946), and E. M. Kulischer, *Europe on the Move* (1948).

national minorities just as death is a "solution" of the problems of an individual.

For a time the liberated nations in east central Europe became free and independent. But not for long. Even in the midst of general rejoicing the menacing shadow of Soviet Russia hovered over the peoples just freed from the fascist terror. It became evident that Communist Russia would engulf them as remorselessly as had Nazi Germany. As described elsewhere, Albania, Rumania, Bulgaria, Poland, Hungary, and Czechoslovakia virtually lost their independence and became satellites of Soviet Russia.[7] Lithuania, Latvia, and Esthonia did not survive even as satellites; they were conquered and incorporated into the Soviet Union. Finland and Austria remained free but within the orbit of Russian influence. Greece and Turkey managed to escape as a result of American intervention. Yugoslavia, though a Communist state, asserted her national independence by refusing to become a Russian satellite. The fierce nationalism that had prevented the small states in east central Europe from forming regional unions resulted in their almost total subservience to their powerful, aggressive neighbors. Nationalism had defeated itself through its shortsighted insistence on the principle of sovereignty.

In Western Europe, nationalism persisted though in a greatly weakened form. All the nations, the large no less than the small, emerged from the war ghosts of their former selves. Not even the strongest among them, such as Britain and France, could assert their sovereignty with anything like their former authority. A sense of common weakness pervaded them all, and, as will be described later, they sought to gather strength by combining into the Western Union and by drawing help from America.[8]

[7] See pp. 301–303.
[8] See pp. 378, 402.

NATIONALISM IN THE ORIENT

The seeds of nationalism sprouted wherever they found lodgment in a favorable soil. For long the soil of the Orient had been unfavorable to nationalism because of the persistence of the ancient ties of family, of tribe, and of religion among the Chinese, the Indians, the Turks, and the Egyptians. But these ties began to loosen and the new political tie of nationalism began to tighten, when the Industrial Revolution was introduced. As elsewhere in the world, the new conditions created by machine production prepared the way for national unity.

Modern industry was introduced chiefly through investments by Western capitalists, supported by their imperialist governments. As a consequence, resentment against alien economic control easily passed into resentment against alien political control. Though backward politically, the Oriental peoples easily became converts to nationalism as the only means by which they could become politically and economically free of foreign control. Hence nationalism made rapid progress in nearly all Oriental countries during the first half of the twentieth century.

The movement for self-government and for the "recovery of national rights" had the support of the industrial classes: capitalists and workers. As elsewhere, these classes had emerged as a result of the great social transformation brought about by the Industrial Revolution, which made headway in Japan, China, and India during the first half of the twentieth century. But this transformation did not affect the entire economy or the great mass of the population. The contrast between the new, which was of the newest, and the old, which was of the oldest, was indeed striking, not to say startling. Medieval, and even primitive, economy existed side by side with Big Business. The great masses of people continued to be farmers, unscientific in their methods; artisans, laboring with their hands; and merchants, engaged in petty trade. But the new industrial centers resembled Manchester, Essen, and Pittsburgh, with a large, native working class and a small though influential class of capitalist-managers, generally foreign. Lucrative returns from their investments induced the Western capitalists to give their powerful support to the imperialist policies of their governments. As commerce and industry developed, a native capitalist class appeared that became bitterly hostile to their Western competitors. The working class, on the other hand, resentful of low wages and long hours, organized trade-unions that became active in demanding better conditions for the workers. These two classes pooled their resentments into a powerful movement against the foreign capitalists; they demanded the end of Western imperialism and the establishment of independent, democratic, national governments.

Though its objective was largely the same in all Asiatic countries, this movement took different forms, depending on the status of each country. The problem of independent Japan was that of forwarding the policy of imperialistic expansion on the mainland. In this way she would attain equality with the great powers. In semidependent China the problem was to unify the country by suppressing the hostilities among the various regions and by ousting the Western powers from their privileged position in the political and economic life of the nation. In wholly dependent India the problem was to compel or to persuade Britain to grant independence or, at least, self-government with Dominion status. The progress of the native nationalist movements in these three important countries held great significance for the progress of all mankind.

The First World War gave a great spurt to these nationalist movements. It was fought, in part at least, to vindicate the principle of nationality. Was this principle applicable only to

Europe? Or was it applicable everywhere? The Oriental peoples, subjected to Western imperialism, now asserted their right of self-determination more vigorously than ever before. Nationalism was strongest in China and in India, countries that had attained a fair degree of industrialization. The native capitalist class in both cases sought to oust the European capitalists from their privileged position in the economy of the country. These capitalists became the financial supporters of the nationalist movements: the Kuomintang party in China and the Congress party in India, both of which grew rapidly in numbers and in militancy.

The wide recognition given by the Conference of Paris to the principle of nationality heartened the nationalists in the Orient. Furthermore, the collapse of the German, Russian, and Ottoman empires was followed by the collapse of their rule in Asia. Germany lost her holdings in the Far East; and Soviet Russia gave up those of the Russian Empire. Arab nationalism flared up, and several Arab states emerged from the ruins of the Ottoman Empire. The cry for self-determination became loud and insistent in China, India, and Egypt. It was heard almost for the first time in French Indo-China and in the Netherlands East Indies. A revolt of Asia against Europe was soon in progress.

China and India became the leaders in this revolt. Though nominally independent, China had even greater difficulty in achieving nationhood than did India, long under British rule. China had to struggle against the growing imperialism of nearby Japan, in addition to the waning imperialism of faraway Europe. The Kuomintang party, inspired by the ideals of Sun Yat-sen,[9] set itself the task of creating a Chinese nation by eliminating the unequal treaties which gave special privileges to foreign nations and by suppressing the separatisms of the various regions. Under the leadership of Chiang Kai-shek, a

[9] See p. 74.

disciple of Sun Yat-sen, considerable progress was at first made in uniting China and in winning concessions from the Western powers. A united, modernized China was accepted, if not welcomed, by those powers who were resigning themselves to the loss of their privileges. Not so Japan, who feared that a united, strong China would frustrate her ambition to become the "lord of the Far East."

Alone among the Oriental peoples the Japanese managed to escape the grip of Western imperialism. Instead of helping to free their fellow peoples in Asia, the Japanese turned imperialist in line with the most aggressive of Western patterns. Japan concentrated on China with the hardened determination to reduce to vassalage this mother of her own civilization. During the First World War, Japan foisted upon China the Twenty-one Demands, which gave to the former important privileges in the latter's government and industry. Japan's obvious purpose to dominate China roused intense national sentiments among the Chinese, who were determined to resist at all costs. Fearing that nationalism would overtake aggression, Japan quickened her imperialist steps. In 1931, Japanese armies invaded Manchuria, and in 1933, China proper. An undeclared war began between the two nations that in 1939 merged with the Second World War.

Nationalism in India faced a problem different from that in China. In Britain the Indian patriots had an enemy, whose traditions were liberal and whose historic policy was to grant concessions when judged opportune and necessary. Therefore, they resolved to make British rule difficult and onerous in order to win freedom for India, even in moderate installments. This they did in a variety of ways: "noncooperation" with the British authorities; boycott of British goods; popular agitation; and occasionally, even rioting. The nationalist movement was dramatized—and advertised—by Gandhi, an extraordinary man who combined in himself the qualities of saint, prophet, and politician.[10] Gandhi's personality and ideals attracted sympathetic attention throughout the world and won many adherents to his cause. The Indian nationalists demanded self-government for India; the moderate element favored Dominion status, but the revolutionary element demanded nothing less than complete independence. So menacing was the nationalist movement that Britain, in order to stay in India, was forced to make concessions. In 1919, Parliament enacted a law that granted considerable power of local self-government to the provinces of British India, and established a national assembly with limited power over legislation. Tariff autonomy was also granted, allowing India to levy duties against Britain. These concessions merely encouraged the Indian nationalists to strive more ardently for independence.

Nationalism in Turkey experienced a new birth with the collapse of the Ottoman Empire. Turkey, now a republic, was shorn of her Arab lands in Asia as before the war she had been shorn of her Balkan lands in Europe. What remained to her was chiefly Anatolia, a fairly solid Turkish region. But the new republic inherited the enmities of the old empire and was beset with foes on all sides. In 1921, Greece attacked Turkey, but was badly defeated. The Turkish hero of the war, Mustafa Kemal, became virtually the dictator of the Turkish Republic, which he had organized according to the most approved pattern of nationalism. After centuries of imperialist aggression, Turkey now resigned herself to the position of a small nation.

Nationalism achieved its supreme triumph in the Orient after the Second World War. In the Far East, in the Middle East, and in North Africa explosive ideas awakened millions from the torpor of centuries to the new belief that poverty and oppression were not unavoidable and that evil conditions due to nature and to man could be controlled. It was this new faith among the colonial peoples that brought about changes result-

[10] See p. 74.

ing in the fall of colonial imperialism. Ancient peoples, long in bondage, became free and independent, sometimes as a result of a successful uprising, sometimes as a result of a voluntary surrender of power by the imperialist nation. In the first place, the war greatly weakened Britain, France, and the Netherlands, who could no longer exert their former authority in the colonies. The weakness of the ruler became the strength of the ruled. In the second place, the Europeans had been badly beaten in battle and driven headlong out of their possessions by the Japanese. Though they had no love for the latter the colonial peoples took pride in the triumph of an Asiatic nation over their European masters. No longer did white supremacy rouse in them a feeling of awe and cause them to bend in an attitude of submission.

By far the most resounding success of Oriental nationalism took place in India. As Britain's weakness became more evident, Indian nationalism became more aggressive. A crisis was fast approaching. It was avoided by the announcement of the British government of its decision to leave India by 1948 and to permit the Indians themselves to decide on their political future. This decision marked a great historic event in the history of British imperialism.[11]

What was to be the future of India? A deep division took place over the issue of religion between the Hindus and the Moslems. This issue, called "communalism," or the organization of religious communities for political ends, threatened to disrupt the newly born nation. The Moslem minority, led by Mohammed Ali Jinnah, absolutely refused to join the Hindu majority, led by Jawaharlal Nehru, to form a united India. Instead, Jinnah demanded the establishment of a Moslem state, called Pakistan, to be entirely independent of the rest of India. Bloody riots broke out between Hindus and Moslems in which thousands were killed. Gandhi was assassinated by a fanatical

[11] See pp. 77, 194.

Hindu because he favored a reconciliation of both elements. So insistent were the Moslems on partition that on August 15, 1947, by mutual consent, India was bisected into the Hindu Union of India and the Moslem Pakistan. Each was given the choice of seceding from the British Commonwealth of Nations or of remaining as Dominions with complete autonomy. Both elected to become Dominions in what was now called the "Commonwealth of Nations." Nearly all the 560 princely states, outside of British India, submitted to the authority of the Union of India. Ceylon became a Dominion in its own right.

The triumph of Indian nationalism was followed by great calamities. In many parts of India, Hindus and Moslems were intermingled and had lived together in peace, though not in amity, during the British occupation. Once the protecting hand of the British army was removed, each element was in danger of being attacked by the other. Communalism in India soon proved to be as brutal and as intolerant as was racialism in Europe. Each side determined to "solve" the minority problem by massacre and deportation. The number of those killed is unknown. About ten million became refugees fleeing for their lives from the one Dominion to the other, leaving behind their homes, their farms, their offices, their factories, and their stores. The greatest mass migration in history followed the recognition of the principle of nationality in India.

Nationalism made extensive gains in eastern Asia. Burma was granted independence by Britain; and the Philippines, by America. Interesting and confusing was the case of Korea, an ancient land that had fallen under Japanese control as a result of the Russo-Japanese war. After the defeat of Japan in the Second World War, Korea was occupied by foreign armies: the north, by Russians, and the south, by Americans. In 1948, a national assembly was elected in the American section, which proclaimed Korea an independent republic. The Americans evacuated their section, an imprudent move as it later proved.

A triumph of Asiatic nationalism, second only to that in India, came with the end of 347 years of colonial rule in the Dutch East Indies. A conference took place at the Hague in 1949 which adopted an agreement of far-reaching importance. This agreement, the Statute of Union, recognized the "United States of Indonesia" as an independent, sovereign republic, and as an equal partner of the Netherlands under the joint headship of the crown. Both countries agreed to cooperate in military, economic, financial, and cultural affairs. Decisions affecting both had to have the consent of both, and special organs were created to ensure regular collaboration. The United States of Indonesia was organized as a federal union of sixteen states, the most important being Sumatra, Java, part of Borneo, and the Celebes.

Western Asia also witnessed a marked advance of nationalism. Especially triumphant was Arab nationalism; a number of Arab states had emerged from the ruins of the Ottoman Empire after the First World War. Saudi Arabia was recognized as an independent nation under an Arab king. Iraq, first organized as a mandate of Britain, became independent in 1932. Egypt, a protectorate of Britain, became an independent kingdom in 1922.

After the Second World War, Arab nationalism made even more notable gains than it had made during the interwar period. Syria and Lebanon, mandatories of France, Transjordania, a mandatory of Britain, and Yemen, a tribal state, were recognized as independent nations. A great conflict arose between Arabs and Jews as to the future of Palestine, a mandatory of Britain. In the Balfour Declaration of 1917 Britain had promised to establish in Palestine a national home for the Jewish people; later, she had given official recognition to the Zionist organization in the government of the mandate. Neither the Jews nor the Arabs wanted Britain in Palestine; even less did each relish being ruled by the other. Actual war broke out between Jews and Arabs soon after the end of the Second World War and ended in the triumph of the Jews. In 1948, as a result of an arrangement made by the United Nations, Palestine was partitioned between Jews and Arabs. The part given to the Jews, called Israel, was recognized as an independent nation.

The political map of Asia now showed divisions into nations, great and small, something novel and unexpected in the history of that continent. The new wine of nationalism from the West had been poured into the old bottle of the East with the result that Asia was definitely out of European control. Colonial imperialism in this oldest of continents is on the wane in the mid-twentieth century, as it was on the wane in the New World in the mid-nineteenth century. Africa still remains largely under imperialist rule. Egypt and Ethiopia are the only independent nations in the second largest continent.

What of the future of nationalism in the Orient? Cut away from the old moorings of Western control, the nations of the Orient are now, in a great measure, free to fashion their own future. During their struggle for independence, the Oriental nationalists had proclaimed high ideals of freedom and equality. Will they be faithful to these ideals now that they are free? Will they show a spirit of moderation in dealing with the many problems bequeathed to them by their subjection in the past and created for them by the internal conflicts of the present? Only the future will tell.

REEVALUATION OF NATIONALISM

For long, nationalism had been accepted almost uncritically by liberals in every land. They had believed that the principle of nationality, if universally applied, would lead to peace and concord among the peoples of the world. Quite the reverse has been the record of history. National hatreds, jealousies, and rivalries were chiefly responsible for the unprecedented calamity of two world wars within one generation. In the light of this experience a reevaluation of the principle of nationality becomes pertinent.

Unquestionably, nationalism made contributions to human progress. In earlier days, it solidified small, scattered feudal areas into a large political unit within which local discords gave way to national harmony. In later times, nationalism became a liberating force by inspiring subjected peoples, such as those in east central Europe and in the colonial empires, to strive for their freedom. In these lands, nationalism roused the inert, apathetic masses and gave them a self-consciousness and a feeling of group loyalty and dignity. It also proved to be a fruitful unifying principle in that individuals of diverse origins, as in America, and independent states with a common heritage, as in Germany and Italy, freely accepted the common bond of a common nationality. Nationalism made a living thing of the map of the world, not merely a flat surface with marked frontiers. Any violent change in the map resulted in "bleeding frontiers" that roused intense feeling. Alsace-Lorraine was a striking illustration. When that region was annexed to France through the wars of Louis XIV, neither the inhabitants, nor the French, nor the Germans were very much concerned over the change. How different was the attitude of these three, when, without a plebiscite, Alsace-Lorraine was annexed by Germany in 1871! And again when it returned to France in 1919!

But nationalism brought also many undoubted evils. What began as an expansion of narrow localisms ended in the narrowness of national egotisms. As described above, national pride was transformed first into the aggressiveness of integral nationalism and imperialism and then into the fearful monster of racialism. Instead of bringing peace and concord, the application of the principle of nationality brought dissension and wars of all kinds, civil, national, and international.

How to retain the undoubted contributions of nationalism

and how to eliminate its undoubted evils has been the great problem in the twentieth century. There can be no solution of this problem without a reconsideration of the very life principle of nationalism, namely, sovereignty. Its full acceptance has made possible the persecution of minorities and the state of "international anarchy" that so often has led to war. Intervention by a foreign state, or even by world organizations like the League of Nations and the United Nations, has been quickly and sharply resented as an infringement of national sovereignty. Has not a nation the sovereign right to do what it wishes with its own? Has not a nation the sovereign right to conduct its foreign policy as it pleases?

It has become evident—to some—that national sovereignty is, in fact, a fiction. Is not the sovereignty of one nation limited by that of all the others? Is it not limited even more by the extent of a nation's resources? The nation, as an independent unit, is as outmoded in the economy of the twentieth century as was the manor in the seventeenth, when feudalism gave way to nationalism. Highly industrialized America and Britain and backward China and Turkey, all are vitally linked in the world economy created by the new Industrial Revolution. Their political independence contradicts their economic interdependence. Not even the greatest powers are self-sufficient. Britain has not a pint of oil; America, not an ounce of tin or natural rubber; and Soviet Russia, little cotton. Some of the weak nations contain resources vital to the economy of the world: Spain has mercury; Turkey, chrome; Italy, sulphur; China, antimony; the Philippines, hemp. Almost every technological development increases the dependence of one nation upon another. The automobile makes Spain dependent on America for gasoline and on Britain for steel. The airplane makes Britain dependent on France for aluminum and on Arabia for oil. In the world of today, unified by the marvelous systems of transportation and communication and by the economic interdependence of all nations, the sovereign, national state has become almost an anachronism. No nation can any longer live unto itself alone, and survive. Economic necessity has often compelled a nation to adopt the policies of another or to make incompatible alliances. A striking illustration has been Italy, which almost completely lacks coal. Italy's diplomatic policies have followed those of coal-producing powers, first of Britain, and then of Germany. Military necessity likewise has compelled a nation to ally itself with others in order to achieve security. No nation, not even the powerful, aggressive, militarist German Empire, has felt strong enough to stand out by itself panoplied in full sovereignty. The sovereign national state is out of date in the economy and politics of the twentieth century.

Equality of nations, like sovereignty, is likewise a myth. How could equality exist between Belgium and France or between Germany and Denmark, when the smaller nation depended for its very existence on the larger one? It was a plain fact, though not frankly avowed, that all the small nations of Europe, and even some of the larger ones, existed only by the right of sufferance. Legal equality was the fiction, actual inequality, the fact, in the hierarchical system of states in which the position of each depended on its military power. Inequality of power negated equality in law. For all that, the fictions of sovereignty and of equality proved to be stumbling blocks to the adoption of a world organization that alone could give security to each nation. Stubborn facts were as babes in the wood when confronted with stubborn theories.

The rise of totalitarianism revealed in a lurid light the shortcomings of national sovereignty in both domestic and foreign matters. Adhering to the principle of nonintervention in the domestic affairs of a nation no move was made to stop the fearful persecution of noncommunists in Russia and the wholesale extermination of Jews in Germany. At the same time these totalitarian states themselves intervened in the domestic affairs of other nations. They organized Fifth Columns to overthrow the governments of neighboring states. Nazi Germany claimed the supreme allegiance of those inhabitants of any country who were of German origin, despite frontiers and citizenship. Asserting that the tie of class was superior to that of citizenship, Communist Russia claimed the supreme allegiance of the workers in all lands. And these were no idle claims, as nations learned to their sorrow. Fifth Columns of local fascists or Communists constantly sought to undermine the land of their birth in the interest of the land of their ideology.

The world of sovereign, national states was disrupted in another way—by the virtual elimination of the balance of power. This principle had played its historic role in the multination system of Europe, wherein each nation had its place, and wherein the leading places were occupied by the great powers. An unforeseen outcome of the two world wars was the elimination or reduction of all the great powers, except Russia. Germany and Austria-Hungary disappeared from the diplomatic scene. France was reduced to a second- and Italy to a third-rate power. Britain was so greatly weakened that not for a long time would she be able to exert the necessary strength required of a great power. Russia emerged as the only great power in Europe, and far stronger than in any previous period of her history. There could be no balance of power in Europe with only one great power dominating the Continent.

This new situation created uneasiness verging upon panic among the nations in Western Europe. They feared that every aspect of their independent existence would be ruthlessly wiped out by Soviet Russia at the first opportune moment. And the military weakness, the political divisions, and the economic disorganization of Western Europe invited aggression. No balance of power existed, as before 1914, that would rouse powerful nations to confront an aggressor. Into this situation America made her dramatic entry as the champion of democracy against totalitarian dictatorship. The Truman Doctrine gave notice that America was ready to aid any democratic nation in defending itself against totalitarian aggression.[12]

A diplomatic revolution followed the Truman Doctrine. Into the vacuum, created by the disappearance of the balance of power, came the bipolar power system of America and Soviet Russia. The "cold war" between them dominated international relations throughout the world; all the other nations supported one side or the other. The sovereign national state could and did find place in a balance of power system, which was based on the independence of all states, great and small. Quite otherwise was the situation under the bipolar power system. Those states that supported Soviet Russia were not independent, political entities but satellites, whose every move, domestic and foreign, was directed from Moscow. Those states that supported America did so voluntarily, it is true, but circumstances compelled them to do so. So weakened were they all, even once powerful Britain and France, that their very survival depended on economic and military help from America. Being democracies they naturally joined forces with America, and they did so gladly because of the generous aid that the latter gave them, freely and promptly. The sovereign national state had become either a satellite or a suppliant.

FUTURE OF NATIONALISM

In the world of two superpowers all talk of national sovereignty has a hollow sound. What is the "sovereignty" of Poland in the Russian bloc? What is the "sovereignty" of France, dependent as she is on American economic and military aid? Neither satellite Poland nor independent France can adopt important policies, domestic no less than foreign, without reference to

[12] See p. 312.

America and to Soviet Russia. That is plain to anyone who reads a daily newspaper. National sovereignty is gone. Is nationalism itself no more?

The great and lasting contribution of nationalism to progress has been primarily cultural. As the various nations came into being and developed, their languages, literatures, arts, and crafts flowered and spread. A nation's culture, unlike its politics, is indestructible. The Germany of Goethe and Beethoven is alive and permanent, but the Germany of Bismarck and Hitler is dead and gone.

How to preserve the enduring cultural values of nationalism, and, at the same time, to discard its encrusted evil of sovereignty, is the basic problem today. The solution lies in the preservation of the cultural aspects of nationalism, or the right of a nation to maintain its cultural heritage intact, and to develop its greatest possibilities undisturbed. Cultural nationalism is possible and desirable, now that economic nationalism is impossible and political nationalism disastrous. It flourishes alike in the old, tiny state of Switzerland and in the new, continental state of the Soviet Union. Each of the three nationalities composing the Swiss people, German, French, and Italian, has cultural autonomy. All three languages are official and are taught in the schools. Despite these cultural differences, the loyalty of the Swiss people to their common fatherland has never been questioned. On more than one occasion have the Swiss shown complete solidarity when confronted by menacing moves on the part of their powerful neighbors.

For all the evils of totalitarian dictatorship, Communist Russia made a notable effort to solve the problem of nationalism. During the period of the Russian Empire there had been a dominant nationality, the Great Russians; the many other national groups had all been subjected to various degrees of discrimination and persecution. A diametrically opposite policy was proclaimed by the Soviet Union in its constitution of 1936, which contained the following provision: "Equality of rights of the citizens of the Soviet Union, irrespective of their nationality or race, in all spheres of economic, state, cultural, social and political life is an indefeasible law." According to this constitution the Soviet Union was a federation of nationalities; each state consisted of a nationality, large or small, and was represented as such in the Council of Nationalities, the upper house of the federal parliament. Each nation-state had cultural autonomy with its language, literature, and folkways officially recognized. Cultural nationalism was encouraged by the government; any national group might organize itself as a nation-state and receive government aid in doing so. The pattern of cultural nationalism, adopted by the Soviet Union in the constitution, marked a great advance in the accepted treatment of national minorities in east central Europe.[13] Unfortunately, however, the provision of the Soviet constitution granting equality of rights to the various nationalities was often violated in practice. During and after the Second World War the government removed national groups from their national homes on the plea of security. Whole communities in the Volga region, in the Crimea, in the Baltic region, in the Ukraine, and in the Caucasus were suddenly torn from their lands and sent elsewhere. Non-Slavic peoples living on the western border were likewise removed, and Slavic groups were sent to replace them. The fate of the displaced has remained unknown.

The cultural integrity of a people is in full harmony with regional federations and even with a world organization. Freed of the need for defense against aggression, each nation would have greater freedom to develop its distinctive national culture. And each nation would have better opportunities to spread its language, its literature, its arts, and its sciences when done freely

[13] See p. 224.

and voluntarily and not, as so often in the past, by means of forceful assimilation following conquest. A varicultured world, living in peace, would create a system of civilization far greater and more enduring than any other in the past or in the present. Then the nation, purified of its egotism and its chauvinism, would truly be the vehicle of human progress.

Chapter 6. Colonial Imperialism, Its Decline and Fall

RISE OF COLONIAL IMPERIALISM

Not least among the forces that created the "world in crisis" during the twentieth century was that of imperialism. It became a world-wide issue that split the great powers into hostile camps and roused the backward peoples of Asia and Africa into national consciousness. As the century wore on, it became all-too evident that imperialism would result in a world conflict, and, whatever its outcome, it would be followed by a revolt of the East against the West.

Imperialism means the rule of one people by another brought about by annexation of territory through conquest. Its main objective is the exploitation of the people, the wealth, and the natural resources of the subjugated land for the benefit of the conquerors. Empires have flourished at all times, in all parts of the world, and under all civilizations. Even pre-Columbian America could boast of the Inca empire in Peru and the Aztec empire in Mexico.

Generally, though not always, the conquerors have had a civilization superior to that of the conquered. In ancient times the civilization of the Romans was superior to that of the Gauls, as was the civilization of the Greeks to that of the Persians. In modern times the civilization of the British was superior to that of the Malayans, as was that of the French to that of the Algerians. In such cases the conquered shared, to some degree, the benefits of the higher civilization of their conquerors. Sometimes, however, the subjugated people had a civilization superior to that of their masters, as was the case when the Greeks were

conquered by the Romans, the Romans by the German barbarians, and the Byzantines, by the Turks. In such instances, the
higher civilization of the subjugated peoples fell into decay, and
human progress suffered a setback.

The essential character of imperialism has always remained
the same: the rule of a militarily weak by a militarily strong
people. But the causes that have led to it, the methods used,
the policies followed, and the forms adopted have varied
throughout history at different times and in different parts of
the world. The classic example of imperialism was that of the
Roman Empire, which, for more than five centuries, ruled
almost the entire world as known in ancient times. Gradually
the Roman Empire disintegrated, its parts fell away, or were
seized by the barbarian invaders. What followed was the turning back of the clock of history for a long period.

The old imperialism of Rome was dead, but its tradition, the
rule of masterful over weak peoples, remained. After the long
interlude of the Middle Ages, when Europe was broken up into
many feudal states, a new imperialism appeared as a result of
the discovery of America. Here were two immense continents
and many islands immeasurably rich in natural resources and
sparsely inhabited by savage and semicivilized tribes that could
offer little resistance to any group of armed Europeans. The
military power and territorial ambition of the new political unit,
the nation, appeared in Spain, France, and England. The policies of the new economy, mercantilism, demanded increased
supplies of raw materials and food for commerce and increased
supplies of gold and silver for money. As these needs could
easily be satisfied in the New World, an expansion of Europe
beyond the seas began, which ushered in the new era of "colonial imperialism." In a short time the New World was conquered and settled by those peoples in Europe, great and small,
that had become nations: the Spanish, the French, the English, the Portuguese, and the Dutch. Each carved out for itself

a colonial empire, exploiting its natural resources, sending settlers to its fertile lands, and enslaving, expelling, or exterminating its native inhabitants. "Colonies" now appeared in far-distant America, each closely tied to the "mother country" in Europe, politically, economically, and culturally.

THE AMERICAN REVOLUTION AND THE DECLINE OF COLONIAL IMPERIALISM

As a colony developed its natural resources and increased its population, the mother country saw great possibilities of becoming richer and stronger as a nation. How? One way was by adding to its colonial possessions through the conquest of colonies belonging to rival nations. Another was by keeping a tight hold on the economic and political activities of the colonists, with the purpose of using them in the interest of the mother country. These two ways were followed by all the colonial powers in the New World during the seventeenth and eighteenth centuries.

The struggle for colonies was not least among the causes of the great European wars that raged during the eighteenth century. Whether they originated in Europe or in the New World, they were fought in both places by the rival colonial empires. And the treaties of peace always marked a shift in colonial power, sometimes in favor of one, sometimes of another. As a consequence of these struggles, France and the Netherlands were practically eliminated from the New World. Spain and Portugal, who had aimed to possess all, had to be content with about half of the Americas. England alone emerged victorious, having won about half of North America.

A colony by its very definition was subordinate to the mother country. But what was the nature and the extent of its subordination in the pattern of colonial imperialism? Politically it was ruled by the mother country, who made laws for it and sent officials to enforce them. This was true for all colonies, but less so for the English, who enjoyed a fair degree of self-government. Economically a colony was integrated in the commercial and industrial organization of the mother country according to the principles of mercantilism then universally accepted. It was limited in its economic activities to that of providing raw materials and foods needed by the mother country, of serving as a market for its manufactures, and of providing cargoes and passengers for its vessels. Except under special circumstances, a colony was forbidden to manufacture goods, to trade with foreign nations, or to ship in foreign vessels.

As the colonies grew and developed, discontent with their subordinate status was rife everywhere in the New World. But more so in the English colonies, where the libertarian traditions were the same as in the mother country. The outcome was the American Revolution, an event of extraordinary historical significance in more ways than one. A new nation, destined to play a great role in world affairs, was born. Moreover, the manner in which America came into existence constituted a precedent of profound significance. The American Revolution was the first successful uprising of a colony against a mother country, the first break in the pattern of colonial imperialism. Early in the nineteenth century, its influence was felt in the revolutions of the Spanish and the Portuguese colonies, which brought into being the Latin-American nations. Later, its influence was again felt in Britain's grant of self-government to Canada, which laid the foundation of that extraordinary development in colonial history, the creation of a free and equal status as between mother country and colony in the British Commonwealth of Nations. By about the middle of the nineteenth century, colonial imperialism was almost dead in the region of its origin, the New World. France and the Netherlands had lost their American colonies to Britain as a result of wars. Britain had lost the Thirteen Colonies, the best in her empire, as a result of revolution. Spain and Portugal had lost their American colonies also as a result of revolution. The separation of a colony from the mother country was now regarded as inevitable; like a fruit, when ripe, it would drop from the mother tree. So why spend money and effort to maintain a colonial empire doomed to disintegrate!

New economic conditions made colonial imperialism unprofitable as well as unnecessary. The progress of the Industrial Revolution during the nineteenth century created an expanding economy that sought markets for its finished goods in thickly populated countries like Germany and Russia, rather than in thinly populated colonies like Canada and Brazil. Unlike the mercantilists, who believed that the amount of trade, in any given period, was limited, the theorists of the Industrial Revolution, the classical economists, believed that trade at any time could be expanded indefinitely, provided markets were freed from artificial restrictions, such as tariffs, navigation laws, and colonial monopolies. A nation could attain wealth and power industrially by increasing production, and commercially by buying in the cheapest and selling in the dearest market, irrespective of what flag floated over them. Trade neither led nor followed the flag. What then was the value of a colony in the new economic scheme? No value at all. On the contrary, a colony was now regarded as a heavy liability in that it constituted a constant threat of war, thereby compelling the mother country to maintain heavy armaments. For both political and economic reasons anti-imperialism became, by the middle of the nineteenth century, the prevailing mood in Europe.

REVIVAL OF COLONIAL IMPERIALISM

This mood, however, passed quickly. Toward the end of the nineteenth century there took place an extraordinary revival of imperialism, far greater in scope and intensity than that of the imperialism of former days. Old nations like Britain and France once more felt the stirrings of empire and resolved to keep what colonies they had and to acquire others at every opportunity. New nations like Germany, Italy, and Japan became eager to make up for lost centuries by acquiring colonial possessions. Even America, born of a protest against imperialism, asserted that her "manifest destiny" lay in annexing new lands, and promptly began a career of expansion overseas. As a result of these new colonial rivalries, great conflicts arose which were far larger in scale and involved far greater issues than those of the rival imperialisms in the eighteenth century. Colonial rivalry was not least among the causes of the two world wars that devastated the world during the first half of the twentieth century.

What brought about this revival of imperialism? In the first place, the discovery, in the sixties and seventies of the nineteenth century, of Central Africa, a vast region containing valuable natural resources and inhabited by weak tribes of aborigines, awakened the cupidity of the Europeans. As in the case of the discovery of America, rich prizes beckoned the militant, adventurous nations of Europe. A scramble for Africa began, and, in a very short time, practically all of Africa, including the northern rim, was divided among the European powers. The partition of Africa was accomplished peacefully through diplomatic agreements and treaties. Some of the powers got more, others less; but all were disappointed with what they got. As a consequence, bitter feelings were engendered among the colonial powers that served to intensify national pride and to revive ancient animosities.

In the second place, an old world, the Far East, was rediscovered about the same time that Central Africa was discovered, which further intensified the cupidity of the Europeans. China and Japan had been known to the Europeans ever since the sixteenth century, but they were closed to foreign trade and settlement except in a few restricted seaports. About the middle of the nineteenth century, China and Japan were "opened up" violently by the Western powers, either through "visits" by threatening fleets or through actual war. China especially was considered a great prize. Here was a vast region rich, thickly populated, highly civilized, but backward politically and economically. Lacking the high degree of national unity attained in Europe, China lacked military effectiveness; hence she was no match in a trial of battle with a European power. She quickly succumbed to the attacks of the European imperialist nations, who seized outlying regions and valuable ports, compelled the Chinese government to accept "unequal treaties" granting special privileges to their nationals, and divided the country into "spheres of influence" each of which was to be dominated by a European power.

By 1914, all Asia, except Turkey and Japan, had been reduced to colonial or semicolonial status. Japan stood out as the only Asiatic country that succeeded not only in establishing herself as a fully independent, sovereign state but also in arriving to the peak of being recognized as a great power. To the dismay of her neighbors, however, Japan joined in the scramble for colonies and became as ruthless in conquering Asiatic peoples as were the European powers. Imperialism knew no brothers.

In the third place, economics played a leading part in the revival of colonial imperialism. As its decline early in the nineteenth century cannot be dissociated from the old Industrial Revolution, with the need to remove restrictions on freedom of trade, so its revival late in the century cannot be dissociated from the new Industrial Revolution with its greatly increased output of goods and its need for new materials. Without large and free markets to absorb the vast supply of manufactures made possible by highly mechanized industry, no nation could hope to achieve prosperity. The manufacturers in highly industrialized nations beheld in the vast populations of Asia potential customers for the goods that rolled off their machines. Furthermore, the new methods, the new techniques, and the new products required new raw materials to keep industries going. Without a plentiful supply of strategic raw materials, such as oil, rubber, tin, chrome, nickel, and manganese, both the industrial and military power of a nation would rapidly decline. Not one of the powers was self-sufficient in this respect. As a consequence, they sought to acquire colonies capable of supplying the needed raw materials, and, at the same time, of absorbing the surplus products of their factories.

Much capital was needed to develop backward regions that would fulfill the needs of the industrialized nations. As a result of the rapid advance of industry, capital accumulated rapidly, and large amounts were exported to backward lands where the return on investments was greater than at home. The export of capital from Europe to Asia and Africa became a prominent feature of the new colonial imperialism. Railways, docks, factories, telegraphs, and telephones, all of the latest types, were built by European capitalists in backward lands. Not infrequently did a newly industrialized country like China and India employ more advanced technology than did the countries where industries had flourished since the old Industrial Revolution. To obtain desired foods and raw materials, large capital investments were made in developing backward regions: tea plantations in Ceylon; rubber plantations in Malaya; cotton fields in the Sudan; phosphate beds in Tunis; and coffee, tobacco, and sugar plantations in the East Indies. To safeguard the investments of their nationals, the European powers established political control over these lands. The flag followed investments.

The conviction became widespread that colonies alone could supply a nation with needed raw materials; with markets for surplus manufactures; with homes for surplus populations; and with investment opportunities for surplus capital. A nation with a colonial empire could snap its fingers at tariff, immigration, and investment restrictions imposed by foreigners. Nationalism now passed into imperialism.

Domination through imperialism was sometimes open, sometimes disguised. The rule of India by Britain, of Madagascar by France, and of Java by the Netherlands was open and direct; laws and officials came from the mother country. Disguised forms of imperialism were many and varied. Some were "protectorates" like Morocco, where the native ruler was kept, but "advised" by French officials. Others were "leaseholds," leased for a number of years by a native ruler to an imperialist power whose authority was full and complete, as when, in 1898, China was compelled to "lease" Port Arthur to Russia and Kiao-chau to Germany. Still another form of disguised imperialism was the "sphere of influence," wherein native political sovereignty was recognized but the ruler was compelled to give exclusive economic privileges to an imperialist power. A notable example was Persia, which was divided, in 1907, into three "spheres of influence": one part was to be exploited exclusively by British capitalists; another, by Russian capitalists; and the third by the capitalists of both powers. Whether open or disguised, imperialist rule was frankly acknowledged and widely practiced.

As the imperialist pace quickened, it became evident that a sharp and bitter antagonism divided the powers into two groups, the "haves" and the "have nots." The former were Britain and France, the old colonial powers, who had managed to acquire large colonial areas and were determined to hold them. The "have nots" were Germany, Italy, and Japan, whose colonial possessions were small and of little value by comparison with those of the "haves." As most of the colonial world was already divided, the "have nots" could gain colonies only at the expense of the "haves." This class struggle between nations implied war on a world-wide scale.

The Far East, because of its rich prizes in territory, in wealth, and in population, became the scene of a great concentration of European imperialism. And the richest prize of all was China, whose weakness invited attack from any quarter. Britain, France, Russia, Germany, and the Netherlands, all had staked out claims in China. But a new imperialist power appeared, Japan, whose ambition overrode those of the Europeans and whose aggressiveness left nothing to be desired even by the most imperialist of the European powers.

One of the phenomenal events in modern history was the rapid rise of Japan from a small, hermit nation to a great world power. Once organized as a nation according to the best European models, the Japanese clearly realized that their island homeland was too small and too poor to be the seat of a great power. Hence Japan felt that she must expand into China in order to realize her ambition of being the "lord of the Far East." Like the Germans the Japanese regarded themselves as a "chosen" race, to whom history had assigned a privileged position among the nations of the world. They dreamed of establishing a "New Order in East Asia" by conquering all the lands in that part of the world, by driving out the European powers, and by organizing a great empire there with themselves as rulers. A half century of careful planning went into this dream, and it was followed by swift, decisive action almost like a time clock in its regularity.

The victory of Japan in the Russo-Japanese war (1904–1905) was an event of the greatest importance in the history of the Far East and of the world in general. As a result, Japan got her first foothold on the continent of Asia, by acquiring Korea and the southern part of Manchuria. These became her "life line." Russia was now virtually eliminated from the Chinese scene. For the first time an Asiatic nation had defeated a great European power, a fact which gave Japan immense prestige among the peoples of Asia. In her aggressive moves to establish the "new order," Japan utilized this prestige by posing as the champion of colonial peoples against European imperialism.

Japan's aggressive moves in the Far East highlighted the rivalries between the imperialist powers throughout the colonial world. The "haves" were determined to keep what they had, and the "have nots" were even more determined to get all that they could. Germany spearheaded the onslaught against the old colonial powers. Infuriated at being at the same time a great power and a "have not" nation, she decided to throw down the gauntlet to Britain and France, her chief rivals. A conflict might now arise anywhere over an "incident"; an altercation about a railway concession, a mob attack on a foreign embassy, an assassination of a foreign prince, any one of these might light the fires of war throughout the world.

DECLINE OF COLONIAL IMPERIALISM

Colonial rivalry played a prominent part in bringing about the diplomatic crises which preceded the outbreak of the First World War in 1914. As the war progressed, the question arose: What would be the attitude of the colonial peoples in this conflict between their masters? So bad was Germany's record in her African colonies and so strident was her militaristic authoritarianism that the colonial peoples feared a German victory almost as much as did their imperialist rulers. Consequently, the British and French colonies rallied to the side of their mother countries and helped materially to bring about the defeat of Germany.

Not unnaturally, the colonies expected benefits for themselves from the victorious outcome of the war "to make the world safe for democracy." And they were not mistaken. A new attitude toward backward peoples found expression in the "mandate system" incorporated in the treaty of Versailles. True it was only an "attitude," but important nevertheless because it held out the prospect of a better future for colonial peoples. According to this system, a backward territory was entrusted to one of the powers, which was to administer it in the interest of the inhabitants, but under the supervision of the League of Nations. Syria, Iraq, and Palestine, formerly ruled by Turkey, became mandatories of designated powers: the first, of France; and the last two, of Britain, all with the promise of ultimate independence. In 1937, Iraq was proclaimed an independent nation. The German colonies in Africa and in the Pacific likewise became mandatories, some of Britain, others of the Union of South Africa, and still others, of Japan; no promise of independence was, however, made to these mandates because of the backwardness of the inhabitants.

Another setback to colonial imperialism—and a very real one —came with the reorganization of the British Empire. In 1931, Parliament passed the Statute of Westminster, as famous in the annals of the British Empire as the Report of Lord Durham in 1839, which had inspired the movement for colonial self-government. The Statute accepted, as a basic principle, that Britain and the Dominions, namely, Canada, Australia, New Zealand, and the Union of South Africa, were equal in status, equally free to decide on domestic and foreign matters, and freely united by a common allegiance to the crown. Imperial control, however, continued in the possessions, apart from the Dominions. Nevertheless, the appearance of the Commonwealth was a promise to all the colonial peoples in the empire of a "procession" from the status of a colony to that of a self-ruled Dominion, now almost indistinguishable from an independent nation.

Still another blow was given to colonial imperialism, this time by Soviet Russia. True to their Marxist principles the Communists repudiated imperialism when they seized power in Russia during the Revolution of 1917. Soviet Russia renounced the special privileges that had been granted to tsarist Russia in Manchuria, in China proper, and in Persia. Furthermore, she issued a call to all colonial peoples to revolt against their European masters. Communist aid was freely given to the revolutionary movements in the colonial world in the belief that the overthrow of imperialism would be followed by the destruction of capitalism everywhere. Soviet Russia's ardent anti-imperialism brought glad tidings to colonial peoples. Here was a great European power, once an enemy, now a friend and ally in their struggle for freedom. Communism for a time gained many converts in Asia, especially in China, because of Soviet Russia's repudiation of imperialism.

These trends away from colonial imperialism became marked during the interwar period. The imperialist rivalries of the Great Powers convinced many in all lands that colonial empires constituted a threat to world peace. After a century of imperialist policies, ardently pursued and stubbornly followed, it now became possible to reevaluate them in the tragic light of the First World War.

BALANCE SHEET OF COLONIAL IMPERIALISM

The debits and credits arising from the possession of a colonial empire were now submitted for a reappraisal. Did the colonies provide the necessary raw materials to the mother country? Were they outlets for surplus manufactures, surplus population, and surplus investments?

Let us examine the record. Careful scientific studies have revealed the fact that colonies had only limited supplies of the important natural resources, such as coal, iron, oil, copper, and cotton, needed by an industrialized nation. In 1937, the estimated total production of all commercially important raw materials in all colonial areas was only about 3 per cent of the world's production.[1] Only rubber, palm oil, copra, cocoa, and tin were produced chiefly in colonial areas.[2] The manufacture of steel requires coal, iron, and such metals as manganese, nickel, and chrome, most of which were, prior to 1939, produced in noncolonial lands. In time of peace, colonial products were as a rule available to all who could pay for them. In time of war, access to colonial products depended on a nation's ability to maintain communications with its colonies as with other lands. During the First World War, Germany, not having control of the seas, was shut out from her own colonies as well as from those of the Allies.

But, argued the apologists of colonial imperialism, noncolonial powers were placed at a great disadvantage in colonial trade by the colonial powers. The latter could and did hamper the trade of their colonies with other powers through onerous restrictions. These restrictions were (1) heavy export duties on goods destined for foreign countries; (2) the system of "imperial preference," adopted by Britain and the Dominions, which laid low tariffs on goods imported from one part of the British Empire to another and high tariffs on foreign goods; and (3) the system of "tariff assimilation," as in the French Empire, wherein there was a common tariff for France and her colonies and a high tariff on foreign imports. Furthermore, colonies were within the currency area of the mother country; hence, purchasers of colonial goods outside this area had the problem of acquiring exchange to pay for these goods. Fear of ever-tightening restrictions on the export of colonial products caused the "have not" nations, especially Germany, to clamor for a place in the colonial sun lest they fall behind in the industrial race.

[1] League of Nations, *Report of the Committee for the Study of the Problem of Raw Materials,* Document A27 (1937), 10.

[2] In 1937, about 91 per cent of the world's rubber and about 58 per cent of the world's tin came from British Malaya and from the Netherlands East Indies. See Lord Hailey, *Future of Colonial Peoples* (1944), 26.

These restrictions on colonial trade were real enough, but their effects were greatly exaggerated by the "have not" nations. A notable instance of the failure of such restrictions was the famous "Stevenson plan," adopted in 1922 by the British owners of the rubber plantations in the Malayan colonies. The plan provided for restrictions on the production and export of crude rubber in order to keep up the price of this essential raw material. For a time, the price of rubber did rise, but only for a time. The great demand for this material, caused by the rapid rise of the automobile industry, led capitalists to develop rubber plantations in noncolonial parts of the world. It also led to the production of synthetic rubber. The "Stevenson plan" was finally abandoned.

In the long run, restrictions on the export of colonial products defeat their own purpose. However, owing to sharp competition, nations, like individuals, consider only the short run. Therefore the solution of the problem of acquiring needed raw materials lies not in the conquest by one nation of the colonies of another but in international agreements through a world organization that would facilitate production and distribution of colonial products for the benefit of all nations.

Are colonies an outlet for the surplus manufactures of the mother country? The record in this respect is not very encouraging. In 1938, only 8.5 per cent of Britain's imports came from her colonial dependencies, and only 12.25 per cent of her exports went to them. Before 1939, India was the third largest customer for British goods, but as self-government was extended, India imposed tariff rates that shut out many imports from Britain. As a result of the Ottawa system of imperial preference, adopted in 1931, Britain's trade with the Dominions considerably improved. However, most of her trade continued to be with foreign nations, not with her colonies and Dominions.

Because of tariff assimilation, 27 per cent of France's total imports, in 1938, came from her colonies, and only 28 per cent of her exports went to them.[3] Prior to 1914, the trade of Italy and Germany with their colonies, was negligible. Japan's colonial trade had a better record. In 1934 it represented about 15.4 per cent of her total external trade, but Japan was obliged to make vast outlays and exert great pressure to hold it.

Are colonies an outlet for surplus population? A great cry was raised, prior to 1939, by the "have nots" that they had people without land, while the "haves" had land without people. Through emigration to foreign lands, asserted the "have nots," Germany, Italy, and Japan, millions of their citizens were lost to them; they therefore demanded *Lebensraum,* or colonies to which their surplus population could emigrate. Again, the record no more substantiated this claim than it did the claim that colonies were the outlet for a nation's surplus goods. In the first place, nearly all colonial areas were in the tropics, and hence not attractive to European settlers. During the first quarter of the twentieth century all the colonies of the world combined received fewer immigrants than the increase in Italy's population for the year 1935. In 1936 there were more foreign-born residents in New Hampshire than the total number of Europeans who had emigrated to Asia during the half century prior to this year.[4] Comparatively few Japanese settled in Manchuria, a large, fertile, empty land. Many preferred to make their new homes in warm, independent Brazil rather than in the cold colonial "outlet" ruled by Japan. During the years 1884 to 1914, an average of about 200,000 people emigrated from Britain annually; two-thirds of them went to the United States and one-third to the lands of the empire. The great emigration from Europe during the nineteenth century did not reduce population pressure at home. The contrary was generally true; population increased rather than diminished. Industrialization, rather than emigration, was the solution of population pressure;

[3] Lord Hailey, *op. cit.,* 28.
[4] Grover Clark, *The Balance Sheets of Imperialism* (1936), 11.

highly developed industries provided increasing employment
for an increasing population. When Germany became highly industrialized, emigration, hitherto very large, became very small.
There was no longer a surplus population in that country.

Colonies became more of an outlet for the export of capital
than for the export of goods or of people. An outflow of capital
went from the Netherlands to the East Indies; from France
to Indo-China and North Africa; and from Belgium to the
Congo. Especially notable was the export of capital from Britain
to the Dominions and colonies.[5] It rose to an extraordinary
height during the first decades of the twentieth century. Of the
annual investment of British capital for the years 1909 to 1913,
only 17 per cent was absorbed by home industry, while 36 per
cent went to the overseas possessions.[6] The reason for the export
of capital to the colonies is not difficult to see. Those who invested their money in colonial enterprises had advantages denied
to those who invested their money at home. One advantage
was that colonial investors were given official preference, directly or indirectly, over foreign competitors. Another advantage was that capital in colonial enterprises brought a higher
rate of profit than that at home. Labor was cheaper and more
docile, and colonial products were sold everywhere at monopoly
or semimonopoly prices. Imperialists argued that the large returns from colonial investments increased the national income;
hence these investments were all-important in maintaining national power and prestige.

Did the colonies benefit from European capital? To some extent they did, as the rapid development of their natural resources fully testifies. However, it was a one-sided development
in that the exploitation of natural resources was not always accompanied by industrialization. The colony was drained of its
primary products, which were sent to industrialized nations to

[5] See p. 36.
[6] *Economist* (London), Vol. 106 (1928), 76.

be processed. The rubber of Malaya was made into tires in America. The oil of the East Indies was refined in Germany. The cotton of the Sudan was made into cloth in England. There was a marked tendency to make a colony a one-crop or two-crop area, and to discourage diversification that would provide more varied foods for the native population. Notable instances were rubber in Malaya, tea in Ceylon, and cotton in the Sudan. As the chief object of colonial development was profit to the investors, the interests of the native population were often neglected. Even the railways in a colony were built with an eye to the transportation of its primary products rather than to the general needs of the colony. The establishment of factories to produce consumers' goods was not encouraged, in fact often discouraged, by the home government.

How fared the natives? In the colonies situated in temperate climates, they were deprived of their best lands, which were given to European settlers. In the tropical colonies, the natives became underpaid, overworked laborers in the mines, plantations, and factories, often under conditions approaching slavery. Their education was almost entirely neglected. Poverty for the natives, wealth for the investors, and lucrative jobs for Europeans in industry and in government became the accepted pattern in nearly all the colonies.

Colonial imperialism undoubtedly had advantages, but these advantages related to war. In the event of a world conflict, a nation having colonies in strategic places could maintain security of communications, have bases from which to attack, and populations to aid in defense. The most famous case was Britain's "life line" in the Mediterranean based upon Gibraltar, Malta, Cyprus, and Egypt. Tunis safeguarded the southern coast of France. Japan's control of Manchuria gave her the necessary bases from which to invade China. Italy's control of Libya enabled the Axis armies during the Second World War to advance upon the British forces in Egypt.

Another military advantage of a colonial empire was its ability to provide a reservoir of manpower for the mother country. In the armament race that raged furiously among the European nations there was great need to fill the ranks of the constantly increasing armies. The colonial populations conveniently satisfied this need of their European rulers. Large numbers of Africans and Asiatics filled the ranks of the French armies both in the colonies and in France. These colonial troops played a great part on the battlefields of Europe during the First World War. A large Indian army was used by the British to police not only India but also the other parts of the empire. This army constituted the bulk of the British forces on the battlefields of Asia during the two world wars. The militarization of colonial peoples became a prominent feature of every colonial empire, large and small.

The balance sheet of imperialism showed more on the debit than on the credit side of the national ledger. Mounting taxation to maintain armies and fleets to protect the colonies brought widespread discontent in imperialist countries. Anti-imperialist movements arose that criticized colonial empires as being unsound economically and as a danger to world peace.

ANTI-IMPERIALISM AND COLONIAL NATIONALISM

Two schools of anti-imperialist writers appeared: one, liberal, and the other, socialist. The liberals, notably the British economist, John A. Hobson,[7] argued that the export of capital to the colonies and to other backward lands was at the expense of domestic economy. Colonial imperialism in the period of the new Industrial Revolution was characterized by the export of capital, not of consumers' goods as in the period of the old In-

[7] John A. Hobson, *Imperialism* (1949).

dustrial Revolution. Lured on by the prospect of large returns
much of the nation's new capital was diverted from home to
build factories, railways, telegraphs, and telephones and to open
mines and oil wells in backward regions. Technology was making rapid progress, and a nation required the latest and best
machinery to make headway in the competitive world market.
But the diminished amount of capital that remained at home
demanded a higher rate of interest, which made difficult, at
times impossible, the necessary renovation of the industrial machine. When British capitalists built cotton factories in India,
they installed the latest machines. From being a customer India
became not only self-sufficient but even a competitor, with ruinous results for the cotton manufacturers of Manchester.

Who then benefited from imperialism? According to the
anti-imperialists it was only the capitalists, who invested in
colonial enterprises, and the officials, who were sent out to rule
the natives. Of the increased national wealth that came from
colonial investments little went to the mass of people at home.
On the contrary, they suffered because of increased unemployment. Far better would it have been, argued the anti-imperialists, for capital to have been invested at home for the purpose
of modernizing the antiquated industrial machine. The resulting increase in production would have brought greater employment and higher wages to the workers, and bigger profits to the
merchants and manufacturers.

Even more drastic were the socialist critics of imperialism.
Socialist anti-imperialism was based on the Marxian theory
that capitalism, in order to survive, must find ever-expanding
markets. Capitalism must expand or perish. The masses, according to Marx, were unable to purchase all the goods produced because of their low wages. In order to dispose of their
surplus goods, argued the socialists, the capitalists had to create
new markets by developing backward lands. Vast amounts of
capital were required to do this effectively, and only great

monopolistic corporations, financed and controlled by the banking interests, could undertake the task of exploiting the colonies, conquered for them by their imperialist governments. Imperialism was, therefore, inevitable in a capitalist economy; it marked the passage of capitalism from a competitive to a monopoly stage. And the latter was the final stage. Capitalism was doomed to perish as a consequence of imperialist wars, arising inevitably among the rival colonial powers.[8]

Both liberal and socialist criticisms of imperialism found support in every country. Anti-imperialism became stronger and more outspoken during the decade prior to 1914, when the international situation became critical. Crisis succeeded crisis, each involving conflicts over colonies, now in the Far East, now in the Middle East, now in North Africa. It became clearly evident that these conflicts between the "have not" and the "have" powers would lead to a world war involving all continents.

Inadvertently, colonial imperialism created the seed of its own destruction by rousing the national consciousness of the colonial peoples. The imperialists envisaged a social order in which the natives would be the hewers of wood and the drawers of water for their European masters. For a time that was so. The natives were trained to be obedient servants, industrious workers, and disciplined soldiers, all, or nearly all, in the lower ranks. The lordship of the white man in a colored world was accepted, at least outwardly, by all sections of the native population. This relationship was romanticized into what was called the "white man's burden," according to which the white man was inspired by a sense of duty to lift the natives to a higher stage of development by assimilating them to the civilization of Europe. Man seldom lacks moral justification for whatever he does, good or bad.

As a colony developed, a native middle class made its appearance. It consisted of business and professional men and white-

[8] Nicholai Lenin, *Imperialism, the Highest Stage of Capitalism* (1933).

collar workers, who were fairly numerous, especially in the
Asiatic colonies. Being literate in the European tongues, they
imbibed European ideas of nationalism and democracy. This
native middle class deeply resented the rule of the European
overlords who kept them in subordinate positions and treated
them as social inferiors. Resentment at being ruled was trans-
muted by some kind of psychological alchemy into a desire to
become the rulers. The ambition of the European-educated, well-
to-do natives to displace the Europeans produced nationalist
movements that grew rapidly during the twentieth century.
Curiously enough at this time when nationalism was being
decried as reactionary in Europe, the land of its origin, it became
the rising hope of the revolutionary elements in the colonial
world eager to liberate their country from European domination.

The revolt of Asia against Europe may be said to have had
its starting point in the Russo-Japanese war. Japan's victory had
sent thrills of hope and had awakened feelings of pride throughout the colonial world, from China to Morocco. An Oriental
people had shown sufficient prowess to defeat decisively one of
the great European powers. The European overlord was then
not invincible! The object lesson of Japan's victory was plain:
any colonial people could overthrow their rulers by adopting
their method of political and military organization. Nationalism
was the only system that could effectively use these methods to
destroy colonial imperialism. Nationalism, hitherto weak and
sporadic, now became a dominant factor in the life of the Asiatic
peoples.

Anti-imperialism in the West, combined with nationalism in
the East, served to discredit colonial imperialism. As already described, it led to the adoption of the mandate system by the
League of Nations, to the establishment of the British Commonwealth of Nations, and the surrender of colonial privileges by
Soviet Russia. Reform, even dissolution, of colonial empires be-

came the hope of many who saw in colonial rivalry the chief cause of world conflicts.

TOTALITARIAN IMPERIALISM

The reaction against imperialism, however, did not last very long. With the advent of fascism came a revival of imperialist sentiments among the "have not" nations, which soon became far more truculent than at any time prior to 1914. Fascism by its very nature was imperialist in every meaning of that word. Discontent with their position in the world, especially with their position as "have nots," gripped the fascist nations. Germany was discontented because she had lost her colonies; Italy, because she had not gained any; and Japan, because she had not gained all that she wanted. Germany's old ambition to acquire a colonial empire at the expense of Britain and France became more intense than ever under the Hitler regime. Her demand for the return of her former colonies had a menacing overtone that plainly implied that she wanted far more than that. Italy, nerved by fascism into imperialist adventures, conquered and annexed Ethiopia and Albania.

Even more imperialist than the European powers was Japan. Almost from the time of her reorganization as a Westernized nation Japan had set her goal on becoming the dominant power in the Far East. This goal could be attained only by conquering China and by eliminating the Western powers from their Far Eastern possessions. On the outbreak of the First World War, Japan saw her opportunity to eliminate Germany from the Far East. She promptly joined the Allies, and conquered Kiao-chau, the German stronghold in China. During and after the war she took advantage of the "time of confusion of Europe" by making aggressive moves in China. She compelled the latter to yield to most of her "Twenty-one Demands," which made China virtually a protectorate of Japan. But nothing would satisfy the Japanese imperialists except the complete subjugation of all China. Once that was accomplished, Japan would be in a position to expand in all directions on the Asiatic continent. Her territorial gains as a result of the war merely whetted her appetite for more. In 1931 Japanese armies invaded Manchuria, all of which was completely conquered. In 1933, they invaded China proper and seized several provinces. Finally, in 1937, a full-scale war began between China and Japan, which two years later merged with the Second World War. Japan openly proclaimed her intention to establish a "new order" in the Far East by conquering the entire region, by ousting the European powers, by nullifying all treaty rights of foreigners, and by closing the door to Western enterprise. The "new order" was on the march with the clear objective of making Japan the heir of three centuries of European imperialism and the "lord of the Far East."

Most surprising of all was that Soviet Russia turned imperialist. Whatever is done in a dictatorship, good or bad, is done quickly and easily; hence it can be undone just as quickly and just as easily. When Stalin became dictator, Soviet Russia abandoned, in practice, her anti-imperialism by taking back what she had given up in the Far East. She even reached out for more. In aiding the native communists, Soviet Russia made effective use of two appeals to colonial people: political nationalism and social revolution. Once a colony was freed through Russian intervention, as in the cases of Outer Mongolia and Northern Korea, it became a "people's democracy" under Communist rule. The change was merely that of form; it was given the role of satellite, having a colonial status in relation to Soviet Russia. Soviet imperialism, dressed in the "new look" of communism, was more onerous in some respects than had been the old colonial imperialism.

FALL OF COLONIAL IMPERIALISM

The Second World War marked the end of colonial imperialism. Ever since the sixteenth century there had been an outpouring from Europe to the colonies, of people, ideas, capital, and manufactures and an inpouring from the colonies into Europe of foods and raw materials. The great shifts of national power that had taken place in Europe were, to a considerable extent, the outcome of colonial rivalries. For almost five centuries Europeans had ruled vast populations in the colonial world. Now the rule of the European overlord virtually ended in Asia and in the East Indies; and it became much weaker in Africa. All the colonial possessions of Japan and of Italy suddenly vanished. Germany's dream of becoming the imperial heir of Britain and France turned into the nightmare of national ruin. Victorious Britain and France were greatly weakened and could no longer maintain a tight hold on their empires. Largely because of this situation, nationalism among the colonial peoples grew stronger, and its demands, more uncompromising. Japan, to no small degree, was responsible for this upsurge of nationalism. During the war the Japanese had appealed to the natives to support them in the war, which they characterized as the revolt of the Asiatic peoples against European imperialism. And the Japanese pointed to their easy victories in the Far East as proof that colored Asiatics were superior to white Europeans. The appeal fell on fertile soil in many places, notably in Burma, Malaya, and the East Indies. Japan succeeded in eliminating the Western powers from these regions but failed to realize her own dream of supplanting them.

A new Asia came into being after the war. Three great centers of imperialism, the Far East, the Middle East, and India, underwent a revolutionary transformation during the short period from 1945 to 1950. The imperial holdings of Britain, France, the Netherlands, and America in the Far East all but vanished. The first separation from the British Empire, since that of the Thirteen Colonies, took place when Burma was permitted to secede peacefully and to become an independent nation. The Malay Federation was organized to which Britain granted considerable powers of local self-government. French Indo-China received a new status early in 1950. The region was divided into three states, namely, Viet Nam, Laos, and Cambodia, each of which was given self-government as an independent nation associated with France in the French Union. Widespread discontent prevailed in the Dutch East Indies. Java, Sumatra, and other islands of the Dutch East Indies organized a union, known as "Indonesia," and proclaimed a republic. After a sharp struggle between the Dutch and Indonesians a compromise was accepted by both. In 1949, the Netherlands recognized the republic of the "United States of Indonesia" as an equal associate under the leadership of the crown.[9] A dramatic repudiation of imperialism took place on July 4, 1946, when America acknowledged the independence of the Philippine republic. For the first time in the history of colonial imperialism a colony became a nation through the voluntary act of the mother country.

A conflict of ideals and interests arose in the Middle East between Soviet Russia and the Western powers. The importance of the Middle East lies in its geographic position and in its vast oil deposits. Being a tricontinental land bridge between Europe, Asia, and Africa the Middle East has always been a region of strategic importance. Especially vital has it been for Britain, with her problem of safeguarding communications with India, Australia, New Zealand, and the Far East. Great as was the geographic importance of the Middle East, it became even more important with the discovery of oil. It is estimated that Saudi Arabia, Iraq, and Iran have the largest oil reserves in the entire

[9] See p. 157.

world. Oil production was in the hands chiefly of British and American companies; hence the British and American governments desired to be on good terms with the Arab rulers, who had granted concessions to the oil companies. During the Second World War, oil from this region had fuelled the Allied fleets and airplanes in the Mediterranean. Palestine, though not a producer of oil, yet occupied a strategic position, being the natural outlet for the pipe lines to the Mediterranean coast. Haifa was the chief center for shipping the oil of the Middle East to the rest of the world.

Iran became the first scene of conflict between Soviet Russia and the West. In order to prevent a pro-Axis party from seizing control of Iran, British and Russian forces had occupied the country during the war. When peace came, Iran demanded the withdrawal of these foreign armies, a demand which Britain accepted and Soviet Russia refused. Reversing her former anti-imperialist policy, Soviet Russia sought to get control of Iran by using her army to back up a Fifth Column of native Communists. A crisis arose, in 1946, which was tided over by the United Nations. As a result of the intervention of the latter, Soviet Russia reluctantly agreed to evacuate her troops from Iran.

Imperialism suffered additional reverses in the Middle East. As already described,[10] Syria, Lebanon, Transjordania, and Palestine emerged from their dependent status to become independent nations. Egypt, a protectorate of Britain in 1914, had been recognized as an independent kingdom in 1922; British troops, however, continued to occupy certain strategic parts of the country. After the Second World War these troops were withdrawn, except from the region of the Suez Canal.

By far the greatest repudiation of colonial imperialism took place in India. That great dependency had for two centuries been the outstanding example of imperialism in general and of British imperialism in particular. India became the very essence

[10] See p. 157.

and symbol of a dependent Oriental country, ruled despotically
by a European power. During the Second World War, India,
despite hostility to the British government, had been on the
whole loyal to the empire and had fought against the Japanese.
The Indians had no intention of exchanging the rule of liberal
Britain for that of despotic Japan; there was hope of freedom
from the former but none from the latter. During the war, the
government had encouraged the rapid industrialization of India
in order to get supplies for the armies in Asia. Furthermore,
British investments in India were sold to native capitalists in
order to get money to pay for war supplies. Industry progressed
rapidly, and, at the end of the war, India for the first time became a creditor of instead of a debtor to Britain. The heavy expense of maintaining British rule was no longer compensated, as
formerly, by the large returns from the investments of British
capital.

India was now rich and discontented, truly a formidable
combination. A change had to be made in the relations between
a weaker Britain and a stronger India. The Indian nationalists
determined to make this change even to the point of complete
independence. As a result of negotiations, amicable on the whole,
Britain in 1948 voluntarily ended her rule in India. The country
was partitioned along religious lines into the Hindu Union of
India and the Moslem Pakistan, each with Dominion status.[11]
Ceylon, too, was given Dominion status. The grant of freedom
to India constituted an historic event of prime importance. It
marked the debacle of colonial imperialism in Asia.

In its long history the British Empire has undergone great
changes. It may be said that "three" British empires have existed.
The "first" began in the age of Elizabeth and came to an end
with the American Revolution. It was characterized by autocratic rule that subordinated the interest of the colonies to those
of the mother country. The "second" began with the American

11 See pp. 77, 155.

Revolution and ended with the Statute of Westminster in 1931. Its outstanding feature was colonial self-government through the grant of Dominion status to those colonies inhabited by people of European origin. The "third" began with the Statute of Westminster and has continued to this day. Its outstanding features are (1) the association of Britain with the Dominions on the basis of almost perfect equality; and (2) the grant of Dominion status to colonies inhabited by peoples non-European in origin, as in the cases of the Union of India, Pakistan, and Ceylon.

What were the fundamental causes that brought into existence the "third" British Empire? As described elsewhere, Britain was greatly weakened economically by the war. The vast expense involved in its conduct and the great losses due to enemy action impoverished the nation whose great wealth had once been the envy of all Europe. Britain's political and strategic interests were now gravely disproportionate to her economic resources. She could not bear the cost of empire and had to retrench by cutting imperial commitments in order to maintain even the "austere" standard of life imposed on the people at home. The threat of strengthened colonial nationalism, notably in India, could no longer be either slighted or repressed by a weakened imperialism.

What facilitated the "new deal" in British imperialism was the triumph of the Labor party in the elections of 1945. Being socialists, the Laborites were, in principle, anti-imperialists, but being also British they favored a policy of granting increasing degrees of self-government to the colonies rather than the dissolution of the British Empire. Confronted, however, with the situation after the war, the Labor government could do no other than cut imperial commitments. The Laborites were not unwilling to do this, and, being socialists, they could do it far more gracefully than could the traditionally imperialist Conservatives. And the latter, being also British, would not undo a great change made by their opponents and accepted by the people.

Like the British, the French and the Netherlands empires took definite and specific steps to change their colonial relationship. Though the methods of the three empires were different, their direction was the same, namely, the substitution of government by association for government by conquest. It involved the granting of a considerable degree of self-government while, at the same time, retaining some bonds of union profitable to both colony and mother country. The French method of colonial transformation was to tighten the bonds that united a colony with the mother country, by contrast with the British method of loosening and even cutting these bonds. But the French colonial bonds were to be tightened, not in tyranny but in friendship. For long the colonies had been represented in parliament but this representation had been nominal only. After the war, colonial representation was increased, and voting rights were extended. In addition, local self-government was established or extended. More important, however, was the creation of the French Union by the constitution of 1946. Its chief purpose was to establish close collaboration between France and her overseas possessions, colonies as well as protectorates. The French Union, already described,[12] created a colonial representation system *within* a national representation system; it was given the right to advise the French government on all legislation pertaining to the overseas possessions.

What was to be the fate of the colonial possessions of Japan and Italy? Would they be divided among the victors of the Second World War? Would they become independent nations? Or would they receive an entirely new status? On this, as on so many other matters, sharp differences arose between Soviet Russia and the Western democracies. Though both repudiated colonial imperialism, they did not agree on the future status of any of the liberated territories, except Ethiopia. That

[12] See p. 192.

unfortunate land, which had suffered so much at the hands of Mussolini's Italy, was promptly recognized as an independent nation. On the other hand, a bitter conflict arose between Soviet Russia and America over the former Japanese colony of Korea. It resulted in a division of the country into two zones of occupation: the northern became Russian, and the southern, American. In 1948 a national assembly, elected in the American zone, proclaimed all Korea an independent republic. North Korea was organized as a satellite of Soviet Russia. Backed by the latter a North Korean army, in 1950, invaded South Korea determined to win the country for communism.

The fate of the Italian colonies was determined by the United Nations. As a result of a resolution adopted in 1949 by the General Assembly, the powers agreed that (1) Libya should receive independence by January 1, 1952; (2) Italian Somaliland should be United Nation's trusteeship territory under the administration of Italy for 10 years; and (3) a United Nations commission should be created to examine the question of the disposal of Eritrea.

The fall of colonial imperialism constituted an event of prime importance in world history. It marked the virtual end of the exploitation and the despotic rule of backward by advanced peoples. Colonial rivalry can no longer become an incitement to a general war; there are no more colonial worlds to conquer. The terrible experience of two world wars in one generation has taught mankind that the path of colonial imperialism, not least among the causes of these conflicts, leads only to national ruin and to world chaos.

NEW ATTITUDE TOWARD BACKWARD PEOPLES

Colonial imperialism was gone, but backward peoples remained in many parts of the world. Unquestionably they could make but little progress without the aid of the more advanced peoples. How could this aid be given without the heavy price of subjection and exploitation? The vital need for reconstructing Europe after the war demanded the rapid development of the backward regions. Without a plentiful supply of the raw materials and the foods of these regions reconstruction would proceed at a very slow pace.

Notable efforts were made to solve this problem by the United Nations, by Britain, and by America. A hint of a better relationship between backward and advanced peoples had been suggested by the mandate system of the League of Nations, which had substituted the principle of trusteeship for that of subjection of a backward nation. The League was dead but the good that it did—some at least—remained after it. As required by the Charter, the United Nations established the "Trusteeship Council" with jurisdiction over the lands called "trusteeships." These were the former mandates in Africa and in the southern Pacific held by Britain, France, Belgium, and Japan; certain territories taken away from Japan and from Italy; and any territory that, in the future, would be voluntarily given over to the Council by a colonial power. Some fifteen million people were now under the trusteeship system.

Was a trusteeship an improvement over a mandate? It was in the sense that the United Nations was given a greater and more direct control over its charges than had the League of Nations. The new principle, established by the Charter, was that a dependent people was an international responsibility, hence the concern of all nations, not of one nation only, as under the mandate system.

The new attitude toward backward peoples was shown in another way by Britain. In her African and West Indian colonies, about all that remained of the empire, Britain inaugurated policies that repudiated the traditional pattern of colonial imperialism. With the advent of the Labor ministry, the Development and Welfare Act, passed during the war, was put into effect. Parliament appropriated about 500 million dollars to be spent by the government in developing the colonies. The new policy aimed, in the first place, to limit the rule of the Europeans by increasing the participation of the natives in the government. In order to train them for self-government, the British introduced popular education, encouraged trade-unions, reformed social conditions, and minimized race discrimination. In the second place, the economic development of a colony was no longer left to private corporations. In many cases the government itself assumed responsibility for the exploitation of natural resources and for the development of industries, but with an eye to the welfare of the inhabitants.

In still another way was the traditional pattern of colonial imperialism repudiated. In the now famous "Point Four" of his Inaugural Address, delivered on January 20, 1949,[18] President Truman asserted the necessity of "a bold new program for making the benefits of our scientific advances and industrial progress available for the improvement and growth of underdeveloped areas." The poverty of the inhabitants of these areas constituted a "handicap and a threat both to them and to more prosperous areas." To carry out Point Four, President Truman recommended (1) the joint participation in the development of backward regions by the United States and other nations through the agency of the United Nations; (2) the pooling of technical knowledge, the "know-how," which was to be made available to peace-loving people, in order to make possible the development of their natural resources; and (3) the financing of development projects, such as irrigation, hydroelectric power, and railways through the investment of private capital, guaranteed by the government. The United States, being pre-

[18] Annette Baker Fox, "President Truman's Fourth Point and the United Nations," *International Conciliation* (Carnegie Endowment for International Peace), June, 1949.

eminent in the progress of industrial and scientific techniques, was to lead in implementing these policies, which aimed to raise the standard of life in backward lands without the exploitation of the native population. According to the President, the old imperialism—exploitation for foreign profit—had no place in the American plan. It was to be a program of development based on the concepts of democratic fair dealing. Point Four was not to be an American government project alone, but a program that envisaged the cooperation of private business, of other industrially advanced countries, of the United Nations, and most important, of the underdeveloped countries themselves.

Point Four aroused great interest throughout the world. Behind it was the power and drive of America, the nation that had boldly chartered the new course. Its implementation, however, required vast outlays of money and the creation of new types of colonial organizations. That evidently was not a matter of a day, or even of a year. The great importance of Point Four, for the present, lies in the official declaration of a new and generous policy toward backward peoples.

After four centuries of aggrandizement, colonial imperialism ended by being universally repudiated. Whether a colony became an independent nation, as in the case of the Philippines; or an associate of the mother country, as in the cases of the Union of India and the United States of Indonesia; or a partner in the French Union, as in the case of Madagascar, the "lesser breeds" rose to the dignity of equality with their former masters. The fall of colonial imperialism marked a great milestone in the progress of mankind toward human equality, the supreme goal of democracy. What now remained was to raise the newly enfranchised to the high level attained by Western civilization.

Chapter 7. Totalitarianism, a Revolutionary Repudiation of Democracy

ECONOMIC DISLOCATION AND TOTALITARIANISM

During the century from 1815 to 1914, democracy had made steady, and sometimes rapid, progress. By 1914, its old enemies, the absolute monarchs and the privileged aristocrats, had been eliminated altogether or relegated to positions of little importance. Their cause became more and more hopeless as more and more countries were won over to democratic principles. Counterrevolution, frequently successful earlier in the nineteenth century, failed signally after 1870. The future of democracy appeared secure.

A new movement, revolutionary in character, but different from all previous revolutionary movements in ideology, in program, and in method, appeared after 1914. Up to this time the term "revolution" had come to signify a definite advance on the road of democracy toward more individual freedom. It might be through an establishment of constitutional in place of autocratic rule, a change from a monarchial to a republican form of government, an expansion of the suffrage from the propertied to the nonpropertied classes, or a winning of national independence. Something startlingly new and completely unforeseen emerged from the First World War, namely, a *revolutionary* movement dedicated to the stamping out of all democratic ideals and practices. It took two forms, communism and fascism, both of which repudiated individual freedom, the fundamental principle of democracy, and established a new order in which the state dominated and directed all political, social, economic, and cultural life. This new order became known as "totalitarianism."

Despite its despotic character totalitarianism made a powerful appeal to many throughout the world, and quickly became the most powerful, the most uncompromising, and the most ruthless enemy of democracy ever yet known. What can be the meaning of the repudiation of democracy in revolutionary terms? An analysis of the situation in Europe during the interwar period will serve to explain the conditions from which emerged this amazing political and social upheaval.

The First World War was followed by economic dislocations that brought widespread disaster. Business failures, unemployment, and general misery were followed by inflation and, to cap the climax, by the Great Depression. Despite many efforts the governments in war-torn Europe were unable to cope with the situation. Especially hard was the blow that fell on the workers, many of whom were reduced to utter helplessness. Starvation stared in the face of millions. In their desperation they were ready to accept any remedy that offered a way out. To these workers communism made a powerful appeal because of its revolutionary program to abolish capitalism and to establish socialism, the long-sought-for workers' paradise.

Economic disaster confronted also the middle class: shopkeepers, artisans, all professional groups, and civil servants. Many were forced to the wall as a result of the war, of inflation, and of the depression; others were forced out of business by the rapid growth of monopolistic combinations. Millions of the middle class were reduced to poverty and were falling to the level of the lower classes whom they despised. The future looked even darker for their children. Those who managed to survive were terrified at the growth of communism that threatened to destroy them altogether. Fascism made a powerful appeal to these groups because of its clear-cut program to curb Big Business and to destroy communism, root and branch, by means of the totalitarian dictatorship of the Fascist party.

In the welter of general misery during the interwar period many distracted people the world over turned a willing ear to the promise of economic security held out by one or the other totalitarian party. How would the nations respond to this new appeal? That depended on whether or not democracy had struck deep roots among the people. In those countries where democracy had become a powerful national tradition, programs of economic reform were put through by radical parties: the Labor party in England, the Socialist party in France, and the "New Deal" Democratic party in America. But in those countries where democracy was not deeply rooted such as Germany, Italy, Hungary, and Spain, communism and fascism struggled for the mastery of the nation.

THE RUSSIAN REVOLUTIONS

The great European nation with hardly any democratic traditions and with no democratic experience was Russia. Hence it is no surprise that Russia was the first to succumb to totalitarian dictatorship. Unlike the other great nations of Europe who, by the end of the nineteenth century, had succeeded in becoming fully or partly democratic, Russia had not taken even the first steps in that direction. All during this century a truceless war had been going on between the tsarist government and various groups of revolutionists who sought to overthrow it. No quarter was asked or given in this struggle between an absolute monarchy of the most reactionary type and revolutionists who, no matter how they differed among themselves, were all united in their common determination to destroy tsarism at whatever cost and by any and all means. But the revolutionists failed to destroy, or even to shake, the autocratic citadel, largely because they received no support from the great masses of Russians, chiefly peasants, who were sunk in poverty, ignorance, and helplessness.

Conditions in Russia began to change with the introduction of the Industrial Revolution. A middle and a working class appeared, both of which were receptive to democratic ideas. New revolutionary forces appeared at the beginning of the twentieth century that received considerable support from these industrial classes. The first popular uprising against tsarism was the Revolution of 1905. Almost all Russia revolted with the result that Tsar Nicholas II was compelled to yield. A constitution was granted, which established a popularly elected parliament, the Duma, and provided for civil liberties. But so deeply autocratic was tsarism that Russia would not, and could not, accustom herself to constitutional methods. Once order was restored, the tsar watered down the constitution that he had granted, and the autocracy was once more in the saddle. Only the shadow of constitutional government persisted in the Duma; its powers were circumscribed, and manhood suffrage was vitiated by numerous restrictions. Tsarism triumphed over nascent democracy, but its triumph was later to spell its doom.

Over and over again has history shown that an autocracy cannot survive defeat in war. The autocrats and "near-autocrats," Napoleon I, Napoleon III, Wilhelm II, Mussolini, and Hitler, all were overthrown when their armies were defeated. Nicholas II was no exception to this general rule. The terrific defeats suffered by the Russian armies at the hands of the Germans during the First World War roused widespread discontent among all classes in Russia. A revolutionary movement was soon on foot, and it had the support of the Duma, despite the fact that this body was controlled by conservative parties. Suddenly, on March 14, 1917, and in the very midst of war, Nicholas II was overthrown by a popular uprising. A provisional government was created by the Duma with the object of establishing a democratic government for Russia.

All the winds of freedom now began blowing throughout Russia. From the very depths of the revolutionary underground emerged men, groups, and parties that for so long had struggled desperately to free their country from tsarism. They varied in their political and social views, all the way from the most moderate to the most extreme. By far the most revolutionary was a socialist group called the "Bolshevists" who favored a plan to overthrow the provisional government by a workers' uprising. A new order would then be inaugurated under the complete domination of the Bolshevist party, which would establish socialism all at once by dictatorial decrees. The Bolshevists were convinced that it would be easier to seize power in a backward, agricultural country like Russia where capitalism was weak than in an advanced, industrial country where it was strong. Therefore, they determined to use the opportunity, offered by the collapse of tsarism, to force Russia to take the steep, untrodden road of Marxist socialism.

Chaos reigned in Russia. Strikes were of daily occurrence. Peasants attacked the aristocrats and seized their land. Soldiers deserted and fled from the front. The provisional government was unable to restore order; hence it failed to inspire confidence. Russia was fast slipping into anarchy. On this scene now appeared the Bolshevist leaders, Lenin and Trotsky, who took command of the situation.

Nicholai Lenin (1870–1924) was one of the extraordinary men of modern times. Early in life he became a professional revolutionist and devoted all his thoughts and activities to the war against tsarism. Prison, exile, underground agitation, conspiracy, and controversy constituted his life as it did that of other Russian professional revolutionists. Unlike his fellow workers, who were impetuous, romantic idealists, Lenin regarded social revolution as a science and an art to be studied and mastered, much in the same way as an engineer plans the construction of a tunnel. Fanatical in his devotion to Marxist principles, coldly shrewd in temperament, and ruthless and unscrupulous in method, Lenin became the mastermind that conceived and planned the creation of Soviet Russia.

Leon Trotsky (1877–1940) was, like Lenin, a professional revolutionist. But, unlike the latter, he was a man of fiery temperament and vivid imagination. An eloquent orator and a penetrating writer, Trotsky won popular acclaim during the Revolution of 1917. He became Lenin's right-hand man in planning the overthrow of the provisional government and the seizure of power by the Bolshevists.

The revolutionary strategy known as "Leninism" succeeded in making the Bolshevist, a minor political party, master of Russia. Several elements contributed to its success, which was as complete as it was unexpected. In the first place, Germany, eager to put Russia out of the war so as to be able to throw all her forces against the Western Front, saw her opportunity in the Bolshevist agitation. In opposition to the provisional government, which loyally supported the Allies, the Bolshevists favored a separate peace with Germany on any terms. In order to give efficient leadership to the Bolshevists, the Germans facilitated the return to Russia of Lenin and Trotsky who were then living abroad. Once in Russia, they were soon at the head of a subversive movement directed against the provisional government.

In the second place, the Russians were tired of the war in which they had suffered so many inglorious defeats. They longed for peace, if not for a separate peace on any terms, then for a general peace on terms satisfactory to both sides. Alexander Kerensky, head of the provisional government, made every effort to bring about a general peace, but without success. The Bolshevists capitalized on Kerensky's failure and increased their propaganda for a separate peace, which made a powerful appeal to many war-weary Russians. Then, also, the Bolshevists promised the land-hungry peasants that, once they came into power, all the estates would be confiscated and land would be given free to the peasants. All over Russia popular bodies, called "soviets" (Russian for councils), appeared and fell under Bolshevist control. The situation began to look desperate for the provisional government as the cry "Peace, land, bread" resounded throughout Russia.

What the Bolshevists called the "November Revolution" was a coup d'état in the best Napoleonic manner. Suddenly, on November 6, 1917, an uprising took place in Petrograd (renamed Leningrad) by an armed band of professional revolutionists, supported by the soldiers of the garrison, who had been won over to the Bolshevists. The members of the provisional government were arrested; only Kerensky managed to escape. A new government, consisting of Bolshevists and their allies, was organized, headed by Lenin and Trotsky.

The new regime, known as "Soviet Russia," proceeded to carry out its program promptly and drastically. It made the separate peace of Brest-Litovsk with Germany. At one fell swoop all private, productive property was confiscated and socialized. The ownership of all productive property in land, commerce, and industry was vested in the state. The possessions of landlords, industrialists, and merchants were confiscated; they either fled for their lives or remained as workers. Not only was the property of Russians confiscated but also that of foreigners who owned property in Russia. All government bonds, whether held by foreigners or by natives, were repudiated.

Revolutionary changes were likewise made in the political system. Shortly after the Bolshevists came into power, the constitutional convention, called by the provisional government, was convened. It had been freely elected by universal suffrage, and the results showed an overwhelming anti-Bolshevist majority. The Bolshevists were disappointed and infuriated because they received only about a quarter of the popular vote. They took prompt and decisive action. A body of troops, dispatched by Lenin, drove out the members and dissolved the convention. Later, an All-Russian Congress of Soviets, dominated by the Bolshevists, adopted a constitution for Soviet Russia, based on a one-party dictatorship without reference to popular majorities. The Bolshevist coup d'état of November 6 succeeded in strangling the newly born Russian democracy.

Though in the seats of power, the Bolshevists faced widespread opposition throughout the country. Civil war raged between the "Reds," or Communists, as the Bolshevists now called themselves, and the "Whites," most of whom were counterrevolutionists who favored a tsarist restoration. After three years of desperate fighting, the Communists succeeded in crushing the Whites, largely because the peasants rallied to the support of the former, who had distributed the confiscated estates. Soviet Russia, now secure from both internal and external attack, was recognized by the powers.

MARXISM

Lenin's revolutionary strategy had proved successful in Russia. A vast empire, ruled for centuries by a powerful autocracy, had collapsed at the touch of a small, well-organized group of revolutionists. And the changes that they made went far beyond those made by the French Revolution. Never in all history had revolutionists altered the entire life of a great nation so deeply and so widely and on so vast a scale as did the Communists.

All revolutions have been propelled by the force of ideas as well as conditioned by historic circumstances. Without what is called an "ideology," a pattern of ideas, revolutionary upheavals have little meaning in history. The Communist party had an ideology to which it adhered fanatically, not only in planning long-range objectives but even in making strategic moves under particular circumstances. This ideology, called Marxism, is based on the writings and teachings of Karl Marx, father of "scientific" socialism. Marxism became the official philosophy of Soviet Russia, where it has been regarded as a creed based on inspired truths, pure, undefiled, and final. It constitutes a tightly integrated system of political and social philosophy resting on five pillars, each one of which is essential to the others and to the system as a whole.

1. *Economic Interpretation of History*

According to Marx, there exist laws of history that regulate the world of human relations just as absolutely as the laws of nature regulate the physical world. And changes in human relations are as universal and as inevitable as are changes in the physical world. In the dynamic process of human progress, the fundamental and determining factor is economic. How does one social order give way to another? Every social order, past, present, and future, asserted Marx, has at its very foundation its own peculiar system of production and exchange, which determines and shapes the institutions, the ideas, and the attitudes of the people. Systems of government, religion, education, philosophy, and law are merely "superstructures" that derive their character from the nature of the economic foundation upon which they rest. Whatever ideals men have concerning their relations in society are "ideological veils" hiding the real forces, which are economic. Marx repudiated morality as a factor in human progress. Anything that was not materialistic was to him nonexistent; hence morality, like religion, was an "ideological veil" that hid from view the rule of exploiting classes.

Different economic systems, according to Marx, create different institutions and promote different ideals. Only when changes take place in the economic foundations of society do changes take place in the institutional "superstructures" and in ideological patterns. Man, declared Marx, does not have the freedom of will to change the social order under which he lives; it is inexorably determined by economic forces beyond his control. Thus far, four economic systems have existed. These have been (1) primitive, in which no property existed; (2) ancient, in which property appeared and with it, slavery; (3) feudal, in which property was based on landlordism, or land tenure and with it, serfdom; and (4) capitalism, in which property was based on industry and with it, wage labor. The property systems functioned in different ways and in the interest of different classes, but always by exploiting human labor.

According to Marx, the economic interpretation of history is the golden key that unlocks all the secrets of the past. It explains why Rome grew, declined, and fell; why Spain was a great power in the seventeenth and a minor power in the nineteenth century; why England became Protestant, and Italy, Catholic; why France was united, and Germany, divided during the eighteenth century; and why America was discovered and settled by Europeans.

2. *Class Struggle*

How did one economic system change into another? According to Marx, the "final causes of all social changes and political revolutions are to be sought, not in men's brains, not in men's better insight into eternal truth and justice, but in changes in modes of production and exchange." This method of progress, called "dialectical materialism," or the conflict of opposing economic forces, presumes that economic life is dynamic; changes, slow at one time, rapid at another, become inevitable. These changes take place, for a time, "under the shell" of the existing economic system. According to the formula of "dialectical materialism," the existing system is called the "thesis," and the emerging system, opposing it, the "anti-thesis." As the productive powers of the "thesis" (existing system) wane, those of the "anti-thesis" (emerging system) wax. In time, a great conflict will arise between them, which will result in the appearance of a new economic system called the "synthesis." In turn, the new economic system becomes the "thesis," confronted by a new "anti-thesis," and the struggle begins all over again.

The "thesis" and "anti-thesis," according to Marx, correspond to classes, hence the class struggle, or the "dialectic" in action. A class is defined by him as a group having common economic interests, fundamentally different from those of other groups. The interests of one class, asserted Marx, are always antagonistic to those of another because the various classes receive unequal shares from the stock of wealth produced. In the Communist Manifesto, he states: "The history of all hitherto existing society is the history of class struggles. Freeman and slave, patrician and plebeian, lord and serf, guildmaster and journeyman, in a word, oppressor and oppressed, stood in constant opposition to one another, carried on an uninterrupted fight, now hidden, now open, a fight that each time ended, either in a revolutionary reconstitution of society at large, or in the common ruin of the contending class."

Under all economic systems based on private property, the classes correspond to the exploiters and exploited. The exploiters under capitalism, according to Marx, are the owners of the means of production, namely, capitalists, or bourgeois; and the exploited are the propertyless wage workers, or "proletariat." Conflicts between them have taken place on other issues, such as war, nationalism, government, and religion; at bottom, however, these have been class conflicts, each striving for a larger share of the wealth produced. Under the capitalist system the ruling class is the capitalist, whether the system of gov-

ernment is democratic or monarchial, constitutional or autocratic. Marx was convinced that republican France, parliamentary Britain, semiautocratic Germany, and autocratic Russia
were all ruled by capitalists. The state under capitalism is merely
an "executive committee" of the capitalists to regulate their
common affairs and to be used as a political means to keep the
proletariat in subjection. In the struggle between the *bourgeoisie*
and the proletariat the latter must, therefore, overthrow the
existing state, as it cannot be reformed in any manner to serve
the interests of the exploited class.

3. *Surplus Value*

Marx's famous book, *Das Kapital,* is an indictment of capitalism as a system of production based on exploitation of the
workers. This exploitation is explained by Marx in the following manner: Articles, produced for the market, *i.e.* "commodities," have market value. These commodities differ in countless ways—size, form, and material—but they all have one
thing in common, namely, human labor which gives them
utility. Therefore, labor is the source of all value; the value of
each commodity is determined by the amount and intensity of
labor time used to produce it. By "labor" is meant not the work
of the individual laborers but that of "social," or collective,
labor directly and indirectly engaged in production. The labor
power of the workers is bought by the capitalist in the form of
wages, always just sufficient to maintain the workers and their
families under existing conditions, *and never more.* The wages
paid are earned by the workers during *part* of the workday;
what they produce during the rest of the time, the unpaid part
of the workers' product, is "surplus value" that is confiscated
by the capitalists in the forms of profit, rent, and interest. Surplus value, therefore, is the difference between what the la-

borers create, namely, all value, and the share that they get, namely, wages. Machinery creates no value; it merely increases the surplus value of the capitalists by enabling the workers to produce more in a given time. To maintain, and even to increase, surplus value by exploiting labor is, according to Marx, the very life principle of capitalism.

4. *Inevitability of Socialism*

The doom of capitalism is, according to Marx, certain and inevitable. It contains within itself the seeds of its own destruction, because of the irreconcilable contradictions in the working of capitalist economy. Capitalism produces vast quantities of goods and pays the lowest subsistence wages; hence the masses of workers cannot buy the goods that they produce. Unable to create an adequate domestic market, assert the Marxists, the capitalists are forced to export the goods not sold at home. Active and bitter competition for foreign markets among capitalist nations leads to imperialism, which in turn leads to war. Within the nation itself, the "anarchy of production," characteristic of capitalism, leads to periods of boom and depression. Periodically, crises arise that bring widespread ruin, with factories and stores closed and millions out of work. As capitalism advances, "its chills and fever" become more and more aggravated. Periodic depressions, declared Marx, "put the existence of the entire bourgeois society on trial, each time more threateningly."

Another contradiction of capitalism, according to Marx, is that its freedom of enterprise leads to monopoly. As capitalism develops, this freedom is limited to fewer and fewer enterprises, as smaller and weaker concerns are wiped out through competition. Production then becomes concentrated in fewer and fewer hands, until finally economic life is controlled by gigantic monopolies that exploit labor more ruthlessly and exact more from consumers through higher prices. Monopoly then becomes "a fetter upon the mode of production," originally established by free enterprise.

Concentration of industry creates a situation in which a small class becomes richer and richer, and the mass of people, poorer and poorer. The middle class is wiped out by being forced into the ranks of the proletariat. And the worker, asserted Marx, "sinks deeper and deeper below the conditions of existence of his own class. He becomes a pauper, and pauperism develops more rapidly than population and wealth." The increasing misery of the masses, according to Marx, is an inexorable necessity in the progress of capitalism. As machinery is improved, the capitalist, in order to compete profitably, is compelled to invest more of his profits in machinery, leaving less for wages. But profits come only from surplus value created by labor; to keep up profits the capitalist is, therefore, compelled to lower the living standard of his workers. But all in vain! Inevitably the rate of profit will keep falling; the capitalists are driven to reduce wages further. There comes a limit to the extent of exploitation to which the workers will submit. Then will arise a revolutionary situation. "The knell of capitalism is sounded. The expropriators are expropriated."

5. World Revolution

The overthrow of capitalism, according to Marx, cannot be effected by a proletarian revolution in one country alone. Being an international economic system, capitalism can be overthrown only by a world revolution of the exploited workers in all lands. Certain conditions have to exist, however, before such an uprising can succeed. In each country there must exist a highly developed, concentrated industrial system; a powerful capitalist class; an organized, well-disciplined body of workers; and an active class struggle. In preparation for the world revolution, the workers of all countries must organize an "international" to which they give primal allegiance. They must not be distracted by patriotism, as workers everywhere have no fatherland, only a "birth place." A war between two nations is of no concern to the workers of either, as they have much more in common as a class than with the capitalists as fellow countrymen. Nor should the workers be distracted by religion, always and everywhere, according to Marx, the "opiate of the masses," dimming their class consciousness and dampening their revolutionary ardor. The final class struggle will be a world revolution of the proletariat against the exploiters, and thus will capitalism be overthrown everywhere. The last "synthesis" will be socialism, the new economic system, which will bring into being a classless society with public ownership of all means of production and exchange; the abolition of wealth and poverty; the end of all discrimination and exploitation; and the establishment of universal peace. At last the age-old dream of peace, plenty, and harmony will be realized.

By "revolution" Marx meant a violent uprising of an armed proletariat. He was convinced that socialism could not be established in a peaceful manner because history taught that only through force were great changes made in society and in government. "Force," he declared, "is the midwife of every old society pregnant with a new one." The political seizure of power through revolution was therefore the essential preliminary to the establishment of socialism. Perhaps Britain would be an exception. Marx expressed the view that Britain, because of her traditional adherence to constitutional methods, might succeed in establishing socialism peacefully through acts of Parliament.

These five pillars of Marxism uphold a philosophic system, all of one piece. Those who accept it, accept all of it. Many intellectual battles have been fought between the advocates and opponents of Marxism. Opponents of the Marxist system refuse to accept a one-eyed economic interpretation of history. They

admit the importance of economics, but as a conditioning not
the determining factor in human progress. At certain times in
history, nationalism, religion, or culture were more important
as factors in progress than was economics. Marx's views of the
class struggle, assert its opponents, is distorted. In modern society there are many classes, whose interests imperceptibly shade
into one another. Class conflicts take place not only between
capitalists and workers but also frequently occur between farmers and town laborers, between organized and unorganized
laborers, and between shopkeepers and great corporations. The
theory of surplus value is flatly denied by anti-Marxists. They
assert that others beside workers create value: capitalists who
initiate new enterprises; technicians who invent new machines;
explorers who discover new lands; and scientists who create
new materials.

Marx was both a true and a false prophet. He was uncannily
right in predicting the concentration of industry into monopolistic corporations and the phenomenon of recurring depressions.
Advanced industrial nations are now engaged in devising ways
and means of preventing the evils of monopoly and of controlling the business cycle in order to forestall economic crises.
Marx's prophecies concerning the increasing misery of the working class proved to be all wrong. As a consequence of greater
production, of trade-unionism, and of social reform the condition of the workers has immensely improved.[1] Equally errone-
ous was Marx's prophecy concerning the doom of the middle
class. As a consequence of the economic changes that came with
the new Industrial Revolution, a new middle class appeared,
consisting of technical experts, scientific workers, administrators,
and small investors. Moreover, there took place a marked increase in the number of members of the professions, civil servants, and white-collar workers. This new middle class became
most prominent in the most capitalistic of all countries, America,

[1] See p. 347.

where it increased seventeenfold from 1870 to 1940. Contrary to the expectation of Marx it is the proletariat, or unskilled workers, who are disappearing. In America, from 1910 to 1940, the unskilled workers dropped from 36 to 25.9 per cent of the labor force.[2]

Despite these limitations, Marxism became the revealed word, a religion, to its adherents. The mixture of truths and untruths, of half-truths and exaggerations, of true and false prophecies contained in the writings of Marx was accepted, every word of it, as "holy writ." It was preached by devoted followers with overflowing enthusiasm and spread with fanatical devotion. Like other religions, Marxism developed divisions between the orthodox and the heretical. Many varieties of socialist groups and parties appeared, each claiming to possess the "true word" of Marx and denouncing the others as false and heretical. What later proved to be the most important division was that between the Social Democrats and the Communists. It first arose, in 1903, among the Russian Social Democrats, who split into a majority faction called "Bolshevists" and a minority faction called "Menshevists."

The origin of the division was not over Marxist ideas; both factions fully accepted them. It was over the methods to be used in making socialism triumphant in the world. Briefly, the position of the Menshevists was that democratic methods, and only democratic methods, were to be employed to make the transition from capitalism to socialism. Gradually, and in successive stages, socialism was to be brought about as a result of measures enacted by parliaments, freely elected by universal suffrage. Nicholai Lenin, leader of the Bolshevists, completely repudiated this democratic approach. He advocated a sudden and violent

[2] On the new middle class, see Lewis Corey, *The Unfinished Task: Economic Reconstruction of Democracy* (1942), 127 *ff*. and 167 *ff*.; and his article in *The New Leader,* May 29, 1948. On the new labor force, see Sumner H. Slichter, *The American Economy* (1948), 12.

overthrow of the existing political system, whatever its nature, and the establishment of the dictatorship of the proletariat to inaugurate socialism at one stroke. To attain this end, Lenin developed a system of revolutionary strategy known as "Leninism," which was applied successfully in the coup d'état of November, 1917, and brought Soviet Russia into existence. Because of its success, Leninism became the classic model of revolution for Communists everywhere throughout the world.

LENINISM

What was the "strategy of revolution," the "art of insurrection," according to Lenin? It was a program of action based on the experience of the various revolutionary movements in Russia during the nineteenth century in the struggle against the tsarist government—hence entirely Russian in spirit. Tsarism was not an autocracy in the Western European tradition, characterized by the culture of the Bourbons, the efficiency of the Hohenzollerns, and the geniality of the Hapsburgs. It was primitive, inefficient, corrupt, and brutal. Passively the Romanov dynasty ruled through the ignorance and helplessness of the masses, and actively, through savage methods of repression. It is not surprising, therefore, that the Russian revolutionists, both moderate and extreme, became convinced that any method was permissible and any act justifiable in the struggle for freedom against tsarism. From this historic experience came an attitude toward government, a method of attaining objectives, and a spirit of intolerance that prepared the way for communism.

Russian history likewise paved the way for the repudiation of democracy by communism. In the struggle for freedom during the nineteenth century, the Russian revolutionists went "to the people" and tried to arouse in them a spirit of revolt against autocracy. But their efforts were all in vain. The common man in Russia was not the radical workman of London or Paris, but a peasant, just out of serfdom, illiterate and superstitious, who paid little if any attention to the appeals of the revolutionists to overthrow the "little father," the tsar. As a consequence, the Communists, unlike the socialists in Western Europe, came to have little respect for the common man, in his reasonableness, his good will, or his effectiveness. They put all their faith in an elite, a selected group of daring, rigidly disciplined, professional revolutionists who were firmly convinced that only through the dictatorship of a communist party would socialism be realized.

Being everywhere a minority the Communists have developed a system of political strategy designed to enable them to seize power whenever a propitious moment offered itself. The following are the main points in the communist system of strategy developed by Lenin. At the very outset the Communists should form a party, a "monolithic" political organization in which no differences of opinion would be tolerated. Any individual or faction that did not wholeheartedly support the party "line," or policy on any given question, was to be eliminated forthwith. Party members were to infiltrate the trade-unions, the historic institutions of the working class, and to get control of their machinery by any and all means. They "must be prepared, if necessary," declared Lenin, "to resort to all sorts of cunning, schemes and stratagems, to employ illegal methods, to evade and conceal the truth in order to penetrate into unions and to conduct the communist work in them at all costs." Especially important were the key industries, such as coal, iron, steel, railways, telephones, electric power, and shipping. A strike in these industries would tie up the whole country and bring on a national crisis. Above all, the Communists were to get control of the national organizations of trade-unions, such as the General Confederation of Labor in France, the Trades-Union Congress in Britain, and the American Federation of Labor and the Congress of Industrial Organizations in America. Should they succeed in becoming the leaders of these bodies, the Communists would be in a position to paralyze the economic life of the country in preparation for revolution.

Lenin's strategy did not fail to realize the importance of using democratic machinery to advance the cause of communism. It was to be done by organizing political parties in every democratic country to contest elections. A communist party, though a minority, could utilize parliament as a forum for making propaganda, and could hinder the smooth working of parliament by resorting to all kinds of filibustering tactics, thus weakening the democratic state.

Important in the general strategy of Leninism was the role allotted to noncommunist individuals and organizations. Those who sympathize generally with the ideas and aims of communism, but are averse to becoming members of the party, are known as "fellow travelers." These willingly lend themselves to serve the Communists by championing causes and reforms advocated by the latter as part of their revolutionary strategy. Equally important are the "front" organizations, such as those favoring the rights of minorities and the promotion of peace, created by the Communists to advocate progressive reforms. It was Lenin's view that Communists should hide their revolutionary objectives by appearing as progressive citizens who take advanced positions by demanding needed reforms of all kinds: in labor, in education, in housing. Either they create "front" organizations that mask their communist control by demanding this or that democratic reform or they infiltrate noncommunist, progressive organizations in order to control them. What they cannot control, they destroy. Ardent, fanatical, well-organized, and unscrupulous, the Communists aim to become the one and only channel of discontent. They exploit whatever injustices exist in any country, such as the treatment of Negroes in America, the misery of the Italian farm laborers, and the grinding poverty of the Chinese workers. The object of the Communists in championing reforms is to aggravate, not to solve, social problems, in order to win for their cause those who suffer from injustice. Reforms, in their opinion, are not indications of progress but steps in the inevitable decay of capitalist society.

Since democracy has always made a strong appeal to all peoples, the Communists have to pretend to be its defenders and upholders. In fact they use the ways of democracy in order to destroy it. Public opinion is a method created by democracy to enlighten citizens as to their rights and duties, and therefore all opinions are permitted to compete in the market places of ideas. The Communists insist that they too represent a body of "opinion"; hence their agitation should be permitted to go on unchecked. In truth, communism is not an opinion, as is socialism, but a strategy of revolutionary action that changes with every shift in the political situation. In carrying out their strategy, Communists endeavor to pervert public opinion in order to protect themselves and to confound their opponents. They are as indifferent to truth as to falsehood; truth is to them a "bourgeois prejudice," and "facts are a political rather than a technical matter." Communists have devised new patterns of intellectual dishonesty of which they have become expert practitioners. Lenin taught them to use any ruse, trick, dodge, and illegality to attain their aims. Once in power, they promptly annihilate all opponents and suppress all views that are contrary to their own. Time and again has history illustrated communist strategy, notably in Russia, in Poland, in Czechoslovakia, and in Hungary.

To what elements are the appeals of the Communists directed? Primarily to the industrial workers, as befits loyal Marxists. However, Lenin extended Marxism to include the peasantry in his revolutionary strategy. Because of his Russian background, Lenin saw the revolutionary potentialities of the land-hungry peasants, especially in the nonindustrialized lands of east central Europe and of the Orient. The Communists hold out the promise of peasant proprietorship to millions of farm laborers by advocating the confiscation of the large estates, from which the peasants would receive small farms, free. But proprietorship is only a bait to lure the peasant to support them. Once in power, the Communists carry out their promise of giving farms to the peasants. But only at first! Soon after, they embark on a policy of "collectivization" by compelling the peasants to give up their land and form consolidated farms. Under a "collective" the peasants become, in fact, tenants of the state. Everywhere this has been the story of the "liberation" of the peasant by Communists.

Why all this communist activity? According to Marx, capitalism is doomed because of the ceaseless conflict of classes becoming ever more bitter and ever more widespread. The capitalists are, therefore, constantly faced with the mortal danger of a workers' uprising. A "revolutionary situation" will arise when the workers repudiate entirely the existing system and when the capitalists will be too weak to maintain it. Depressions, becoming ever greater and ever more ruinous, will goad the proletariat to revolutionary action. Wars will become more frequent, more widespread, and more devastating. It was Lenin who developed this Marxist thesis into a program of action. According to Lenin, capitalism, in becoming monopolistic, turns from national to international fields of action. A world economy emerges, with some nations highly industrialized; others, backward; and still others, primitive, but all within the orbit of capitalism. International cartels appear that seek to control world markets, investments, and sources of raw materials. Behind these cartels are the capitalist nations, whose rival imperialisms sharpen and extend the contradictions inherent in capitalism. World wars, under these circumstances, become inevitable.

World war, according to Lenin, is the midwife of world revolution. Uprisings will begin not in highly industrialized nations where the *bourgeoisie* is numerous and strong but in backward nations where it is small and weak. In case of war, the Communists in belligerent, capitalist countries should work for the defeat of their own nation by means of strikes, mutinies, sabotage, and peace demonstrations, all with the object of turning a foreign into a civil war. When the government is discredited by defeat and when the misery of the people is intensified by economic disruption, the hour of revolution will strike. A general strike of all labor led by communist-controlled trade-unions will paralyze the country and create chaos before which the government would be helpless. Compact, well-organized, rigidly disciplined, and fanatically devoted to their Marxist faith, the Communists will lead discontented masses in a revolution to "take over" the rule of the nation. Opposed to them will be a weak, discredited government and political parties that are disorganized or under secret communist direction. A communist victory will then be swift and certain. Leninism worked to perfection in the coup d'état of November, 1917, when the Bolshevists seized power in Russia.

TOTALITARIAN DICTATORSHIP IN SOVIET RUSSIA

Since Soviet Russia has become the model communist state, what was the new system established in that country? A series of constitutions were formulated to lay the foundations of the new regime: one in 1918; another in 1924; and the latest, the "Stalin constitution" of 1936. These documents made important changes, but always in line with communist principles. The constitution of 1936 created a federal state, the Union of Soviet Socialist Republics (USSR) consisting of about 16 states, the

chief being Russia, which has about two-thirds of the population of the Union. Each state corresponds to a nationality, with
its own language officially recognized. It enjoys local autonomy,
and since 1944, control of its army, foreign trade, and diplomacy.

The highest organ of the Soviet Union is the Supreme Soviet.
It is a bicameral legislature consisting of the Council of the
Union that represents the people and the Council of Nationalities that represents the states. Executive authority is exercised
by two bodies: a small one, the Praesidium, and a larger one, the
Council of the People's Commissars; both are chosen by a
joint session of the two houses. Judicial power is exercised by a
supreme court, chosen by the Supreme Soviet and by popularly
elected lower courts.

Voting for all local and federal offices is based on direct,
universal suffrage by means of the secret ballot. In line with
totalitarian principles, widely different from those in democratic countries, everyone votes for the same candidates; no
opposition is allowed. Most of the candidates are nominated
by the Communist party, the only political party permitted to
exist; other candidates may be nominated by trade-unions,
cooperative societies, and cultural groups, all of them, however, controlled by the Communist party. A "voter" receives a
ballot containing one list of candidates. His choice is either to
vote for it or to "scratch" the list, namely, by not voting for it.
The list is almost always universally approved; to scratch it
would be useless and even dangerous, as reprisals might follow.
The constitution contains an elaborate bill of rights guaranteeing every citizen equal rights, irrespective of race, sex, or nationality. These rights are freedom of speech, of the press,
and of assembly; the right to work; and the right to social
security.

Despite its elaborate democratic provisions, the constitution
is only a façade, and was intended to be such by its authors, the
chief of whom was Stalin. The reality of government in the

Soviet Union lies in the power of the Communist party. In theory, the party and the government are separate; in practice, they are one and the same. All important officials, local and federal, in all branches of the government are party members. Whatever the government does merely echoes the decision of the party. The Communist party is not a political party in the democratic sense: a free and open organization of citizens which endeavors to win a majority of the voters to its policies in order to get into power. The Communist party is neither free nor open. It is highly restricted in membership; only a small fraction of the citizens, about 3 per cent, are permitted to join. Members are recruited from the graduates of youth organizations, formed by the party to indoctrinate the rising generation with communist principles. The organization of the party is pyramidal and hierarchal in character. At the base are district "cells," from which rise regional, state, and federal bodies. In theory, supreme authority of the party is vested in its All-Union Congress, which appoints the executive Central Committee. In turn, the Central Committee appoints three small bodies: the Secretariat, a body of administrators; the Orgburo, concerned with methods of organization; and the Politburo, concerned with political policies. The Politburo, consisting of about 14 members, is the real core of power in the Soviet Union. Its leading member, Joseph Stalin, is at the very apex of the political pyramid; in effect, he appoints and dismisses his associates. Decisions of the party, or party "line," are made by the Politburo, and these decisions automatically become the laws and policies of the Soviet Union.

Whatever the "line," party members follow it implicitly. The iron discipline of the "monolithic" Communist party is unparalleled in political history. It is hard to be admitted and easy to be expelled. To keep the ranks solid and the doctrine pure, periodic inquisitions of the members take place, resulting in expulsions, or "purges." Those "purged" disappear and are never heard of again. Not infrequently a member leaves the party and the world at the same time. Party members are a carefully selected elite, who are constantly active in promoting the "cause," *i.e.,* communism, and are ever ready to undertake any assignment no matter how arduous and how dangerous. But there are compensations. Party members are given preference in all positions in the Soviet Union, receive higher salaries, and are given special perquisites denied to other citizens. In effect, they constitute a privileged ruling class, the successors of the aristocrats under tsarism.

The Soviet Union is a totalitarian dictatorship. What makes it totalitarian? What makes it a dictatorship? Nothing resembling the totalitarian state had ever existed before. In every other system of government, whether democratic or authoritarian, republican or monarchical, constitutional or autocratic, two spheres of life have been recognized: one in society, or private life, and another in government, or public life. The autocratic rule of Louis XIV, the classic example of absolute monarchy, was confined chiefly to the sphere of government and reached only to a limited degree into the private life of the people, their occupations, their social relations, their cultural preferences. With democracy came an extension of the area of freedom through the establishment of civil, religious, cultural, and economic rights. By contrast with the state under absolute monarchy or democracy, the totalitarian state is all-supreme and all-inclusive. Legally, its authority can neither be questioned nor challenged by anyone for any reason. Therefore it denies to the individual any right whatsoever, whether it be in the realm of judgment, such as formulating a public policy, or of conscience, such as refusal to accept the party line on religion. For the same token, it denies autonomy to any group of whatever kind, organized outside the state, such as literary and sporting clubs. The state is made identical and coextensive with society. Private life does not exist under totalitarianism. What materials should go in the making of hats; what kind of automobiles should be manufactured; what biologists should think concerning heredity; what historians should write concerning any country of any period; what rules should be adopted by a tennis club; what compositions should be played at a concert; what stories should be told to children; all are prescribed by the government. These tremendous powers are concentrated in a dictatorship that is responsible to no one, neither to a privileged aristocracy, nor to the people, nor even to God.

The totalitarian state is the distinctive creation of communism. It functions in Russia by the following methods:

1. Marxism is recognized as the official philosophy, the only body of ideas having validity in the political, social, and economic spheres of life. All citizens are required to uphold, at least not to deny, Marxist principles. No one can be a member of the Communist party who does not fully and completely accept Marxism. The established Orthodox church under tsarism was succeeded by an established Marxist philosophy.

2. The views of scholars, scientists, writers, composers, and artists have to be in harmony with those formulated by the government.

3. Teachers and textbooks in all schools, from the kindergarten to the university, have to accept Marxism and to uphold the Soviet system and its policies.

4. All means of communication—books, journals, theaters, radio, motion pictures, telephone, and telegraph—are under government ownership and control.

5. All means of production and distribution—factories, mines, land, stores, railways, and banks—are directly or indirectly owned and controlled by the government.

6. All associations, whether social clubs, literary and scientific societies, trade-unions, or churches are controlled and directed by the government.

Especially effective is the system of thought control established in the Soviet Union. It is far more complete and far more rigid than had been the censorships of the past. Under the latter, only those opinions, considered inimical to the government, were denied expression. But under a totalitarian dictatorship all intellectual activity is a government monopoly. Every expression of opinion, of knowledge, of sentiment comes directly from the government itself.

Most revolutionary of all in the totalitarian scheme of life has been the economic system inaugurated by the Communists. It has operated on the principles of a "planned" economy in contrast with the "free" economy of capitalism. The government of Soviet Russia owns and operates all means of production and distribution. Foreign trade is a government monopoly, and domestic trade is largely in the hands of government stores. Finance and banking are government monopolies. Industry is organized into units called "trusts," a group of enterprises in the same industry, such as coal, cotton, or rubber. These trusts are directed by managers, who buy raw materials and machinery, pay wages, and fix prices on the business principle of making profit. All economy is centrally planned in order, according to the Communists, to eliminate the waste, the inefficiency, and the depressions of capitalism.

Nearly all the workers are employees of the government, directly or indirectly. They are organized into trade-unions, which, however, do not correspond to those in democratic countries because they are controlled and directed by officials and serve primarily to carry out the labor policies of the government. Strikes are forbidden, and "collective bargaining" between union and management is perfunctory. Wages are determined by the skill and industry of each worker, since piecework is the general rule. Members of the professions are grouped into unions similar to those of the workers, and their remuneration is, likewise, fixed by government authority.

A different system obtains in agriculture, most of which is collectivized but not nationalized. A "collective" consists of a large plot of land worked and "owned" by a cooperative group of peasants. Farm machinery is rented at a price from government stations. Each collective must sell to the government about one-half of its product at prices fixed by the government. The rest is divided among the peasants in accordance with the amount of labor that each contributed. Every individual member of the collective is permitted to own a plot of about half an acre of land, farm animals, and poultry. Whatever a peasant raises on his plot he is allowed to sell in the "open" market.

How does the government get revenue? As in other countries, there are many taxes in the Soviet Union, but the chief source of revenue comes from extremely high sales, or turnover, taxes on consumers' goods. These taxes are levied on the cost of the articles produced on the farm and in the factory. In some years the turnover tax has been as high as 75 per cent on bread, 70 per cent on meat, 87 per cent on sugar, 83 per cent on salt, and 75 per cent on textiles. Another important source of revenue is derived from the sale of food. The government "buys" food from the collectives at nominal prices and sells it to consumers at high prices. Thus the economic life of the entire nation, as well as its cultural and political institutions, is determined and directed by the totalitarian state.

What makes the Soviet Union a dictatorship? Authoritarian government is as old as history, and it has had many forms, from that of the primitive tribal chieftains to the adventurous generals like Cromwell and Napoleon, from that of the emperors of the Roman Empire to divine-right monarchs of modern Europe. Authoritarian government under communism differs from all these in one important respect; it has a popular base in the Communist party, with its wide ramifications throughout the country. In theory, authority is based on the principle of the dictatorship of the proletariat, which implies government by the vast majority of the people. In practice, as already described, it means government by the Communist party, a small minority of the people. According to Lenin, the dictatorship of the proletariat is substantially the dictatorship of the Communist party. At first, democratic methods were followed *within* the party; the party "line" was adopted after free debate by the All-Union Congress. A contradiction then existed between dictatorship by the party and democracy within it. This contradiction was resolved when, in 1929, Stalin became the leader of the party. Soon thereafter, dictatorship within the party was established by Stalin, who completely controlled its machinery. After that, congresses seldom met; in the seventeen years from 1933 to 1950 the All-Union Congress met only twice, and then merely to pass resolutions, already cut and dried. The party, like the government, became a façade, behind which was the real power, the Politburo controlled by Stalin. Dictatorship of the proletariat came to be that of the Communist party; the dictatorship of the Communist party came to be that of the Politburo; and the dictatorship of the Politburo came to be that of Stalin. Whatever its theory, dictatorship inevitably ends in the rule of one man. The absolute monarch of the past, however, never ruled as absolutely as does a totalitarian dictator. What frequently served as a check to the monarch's power were the traditions of the people, the privileges of the nobility and the clergy, and the rights of the guilds and corporations. A totalitarian dictatorship is almost a perfect example of power without responsibility and of government without law.

The constitution of 1936, so democratic in many of its provisions, means little or nothing in actual practice. Local autonomy in the Soviet Union is, in effect, nullified by the highly centralized Communist party with its center in Moscow and its branches in every part of the Union that promptly and unquestioningly carry out the orders of the Politburo. Elections, as already described, are farcical as a result of the absence of opposition parties. Laws are not "passed" by the legislature as they are in democratic countries; they are formulated by party officials and quickly ratified by unanimous vote. The Supreme Soviet has few sessions, and these are short. Important shifts in the policy of the government are made quickly, often suddenly, without preparing the people, as is done in democratic countries, through the means of a free press and free elections. A striking illustration was the devaluation of the ruble in 1948. Suddenly, the government decreed that the ruble was now worth one-tenth of its full value, thereby drastically reducing the savings of millions by 90 per cent.

Where there is no political liberty, there is no civil liberty. The provisions of the constitution guaranteeing civil rights mean nothing, less than nothing. Communism has created a system of secret police far greater in extent and in power than that of the tsars. Under various names, the latest being the MVD, a vast network of spies operates in every nook and cranny of the Soviet Union. No man's life, liberty, or property is held inviolable; individuals suddenly disappear and are never afterwards heard of by their friends and relatives. Everyone is encouraged, even forced, to send secret reports on his associates, even on members of his or her family. It has been said that, in Russia, no one has a friend. An extensive system of slavery has been established, called "forced labor." Millions of the "politically unreliable" are herded into concentration camps, and are compelled to perform arduous labor under harrowing conditions.

Will the system change? Not so long as the Communists are in power in Russia. The party "line" has changed frequently, sometimes drastically, but only in tactics, never in the supreme aim of establishing a communist world with Russia as the center and model. To gain their ultimate goal, the Communists will hold fast to Marxism, which is their very soul, and to Leninism, without which they can never get into power.

After its success in Russia, communism became a world crusade that spread throughout the world. The genii of social
revolution, let out of the bottle by the Bolshevists, now roamed
everywhere threatening to destroy the existing political and
social order and to bring civil strife in every land. Communist
parties appeared in nearly every country, with the avowed purpose of planning to overthrow their native government, whether
democratic or not. Soviet Russia made its first bid for world
revolution by organizing the Third International, or Comintern, in 1919. This revolutionary body, representing the Communist parties in the various countries, was directed from Moscow, chiefly by Russians. It became very active in fomenting
revolutions, especially in countries like Italy, Spain, and Germany, where opposition to the existing regimes was bitter and
widespread. Soviet Russia was recognized by Communists
everywhere as their fatherland. Undivided in their allegiance,
they labored in all ways to advance her interests and to uphold her policies. In case of war between their own country
and Soviet Russia, Communists openly declared their intention of supporting the latter against their own country and of
welcoming as liberators Russian armies of invasion.

FASCISM VERSUS COMMUNISM

The communist crusade greatly alarmed the world. Not since the
French Revolution had a revolutionary movement appeared
that threatened the very existence of the social order and of all
established governments. Fear was felt not only by the wealthy
classes but also by the numerous small property owners in the
lower middle class, who, in the case of a communist triumph,
would suffer the loss of their property no less than the capitalists
and the landowners. Moreover the uncompromising hostility
of the Communists toward all religion caused great concern

among religious people of all classes. Marxist materialism now offered a far greater challenge to Christianity than had Voltairean rationalism in the past. A new movement appeared that everywhere threw down the gage of battle to communism. It originated in Italy, where it became known as "fascism."

Fascism arose as if out of the void. Neither the Communists nor their democratic opponents had any inkling of its coming and of its nature. Ideas are born in the brain of great thinkers, but they have little influence until conditions in society favor their development. As already described, conditions everywhere in Europe bordered on chaos, especially in Italy and in Germany. Would these countries follow Soviet Russia? Perhaps not, for the situation in the former countries differed markedly from that in the latter. There existed in Italy and in Germany what did not exist in tsarist Russia, namely, a numerous middle class that could and would fight to maintain its property and position in society.

The first test in this conflict came in Italy. A general strike took place, in 1920, that was organized by the trade-unions under communist influence. Carried away by revolutionary ardor the workers in the Milan steel works ousted the managers and seized control of the plant. Though this revolutionary attempt proved unsuccessful, it nevertheless roused widespread alarm throughout the nation. The government had shown itself weak and helpless during the crisis, and many feared that Italy would soon go the way of Russia. Then it was that the ex-socialist, Benito Mussolini, leader of a group called "Fascists," came forward as the uncompromising, unflinching opponent of communism. Lack of confidence in the government caused thousands to rally to Mussolini's banner; from a small and insignificant group the Fascists quickly rose to be a powerful, nation-wide movement. In 1922 King Victor Emanuel III appointed Mussolini as premier, with full power to protect the nation against revolutionary onslaughts.

Once in power, the Fascists revealed themselves, not as counterrevolutionists but as revolutionists. They promptly proceeded
to destroy the existing political system, and to establish a new
one, based more or less on the Soviet model. Fascism removed
the menace of communism and, at the same time, destroyed
every vestige of democracy. The Italians were saved from one
revolution only to succumb to another. This was a novel and
disturbing way of "saving society"; yet it spread widely on the
Continent. Confidence in democracy as a protector of property
rights sank to a low ebb, and all men of property, large and
small, capitalists, shopkeepers, peasant proprietors, professionals,
and artisans, turned to fascism as the only protection against
universal confiscation proclaimed by communism.

Wherever communism raised its head, fascism appeared to
combat it. For the first time in modern history, competitive
revolutionary movements struggled for mastery: communism,
claiming to represent the workers, and fascism, the middle class.
Of the two, fascism at first proved to be far stronger than communism. Its greatest success came in Germany, where the
Communist party had more adherents than in any other country of Western Europe. Fear of communism caused millions of
Germans to rally to the support of the National Socialist, or
Nazi, party, a fascist group, led by Adolph Hitler. In March,
1933, the Weimar Republic was overthrown, and Nazi Germany
arose to challenge the world. As in Italy, the Communists had
merely held the stirrup for the Fascists to mount to power.

What were the methods used by the Fascists to gain power?
They studied Leninism very closely, and resolved to follow its
"strategy of revolution" whenever suitable. Like the Communists, the Fascists were a minority in every country, a small
one in Italy, a large one in Germany; hence they could attain
power only through a violent uprising. So it seemed. But there
was an alternative open to them, not open to the Communists.
The Fascists might be put in power by the heads of the very

governments that they planned to overthrow, on the plea that they, and they alone, could "save society" from the danger of a communist revolution. In order to win over the heads of governments, the Fascists resorted to violent attacks on Communists; to appeals for support from the propertied classes, high and low; to infiltration of conservative associations in order to control them; and to conspiracies with the army chiefs. This "strategy of revolution" proved successful. Although the parliamentary elections in Italy, in 1921, gave the Fascist party only about 5 per cent of the total vote, Mussolini was put into power by the king. When, in January, 1933, Hitler became Chancellor of Germany, the Nazi party did not have a majority in the *Reichstag*. In the hope of winning a majority, the *Reichstag* was dissolved, and new elections were ordered. The outcome was a majority for the combination of Nazis and their allies, the Nationalists. This combination then overthrew the Weimar Republic and made Hitler the dictator of Germany.[3]

THE FASCIST SYSTEM AND ITS IDEOLOGY

The system of government established by Fascist Italy and by Nazi Germany was a totalitarian dictatorship. As a whole, it was almost a replica of that in Soviet Russia: a façade parliament, "elected" by universal suffrage under the dictatorial power wielded by the Fascist party in Italy and by the Nazi party in Germany. Like the Communist party in Russia, a small group at the top, dominated by the "Duce," Mussolini, controlled the party in Italy; and a similar one, headed by the "Fuehrer," Hitler, dominated the party in Germany. As in Soviet Russia, all activities of whatever kind were put under strict governmental control. Democracy was excoriated in theory and repudiated in practice. The Fascists had contempt for the com-

[3] See p. 269.

mon man, but, unlike the Communists, they frankly expressed their sentiment. "By clever, persistent propaganda," declared Hitler, "even heaven can be represented as hell and the most wretched life as paradise."

Fascism, both in theory and practice, glorified the state as an all-inclusive, eternal power, a kind of deity. The state was omniscient, omnipotent, and ubiquitous, and led a life apart and above the people. "Everything in the state, everything for the state, nothing against the state," was Mussolini's famous apothegm. The individual, under fascism, could be arbitrarily moved from place to place, from occupation to occupation, from duty to duty, from life to death. Popular sovereignty was contemptuously repudiated, and the people were exhorted to "Believe! Obey! Work! Fight!"

The fascist economic system was based on the principle of national planning. It resembled communism, but with an important difference. Instead of government ownership, fascism established government *control* of all enterprises. The owner of a concern was directed as to the amount of goods to be bought and sold; the rate of profit to be made; the location and size of the establishment; the amount to be invested; the prices to be charged; and the number of workers to be employed and at what wages. The owner, in fact, became a manager, whose every act was minutely supervised by officials. Foreign trade was made a government monopoly; all goods imported were purchased by the government, and all goods exported were sold by the government. Often trade with a nation was put on a barter basis: the exchange of a bulk of imports for a bulk of exports.

Labor, like capital, was strictly regulated. All employees in an industry had to join a union. As in Soviet Russia, trade-unions were official bodies, controlled and directed by the government through party members. Wages and conditions of labor were fixed by compulsory arbitration between trade-unions and management, both controlled by the government. Strikes and lock-outs were forbidden under severe penalties.

Agriculture, like commerce and industry, was placed under government control. Private ownership of land was maintained, but the farmer, like the businessman, was strictly regulated. He was directed as to the kind and the amount of the crops to be planted; how much of the harvest was to be sold, in what manner, and at what prices; the pay of agricultural laborers; and the amount of capital to be invested.

What was the aim of this elaborate system of economic control? It was to establish, as far as possible, national self-sufficiency, or autarchy, so that the nation would depend as little as possible on foreigners in matters economic. Once autarchy was attained, the nation would be in a highly advantageous position to wage war. Industry and labor would be channelized in the direction of producing munitions of war. Commerce would be directed to create stockpiles of essential raw materials and manufactures produced abroad. Agriculture would be stimulated to produce sufficient food to nullify the effects of a blockade. War to dominate the world was the over-mastering motive of fascist economic planning.

Like communism, fascism had a pattern of ideas, or ideology, which was the driving force behind its activities. This ideology came from Germany, despite the fact that Italy was the land where fascism was born. Nazism developed an integrated philosophy, which was universally recognized as the classic pattern of fascism, much as Bolshevism was recognized as that of communism.

As Marxism was the soul of communism, racialism was the soul of fascism. What the fascists meant by "racialism" can best be understood by contrasting it with nationalism. As already explained, the nation had been generally accepted as the collective unit in the modern world. It is political in character, and the tie that binds the people is citizenship, easily acquired through birth or naturalization. The citizens may be of different racial and national origins, may hold widely different views on politics, religion, or economics, but all owe supreme allegiance to the nation as established by its constitution. The Fascists, however, insisted that the collective unit of mankind was not the political and changeable nation but the biological and permanent "race."

Racialism was first promulgated by the Nazis, and it was later accepted by Fascists everywhere. Mankind, according to the Nazis, consists of a hierarchy of races, high and low; each race has produced its characteristic civilization, high and low. Race mixture through intermarriage is always bad, as it leads to the degeneration of the higher race and to the consequent decline of its civilization. Western civilization, the most advanced in history, is, according to the Nazis, the creation of the Aryan race in Europe. Though parts of different nationalities, all Europeans are by descent members of one race, the Aryans. Not all of the latter are, however, equal in worth. The best of them are the Teutons, and the best of these are the Germans. The latter are a "master race," who have been the creators of the best elements in Western civilization, and who are the "chosen people" destined to create the supercivilization of the future. Because of the great role played by the Germans in history, they should be made conscious of their high mission in all manner of ways, especially through education. "All education and training must be so planned," declared Hitler, "as to give the German child the feeling that he is unquestionably superior to the children of all other races. His physical education must leave him with the conviction that his nation is unconquerable. . . . The teaching of history must be completely changed and the race question must take a dominating place."

Unlike nationalism, which encourages assimilation, racialism forbids it. The Germans, insisted the Nazis, should keep themselves "pure" by erecting barriers between themselves and non-

Germans. The latter were to be relegated to their appropriate inferior status. All those of German origin in whatever land, according to the Nazis, were "racial comrades" who owed allegiance to Germany, not to the country of their birth or adoption; hence, they should work for the promotion of Germany's ultimate domination of the world. Non-German Aryans, such as the French, the Poles, and the Russians, were to be conquered and reduced to permanent inferiority by being made hewers of wood and drawers of water for their German masters. Part of their territory was to be seized, the inhabitants driven out or exterminated, and their places taken by Germans.

Racialism's chief driving force was anti-Semitism, which became the fundamental principle motivating the Nazis. Hatred of the Jews was not based on religion but on race; the Jews were considered non-Aryans living in Europe. A "Jew" was one who was descended from Jews, in whole or in part, irrespective of his religion, whether Jewish or Christian. All Jews were to be exterminated; they were regarded by the Nazis as the very antithesis of the Germans in all ways of life and thought. Anti-Semitism, propagated by the Nazis, became the hallmark of fascism the world over.

The racial ideology of fascism was based, according to scientific and historical students of the subject, on a myth, that of an Aryan "race." No such race exists, or, as far as it is known, has ever existed. Yet the myth became more potent than scientific and historical truth, as it was widely and passionately believed, especially in Germany. Racialism found adherents in all classes of German society, even among the highly educated.

Another fundamental doctrine of fascism was militarism. "Mankind has grown great in eternal war, it will decay in eternal peace," said Hitler. "War alone brings up to its highest tension all human energy and puts the stamp of nobility upon the peoples who have the courage to meet it," said Mussolini. Peace was merely a trying-out period in preparation for war, in which

man rose to his highest and to his best. Before the advent of
fascism, militarism meant the supremacy of the military over
the civil powers in the government of a nation. Examples of
militarist states were the German Empire and the Japanese
Empire, wherein the military exercised predominant influence
in the government, Fascism went one step further; it abolished
the distinction between the civil and the military powers altogether. Every aspect of national life was organized on military
lines and imbued with the military spirit. The supreme objective of total militarism was to conquer and to annex territory,
whenever and wherever feasible, with or without reasons,
justified or unjustified. Eventually the whole world would become fascist through conquest.

Fascism, like communism, became an international move-
ment. It was organized and directed by Nazis from Berlin and by
Fascists from Rome. Fascist groups and parties, drawing their
strength from fear of communism, appeared in every country.
Corresponding to the communist fellow travelers was the fascist
Fifth Column,[4] local sympathizers who agitated in favor of
fascist ideas and conspired to overthrow their own government.
Fascism proved to be far more successful during the interwar
period than did communism, which did not march out of Russia.
Spain, Portugal, Austria, and Hungary became fascist; and semifascist regimes were established in Poland, in the Baltic states,
in the Balkan states, and in some of the South American states.
The pulsating center of fascism was Nazi Germany, as Soviet
Russia was that of communism. The extraordinary successes
of Nazi Germany, her open avowal to dominate Europe, created
a series of crises that reverberated throughout the world. The
inevitable outcome was the Second World War.

---

[4] The term "Fifth Column" was first used during the civil war in Spain.
General Francisco Franco, the Fascist chief, when leading an army consisting
of four columns against republican Madrid, boasted that he had a "fifth column" of supporters within the city itself.

EVALUATION OF TOTALITARIANISM

Totalitarianism, whether communist or fascist, became the uncompromising enemy of democracy. Though deadly enemies, Communists and Fascists made common cause against democracy; wherever either came into power, democracy was annihilated, swiftly and completely. However, each appealed for support to different classes: the communists, to the workers; and the fascists, to the middle class. To accomplish their objective, both put their trust in a revolutionary elite, backed by popular support organized as a monolithic political party. Both believed in the efficacy of a propaganda machine, established officially by the government to break down mental resistance to their ideas and policies. The same thing, repeated every day in every way without contradiction, would in the end cause even the most skeptical to become reconciled to the totalitarian regime.

The stress placed on propaganda by the Fascists and Communists reveals the low esteem in which they hold the common man. By contrast, democracy has profound faith in the essential goodness of human nature, in the good will of the average man, and in the efficacy of the appeal to his reason. The evils in the world, according to democracy, come from bad institutions inherited from an evil past, outworn traditions, and general ignorance. Therefore democracy has made every effort to reform the social and political order, to promote popular education, and to stimulate the reasoning faculty through freedom of speech and of the press. Totalitarianism has no such faith in the common man, in his goodness, his good will, or his reasonableness. In the view of Fascists and Communists, the common man is foolish and childish at best, stupid and brutal at worst. A bundle of prejudices, quick to react emotionally when his hopes or fears are aroused, he will act without reason and without conscience. Therefore an elite, in full control of the government and of the organs of public opinion, is necessary to rule the unthinking masses. This elite constitutes the "party" in a totalitarian state. Hence the necessity for "propaganda" to convince or to coerce the masses to follow the "party line" unswervingly. The "party line" of today may be just the opposite of that of yesterday or of that of tomorrow, and yet the masses are expected to follow it.

Such use of propaganda by Nazi Germany and by Communist Russia was strikingly illustrated during the Second World War. Hitler had made a pact of friendship with Stalin, and the German propaganda machine was set at full blast to show that he was "right" in so doing, despite the well-known fact that Nazi Germany had vowed to destroy Communist Russia. And the Russian propaganda machine proclaimed to the world that Stalin was also "right" in making a pact with the mortal enemy of communism. When, in 1941, Hitler turned on Stalin and attacked Soviet Russia, the Communists suddenly changed their "party line." The war, which they had denounced as an imperialist war between capitalist nations, now became a holy crusade of democracy to extirpate fascism. Communists, the world over, suddenly, almost automatically, switched when the propaganda command was given. And the masses were expected to do likewise.

The methods used by Communists and Fascists were all of a piece. They did not shrink from any form of violence, whether that of a general uprising, organized rioting, or individual assassination. Along with violence and terrorism went an adroit manipulation of both allies and enemies. Every concession, every act of good will, every gesture of toleration was deemed by them a sign of weakness to be utilized for the destruction of those who made it. Communists and Fascists kept no promises, no agreements, no treaties that stood in the way of their objectives. They would turn as promptly and as ruthlessly on a friend as on an enemy when the "party line" demanded it. "Communists and Fascists may assert different objectives. This does not obscure the identity of the means which both are willing to use to further themselves. Both often use the words and symbols of democracy to mask their totalitarian tactics. But their concern for civil rights is always limited to themselves. Both are willing to lie about their political views when it is convenient. They feel no obligation to come before the public openly and say who they are and what they really want." [5] Communist and Fascist parties strenuously insisted on their right to oppose the government. In truth neither was a political "party," but an organized conspiracy to overthrow the existing order. Once in power, they ruthlessly suppressed the democratic liberties that had enabled them to win supporters and to organize effectively.

Communist and Fascist parties stood ready to overthrow their own government in the interest of the "fatherland" of their special ideology. Totalitarianism succeeded in sanctifying treason to many because of its universal ideal of race or class loyalty. This new type of loyalty arose because both communism and fascism were predicated upon the existence of hero and villain groups everywhere in the world: to the Communists these were the proletariat and the *bourgeoisie;* and to the Fascists, the Aryans and the Jews. Collective guilt was in this manner fastened on a group because of its mere existence. A class, the capitalists, was guilty because they were capitalists, declared the Communists. A race, the Jews, were guilty because they were Jews, declared the Fascists. Extermination, swift, thorough, and frightful, was the punishment in each case.

Another similarity characterized communism and fascism. Both maintained democratic forms of government through con-

[5] "To Secure These Rights," *Report of the President's Committee on Civil Rights,* 1947.

stitutions that provided for parliaments, popular elections, and civil liberties, all of which they cynically flouted in practice. Especially did they insist that every citizen go to the polls during "elections." In truth, universal suffrage was a form of terrorism exercised by the government over the people. No one dared to stay away from the polls lest he be stigmatized as an opponent of the regime. And when the one-party list of candidates was "elected," the government claimed that it had the solid support of the nation. The totalitarian dictatorships made good use of their constitutions as a means of deceiving foreigners. They pointed with pride to the liberal provisions as proof that they, too, were democracies.

Still another similarity existed between communism and fascism, namely, their attitude toward religion. Unlike the secularist liberals, who respected religion as a form of opinion and sought to confine the church to purely religious functions, the totalitarians hated religion in general and Christianity in particular. The Communists, being Marxist materialists, regarded religion as the "opiate of the masses." The Fascists, particularly the Nazis, were pagans; they regarded Christianity as a national evil because, in their view, it preached a "slave morality," thereby weakening the national will to power. As a consequence, the Communists and Fascists sought by every means in their power to extirpate religion from the hearts and minds of the people. Persecution of all faiths, Christian, Jewish, and Moslem, became the order of the day in totalitarian lands.

There were contrasts as well as similarities between communism and fascism. If their methods were the same, their objectives were different. Communism proclaimed the solidarity of the human race and aimed to establish one world in which there would be no subjection and no exploitation. The Communists, therefore, repudiated the rule of one nation by another and the exploitation of one people by another. They denounced colonial imperialism in backward lands and aggressive nationalist policies in Europe. The Fascists, on the contrary, glorified conquest and overlordship, and sought to aggrandize national power at every turn. Again, communism forbade discrimination of individuals within a nation because of racial or national origin. Equality of opportunity for individuals of all groups was offered in the party and in the government. On the other hand, racial and national discrimination was the very soul of fascism, which sought to establish the arbitrary rule of the "master race" within and without the nation.

The most important contrast between communism and fascism, however, lay in the kind of one world that each aimed to create. According to communism, the future would see humanity freed at last from the exploitation of man by man. Poverty would be abolished. Class rule would cease. War would be banished. Quite otherwise was the Fascist vision of the future one world. There would be peace, the peace of universal conquest. In the seat of power would be the "master race," living in luxurious ease as overlords of the "inferior races" reduced to slavelike existence of arduous labor and grinding poverty. This contrast between the vision of communism and that of fascism contributed not a little to the success of the former in gaining many adherents.

These differences in objectives, stridently proclaimed by both totalitarian groups, were not as great in practice as in theory. Methods tended to obscure objectives, and only too often the means became ends in themselves. Communist Russia, like Nazi Germany, sought world dominion, which inevitably led to the subjection of other countries. Being militarists, the Fascists frankly avowed their intention of using war, even a world war, to impose their faith on mankind. Though far from being pacifists, the Communists denounced militarism and disavowed war as an instrument of their faith. What they repudiated, however, was war between nations; they strongly favored and promoted, by every means at their command, civil war between the classes. Aggressive nationalism, imperialism, and ruthless treatment of conquered peoples became the practice alike of communism and fascism. And the fundamental explanation lies in the fact that both rejected democracy and accepted totalitarian dictatorship, which precluded civil liberty and legal equality.

The phenomenon of totalitarian dictatorship was startlingly new in history. Neither communism nor fascism can be fully understood unless regarded as political religions, having the attitude, the paraphernalia, and the organization of a revealed faith. Each had an infallible bible—the writings of Marx and Lenin for Communists, and those of Hitler and Mussolini for Fascists. Each had an infallible guide in the leader of the party, who was "always right." Each believed in dogmas, absolute truths valid at all times and in all places. Each had a "church," the party, the adherents of which were divided into the "clergy," or the members, and the "laity," or the mass of people. Each visited fearful punishment on "heretics," those who lapsed from the party doctrines. Both were missionary religions and aimed to convert the entire world by spreading their doctrines with fanatical zeal. Fascists and Communists were not content merely to preach their faith; they came, like other missionaries, bearing a bible in one hand and a sword in the other. However, these political religions did not have what spiritual religions always have had, namely, an abiding love of mankind and an anxious regard for the eternal welfare of each individual. Lacking a common love, they had a common hate for democracy, which both regarded as the weak instrument of a decadent *bourgeoisie*.

Unlike other authoritarian states in history, the totalitarian dictatorships lacked all moral foundations. No matter how tyrannical their conduct, the god-emperors of pagan Rome and the divine-right kings of Christian Europe at least had the saving grace of a moral ideal. Being a government without law and without any responsibility to man or to God, the totalitarian dictatorship justified any act of the state, no matter how monstrous. One illustration concerns Communist Russia, which, in carrying out its policy of collective farming, resorted to a "managed famine" in deliberately leaving millions of recalcitrant peasants to die of starvation by preventing aid from reaching them. Another concerns Nazi Germany, which, in carrying out racial policies, deliberately exterminated six million Jews by burning and asphyxiating them wholesale.

Inevitably totalitarianism leads to the "police state." Since the totalitarian state has no moral justification and is rejected by a majority of the people, it is not "legitimate." The people do not spontaneously and willingly accept it; hence the authorities are pervaded by constant fear of uprisings, conspiracies, and sabotage. Because of its very nature, dictatorship of any kind at any time cannot achieve legitimacy. It does not govern according to laws, uniform, regular, and impartial in their application. It does not provide for an orderly succession of the head of the state, as do the monarchies through heredity, and the democracies through election. Everything in a dictatorship is uncertain, irregular, and insecure. To keep themselves in power, totalitarian rulers use terrorism on a scale unparalleled in history. Veritable armies of secret police, with unlimited powers, keep constant watch over everyone, including government officials. An atmosphere of mysterious terror pervades the nation, and no one trusts another. In Soviet Russia the secret police became so terrifying that it was officially "abolished" several times. But it continued to function under different names, the Cheka, the OGPU, the NKVD, and the present-day MVD. In Nazi Germany the secret police became notorious as the Gestapo; and in Fascist Italy, as the Ovra.

In some respects the totalitarian dictatorship of communism was more formidable than that of fascism. Soviet Russia had an appeal to many that Nazi Germany, with her repressive racial and labor policies, lacked entirely. Because her laws granted equal treatment to all races, peoples, and nationalities,

Soviet Russia found supporters among those who had undergone subjugation and discrimination in every land. Though
equality in Soviet Russia was the equality of misery, yet the
human passion for equality is so great that many prefer equality
in misery to inequality under favorable conditions. Furthermore, the Communists, because of their hostility to capitalism,
made a powerful appeal to the laboring masses, to whom they
promised security against want. Though the security, established
in Russia, was the security of a prison, yet the ever-present fear
of unemployment and of dire need influenced many workers to
support the Communist parties in their native land.

Democracy was bewildered when confronted by its totalitarian enemies. For a time it was rendered almost defenseless
by its unwillingness to use drastic measures to safeguard its very
existence. Would not suppression of communism and fascism
violate the cherished principles of civil liberty? Fear of one more
than fear of the other caused many either to take sides with
one against the other or to tolerate both. Whichever policy was
followed, it led straight to the triumph of totalitarianism. In
despair, some statesmen hoped that Communist Russia and Nazi
Germany, being deadly enemies, would destroy each other in
war. And thus democracy would be saved by default. What
astonished these statesmen was that suddenly, in 1939, Hitler
and Stalin entered into a pact directed against the democracies.
The outbreak of the Second World War found democracy in
a death struggle with its totalitarian enemies.

Chapter 8. Germany's Bid for World Dominion; the Two World Wars

RISE OF GERMANY

When the twentieth century opened, all seemed stable and peaceful. And many looked hopefully forward to continuous peace which, in time, would create an international order based on universal security. Two great pillars upheld the international structure: the balance of power in Europe and the Monroe Doctrine in the Americas, both of which were generally regarded as guarantees of peace in both the Old and New Worlds. All of Africa and most of Asia were dependencies of Europe, and hence played no active part on the international scene. Japan, having just emerged from feudalism, turned all her energies toward consolidating and remodeling her institutions on the Western pattern. Europe was the center of world diplomacy; hence the balance of power doctrine, though confined to that continent, had world-wide significance. Whatever shuffle or conflict arose in Europe was bound to have a resounding echo throughout the world.

The sudden emergence of Germany in 1871 as the greatest power on the Continent created an unprecedented situation. What was to be her place at the council table of Europe? What would she demand as her rightful due? What methods would she use to assert her claims? The balance of power had aimed to maintain the equilibrium of existing states; it had made no provision for the appearance of new states. Certainly there was no place for a new great power such as the German Empire.

249

An adjustment of the latter to the European diplomatic system was happily made through the genius of Bismarck. As long as he was at the helm, Germany was a "satiated" nation, happy in the achievement of her unity and content with her position as a great power. All of Bismarck's foreign policies had, as their supreme aim, that of making secure what Germany had gained in the wars for unification. Therefore, with some shuffling at the expense of France, Germany was given a seat at the council table of Europe along with the other great powers.

Germany developed sources of strength far greater than those of any other nation in Europe. Her economic progress proceeded at a pace so astounding that in one generation she was at the heels of pioneer Britain. As a rival "workshop of the world," Germany succeeded in superseding Britain in many foreign markets. Her merchant marine in 1914 was second only to that of her rival. Steel production, the index of modern economic progress, was far greater in Germany than in Britain. Like the latter, the former now lived by importing raw materials and food and by exporting manufactures; the excess of imports over exports was made up from the income earned by capital invested abroad and from the earnings of the merchant marine. But, unlike Britain, Germany had a flourishing agriculture, which made her almost self-supporting, a great advantage in case of a blockade during war.

Military power advanced with a pace equally rapid. Germany had the most powerful standing army in the world, superbly equipped, trained, and officered. A threat by this mighty force was sufficient to bring terror and dismay to any nation in Europe that dared to challenge it. German naval power did not arise until the twentieth century. Early in that century a German navy appeared, of the latest pattern, and it grew rapidly to be the second largest in the world. Though inferior in size to the British navy, it was not at all inferior in quality; in some respects it was even superior. Never before in modern times had a nation succeeded in being, at the same time, both a great military and a great naval power.

The class structure of Germany was another great source of strength. In Britain and France, the landed aristocracy had lost its power and become subordinate to the rising capitalists. Not so in Germany, where the Junkers, the powerful, feudal, landed aristocrats of Prussia, east of the Elbe, dominated the government of the empire. They were given key positions in the army and in the civil service, and their economic interests received special protection through high tariff rates on food imports. These privileges did not, as in Britain and France, lead to a class conflict with the industrialists. As a result of a "marriage of iron and rye," arranged by Bismarck, the industrialists of the Rhineland joined with the Junkers of eastern Prussia to uphold the government. But the former had to play second fiddle to the latter. The capitalists consented to do so because they, like the aristocrats, received tariff protection for their products and special inducements to invest their money at home and abroad. The joint interests of these powerful classes became identified with national policies.

A similar reconciliation took place in Germany when the new class conflict, that between capitalists and workers, came to the fore. Though socialism, which emphasized this class conflict, spread more rapidly in Germany than in Britain or France, it did not constitute a revolutionary threat to the government of the empire. Appearances on the surface belied the realities in the depths. With great foresight, Bismarck had, during the eighties of the nineteenth century, put through social insurance laws giving security to the workers against sickness, disability, industrial accidents, and old age. Largely because of these laws the German workers, despite their socialist beliefs, gave their prime loyalty to the nation. They came to feel that they, too, had a stake in the country, and this feeling became intense whenever an international crisis arose. The loyalty of the Social

Democrats to the empire became evident during the Balkan crisis of 1912–1913 when, for the first time in their history, they voted for a military budget. During the great crisis of 1914, which led to the First World War, the Social Democrats rallied to the side of their government by unanimously voting war credits. And, with the exception of a small faction, they loyally supported the government throughout the war.

The political structure of the empire was still another source of German strength. Essentially it was an autocracy with a democratic façade. The popular body, the *Reichstag,* was elected by secret, equal, manhood suffrage. Its powers, however, were anomalous and confusing, having been deliberately made so by its chief author, Bismarck. The *Reichstag* had no control over the ministry, which was responsible to the Kaiser, not as in Britain, to the House of Commons. The will of the *Reichstag* was not translated into law. It could be paralyzed by the *Bundesrat,* which was controlled by the princes of the various states; as the upper house it could defeat all bills passed by the *Reichstag.* In truly democratic Britain the will of the House of Commons was supreme; the House of Lords exercised little or no power over legislation. At most, the *Reichstag,* derided as the "fig leaf of autocracy," could exercise negative power by refusing to pass laws demanded by the government. An even more antidemocratic feature of the constitution of the empire was the privileged position of Prussia, whose king was Kaiser, whose prime minister was Chancellor, and whose veto in the *Bundesrat* could paralyze important bills and prevent the federal constitution from being amended. So decisive was Prussia's control of Germany that, curious as it may sound, it could be said that, politically, the part was greater than the whole. The will of the Prussian government, not that of the German people, determined in the last analysis the policies of the nation. And the Prussian government was a divine-right monarchy with a few constitutional trimmings.

For almost two generations, the Germans lived under this system, and the great majority became reconciled to it. Germany was powerful, prosperous, and socially progressive, though politically the "kindergarten of Europe." The semiautocratic German Empire gave tremendous power to those elements—the Junkers and capitalists—who controlled the government, whose will automatically became the will of the nation. Once committed to a policy of aggression, the rulers of Germany could count on the united support of seventy million people, highly disciplined, obedient, capable, resourceful, and fanatically devoted to the Fatherland. The Bismarckian system had become associated with the unification of Germany; hence any break with it caused the Germans to fear for their national unity. The party in the *Reichstag* that opposed the government, the Social Democratic, was always in opposition, never in power. Every ministry during the entire life of the German Empire represented the conservative parties.

GERMANY'S WELTANSCHAUUNG

Behind political institutions and economic systems in a country there always exists an attitude toward life characteristic of the nation. Germany proclaimed a *Weltanschauung,* or world outlook, that inflated her soul and steeled her arm in the bid that she twice made for world dominion. This German world outlook contained three fundamental elements: militarism, racialism, and authoritarianism. Germany was the only truly militarist state in Europe. By militarism is meant the supremacy of the military over the civil power through special privileges given to the army. In the German Empire, universal conscription was established, not by law but by the constitution itself. The officers constituted virtually a caste, formed from members of aristocratic families, chiefly Prussian. Appropriations for the army,

generally made annually in democratic countries, were made
by the *Reichstag,* at first for a period of seven years, later reduced to five. This greatly limited the control of the civil authorities over the military. The prestige enjoyed by the army
was enormous. Military ideals dominated almost every phase
of national life and thought. The energies, resources, and institutions of the nation were devoted, directly and indirectly, to
strengthening its military power. In order to make militarism
an antidote to revolution, the German soldier was trained to
"corpselike obedience." At the word of command he was ready
to commit any atrocity, any inhumanity, on the plea of "orders."
He became a robot, demoralized and dehumanized, accustomed
to obey the command of those in authority, no matter what the
command and who the authority. There was nothing gallant
and romantic about German militarism; it was hard, cold, ruthless, and inhuman. Democracy, with its ideals of liberty and
equality and its love of peace, was despised and derided as being
characteristic of weak, and even of degenerate, peoples. "Universal peace is a dream, and not even a beautiful dream," declared General Helmuth von Moltke, the hero of the Franco-
Prussian war. Militarism, more than any other factor, was
responsible for the soul erosion of the German people, which
made them the potential enemy of every nation.

Nationalism was generally confused by Germans with racialism. What is meant by racialism and how it differs from nationalism has already been described.[1] A veritable cult of the
"superior Teuton" flourished in Germany, and had for its
votaries famous thinkers, such as Hegel, Fichte, Wagner,
Treitschke, and Sombart, whose views found wide acceptance.
The Germans were taught to regard themselves as a superior
race, Germany as an invincible nation, and German culture as
the supreme achievement of mankind. All other races, nations,
and cultures were relegated to various degrees of inferiority.

[1] See pp. 237–239.

England and France were especially regarded as Germany's mortal enemies, jealous of her success, resentful of her superiority, and constantly plotting her ruin. The naturally superior Germans need only to gird themselves for the coming fray, from which they would inevitably emerge victorious. Once these enemies were conquered, they would cease from troubling, and Germany as ruler of the Continent would be free to reorganize Europe.

The race myth seized hold of the German mind. It became an intoxicant. The Germans, declared Nietzsche, were "a dangerous people; they are experts in inventing intoxicants." A driving search for heroic origins began, and the Teutonic barbarians of ancient times were glorified as heroes in song and story—even in law and history. Wagner's famous operas celebrating the feats of Teutonic gods and of medieval German knights had an immense vogue. Curiously enough, along with the cult of the primitive there existed a great devotion to science. In no other country was science studied so much and applied so widely as in Germany. The passionate adoration of the primitive joined with the cold objectivity of science created among Germans a mood of romantic exaltation and of confidence in their prowess that boded ill for the peace of mankind.

German political ideas differed as strikingly from those in democratic countries as did the cultural and racial ideas. The German conception of government, derived chiefly from the writings of Hegel, was based on the belief that the state was a sort of divinity, existing apart from the people and responsible to no one. Whatever it did was right. Its welfare constituted the highest criterion of justice; hence there could be no conflict between morality and political necessity. The function of the people was to obey the state unquestioningly, to serve it loyally, and to support it at any and all cost. The Hegelian state, according to its upholders, was strong because it was "natural," authority being exercised by an hereditary monarch. The democratic state, they asserted, was weak because it was "artificial," authority being exercised by shifting majorities in parliament. It was the lifelong view of Bismarck that the state was power, supreme and responsible to no one, whether it smote socialists or gave benefits to the working class.

This idolatrous state was almost universally accepted in Germany, as loyally by the socialists, the Hegelians on the left, as by the conservatives, the Hegelians on the right. Liberal democratic ideas found few adherents, an astonishing fact in a highly industrialized, progressive, modern nation like Germany. It is well to keep in mind that Germany had never experienced a democratic revolution; hence there existed no democratic tradition among the people, like that associated in England with 1688, in America with 1776, and in France with 1789. The liberal Revolution of 1848 ended as a fiasco in Germany, and discredited liberals and liberalism. Bismarck's success in uniting Germany by "blood and iron" left an evil heritage: the general belief that power, and power alone, succeeds in achieving desirable objectives.

THE DIPLOMATIC REVOLUTION

As long as Bismarck was at the helm, Germany remained a "satiated" power. The situation, however, changed markedly when, in 1890, Bismarck was dismissed by Kaiser Wilhelm II. Germany became the discontented nation of Europe, bitterly resentful of her subordinate political position in relation to her economic importance and to her military might. She resented her narrow confines in Europe, and demanded *Lebensraum,* looking with jaundiced eyes at the great colonial empires of Britain and of France and at the vast spaces in Russia. The Kaiser, who became the spokesman of the now discontented nation, laid out a "new course," according to which Germany would seek "a place in the sun" by acquiring colonies, by expanding her territory in Europe, and by advancing her *Kultur,* her special brand of civilization throughout the world.

As a consequence of her aggressive policies, Germany became the center of every diplomatic crisis from the beginning of the twentieth century to 1914. From all, except the last, Europe emerged peaceful but fearful. Germany's truculence always increased, whether she had made gains or had suffered losses. Almost every year witnessed an increase in her military and naval armament, an augmentation of her prosperity, a deepening of her discontent, and a hardening of her determination to destroy the European system unless she succeeded in dominating it. The balance of power, so carefully maintained during the nineteenth century, now faced a new threat in the aggressive Germany of Kaiser Wilhelm. Fear of Germany reverberated throughout Europe. When, where, and how would the lightning of war strike? Would it be confined to Europe or would it spread throughout the world? These were the anxious questions in everyone's mind as the year 1914 drew near.

Even a militarist nation like Germany does not strike in a vacuum. Conditions in the world during the twentieth century had reached a point of development wherein conflicts on a world-wide scale became, if not inevitable, at least probable. As already described, every industrialized nation had need of free access to the raw materials of the world: the tin and rubber of Malaya; the nickel of Canada; the chrome of Turkey; the oil of America and of the Middle East; and the coal of Britain and of Germany. How was this need to be met? By the acquisition of a colonial empire, answered the colonial imperialists.[2] The struggle that began between the "have" and "have not" nations was focused on a bitter rivalry between the young industrial giant, Germany, and the old industrial giant, Britain. Always in the past the British and German peoples had been

2 See p. 180.

friends; they had never met as enemies on a battlefield. But the commercial and colonial rivalry that arose between them turned an historic friendship into mutual suspicion and bitter hostility. Every move of the British Empire to adopt restrictive economic measures in a system of imperial preference raised anxieties and fears in Germany. What if this great market were closed to German goods! What if this great source of raw materials were closed to German factories! When, in the twentieth century, a great German fleet appeared on the seas, a wave of alarm spread throughout Britain. For the first time since the Napoleonic Wars Britain's mastery of the seas was openly and defiantly challenged.

It has been said that Britain has no permanent friends and no permanent enemies, only permanent interests. This became more evident in the twentieth century than in any previous time. Britain realized that she could not afford to lose a war, least of all to her economic rival, Germany. In case of a defeat, she would be deprived of her chief sources of livelihood: foreign trade, foreign investments, and merchant marine. Her empire would be partitioned, and her fleet, eliminated. An island, no greater in area than Minnesota, Britain contained a population of 45,000,000, and produced only one-third of the required food. Without a flourishing commerce and industry, the population would soon dwindle, and Britain would sink, rapidly and permanently, to the level of a small, insignificant nation. In this respect she was unlike France, who, because of her flourishing agriculture, could always support her 40,000,000 people, at least modestly. Even after her severe defeats in 1815 and 1871, France recovered, and rapidly regained her position as a great power. No such national resurrection was possible for Britain.

Fear of Germany dominated the diplomacy of all the other European states. In view of the German challenge, Britain made changes in her foreign policy that resulted in a veritable diplo-

matic revolution. The German menace was directed also against
France and Russia; against France because Germany had
determined to eliminate, once and for all, an irreconcilable
enemy that insisted on recovering Alsace-Lorraine; and against
Russia because Germany sought to expand her frontier by re-
viving the historic *Drang nach Osten,* or movement of the Germans eastward. Every move made by Germany on the European
chessboard was inspired by her old hatred of France, by her new
hatred of Britain, and by her distrust and fear of Russia. As
a consequence, Britain, France, and Russia, enemies for centuries, became friends and allies. Britain beheld in the Germany
of the Kaiser an even greater menace to her safety than she had
encountered in the France of Napoleon. The scattered British
Empire, with its vital lines of supply and communication, could
be attacked at many points by German submarines and raiding
fleets. Though large and powerful, the British navy could not
be on all seas at once. Britain had need of the French navy
to guard the Mediterranean, the most vital of all her lines of
supply and communication. The French and Russian armies,
aided by British expeditionary forces, would compel Germany
to fight a war on two fronts. Such a war, the "nightmare" of
Bismarck, would seriously weaken even the mighty German
army by dividing its forces.

France, too, made a revolutionary departure from her historic
policies by joining with Britain. For centuries she had regarded
"perfidious Albion" as her hereditary enemy, but now a new
and greater enemy appeared in Germany. France could not
forget her defeat in the Franco-Prussian war. After a conflict
lasting only 10 months she was compelled to sign a treaty that
imposed the heaviest indemnity on a defeated nation in modern
European history up to that time; and, in addition, she was
obliged to cede Alsace-Lorraine. Because of these severe terms,
France came to regard Germany as an enemy from whom no

mercy, no consideration of any kind, could be expected. A
second defeat at the hands of Germany would prove so disastrous
that France would not live to fight another day.

From the days of Frederick the Great to those of Bismarck,
friendship with Russia had been a cardinal point in the foreign
policy first of Prussia, later of Germany. What caused a break
in this historic friendship and a shift of Russia's policy in favor
of Britain and France, her historic enemies? It came partly
because of the need for defense against threats of German aggression, and partly because of a revival of Russian aggression
in the Balkans. As Germany became more and more industrialized, the Junkers feared that the control of the government
would fall into the hands of the industrialists, who were becoming more and more influential. A disintegrating agrarian
class, as were the Junkers, could not for long rule that exuberant,
industrial nation. How could the Junkers extend Germany's
agricultural area and thereby continue to maintain their political
hegemony? By the conquest of the Baltic states and the Ukraine,
which would give to Germany great agricultural wealth and
a large agrarian population, both under Junker control. The
Kaiser's anti-Russian policy was in clear harmony with Junker
class interest, and was so regarded by the German industrialists
who aimed to counterbalance this policy by favoring the annexation to Germany of the industrial regions of France and
Belgium, which would strengthen their power in the government. This situation in Germany sent tremors of fear down
the spine of the tsar, and caused him to look to Britain for aid.

Furthermore, Russia had aggressive plans of her own. After
her defeat in the Russo-Japanese war, her ambition in the
Balkans again reasserted itself. Once more the dome of Saint
Sophia glittered before the eyes of the Russian imperialists.
Britain, hitherto the great obstacle to the realization of this
ambition, now agreed to let Russia have control of Constantinople and the Straits in return for military support in case of

war with Germany. But a new obstacle arose, namely, Austria-Hungary, who feared that Russia's march toward Constantinople would be over her own dead body. The ramshackle empire of the Hapsburgs could not for long, by itself, contain Russia. Behind Austria-Hungary, however, came mighty Germany, who was determined to maintain the Hapsburgs, the only reliable ally Germany had in Europe. Russia's imperial ambitions now clashed with Germany's interests, as a consequence of which the tsar swung to the side of Britain and France.

The outcome of this diplomatic revolution was the Triple Entente of Britain, France, and Russia, united to resist German aggression. Fear of Germany was so widespread in Europe that it found an echo even in America. All during the nineteenth century, America had followed a policy of isolation, feeling secure behind the shelter of the Monroe Doctrine, which kept aggressive European powers out of the New World. However, it was the power of the British navy that made the Monroe Doctrine effective during the nineteenth century. Britain had important interests in Latin America, which she feared would be jeopardized by rival colonial powers, and hence supported the Monroe Doctrine. When, in the twentieth century, a great German navy appeared on the seas, America's isolation began to appear as a policy fraught with danger to the New World. What if the British navy was destroyed in the war between Britain and Germany! That a triumphant Germany might challenge the Monroe Doctrine became the anxious thought of American statesmen.

After a century and a half of mutual dislike and distrust, friendly, and even cordial relations began between America and Britain. The hostile traditions of 1776 and 1812 became softened, and a policy of friendly cooperation was pursued by whichever party was in power in America or in Britain. After the Venezuela crisis of 1895, which brought both nations to the verge of war, this friendly cooperation between America and Britain became marked on many occasions. They were drawn together inevitably and insensibly because Germany threatened them both: Britain, immediately; and America, eventually. In case of war between Germany and Britain, America could now be counted on the side of the latter, whether as a friendly neutral or as a belligerent. When, during the administration of President Theodore Roosevelt, a new and powerful American navy made its appearance, it was tacitly assumed that the British fleets could safely concentrate in the European Atlantic because the American fleets would police the American Atlantic. This understanding gave a tremendous prop to the security of Britain. Seen in retrospect, the friendly relations between Britain and America appear truly remarkable. German aggression was primarily responsible for bringing about this historic reconciliation.

Like her rival, Britain, Germany too had allies that needed her help. She was allied with Austria-Hungary and Italy in the famous Triple Alliance, originally formed by Bismarck to protect the integrity of the newly formed German Empire. The hard core of the Alliance was Germany, which almost by herself determined its policies. Austria-Hungary pursued a diplomacy of existence; her one aim was to keep alive and intact. During the twentieth century, her many peoples, inspired by nationalistic sentiments, sought to loosen the bonds that tied them to the Dual Monarchy. In addition, Russia and Serbia were determined to disrupt the Dual Monarchy by encouraging irredentist movements among the Slavic elements. Austria-Hungary clung to Germany as the great power that could preserve her existence, threatened by nationalistic forces from within and by Russia from without.

Italy joined the Triple Alliance in the hope of getting Tunis from France. Her strategic position in the Mediterranean made her important as an ally of Germany; she could endanger the

British line of communication in the Mediterranean; and she could immobilize a French army on her northwestern frontier. However, the ties that bound Italy to her allies were very tenuous; even a modest satisfaction of her colonial ambitions by France would cause her to switch sides in case of a conflict. When Italy acquired Tripoli, in 1912, largely by the grace of France and Britain, she was lost to the Triple Alliance. But the great strength of Germany, which would be energized to the highest point, more than made up for whatever weaknesses were shown by her allies.

GERMANY'S FIRST BID FOR WORLD DOMINION

Did the diplomatic revolution result in a new balance of power? So it appeared; the force of the Triple Entente balanced the force of the Triple Alliance. Neither was strong enough to challenge the other; hence peace seemed assured. Nevertheless an irrepressible conflict was brewing, and it was destined to involve not only Europe but most of the world. As already described, the world had become more united as a result of the modern systems of transportation and communications, and the nations had become mutually dependent as a result of the progress of industrialization. A war between two nations could no longer, as formerly, be isolated; it was bound to spread. Let an incident arise anywhere in the world, in Morocco, in the Balkans, in Manchuria, on an islet in the Pacific, and the world would face a crisis. With the two great military coalitions confronting each other, the possibilities were excellent that a conflict between a member of one and a member of the other would bring on a world war.

Such an incident did arise. On June 28, 1914, Archduke Francis Ferdinand, heir to the Hapsburg throne, and his wife were assassinated in Sarajevo, a little town in Bosnia. The murder was committed by Serbian nationalists as a protest against Austria's opposition to Serbia's nationalist policies. The crisis that followed soon involved the Triple Alliance and the Triple Entente, and led straight to the First World War.

The immediate cause of the war was the reckless attempt of Austria-Hungary, backed by Germany, to suppress the national movement among the southern Slavs. Far more important, however, were the deeply rooted causes of this world conflict, the first since the Napoleonic Wars. The diplomatic moves during the Sarajevo crisis were soon enveloped by the hatreds, the rivalries, and the aspirations that had for long divided Europe: France's desire for the return of Alsace-Lorraine; the economic rivalry between Britain and Germany; the struggle for colonies between the "have" and "have not" powers; the national aspirations of the subjected peoples in east central Europe; the conflict between Russia, on one side, and Austria-Hungary and Germany, on the other, for hegemony in the Balkans; and, most important of all, the menacing militarism and the overwhelming ambition of Germany which stood out, sharp and clear, all during the crisis. Whatever the immediate cause, once war broke out, the real issue would be German world supremacy. A peaceful solution of international problems through concession and compromise became impossible because Germany was determined "to hack her way through" the precarious system of international relations in order to dominate Europe. And with Europe as the heartland of the world, the mastery of the Continent would be only a prelude to world mastery. For Germany it was *Weltmacht oder Niedergang* (world dominion or downfall). Whatever concessions that she made or was willing to make during the crisis were far outweighed by her iron resolve not to let this opportunity pass for a decisive showdown between herself and her enemies. War not peace could be the only outcome of Germany's attitude.

The First World War was world-wide in extent. Most of the nations were involved, either directly or indirectly. The victories of the German armies astounded the world. They swept all before them; several times they were within sight of complete victory. But Germany failed in her first bid for world dominion, and the chief credit belongs to the blockade and to the intervention of America. The blockade, applied by the British fleet in Germany's home waters, slowly strangled her into submission. Never before had the British navy met so redoubtable a foe as the newly created German navy. The battle of Jutland, a very costly victory for the British, and the success of the German submarines in sinking Allied merchant vessels bore witness to German naval power. The British fleet, allied with the French in the Mediterranean, with the American in the Atlantic, and with the Japanese in the Pacific, managed, not without great difficulty, to keep open Allied lines of supply and to close those of Germany.

With all her careful planning and thorough preparation for the conflict, Germany had not counted on America as a possible foe. She saw only that, before 1914, America was a peaceful democracy, traditionally isolationist, and practically without an army though with a fair-sized, efficient navy. Widespread isolationist and pacifist sentiment and large numbers of Americans of German origin could then be counted on to keep America strictly neutral. This was the German reasoning, and it was wrong. When war broke out, the overwhelming sentiment in America favored the Allies, and the government, though officially neutral, gave every possible nonmilitary aid to Britain. When, on April 6, 1917, America entered the war on the side of the Allies, Germany was convinced that American aid would be too little and too late to prevent the defeat of her enemies. Again, Germany was wrong. America mobilized her tremendous resources in materials and men with a swiftness and an effectiveness that astonished the world. Immense armies and vast stores of munitions and of supplies quickly and continuously crossed the Atlantic on a "bridge of ships." The tide of war now definitely turned in favor of the Allies. The hitherto victorious German armies were defeated, and they retreated, giving up the territory that they had won at such great cost. Germany's strength was ebbing fast, and, suddenly, on November 11, 1918, she surrendered and asked for an armistice.

RISE OF HITLERISM

According to the treaty of Versailles, Germany was rendered harmless. Her army was reduced to 100,000 men; her navy, in order to avoid surrender, sank its ships; and the manufacture of war planes was forbidden. Germany lost her colonies, her merchant marine, and her foreign investments. She ceded parts of her home territory to her neighbors. The left bank of the Rhine and the Saar were occupied by Allied troops. Economically, Germany suffered a serious setback by the requirement to pay enormous reparations. A smaller, a weaker, and a poorer democratic republic succeeded the militant, semiautocratic empire. Many now believed that the peace of Europe and of the world was at last safe from German aggression.

So it seemed. But, as seen in retrospect, the treaty of Versailles left Germany's main source of economic power intact, and therefore provided a basis for rapid recovery, of which she took full advantage. The Ruhr, the greatest source of industrial power in Europe, was left with Germany, as was East Prussia, her greatest source of food supply. Hence the Bismarckian "marriage of iron and rye" had not been dissolved. Though the strategic left bank of the Rhine and the coal-producing Saar were occupied by the Allies, Germany fully expected their return. What she needed most was to recover from the economic wounds inflicted by the war. And British and American capitalists readily loaned vast sums to Germany, and thus greatly aided in her astonishingly quick rehabilitation. Germany's recovery spelled preparation for another war.

The situation in postwar Europe was more favorable to German aggression than that before 1914. No powerful combination of great powers, such as the Triple Entente, would again confront a would-be aggressor. Russia was greatly weakened by revolution. France, seemingly strong, was in reality weak, divided, and pacifist. Britain again asserted her balance of power diplomacy by favoring Germany against France. Italy was demoralized by internal difficulties. Central Europe consisted of weak, mutually hostile small nations. A new and strengthened Germany might succeed where the old Germany of 1914 had failed.

The problem of Germany was Germany. That nation, created by "blood and iron" and fanatically convinced of her "world mission," did not and could not believe that she had suffered defeat on the field of battle. To maintain intact the tradition of invincibility, the German army chiefs had asked for an armistice as the Allied armies were nearing the German frontier. When fighting ceased, German soldiers were on Allied soil, but no Allied soldiers were on German soil. After the armistice, the German armies returned with drums beating and banners flying. *Im Felde unbesiegt* (unconquered on the field of battle) was the proud slogan. Then why had Germany surrendered? She was forced to do so, declared the militarists, because of a "stab in the back" by disloyal elements: the Socialists and the Jews.

The German people had not been won over to democracy as a result of the war, as many erroneously believed. They established the Weimar Republic as a concession to the demand of the Allies, especially that of Woodrow Wilson, who insisted that the Kaiser be ousted, as no peace would be made with those that had made the war. It was fully expected in Germany that the Weimar Republic would be granted generous peace terms. When the severe treaty of Versailles was adopted, a wave of embittered disappointment and fury swept over Germany. Many now turned against the Weimar Republic, which they accused of having been responsible for the *Diktat* of Versailles. They denounced the Kaiser for having lost the war and the Republic for having lost the peace. Were a movement to appear that promised to undo the failures of both regimes and to give Germany the power to make another bid for world dominion, it would be welcomed by a resurgent nation that had never lost faith in its invincibility.

The "strange interlude" of the Weimar Republic, with its unexpected birth, its short life, and its sudden death can be explained in the light of history. For almost two generations, the Germans had lived under the semiautocratic empire, which, on the whole, satisfied them. And then these very Germans were expected to accept a democratic republic, and one having the most democratic constitution of any then in existence. They had neither the liberal traditions nor the experience in self-government necessary to make democracy work satisfactorily. Incredibly weak and inept were the parties in power during the Weimar period: the Social Democrats and the Center. Before long, the old military caste began to operate behind the façade of the Republic, which proved to be an effective screen for rearmament in preparation for war. As it was then said in Germany, "The Kaiser had departed but the generals remained." The Social Democrats, the party most loyal to the Weimar Republic, could draw no strength from national traditions to support the democratic regime. Authoritarianism had become deeply embedded in German political thought; hence, it was widely diffused among all classes of society. Only a party espousing authoritarian ideas could have a popular appeal in Germany. Such a party did appear in the National Socialists, popularly called the "Nazis," led by Adolph Hitler. It made a powerful appeal to the nation, and especially to the lower middle class. Fear of ruin haunted this class during the inter-war period. War was followed by inflation and by the Great Depression, which drove to the wall millions of the lower middle class; and, along with these calamities, the growing communist movement threatened social revolution. The elections of 1930 emphatically registered this middle-class fear by making the Nazis the leading party in the *Reichstag*.

Hitler now openly prepared to overthrow the Weimar Republic and to establish a dictatorship. His quick and easy success astonished and dismayed the democratic world. Fear paralyzed the defenders of the Weimar Republic into inaction; they took no measures against their deadly enemies. Let it be recalled that the Weimar Republic collapsed, not as a result of a coup d'état, as did parliamentary Italy in 1922, but as a result of democratic elections. Hitler rightly claimed that he came into power constitutionally. In the last elections under the Weimar Republic, in March, 1933, a large majority of the voters supported those parties, the Nazis, the Nationalists, and the Communists, who openly advocated the overthrow of the Weimar Republic. The Nazis alone received 44 per cent of the vote, which together with their allies, the Nationalists, who received 8 per cent, gave a majority to this combination. After outlawing the Communists, the *Reichstag,* supported by all the parties, except the Social Democrats, joined in voting dictatorial power to Hitler. The Weimar Republic then suffered swift destruction.

Never before in modern history had a democratic regime been overthrown by a popular mandate. Were the German people incurably addicted to authoritarian government? The answer is "no," despite Nazi philosophy, which said "yes." Capacity for self-government is acquired after a long and painful process, as the history of the English people bears witness. The Germans of 1848 gave ample evidence of their desire for democracy. The millions of Germans who had emigrated to America easily acquired democratic ways and ideas, and became loyal citizens of the American Republic. Once, under the German Empire, in the elections of 1912, a large majority of the voters had supported the parties that favored the democratization of the Bismarckian system. The love of Germans for authority was due to "nurture" not to "nature." They had been nurtured politically for a half century by the constitution of the German Empire, a cunningly devised political strait jacket that effectively prevented progress toward greater freedom. Though it contained an amendment clause, the constitution in practice could not be amended, and in fact was not amended in any important respect during its entire existence. As a consequence, two generations of Germans became politically illiterate, and even prided themselves on being *unpolitisch*. Escape from political responsibility even became an ideal among highly educated Germans.

Once in power, the control of Germany by the Nazi party was quickly realized. And it was never openly challenged all during the period of the "Third Reich," as Nazi Germany was called; there was little opposition to the Hitler regime aboveground or underground. At best there was a passive acceptance, not a passive resistance. This complete mastery of Germany by the Nazis was, in part, due to the ruthless suppression of all opposition, but only in part. Even more was it due to the habituated obedience of the Germans to the voice of authority, which had been ground into their bones by militarism. And the authority of the Nazis was greater than that of any other party in the German past, because their ideology constituted a complete fusion of the three ideals that had profoundly influenced German life and thought: militarism, racialism, and authoritarianism. Strangely enough the Nazis appealed to conservative, even to primitive, ideals in order to launch their revolutionary program.

How did Germany, disarmed, occupied, burdened with reparations, with "bleeding frontiers" manage, in a short time, to become strong enough to make another, and even greater, bid for world dominion? The chief answer lies in the fact that the treaty of Versailles had not been fully enforced. The disarmament clauses were violated secretly by the Weimar Republic, and openly by the Third Reich. Reparations were constantly whittled down and finally ended altogether. Germany paid no money reparations at all; she borrowed as much from the Allies as she paid them, and then repudiated the balance of her debts. The occupation of the Rhineland, a vitally strategic region, ended five years before the date fixed by the treaty of Versailles. Most important of all was the fact that Germany was permitted to keep the Ruhr, the industrial heart of the country and of the Continent. In the tremendous steel and chemical works of the Ruhr, Germany had a sure basis for rapid rearmament on a large scale. As soon as Hitler came into power, all the treaty limitations on Germany's armament were openly flouted. Germany now devoted her resources, her industry, her science, her superb technique of organization to rearmament that proceeded fast and furious. "Guns not butter" was the Nazi slogan.

Why had the treaty of Versailles not been enforced? The diplomatic history of the period between the two world wars makes instructive reading. Almost every move of the Allies in reference to Germany was a bad move. No sooner was the treaty signed than the Allies began falling apart. Britain and France resumed their historic mistrust of each other. France was now the strongest power on the Continent, and Britain, true to her balance of power tradition, began to oppose France and to favor weakened Germany. Once again France railed at "perfidious Albion." America relapsed into her traditional isolation by refusing to join Britain and France in an alliance to prevent the resurgence of Germany. American isolationism deepened

when Britain and France refused to pay their war debts. At
the peace conference, America had asked for no territory and
no reparations, and got what she had asked for. Now she was
saddled with the great burden of paying a large part of the
cost of the war. In deep resentment, America firmly resolved
that in the future she would let Europe "stew in its own juice."
Under such circumstances, Germany was free to defy the *Diktat*
of Versailles.

GERMANY'S SECOND BID FOR WORLD DOMINION

The very existence of Nazi Germany constituted a threat to
world peace. Hitler had come into power on the promise of
undoing the treaty of Versailles and, as he put it, even of the
treaty of Westphalia (1648), which had split Germany into so
many pieces. As his rise to power in Germany was due largely
to the weakness of the Weimar Republic, so his rise to power
in Europe was due largely to the weakness of the Versailles
system. The defenders of the latter, like the defenders of the
former, were paralyzed by fear into inaction. One terrific blow
after another was struck by Germany at the Versailles system:
repudiation of reparations, rearmament, remilitarization of the
Rhineland, annexation of Austria, and, finally, the partition of
Czechoslovakia by the infamous treaty of Munich. All these
blows were delivered without a hand being raised to uphold
the treaty of Versailles.

Germany's immediate aim was to dominate Europe. But her
ultimate aim, as openly proclaimed by Hitler, was world dominion, "tomorrow the world." Because of their obsession that the
superior German race was destined to rule the world, the Nazis
were ready to challenge the world, even if it resulted in Germany's ruin. Rather would they see Germany die as a nation

than live in a world not dominated by her. Germany must then prepare for a world war; hence she must find allies to ensure her success. In Europe, Fascist Italy was a likely ally, who might be satisfied with a minor share in the spoils. In 1936 Hitler and Mussolini formed a military alliance that became known as the "Axis." Hitler looked beyond Europe for another and stronger ally, which he found in Japan, militarist, authoritarian, and racialist like Germany. The ambition of Japan to become the "lord of the Far East" could be utilized by Germany in her ambition to become the lord of Europe. In case of war with the Western powers, Japan could weaken the latter by seizing their colonial possessions in the Far East and by holding Soviet Russia in check. So important were the Japanese to Germany's ambitions that they were "elevated" racially by the Germans to the position of "honorary Aryans." As war drew nearer, Japan joined the Axis powers and prepared to play her part in the drama.

All was now ready for the Second World War. If ever a period in history could be characterized as bankrupt, it was the interwar period. High were the hopes of humanity, after the terrible ordeal of the First World War, to establish universal peace, freedom, and equality. But the "war to end war" was followed by the greatest of all wars. The war "to make the world safe for democracy" was followed by the establishment of totalitarian dictatorships, the most ruthless and most despotic of all authoritarian governments. The war for "national self-determination" was followed by the destruction of the independence of the states in Central Europe. A cynical younger generation succeeded a bewildered older generation.

There now existed two formidable dictatorships: Communist Russia and Nazi Germany. Everywhere, anywhere, and in any and every way, the totalitarian dictatorships sought to extend their power and influence. As might be expected, their neighbors were the first to suffer. Russia conquered and annexed the

Baltic states—Esthonia, Latvia, and Lithuania—and reduced
Finland to subservience. Germany conquered and annexed
Czechoslovakia and Austria, and reduced Hungary, Yugoslavia,
and Rumania to subservience. Both Germany and Russia conquered Poland and divided her territory between them. Not to
be put in the shade by her fellow dictatorships, Italy conquered
and annexed Ethiopia and Albania. The new yoke of totalitarian
dictatorship that each established weighed far more heavily than
had the yoke of absolute monarchy.

The situation in Europe during the interwar period favored
Germany's aggressive designs. Once Hitler was in power, diplomatic policies were adopted and plans formulated, with all the
care and definiteness that had long characterized the Germans.
The objective was the conquest of Europe. There existed a German tradition, first established by Frederick the Great and later
reinforced by Bismarck, that relations between nations were un-
alterably relations of enmity; even a friendly nation was to be
regarded as a potential enemy. No security was, therefore, possible except by a constant increase of power through conquest,
and only through conquest. Germany must always be on the
watch, and wait for the opportunity to strike. And that opportunity would surely come in the game of power politics so characteristic of international relations. After the First World War
an unstable power equilibrium had come into existence in the
Europe of "dead empires and sick republics." The balance of
power was in the melting pot, and a bold stroke by Germany
would meet no such solid resistance at the hands of the great
powers as it had met in 1914. Furthermore, Germany's old fear
of a two-front war was allayed by the Hitler-Stalin pact of 1939,
which assured a friend, not an enemy, on the eastern frontier.
Fascist Italy was a jackal partner of Nazi Germany, and hence
sure to be loyal for the sake of the pickings. Might not America
again intervene in Europe against Germany as in the First
World War? In such a contingency, Japan's part in the Axis

would come into play and divert American war efforts to the far Pacific. The system of collective security, built up by the League of Nations, collapsed, when that body shriveled into nothingness after its refusal to take action against Japan, in 1931, for invading Manchuria. As the menacing shadow of Germany became ever darker and ever larger, France, paralyzed with fear, sought safety behind the Maginot line. Britain, muddled and unprepared, sought safety in appeasing Hitler. Both Britain and France were bent on maintaining peace at any cost—to others— and this led straight to Munich. In view of the weakness of the great powers, the smaller nations on the Continent either made common cause with the Axis or huddled together in terror awaiting the onslaught. Germany's second bid for world dominion had every prospect for success.

The responsibility for starting the Second World War rests squarely and solely on Germany. There is no question of Germany's guilt in the Second as there had been in the First World War. Hitler, it is true, did not believe that a world conflagration would result from his continual aggressions. Munich had convinced him that neither Britain nor France had the courage or the will to stop him. His strategy was to seize Germany's neighbors by the deadly method of "one by one," using threats of invasion and the terrorist activity of fascist Fifth Columns. Anyone who opposed Hitler's "peaceful" methods was loudly denounced as a "warmonger." Austria, Czechoslovakia, and Danzig, each in turn, succumbed, and this gave Hitler a great reputation for "timing." When, in 1939, Germany attacked Poland, he was confident that the same good fortune would attend him and that he could continue his conquests unopposed. Hitler was, therefore, surprised and infuriated when Britain, under Neville Chamberlain, and France, under Daladier—both men of Munich—declared war against Germany.

The Second World War (1939–1945) was the most widespread and most devastating in modern history. Virtually every nation in the world was a belligerent. The few neutral nations in Europe—Spain, Portugal, Sweden, Eire, Switzerland, and Turkey—were not very neutral. All of them, except Eire, aided Germany, willingly or unwillingly, at one time or another. In another aspect the war was a world revolution. As already described, fascism was a revolutionary movement that aimed to overthrow the existing system of society and government everywhere and to establish a new one, based on a totalitarian dictatorship. And the model of the new order was Germany, which had succeeded in destroying democracy and in establishing fascism, quickly, ruthlessly, and thoroughly. As a consequence, the fate of individuals, as well as that of nations, was intimately involved in the world-wide struggle between the Axis and the Allies. On its outcome depended the personal future of a steelworker in Pennsylvania, of a peasant in Manchuria, of a professor in Oxford, of a shopkeeper in Antwerp, of a writer in Paris, or of a planter in Brazil.

Germany's war plans called for a blitzkrieg, successive attacks by overwhelming forces with lightning speed. Its success astounded the world, and even the Germans themselves, as their armies swept quickly from victory to victory. Norway, Denmark, Holland, Belgium, Poland, and the Balkan states were overrun. Even powerful France crumpled up swiftly and ignominiously. The Germans were elated with the success of the blitzkrieg, and they determined to get rid of their competitors for world dominion, namely, the Russians. So arrogant were the Germans, so convinced were they of the invincibility of their army, especially after the swift collapse of France, that they felt confident of being able to destroy both democracy and communism at the same time, and that quickly. Suddenly, on June 22, 1941, German armies invaded Russia, and both dictatorships were locked in mortal combat. Hitler's colossal error threw Soviet Russia from the side of the fascists to that of the democracies.

The Axis powers came within a hairbreadth of complete success in 1942. Germany bestrode almost the entire Continent, from the Atlantic to the Caucasus. Still unconquered were Britain and Soviet Russia. What saved Britain was the Channel, as the German army could not follow up air attacks; the British fleet still controlled the waters. What saved Soviet Russia was her huge land mass, which enabled the Russian armies to retreat and to re-form their lines after every German advance. The success of Japan rivaled that of Germany. Japanese forces swiftly conquered and occupied all eastern China, Siam, the Malay peninsula, the Netherlands East Indies, the Philippines, and Burma. A Japanese army even crossed the border into India. Japan was far on the way to realizing her dream of being "lord of the Far East."

The policies inaugurated by Germany in the occupied territory gave a vivid and terrifying picture of the fascist order. Basic and fundamental was the aim of making the Germans the "master race" of a Europe united under their rule. The conquered states in east central Europe were organized as "satellites." A totalitarian dictatorship was established in each state, the government of which was administered by local fascists, directed and supervised by their German overlords. The interests of the satellites were made subordinate to those of Germany in all ways, but especially in economic matters.

According to the plan, Germany alone was to be the highly industrialized nation of Europe; the economy of the satellites was to be geared to the needs of Germany, largely to the production of food and raw materials, to be purchased by the Germans at their own prices. Whatever local industry was permitted was directed and controlled by the Germans. The satellites were given a colonial status in the scheme of fascist imperialism.

The inhabitants of the conquered regions were maltreated by the Germans with a ferocity unparalleled in the history of

Christian Europe. All non-Germans were to be exterminated, subjected to slavery, or reduced to inferiority. And the Germans proceeded to carry out this aim with cold, tigrish ferocity. Anti-Semitism was applied in a manner that horrified mankind. Every Jew in lands under German control was marked for death. Few escaped. It is estimated that six million Jews were put to death, chiefly by wholesale asphyxiation. So stupendous a crime against humanity had no name, and one had to be invented. "Genocide" is now the term used to describe the wholesale destruction of a people. Millions of Poles, Czechs, and Russians were massacred or driven out of their homes to work as slaves in German fields and factories. Their places were taken by Germans sent in as colonists. A veritable substitution of population took place in some of the occupied regions in the east. The Germans hated and feared the French as their mortal enemies. When France was conquered, they deliberately planned to starve the French people, slowly and gradually, with the object of devitalizing the nation by reducing its numbers and by enfeebling those who survived. The atrocities committed by the Germans against the civilian population in the occupied territories and against prisoners of war were not only inhumane but inhuman. Horror piled upon horror, and mankind stood aghast at German inhumanity.

What saved mankind from domination by the Germans was their genius for making big mistakes, not small ones. This quality became even more pronounced during the Second than in the First World War. All of Germany's carefully laid plans went awry because of this failing, which was strikingly illustrated in her attitude toward Britain, Russia, and America. After the British disaster at Dunkerque in 1940, the moment was propitious for Germany to challenge British sea power by invading Britain, which then had few coastal and road defenses and only one fully equipped army division available for defense. But the propitious moment passed. Later in the year, when France fell, the Germans expected that Britain, seeing the hopelessness of her lone fight, would surrender. But Britain kept up her fight undaunted, under the inspiring leadership of Winston Churchill. Another great German mistake was the attack on Soviet Russia. Despite every effort on the part of Hitler and Stalin to collaborate because of their common hatred of democracy, their fundamental rivalry for world dominion caused mutual distrust between them. Though linked by a pact, solemnly entered into, each feared the other more than both feared the democracies. When the Second World War broke out, Germany dreaded that, if successful, she would face a greatly strengthened Russia. And the latter dreaded exactly the same thing regarding the former. Elated with the many victories in the western campaigns, Germany suddenly made war on Soviet Russia, feeling supremely confident of defeating both the democracies and her fellow dictatorship. After carefully laying plans to fight on one front only, Germany was now fighting on two fronts, as in the First World War. Hitler fully expected Soviet Russia to collapse under the hammer blows of the German armies, but the Russians kept on fighting stubbornly. The greatest of all German mistakes was to draw America into the war. As already noted, Germany's alliance with Japan was based on the belief that, should America enter the war, her main forces would be concentrated in the Far East; whatever forces America could spare for Europe would not be sufficient to prevent a Nazi victory. When, after the attack on Pearl Harbor (December 7, 1941), Japan and America were at war, Germany declared war against America, feeling certain that any aid from that source would be too little and too late. The miracle of American production now proved far greater than in the First World War; she produced armies, fleets, and airplanes sufficient to fight both in Europe and in the Far East. And, to the consternation of the Germans, the Americans concentrated their main forces in Europe.

The tide of war turned in favor of the Allies in 1942. On June

6 the Americans won a great naval battle over the Japanese at
Midway, in the Pacific. On November 12, the British won the
great battle of El Alamein, in Egypt, over the Germans and
Italians. On February 2, 1943, the Russians scored a great victory
over the Germans at Stalingrad, in Russia. An Allied invasion of
Italy began, in July, 1943, which met stout resistance from German and Italian armies. As the Allies advanced, the "sawdust"
Caesar, Mussolini, was overthrown, and Italy made a separate
peace. On June 6, 1944, an American army landed in northern
France, and the Allied invasion of "Fortress Europe" began in
the west. At the same time the Russians attacked the Germans
fiercely in the east. Fighting desperately and retreating slowly,
east and west, the Germans finally surrendered unconditionally,
on May 8, 1945. Japan kept on fighting, but not for long. Atomic
bombs, the newest and most destructive of all weapons, were
hurled by the Americans on two Japanese cities, one on Hiroshima and another on Nagasaki. The bombs caused unprecedented losses in life and property. On August 14, 1945, Japan
surrendered, and it was occupied by American forces.

THE PARTITION OF GERMANY

The defeat of the Axis powers was complete. Italy and Japan
barely escaped with their national lives. They lost all the territory that they had acquired since 1870, and were reduced to the
position of third-rate powers. Even more severe were the terms
imposed on Germany. The Allies decided to weaken Germany
to such a degree that never again would she be able to disturb
the peace of mankind. No government immediately succeeded
that of the Third Reich; no central political authority was permitted to maintain national unity, as at the end of the First
World War.

The Allies were determined to bring home to the German

people their responsibility for the Third Reich. Heavy reparations were demanded because, as was officially stated at the time,
"the German people cannot escape responsibility" for the fearful acts of the Nazis. Many of the German industrial plants were
dismantled in order to give reparations in the form of machinery
to the Allies, and, at the same time, to remove the industrial
basis for rearmament in order to avoid a recurrence of what had
happened after the First World War. These measures, far more
severe than the *Diktat* of Versailles, were taken because of the
almost universal belief that Germany was a nation, without conscience and without humanity, whose existence as a great power
constituted a danger to all mankind.

Germany was, in fact, partitioned. All her territory in the east,
up to the Oder-Neisse rivers, was given, until a definite decision
by a peace treaty, to Poland and Soviet Russia, chiefly to the
former. The remainder was divided into four occupation zones:
Russian, American, British, and French. The period of occupation was left indefinite. Economic control of the Ruhr was
turned over to an international commission, representing Britain, France, America, Belgium, the Netherlands, and Luxemburg, with power to direct the production and distribution of
the resources of the region. Economic control of the Saar, a great
coal center, was definitely given to France.

The defeat of militarist Germany and Japan was highly
dramatized by the punishment of those responsible for the war.
For the first time in history, an international tribunal was created to try the heads of a nation for starting a war and for committing outrages in violation of international law. This tribunal,
sitting in Nuremberg, consisted of judges representing America,
Britain, Soviet Russia, and France. It indicted twenty-four of the
chief leaders of Nazi Germany, among them Herman Goering
who, next to Hitler, was the most powerful of the Nazi chieftains. Hitler and Goebbels had committed suicide during the last
days of the Third Reich. In 1946, nearly all of those indicted were

found guilty; some were executed, and others, sent to prison for long terms. Goering cheated the gallows by committing suicide.

The Japanese militarists suffered a like fate. In 1948, 25 high civil and military officials of the former empire were indicted by an international military tribunal, sitting in Tokyo, charged with the same crimes as those of the Nazi leaders. Nearly all the defendants were found guilty. Some, among them former Premier Tojo, were sentenced to death and executed; nearly all the others received life imprisonment.

These trials were unprecedented in international relations. The accused were permitted to have defense counsel and witnesses, and were given every opportunity to present their side. Two new principles were established by the convictions: (1) that starting and waging aggressive war was declared to be a crime for which *individuals* were responsible and (2) that violations of the laws of war, such as extermination of civilians and the enslavement, deportation, and torture of prisoners, were crimes for which *individuals* were responsible, even when done under orders of a superior. No longer was a chief of state to be immune because he represented a sovereign nation. And no longer was an official shorn of responsibility because he obeyed the orders of his chief.

In 1949, important political changes were made in Germany. The three zones occupied by the Western powers were united to form a federal union of eleven states called the German Federal Republic.[3] The powers of the new state were limited in many ways by the Occupation Statute adopted by Britain, France, and America. A commission representing these powers was given supreme authority over foreign affairs, foreign trade and exchange, military security, and constitutional interpretation. Another state, the German Democratic Republic, was created by the Russians in their zone. It was completely controlled by the Communists, who established a government in the man-

[3] See p. 85.

ner and according to the principles of totalitarian dictatorship. In reality, the German Democratic Republic became a satellite of Soviet Russia. The united Germany that had played so great a part in the world since 1871 was dissolved in history.

It has been said that nothing fails like success. The history of Germany gives point to this saying. No nation achieved success so quickly as did the German Empire which dominated Europe and profoundly influenced the entire world. Defeated in the First World War, Germany quickly rose again, and under Hitler almost succeeded in conquering Europe. Never in modern times was a defeat so complete and so overwhelming as that suffered by Germany in the Second World War. Battered and truncated, its government subjected to foreign control, the Germany of 1950 was not even a ghost of the Germany of 1914. And when that once mighty power sank into decrepitude, its fate aroused little sympathy among the other nations. Germany vanished from the scene of her greatness, "unwept, unhonored, and unsung."

Chapter 9. Russia's Bid for World Revolution

All seemed well after the Second World War. Democracy, both political and social, was advancing. Colonial imperialism was on its way out. Fascist Germany and Italy were crushed, as was semifascist Japan. A new and stronger world organization, the United Nations, was established. But these prospects of universal democracy and peace vanished when the defeated totalitarianism of fascism was succeeded by the triumphant totalitarianism of communism. Soviet Russia became the new menace to democracy and peace.

The democratic world was dismayed. Soviet Russia had been a doughty ally in the war, and a potent factor in the defeat of Germany. Many were convinced that she would now cooperate with the democracies in restoring a ruined world, in promoting friendly relations among nations, and in supporting the United Nations. Had not Soviet Russia, like the democracies, faced total annihilation in the war against fascism? Then why should not both join hands to create a new and better world? But that was not to be.

The present conflict between East and West was not improvised by the Communist dictatorship. Its roots lie deep in history, not only in the history of Russia but in that of all Europe. The demarcation between Eastern and Western Europe, now so evident, began long, long ago. In origin, it was neither political nor economic, but religious. The split between the two European regions arose from the great schism in the Christian church during the eighth century, known as the Iconoclastic Controversy. It divided Christianity into two parts: Western, or Catholic, with its center in Rome; and Eastern, or Greek, with its center in Constantinople. This schism, which deepened with the years, was the origin of a type of civilization in Byzantine, or Eastern, Europe, markedly different from that in Western Europe. The two parts of the Continent became even more separated when Russia was conquered by the Tatars in the thirteenth century and the Balkans were conquered by the Turks in the fifteenth century. An "iron curtain," then as now, separated East from West.

This separation seriously retarded the progress of Eastern Europe. It had no share in the Renaissance, which gave a new direction to Western culture; in the Protestant Revolution, which gave a new direction to Western Christianity; in the Commercial Revolution, which gave a new direction to Western economy; in the expansion of Europe, which brought Western civilization to the New World; or in the eighteenth-century Enlightenment which proclaimed rationalism in thought and secularism in life. "Europe" came to mean Western Europe.

Russia and the Balkans had no part in these vast changes. The Balkans remained much as they had been, clamped down under the iron rule of the Turks. Russia during the sixteenth century had succeeded in freeing herself from Tatar rule, but not from the Byzantine heritage of absolutism in government and Orthodoxy in religion. During the eighteenth century, Russia tried to "enter" Europe, first through Peter the Great and then through Catherine the Great, but these efforts were tentative, and their results were relatively slight. Russia remained definitely separated from Europe in all essential matters. Her government continued to be an absolute monarchy by divine right; her economy remained agricultural, along feudal lines; and her culture was medieval in spirit and in organization.

The wars of the French Revolution and of Napoleon produced great changes in the relations between Russia and Western Europe. To save themselves from defeat, the rulers of the Western nations, at war with France, had great need of the vast armies of Tsar Alexander I. They literally dragged Russia into Europe by a close alliance with the Tsar against France. The defeat of Napoleon had important consequences for Russia: she became an integral part of Europe and the dominant power on the Continent.

An unexpected outcome of the association of Russia with the West was the lifting of the iron curtain. Russian intellectuals now caught glimpses of Western civilization, and were fascinated. The "westerners," as these Russians were called, were convinced that the only salvation for Russia lay in repudiating her Byzantine heritage and in reorganizing herself on the model of Western liberalism. Their first effort in that direction was the abortive Decembrist uprising in 1825. The reaction that followed lasted until the reign of Alexander II (1855–1881), when liberalism, for the first time, scored great triumphs: the emancipation of the serfs; the establishment of local government; and the reform of education on Western models. But the westerners were not satisfied. They strove for the complete overthrow of tsarism by a revolutionary upheaval. Revolution, too, was Western. The Russian revolutionary movements during the nineteenth century were generally inspired by Western ideals, and directed toward Western objectives in government and society.

But old traditions continued to influence the nation. Opposed to the westerners were the easterners, called "Slavophils," who stoutly championed the Byzantine heritage of absolute monarchy and the Orthodox church. The Slavophils argued that Russia had a civilization of her own, peculiar to her history and to the Slav race, and superior to that of the liberal West, which they denounced as degenerate and un-Christian. Later, they adopted a policy of racial expansion, called "pan-Slavism," which sought to include under Russian hegemony the Slav peoples in Austria-Hungary and in the Balkans.

Russia herself was now divided between those who championed the West and those who championed the East. This division found echoes even in literature where two intellectual giants confronted each other: the westerner, Turgenev, and the easterner, Dostoievsky. During the last decades of the nineteenth century, Western influences made headway with the introduction of the Industrial Revolution. As elsewhere, modern industrialism made inroads on the ancient political and social order. New social classes, capitalists and workers, appeared, both influenced by Western ideas. As in Western Europe, the former became liberals, and the latter, socialists. A revolutionary movement against tsarism quickly became widespread.

But old traditions proved stronger than new revolutionary ideologies. Before long, the revolutionists themselves were split into easterners and westerners. A revolutionary group, called "Social Revolutionists," appeared and repudiated both the liberalism and the socialism of the West. These new easterners maintained that a revolutionary movement in Russia, to be successful, must be based on the needs of the vast majority of the people, the peasants, who were discontented because they had received insufficient land at the time of their emancipation. The future in Russia, according to the Social Revolutionists, was to be a new agrarian economy based on cooperative peasant communes, not a new industrial economy based on capitalism, as advocated by the liberal Constitutional Democrats, or based on socialism, as advocated by the Marxist Social Democrats. This bitter antagonism between eastern and western revolutionists accounted, to a considerable degree, for the failure of the Revolution of 1905 to overthrow tsarism.

The failure of this great upheaval caused Nicholai Lenin to reflect on the basic problems and necessary methods of revolution in Russia. Out of his reflections came the ideology, the policies, and the tactics known as "Leninism," destined to play so decisive a role not only in Russian but in world history. Lenin clearly realized that a revolutionary movement designed for advanced industrial countries, as was Marxism, would have to be considerably modified to meet the needs of a backward agricultural country like Russia. There, the peasants, rather than the industrial workers, constituted the "proletariat." And the Russian peasants were ignorant and backward but intensely land-hungry. Therefore, promise of land to the peasants, as well as the overthrow of capitalism, would have to be the rallying cry of the revolution. Democracy, a purely Western concept, had hardly gained a toehold in Russia. Hence, it found no place in Lenin's plan to overthrow tsarism and to establish a new order. Instead, irresponsible rule and abject submission, Russia's Byzantine heritage, became the basis of Lenin's vision of the new order in Russia. The revolutionary movement was to be directed by an elite of professional revolutionists who were to seize power and establish themselves as the new rulers by making use of repression and terrorism, the time-worn instruments of tsarist control. Leninism was in essence an easternized version of Marxism, retaining its objectives of world revolution and the abolition of capitalism, but applying tactics, worked out in a clear, ruthless pattern, designed to achieve immediate results in Russia, not the vague program of Marx for some distant future.

Lenin, as chief of the Bolshevists, or those Social Democrats who had rejected democracy, succeeded in forming a combination with the left wing of the Social Revolutionists. It was this combination that came into power with the coup d'état of November, 1917, which overthrew the provisional government and established Soviet Russia.

The ruthless tactics of Leninism were soon brought into play. Once secure in power, the Soviet government, headed by Lenin, suppressed all opposing parties. Then the "Communists," as the

Bolshevists were now called, turned on their allies, the left-wing Social Revolutionists. They were suppressed as mercilessly as had been the opposing parties. Both opponents and allies having been eliminated, the Communists were left in full control of "all the Russias." How complete and thorough has been the totalitarian dictatorship in Soviet Russia since then, the world knows only too well.

Control of Russia was but a step toward world revolution, the central and never-changing objective of communism. Their easy and quick success in seizing power in the vast empire of the tsars convinced the Communists that their methods constituted a classic model for social revolution everywhere. With this in view, they organized the Communist International (Comintern).[1] It was a highly centralized body representing the Communist parties of the various nations, and was directed from Moscow chiefly by the Russians. However, its activities in Western Europe—attempting to overthrow existing governments—proved to be unsuccessful, despite the disintegration, political and economic, that followed the First World War. The numerous middle class in the industrialized West, fearing total ruin, offered stout resistance to the Communist onslaught. No such middle class had existed in Russia to resist the Bolshevists. Fascism, a new and powerful movement, arose and declared war *à outrance* against communism.

The failure of the Comintern in Western Europe created a serious problem for the Russian strategists. Would the party "line" have to change? The original "line" was predicated on the belief that a communist triumph in Western Europe would establish governments that would aid Russia, economically and militarily, to forward world revolution. Since this triumph had not come to pass, would world revolution have to be abandoned? If so, would Soviet Russia be able to survive in a capitalist world?

[1] See p. 232.

After Lenin's death in 1924, a sharp division arose in the Russian Communist party as to the "line" to be followed. Strangely enough, the historic conflict between East and West now reappeared, this time within the Communist party itself, in the struggle between Leon Trotsky and Joseph Stalin. Trotsky's views revealed clearly that he was a westerner. As a result of his experience in Western Europe and America, where he had lived for a number of years, he was convinced that world revolution would succeed only when harnessed to the disciplined industrialism of the West. Therefore, he favored what he called "permanent revolution," or policies to intensify the communist movement in Western countries. A communist Western Europe would then effectively cooperate with Soviet Russia. Stalin, on the contrary, was essentially an easterner. He had never been out of Russia, and his knowledge of the West was limited. He believed that, before all else, the revolution must be carried through completely in Russia. As a consequence, he advanced the idea of establishing "socialism in one country" first, namely, in Russia, which had extensive territory, a large population, and the natural resources essential for industrialization. Once Soviet Russia was established as a mighty industrial power, she could effectively aid and direct communist movements in all countries. Unlike the westerner, Trotsky, who visualized a communist world of independent nations, the easterner, Stalin, visualized a communist world of nations subservient to Soviet Russia, dependent on her, and exploited by her—all for the greater glory of the "socialist fatherland."

The victory of Stalin over Trotsky again marked the triumph of the easterners over the westerners. Stalin emerged from this struggle as the new "autocrat of all the Russias." All those who favored cooperation with the West were eliminated from the government. A notable example was the removal, in 1939, of Foreign Minister Maxim Litvinov, the last westerner. Viacheslav Molotov, his successor, was an uncompromising easterner.

It must not be supposed that Stalin's victory over Trotsky denoted a repudiation of Soviet Russia's bid for world revolution. Never at any time in the history of Soviet Russia has the vision of a communist world been obliterated or even darkened. Stalin's policy of "socialism in one country" denoted merely a strategic retreat; his objective, world revolution, remained fixed. He realized, as Trotsky did not, that Soviet Russia was as yet too weak to engage in a world conflict to establish universal communism. Before embarking on such a career Russia must become strong by developing her economy, establishing her military might, and uniting all elements of the population behind the government. Once this objective was attained, Soviet Russia would be consolidated as the citadel of world revolution from which would sally forth the shock troops of communism. Stalin himself plainly asserted that the "existence of the Soviet Republic side by side with imperialist states for a long time is unthinkable. One or the other must triumph in the end. And before the end comes, a series of frightful clashes between the Soviet Republic and the bourgeois states is inevitable." For the time being, however, Soviet Russia must bide her time, and strengthen herself by establishing "socialism in one country."

Stalin covered his strategic retreat in a masterly fashion. The Communist party "line" took a sudden switch in favor of parliamentary action in democratic countries. "Popular Front" movements, organized by the Communists, vociferously advocated an alliance of all opponents of fascism, Communists, socialists, and liberals, in order to present a common front to their common enemy. The Popular Front proved very successful, especially in France, where, in 1936, Léon Blum became premier, supported in the Chamber of Deputies by the Socialist, Radical Socialist, and Communist parties. The "democratic" constitution of 1936 was adopted by Soviet Russia in order to align that dictatorship with the democracies.[2] This new party "line"

[2] A similar policy was followed after the Second World War. See p. 314.

served, for the first time, to create a friendly attitude in democratic lands toward Soviet Russia. When, in 1941, Germany
attacked Soviet Russia, the latter was welcomed by the democracies as an ally in the war against fascism. In deference to
democratic opinion, the Comintern, dedicated to world revolution, was officially "dissolved" in 1943.

Soviet Russia's victory in the Second World War did not, as
many then believed, orient her toward the West which had
aided her so greatly in that fateful struggle. More than ever did
she confirm her Eastern orientation. She felt that her victory
was not only over Nazi Germany but over the entire West.
Even while the conflict was raging, the Russians were preparing
moves against the West by entrenching themselves in Eastern
Europe to prepare the countries of that region for their satellite
future. They slighted, and sometimes even ignored, the part of
the West in the "Great Patriotic War," as the Second World War
is called in Soviet Russia. Nationalism was now to the fore.

In marked contradiction to Marxist internationalism, the
Soviet government conducted propaganda in the press, the
schools, the theater, radio, and motion pictures patriotically
extolling the Russian past. Ivan the Terrible and Peter the Great
became national heroes. The historic struggles of Russia against
invaders—the Prussians, the Poles, the Swedes, the French, and
the Germans—were glorified in strident patriotic terms. The
national anthem, the *Internationale,* French in origin, was
abandoned for a new anthem, Russian in origin. Even more
striking was the revival of the Orthodox church and of pan-
Slavism. In 1943 the synod of the Orthodox church was restored,
and the power of the head of the church, the Patriarch, was
greatly increased. As in tsarist days, the church was now controlled by the government, and the compliant Patriarch voiced
full confidence in Soviet Russia. In 1946 an all-Slav Congress,
representing the Slavic peoples of Europe, was called by Soviet

Russia. It met in Belgrade and proclaimed the unity of the Slavs everywhere in protecting their racial ideals and interests. The Congress hailed Soviet Russia as the leader of a new pan-Slav movement against the West, the culture of which was denounced as bourgeois, decadent, false, and corrupt. Russian writers, scientists, artists, and composers were compelled, on pain of severe punishment, to abjure any sympathy whatever with Western ideals. Russia was now definitely Eastern. The most far-reaching of all revolutions resulted in confirming Russia in the way of life marked out for her in the eighth century by the Iconoclastic Controversy. What may happen in the strange whirligig of history has often baffled the wisest and the most farseeing.

RUSSIA VERSUS THE WEST

This resurgence of Russian nationalism by no means precluded revolutionary activity on a world-wide scale. After the Second World War, Russian intervention everywhere to promote the communist movement took a new spurt, much to the surprise and chagrin of the world. It was then widely believed that Soviet Russia had abandoned world revolution and was now ready to cooperate with the other nations to reconstruct a war-torn world. She herself had suffered tremendous losses and needed all possible aid, especially from America. During the war, America had given immense assistance to Soviet Russia through lend-lease, and was now willing to extend new aid in the Marshall Plan. Great concessions had been made to Stalin by President Roosevelt in order to convince him of America's friendship. At the founding of the United Nations in San Francisco, Soviet Russia was universally welcomed by the democracies. Many hoped that one world in which different political and economic systems would exist side by side and freely cooperate to preserve world peace and to speed world recovery would at last come into existence.

But these hopes soon turned to ashes. By her actions Soviet Russia made only too plain that she had no intention of co-operating with the Western democracies, except on her own terms. In the field of international relations, the conduct of Soviet Russia caused consternation, confusion, and dismay. Soviet diplomacy, remarked Winston Churchill, was "a riddle wrapped up in a mystery inside of an enigma." The Russians would begin negotiations in a cordial atmosphere; then they would become more and more obdurate; and finally would reach an adamantine decision to agree only when all their demands were granted. What angered the Western powers especially was the cool violation of solemn agreements, such as those entered into by Stalin himself at Teheran, Yalta, and Potsdam. Violations of treaties have been familiar in history; almost every nation could justly be held guilty of such conduct, at one time or another. But when a nation violated a treaty, it *knew* that it was doing so, and defended itself by giving excuses, as when, in 1914, Germany violated the neutrality of Belgium, and when, in 1938, France deserted Czechoslovakia at Munich. Soviet Russia, however, did not seem to be aware of her violations, and if she was aware of them she did not appear to care very much. The "opinion of mankind" exerted little or no influence on the Russians.

Here history comes in to explain this seemingly inexplicable conduct. During the long centuries of tsarism, there did not exist in Russia the system of economic relations based on freedom of contract, which had been established in the West through the growth of commerce and industry. Free contract is a business way of making an agreement through bargaining. The transaction is the result of give and take between the parties for their mutual benefit. Once the contract is made, both parties are required to live up to it, even if it proves to be more advantageous to one than to the other. Violators are held responsible at law and are condemned by public opinion. Only those countries that have well-established business traditions accept the sanctity of contract, which reaches beyond business and influences the political and diplomatic activities of the nation. Business life in tsarist Russia was very limited. The vast majority of the people were peasants and craftsmen, and the ruling groups were landlords and officials. Their relationships were fixed by their status and by established customs; hence, they were not habituated to the free contract ways of business. Those who were so habituated, the capitalists and merchants, were relatively few in number, generally foreigners, and hence outside the main stream of Russian economic life. Under such conditions the principle of freedom of contract did not, and could not, develop, and consequently no strong public opinion existed that upheld the sanctity of contracts once made.

When backward, semimedieval Russia fell under the rule of the Communists, freedom of contract, as a principle, was repudiated *in toto*. Being Marxists, the Communists believe that under capitalism economic contracts are entered into under duress. Between capitalist and capitalist a contract, in their view, is a method used by one party to ruin the other; between capitalist and worker a contract is a method used by the former to exploit the latter. To abide by the terms of a contract that is not wholly advantageous shows a naive willingness to sacrifice one's own interest for the benefit of another. On their accession to power, the Communists showed their contempt for contractual obligations by repudiating all Russian national debts, foreign and domestic, whether owed to governments, corporations, or individuals.

This attitude toward matters economic found expression also in matters political and diplomatic. According to the Communists, the capitalist nations are always and ever the "enemy";

hence they regard treaty negotiations merely as moves on a chessboard, not efforts to solve pressing problems in order to promote the good life among nations. The Russians will sign agreements, but the extent to which they will honor them depends upon circumstances. Always will they insist that the other party live up to the letter of those provisions of the agreement which are advantageous to Soviet Russia. On the other hand, they will completely disregard those terms which constitute the price of the concessions made to them. The Russians will also sign an agreement in order to gain a special objective, but without the slightest intention of keeping their part of the obligation. At all times they strive to get the best of the "enemy," the capitalist. Moreover the capitalist is not only an "enemy" but also a "heretic." As Marxists, the Communists regard all non-Marxists as being without the blessing of the one true, secular religion. And faith need not be kept with heretics.

Soviet diplomacy has applied the doctrine of the class struggle to international relations. As, according to Marxism, an inevitable conflict exists between capital and labor in a capitalist economy, so there exists an inevitable conflict between capitalist and communist nations. No compromise is possible in either case. There cannot be one world of capitalist and communist nations any more than there can be one nation of bourgeois and proletariat. According to Lenin, it is impossible, even unthinkable, that Soviet Russia can for long flourish side by side with capitalist states. Either one or the other must be eliminated. And the triumph of Soviet Russia is inevitable, according to his followers. The "sword of history" lies in her hands.

To speed up the inevitable became the communist policy. And the best way to do it was to bring economic chaos to every democratic land. Loss of production through strikes fomented by communist labor leaders and diversion of production to armament would prove ruinous to the democracies.

THE "COLD REVOLUTION" IN EAST
CENTRAL EUROPE

The strange combination of historic nationalism with communist internationalism puzzled, confused, and dismayed the world. Regardless of revolution and of ideology, Soviet Russia could not escape history. That invisible hand leads even the most recalcitrant revolutionists into the path marked out by centuries of national experience, national traditions, and national ideals. All that new forces can do is to broaden or to narrow this path, to accelerate or to slow down the pace of travel. In Soviet Russia the historic path of tsarist imperialism was broadened and its pace accelerated by messianic Marxism. Whatever was the deficiency of one was made up by the abundance of the other.

Soviet Russia is historic Russia plus Marxism. These two streams, flowing from opposite directions, mingled into one as a result of the confluence brought about by the situation in which Soviet Russia found herself. Once the Revolution was stabilized, the historic drive for expansion could not be denied by the Communists in power. And the historic fields of Russian expansion were Central Europe, the Balkans, the Middle East, and the Far East. These lands were predominately agrarian; hence, communism must make its supreme appeal to the peasants. By promising land from confiscated estates to the impoverished peasantry, the Communists could win the support of the traditionally conservative masses in these regions. The overthrow of the existing governments would be followed by social revolution and, at the same time, by the expansion of Russian influence. Tsarist Russia had no such powerful ally as Marxism; hence, its expansion was limited in scope and in appeal. Marxism, as a political religion, was plainly not limited to the preaching of doctrines. A mighty power, Soviet Russia, stood ready at all times to spread them with all the force at her command.

Communist imperialism proved far more successful than had tsarist imperialism. As a result of the First World War, Russia lost practically all the territory that she had gained since Peter the Great. Soviet Russia became assiduously active in her efforts to recover Russia's lost territories. By using the old and tried imperial methods of military conquest, intervention, and diplomatic deals, she succeeded in reincorporating former territory and in annexing new lands. During the interwar period, Esthonia, Latvia, and Lithuania lost their independence and were incorporated into Soviet Russia. As a consequence of the Hitler-Stalin pact (1939), Poland underwent a fourth partition; her territory was divided between Germany and Russia. During and after the Second World War, Finland was compelled to cede to Russia the Karelian isthmus, strategic islands in the Gulf of Finland, and the strategic towns of Porkkala and Petsamo. Rumania was compelled to give back Bessarabia. Poland was restored in 1945, but not with her former boundaries; she was compelled to cede a large region to Russia.

Russia's recovery of former territory did not restore her pre-1914 boundaries. However, she managed, during and after the Second World War, to more than make up for it by acquiring territory that had never been under tsarist rule. In Europe, she acquired from the Allies the right to occupy half of East Prussia; from Rumania, she acquired northern Bukovina; and from Czechoslovakia, the sub-Carpathian region. Russia's gains in the Far East at the expense of Japan were strategically very important. She annexed the Kuril Islands and the southern half of the island of Sakhalin, and occupied the northern half of Korea. Under Russian pressure, Outer Mongolia seceded from China and became an "independent" republic.

Soviet imperialism curiously enough had a Marxist objective, namely, world revolution. By expanding its frontier, the fatherland of all Communists would become so powerful that no nation or combination of nations would dare to attack it. At the same time, Soviet Russia would threaten every noncommunist nation. Local Communists would no longer have to depend on their own efforts to seize power, but could depend on the ready support of the most powerful state in Europe. Especially effective would this support be in the states that were on or near the Russian borders. Nearly all of these states had been liberated from the Germans by the Red army, which then became an army of occupation. Though the local Communist parties attracted little popular support, they were aided, openly and secretly, by the Red army. And the menacing shadow of their powerful neighbor was always present to remind the small nations in east central Europe of their precarious situation.

Conditions in Europe and in Asia, after the Second World War, favored Soviet Russia's expansionist aims. Germany and Austria-Hungary, long the great bulwarks against Russian expansion toward the West, had disappeared. Britain, the great opponent of Russia in the Balkans, was seriously weakened. Asia was now out of European control. But the independent national states that arose on the ruins of colonial imperialism were in a condition of instability and uncertainty. Ravaged by war and deprived of colonial foods and raw materials, the European nations were in a condition bordering on chaos. The capitalists had neither the means nor the will to undertake the great task of rehabilitation. The cost of living was rising rapidly, far more rapidly than wages. Workers in all trades were bitterly discontented, and gave ready ear to revolutionary appeals. Inflation and the black market demoralized buying and selling, and many businessmen were ruined. The economic fabric of Europe was dissolving, and seemed to bear out Marx's prophecy of the final ruin of capitalism.

Soviet Russia quickly took advantage of this chaotic situation. She embarked on policies of westward and eastward expansion, which were pursued with skill, determination, and persistence. The tactics followed the pattern of "cold revolution," according to which the government of a neighboring country would be overthrown by the local Communists without resorting to a popular uprising. An essential part of these tactics was the method of taking over "one by one," made familiar by the Nazis in their conquest of east central Europe.

The cold revolution was carried through according to a set pattern. Under the leadership of the local Communists a Popular Front was organized, which included some noncommunists. This combination aimed to get into power without using the democratic process of free elections. Stalin frankly admitted that a "freely elected government in any of these countries would be anti-Soviet, and that we cannot allow." Elections were then called, and by using terrorism, pressure, and even intervention by the occupying Red army a Popular Front majority would be elected to the national assembly. A ministry was then formed, representing the various elements composing the Popular Front, but the key positions, those departments in control of the army, the police, and communications, were given to the Communists. Promptly the Communist ministers filled the positions under them with their followers, and used the powers of the government to forward communist objectives. Those in the assembly who opposed the ministry were denounced as "traitors" and "fascists." Their activities were seriously hampered, and their leaders were imprisoned or executed on trumped-up charges.

The next step of the Communists was to eliminate their allies from the ministry. At the proper time a "crisis" was created through Communist-led strikes and organized mob demonstrations. The menacing attitude of the Red army, inside or near the border, aggravated the crisis. As a consequence, the noncommunist ministers fled for their lives; those who did not were imprisoned or executed. The government was now completely in the hands of the Communists and their close allies, the left-wing Socialists.

Then came the third and final step of the "cold revolution." New elections were held in which only one list of candidates appeared consisting of Communists and left-wing Socialists. The electors could vote only for this one list. The outcome of these "elections" was a foregone conclusion. It was followed by savage suppression of all opponents of the government and by wholesale confiscation of the property of capitalists and of landlords. Even the left-wing Socialists were eliminated as a separate group by being forced to "unite" with the Communists. When everything was fairly secure, the all-Communist government entered into close political, economic, and diplomatic relations with Soviet Russia.

The Communist method of cold revolution was first tried in Yugoslavia. After liberation from the Germans, in 1945, the various steps, outlined above, were followed by the Communists, headed by Joseph Brosz, popularly known as "Tito." A constitutional assembly dethroned Peter II, proclaimed a republic, and adopted a constitution modeled on that of Soviet Russia. Tito became the dictator of Yugoslavia, now completely controlled by the Communists. The next country to fall under Communist control was Albania. The Communists, led by Enver Hoxha, organized a Popular Front and won control of the national assembly, "elected" in 1945. This body proclaimed Albania a republic; in fact, it became a dictatorship under Hoxha. The next was Bulgaria. In 1946 a plebiscite resulted in the creation of a republic and the ousting of King Simeon II. As in the cases of Yugoslavia and Albania, the Communists, led by George Dimitrov, got control of the government, which was then organized as a dictatorship.

The next was Poland. After the war Poland was once again resurrected, and with new and enlarged boundaries. But her strategic position in reference to Russia remained the same: she was the gateway between Russia and Western Europe. The Yalta agreement of 1945, entered into by Stalin, Roosevelt, and

Churchill, explicitly stated that a government of Poland was
to come into existence as a result of "free and unfettered elections" in which "all democratic and anti-Nazi parties" were to
take part. Especially in Poland, traditionally hostile to Russia,
was Communist control all-important. Therefore Russia exerted
every influence in favor of the Polish Communists and their
allies, the left-wing Socialists. A provisional government was organized representing a coalition of parties, called the National
Union, which was, however, dominated by Communists. Elections in 1947 for a national assembly were anything but "free
and unfettered." Every form of pressure and of terrorism was
used by the Communists, who were aided openly by the Russian
army of occupation. As a consequence, the assembly contained
an overwhelming majority of Communists and their allies. The
noncommunists in the National Union were expelled; their
leader, Mikolajczyk, fled for his life to America. In 1948 the
Communists compelled their Socialist allies to "unite" with
them to establish one party.

The next was Hungary. After the war a republic was proclaimed, and elections were held in 1945 for a national assembly.
These elections were free, and the result was an overwhelming
success for the noncommunist parties. A ministry was formed,
representing the leading parties, headed by Ferenc Nagy, leader
of the Smallholders party. In this ministry, Communists were,
however, given key positions, because of the pressure exercised
by the Russian army of occupation. As elsewhere under similar
circumstances, the Communists laid plans to overthrow the government of which they were part. In 1947 the familiar "crisis"
was created by the "discovery" of a plot to overthrow the republic. The Communists, led by Mathias Rakosi, ousted their associates and seized control of the government. Noncommunist
leaders were imprisoned or executed on trumped-up charges of
treason. New "elections" returned a majority in favor of the

Communist party, which was now in full control of the government.

The next was Rumania. Elections, held in 1946, resulted in a victory for the Popular Front, headed by Peter Groza. Then followed the various steps in the elimination of noncommunists from the government. When that was accomplished, "elections" took place for a national assembly that resulted in a Communist victory. King Michael was exiled, and Rumania was proclaimed a republic.

The next was Czechoslovakia. From its very birth, in 1919, Czechoslovakia was an unwavering good neighbor and loyal friend of Soviet Russia. But this did not save her from being steam-rolled into a dictatorship like the others. In 1946 fairly free elections were held, which resulted in a noncommunist majority, but with considerable support for the Communist party. The ministry consisted of representatives of the various parties, but key positions were given to Communists. President Eduard Benes, however, was not a Communist, nor was the Foreign Minister, Jan Masaryk, son of Thomas Masaryk, father of the republic. Czechoslovakia stoutly sought to maintain her democratic liberties and her national independence. Before long, however, the familiar Communist pattern of pressure, coercion, and terrorism made its appearance. In 1948 the Communist Premier, Klement Gottwald, denounced his noncommunist associates in the ministry as "traitors." The police "discovered" a "fascist plot" against the republic. The unions called strikes. Threatening demonstrations took place in Prague. The opposition leaders fled or were arrested, and the ministry came under full control of the Communists. As a dramatic protest against the suppression of democracy, Masaryk committed suicide. The Communist seizure of Czechoslovakia caused world-wide indignation and anxiety. Czechoslovakia had been the only truly democratic country in east central Europe, and had adhered to the ideals of the Western democracies, especially to those of America.

Communist influence reached out to that other historic field of Russian expansion, namely, the Far East. Two powerful appeals could be made by Soviet Russia in that region: nationalism, in opposition to Western imperialism; and socialism, in opposition to foreign capitalism and to native landlordism. Lenin had long before realized the possibility of directing native nationalism into socialist channels, and had formulated policies designed to call into existence an anti-imperialist, anticapitalist Asia as an ally of Soviet Russia in her bid for world revolution.

Stalin faithfully followed Lenin's policy. The Communist party of China, in opposition to the Nationalist government of Chiang Kai-shek, received Russian support, directly and indirectly. Chinese Communists, trained in Moscow, assumed the leadership of their party. The great opportunity came with the defeat of Japan in the Second World War. A power vacuum now existed in the Far East, as it had in east central Europe after the defeat of Germany. Soviet Russia promptly sought to fill this vacuum, as it had the other, in Europe. In the struggle between the Communists and Nationalists for the control of Manchuria, the richest province of China, the former were successful because they were aided by the Russians, who gave them the arms captured from the Japanese. The civil war now increased in intensity, with the Communist armies constantly gaining. Great alarm was felt in the democracies at the prospect of the most populous nation of the world falling under Communist control. But only America had the power to aid the Nationalists, which she did, though intermittently and indecisively. In 1949, the Communists scored a great triumph over the Nationalists, and entered Nanking, the capital of China. Most of the country was overrun and, later in the year, a Communist-controlled government was established in China, headed by Mao Tse-tung. Because of the importance of China, the Communist triumph gave immense prestige to Soviet Russia in Asia, and aroused great fear everywhere in the world.

THE PEOPLE'S DEMOCRACIES

The system of government established in the new Communist states in east central Europe and in the Far East became known as a "people's democracy." It was not democracy in the Western sense or a totalitarian dictatorship in the Russian sense. A "people's democracy" may be described as a halfway house in the direction of complete sovietization. Its government was based on the principle of the "dictatorship of the proletariat though not in the soviet form." As all but a small percentage of the citizens in a "people's democracy" were opposed to the Communists, it was essential for the latter to disguise their control. The country was, therefore, nominally ruled by a coalition, actually by the Communist party. Front organizations were utilized in many fields to veil the fact of Communist dictatorship. In order to win popular adherence to the new regime, all means of communication—schools, journals, books, theaters, radio, and motion pictures—were continually and fervently engaged in spreading Communist doctrines. As in Soviet Russia, the strong, who might become an opposition, were eliminated through death, prison, or exile; and the weak were indoctrinated through propaganda and cowed by intimidation.

Only one barrier to complete Communist control remained: the Roman Catholic church. In Catholic Poland, Hungary, and Czechoslovakia a bitter feud raged between church and state. The governments in these countries were willing to permit religious worship—for a time—but on condition that they were given control of the church organization. But Roman Catholics recognized the pope, and none other, as the head of their church; hence the Catholic hierarchy refused to submit to the demand

of the Communist governments. In this they were supported
by Pope Pius XII and by the entire Catholic world. The outcome has been a policy of unrelenting persecution of the church
by the Communist governments. World-wide attention was directed to two famous cases. During 1948–1949, Cardinal
Mindszenty of Hungary and Archbishop Joseph Beran of
Czechoslovakia were imprisoned on trumped-up charges of
treason. The struggle for survival by the Catholic church against
the Communist governments was, in essence, a struggle for religious freedom.

What about the economic system in a "people's democracy"?
All heavy industry and all banking were confiscated and nationalized outright. All estates of the landowners and of the
church were confiscated; part was given to the peasants, and
part, nationalized. Peasant proprietorship and small business
were permitted to continue, though with many restrictions.
However, the Communists were convinced that as long as small
property owners continued to exist, the dictatorship was not
safe. But they feared to follow Soviet Russia's policy of wholesale and immediate liquidation of the small proprietors. There
were too many of these in the "people's democracies." Therefore the Communists resorted to the gradual collectivization
of farms, preferring intimidation to outright force. The small
businessmen have been gradually squeezed out by all sorts of
restrictions on their activities. The final objective of a "people's
democracy" is to establish a totalitarian dictatorship on the model
of that of Soviet Russia.

What is the relation of a "people's democracy" to Soviet
Russia? It is that of a "satellite" following the model established
by Nazi Germany.[3] Behind the government of each satellite
are Russian representatives whose "advice" on all matters, national and international, must be followed. Russian officers are
given the power to coordinate the army of a satellite with that

[3] See p. 277.

of Soviet Russia. Especially important are the economic relations between the latter and her satellites. In order to develop economic cooperation among the countries of the "people's democracies" and the Soviet Union, new economic ties were created. These ties subordinated the economic life of the satellites to that of Soviet Russia. Commerce and industry were controlled and regulated chiefly by Russians. Financial privileges in the satellites were gained by the Russians through the stratagem of seizing German assets in these countries. On the basis of these assets, Soviet Russia, without investing any money, was given half interest in industrial corporations called "mixed companies," the profits of which were shared equally between Soviet Russia and the satellite. Commerce between them was regulated by a treaty dictated by the Russians. The satellite was compelled to send most of its exports to Soviet Russia, at prices fixed by the latter. These prices were lower than world prices, whereas the satellite was compelled to import certain Russian goods at higher than world prices. In order to maintain this system of exploitation, Soviet Russia forced her satellites to restrict their trade with the West. The satellite system was integrated politically as well as economically. In 1947, the Communist Information Bureau, popularly known as the "Cominform," was organized, representing chiefly Soviet Russia and her satellites. Its main function has been to support Russian policies and objectives in east central Europe. These methods created a powerful Eastern bloc, unified economically and politically, and dominated by Soviet Russia.

The division between the Eastern bloc and the democratic West was sharply emphasized by what Winston Churchill aptly called the "iron curtain." It was erected by Soviet Russia to isolate the Communist world, lest it be contaminated by democratic influences. Communication and travel, other than official, between the iron curtain countries and other lands were severely restricted. This secrecy and aloofness have prevented the peoples

in the West from peering behind, and the peoples in the East
from peering in front of, the iron curtain. The Communist
governments did not wish their peoples, whose standard of
living was desperately low, to learn of the superior living
standard in the West. Neither did they wish the ideas of democratic freedom to circulate among their peoples, who suffered
from the tyranny of totalitarian dictatorship.

CHECKS TO RUSSIAN EXPANSION

Soviet imperialism, despite its many successes, has failed to
achieve full control of east central Europe. Finland, Austria,
Greece, and Turkey have managed to remain free. Because of
the strategic importance of these lands, Soviet Russia has made
every effort to bring them within her orbit, thus far without
success. The pattern of the cold revolution, through the agency
of local Communists, has failed to achieve its purpose, in each
case for special reasons. Let it be kept in mind that its success
in the other countries has been due in no small measure to
the fear that, unless the local Communists were permitted to
come into power, the Red army itself would "take over."

In the case of Finland, Soviet Russia had to watch her step.
Finland might show vigorous opposition, as in 1939, when that
little nation boldly fought against mighty Russia. After the
Second World War, the Finnish Communist party made ready
to seize power by the well-known methods of the cold revolution. In this instance, the government was determined to oppose them vigorously, even at the risk of invasion by the Red
army. Elections, held in 1945, resulted in a large noncommunist
majority. Because of Russia's insistence, Communists were included in the ministry, but their activities were closely watched.
As Finland's position on the Baltic was important strategically,
Soviet Russia sought to influence her foreign policy, even at a

distance. In 1948, she compelled Finland to sign a treaty which declared that in "the event of the existence of a threat of military attack" Finland would "consult" with Soviet Russia. Despite this concession, Finland did not become a satellite.

Only Austria was left of the formerly free nations in Central Europe. As it was occupied by Britain, America, France, and Soviet Russia, that country could not be "taken over" by the local Communists without danger of a general war. Another method had to be tried. In every way possible the Russians sought to impoverish and to weaken Austria, to force out the other occupying powers, and to bolster the Austrian Communist party, but all without avail. Consequently, they adopted a policy of waiting patiently and watching constantly for the opportune moment when they could strike safely. Austria thus far has remained outside of Soviet Russia's sphere of influence.

As in past centuries, the Balkans now occupied the center of the Russian field of expansion. Control of this region would satisfy Russia's historic quest for ice-free ports on the shores of the blue, warm waters of the Mediterranean. At the same time, Communist hegemony in the Balkans would give a great impetus to the progress of world revolution. Italy could then be outflanked and might succumb to a coup staged by the local Communists, aided by the menacing shadow of a Red army, ready to embark for Italian shores. In full control of Central Europe, of the Balkans, and of Italy, Soviet Russia would be in a position to execute a gigantic pincer movement against Western Europe. In such a situation there might not even be the necessity of an attack; the Western nations would collapse with fear and fall into the waiting arms of the local Communists.

Highly important strategically in this design were Greece and Turkey. Whatever great power controlled the former controlled the eastern Mediterranean. Even more important was Turkey because of the Straits, the only entrance to and the only exit from Soviet Russia in the Mediterranean. For centuries,

Russia had sought to gain control of the Straits in order to prevent the warships of the Western powers from reaching her shores in time of war. Once Greece and Turkey were controlled by local Communists, the Straits would be open to Soviet Russia and closed to the Western powers. The former would in that case be safe from invasion by sea and at the same time be free to invade the Mediterranean lands.

How to get control of Turkey and Greece? That was the question for Russia. Turkey had been neutral during the war, and consequently had no problem of reconstruction. Her government was a military dictatorship, which suppressed all Communist activities; hence there was no native fifth column in Turkey. The situation was different in Greece, which had been frightfully devastated by the Germans. The acute problem of reconstruction created sharp divisions among the people. A fairly large and active Communist party made several desperate efforts to seize power. They were foiled, largely through the efforts of a British army which remained after the Germans had been driven out. In 1946, King George II was recalled from exile as a result of a plebiscite. Elections to parliament gave the monarchist parties an overwhelming majority. Dread of the Communists, not love of the King, was chiefly responsible for these expressions of popular opinion. The Communists refused to accept the verdict of the polls and rose in rebellion. Civil war raged in Greece. Communist guerilla bands operated chiefly in the mountainous north, where they attacked towns causing the inhabitants to flee for their lives.

A new technique of aggression was adopted by Soviet Russia to get control of Turkey and Greece. It was to exhaust these states economically by compelling them to make large and continuous military outlays. An impoverished people would then compel a bankrupt government to make terms with Soviet Russia. As no Communist party existed in Turkey, the method of "cold revolution" gave way to one of threatening demands.

The Russian government demanded of Turkey the right to erect fortifications in the region of the Dardanelles. Fully realizing that Russian fortresses on the Dardanelles would reduce her to the position of a satellite, Turkey resolutely refused the Russian demands. Because of repeated threats, Turkey was compelled to keep her armies constantly mobilized, a costly process that drained the resources of that poor country.

In Greece, since the cold revolution had failed, the method of a "hot" revolution was tried. This method depended for its success on keeping up the activities of the Communist guerillas. The satellites—Albania, Yugoslavia, and Bulgaria—gave every aid to the guerillas in their struggle against the Greek forces. Behind the former was Soviet Russia doing her utmost to prevent action by the United Nations to stop the civil war. At one time the situation in Greece became serious, even critical, for the government. Thousands of refugees from the towns, captured or destroyed by the guerillas, had to be supported. Armies had to be kept in the field. The scanty resources of impoverished Greece were being strained to the point of bankruptcy. It was fully expected by the Communists that, out of sheer necessity, the government would agree to "collaborate" with them. Then would follow a Communist dictatorship, as inevitably as in other Balkan states.

It became all too clear that once Turkey and Greece were reduced to the position of satellites Soviet Russia would be well on the way toward realizing the old dream of tsarist expansion and the new dream of world revolution. Already the strongest land power in the world, control of the Mediterranean would give Soviet Russia easy access to southern Europe, northern Africa, and western Asia. The historic opponent of Russian aggression in the Balkans, Britain, was now too weak to undertake the task of containing the Russians, as she had done so often in the past.

Like a "knight in shining armor" America suddenly appeared

on the scene. On March 12, 1947, President Truman delivered an address to Congress that resounded throughout the world. The President formulated what has become known as the "Truman Doctrine," which is destined to become as famous in history as the Monroe Doctrine. He stressed the urgency of American aid to Turkey and Greece, especially to the latter, where "a militant minority, exploiting human want and misery" made impossible the economic recovery of the country. "One of the primary objectives of the foreign policy of the United States," he declared, "is the creation of conditions in which we and other nations will be able to work out a way of life free from coercion." Totalitarian regimes, "imposed on free peoples by direct or indirect aggression, undermine the foundations of international peace and hence the security of the United States." America stood ready, he declared, to support free peoples everywhere who desired "to work out their own destinies in their own way" in "resisting attempted subjugation by armed minorities or by outside pressure."

President Truman requested the Congress to appropriate funds for aid to Greece and Turkey. Promptly and overwhelmingly the Congress endorsed the Truman Doctrine, and implemented it by making generous appropriations. The New World now appeared to redress the balance of the Old. American military and civil missions were sent to advise the Greek and Turkish governments and to direct the expenditure of the money appropriated by the Congress. Help from America enabled Turkey to resist Russian pressure more effectively. Even more decisive was American help to Greece. Slowly but surely the guerillas were driven out of their strongholds in the mountains of northern Greece. By 1950 the civil war had virtually ended with the triumph of the Greek government.

Another check suffered by Soviet Russia in her plan to subjugate east central Europe was the secession of Yugoslavia from the Eastern bloc. In 1948 the Communist dictator, Tito, refused to follow the dictates of Moscow and proclaimed Yugoslavia's intention to pursue her own national policies. What had brought about this rift was the system of economic exploitation imposed by Soviet Russia on her satellites. Yugoslavia refused to assume the humble economic part assigned to her. Furthermore, Moscow insisted that Tito's government speed up the collectivization of farms. As there were many peasant proprietors in Yugoslavia, the government refused to obey, fearing that a peasant uprising would follow too rapid collectivization. Tito's defiance of Moscow produced a serious crack in the monolithic bloc of communist states.

The defection of Tito caused consternation among Communists everywhere, especially in Soviet Russia. Titoism now rose to challenge Stalinism in the Communist world. Influential Communists in the satellite states, where nationalism was a powerful sentiment, made efforts to emulate Tito's example. But these efforts were sternly repressed by the governments at the command of Moscow. Yugoslavia's bold move had succeeded because, unlike the other satellites, she had neither a Russian army of occupation nor a common frontier with Soviet Russia.

Tito's defiance of Moscow resulted in an economic boycott of Yugoslavia by Soviet Russia and her satellites. Fearing ruin, Tito turned to the West for help. America and Britain realized the great importance of an independent, though Communist, Yugoslavia in the cold war between East and West. They gave generous economic aid to Yugoslavia, which more than balanced the losses suffered by the latter as a result of the economic boycott.

Yugoslavia's secession from the Eastern bloc made another serious puncture in the line separating the iron curtain countries from the West. This line, which runs from Murmansk on the

Arctic to Trieste on the Adriatic, contains important "holes" consisting of countries hostile to Soviet Russia. These "holes" are Finland in the north, Austria in the center, and Yugoslavia, Greece, and Turkey in the south. In case of a war between East and West, these countries would prove to be a serious military weakness for the former and a great military advantage for the latter. It may be fully expected, therefore, that Soviet Russia will make every effort to fill up these "holes."

DEFEAT OF COMMUNISM IN WESTERN EUROPE

Despite the defeat of Soviet Russia in Austria, Turkey, and Greece, and despite Titoism, communism has made notable gains. A new bid for world revolution by Soviet Russia would have at the outset the support of her satellites. But world revolution could not be achieved without the aid of a communist Western Europe; therefore it became imperative to gain control of the countries in this highly important region. Chaotic conditions and widespread discontent offered a favorable opportunity for communist penetration in Western Europe. But a new strategy had to be devised, one in harmony with the democratic traditions and the long-established parliamentary institutions of the nations in the West. How could the Communists make use of constitutional methods to establish a totalitarian dictatorship?

The new strategy, devised by the Communists, sought to utilize democratic techniques in order to win popular support. Violence and dictatorship were temporarily repudiated and Communist parties entered the political arena as constitutional groups advocating advanced programs of social reform. As they did not expect to win a majority by themselves, the Communists made every effort to ally themselves with the Socialists. Together they had every hope of winning control of parliament.

What would follow after such a victory was best known only to the Communists.

Elections in nearly all of the countries in Western Europe showed a marked drift to the parties on the left, especially to the Socialists and Communists. The parties on the right and the propertied classes supporting them were discredited because, in general, they had collaborated with the Germans during the occupation. Socialists and Communists, who had led in the resistance movement, now appealed to patriotism as well as to the need for radical reform. As a consequence conservative and reactionary parties were almost wiped out. So marked was the drift to the left that radical parties, other than the Socialists and the Communists, were organized, notably the Mouvement Républicain Populaire (MRP) in France and the Christian Democrats in Italy.

Labor now ruled most of Western Europe. Its greatest triumph came in Britain, in 1945, when the Labor party took office supported by a large majority in Parliament. In 1946 the French elections took place for the first legislature of the Fourth Republic. Out of a total of 574 seats the Communists won 163; the MRP, 160; and the Socialists, 93. A ministry, representing chiefly these three leading parties, was formed. In the Italian elections for the Constituent Assembly, in 1946, the Christian Democrats, Socialists, and Communists together won about three-quarters of all the seats. A ministry was formed representing these parties.

Though political allies in France and in Italy the Communists and the Socialists were bitter rivals for the control of the trade-unions, the prime source of their electoral support. In Britain the socialist Laborites had all but complete control of the Trades Union Congress, the national organization of the trade-unions; hence the Communists played an insignificant role. It was quite otherwise in France and Italy, where the General Confederation of Labor in each country was dominated by Communists. In their hands lay the power to paralyze the country by a general strike of all organized labor, in case a "revolutionary situation" suddenly appeared.

The great question now was: Would Communist strategy succeed in France and in Italy? If so, the fate of democracy on the Continent would be doomed. It was almost certain that once the governments of these countries fell under the control of the allied Socialists and Communists, the former would be eliminated by the latter as ruthlessly as in east central Europe. Communist control of Italy would bisect the Mediterranean and prevent the Western powers from coming to the aid of Turkey and Greece, in case these nations were attacked by Soviet Russia. Communist control of France, the most important of the Western powers on the Continent, would mark a decisive step toward a Communist Europe. Moreover, a Communist France would have serious implications for the security of America. French Guiana and Martinique would then constitute a serious threat to the Panama Canal. The French African port of Dakar, about 2,000 miles from Brazil, would then become a basis for Communist moves against South America. As a consequence, America became vitally interested in the politics of Italy and France.

The success of Communist tactics in Western Europe depended, to a large degree, on the attitude of the Socialists. Curious as it would have seemed prior to 1914, the Socialists were now considered in Europe to be the strongest bulwark against social revolution; they were committed wholeheartedly to the democratic process. Because of their opposition to dictatorship and their fear and distrust of the Communists the French Socialist party, in 1947, broke relations with the former. A new ministry was formed, from which the Communists were excluded. Though the largest party the Communists were now isolated, as the ministry was supported by all the other parties.

Infuriated at the failure of their strategy, the Communists

threw aside their constitutional mask. During 1947–1948 they sought to undermine the Fourth Republic by all methods and in all ways. In parliament, they endeavored to hamstring the government by obstruction, delays, and filibustering. Outside of parliament, the Communists aimed to paralyze the country economically in order to bring about general chaos as a prelude to a general uprising. Through their control of the General Confederation of Labor (CGT) the Communists organized a continuous series of strikes, now in one industry, now in another, accompanied by sabotage and organized rioting. These "chain" strikes were to culminate in a general strike of all labor in France. Then a "revolutionary situation" would arise.

The government was determined to meet the Communist threat with all the resources at its command. It promptly and firmly suppressed all disorders, and assured protection to those workers who refused to follow the strike orders of their Communist leaders. A large number of trade-unionists, resenting political strikes, seceded from the CGT, and formed another labor federation, the *Force ouvrière,* led by Léon Jouhaux, the former head of the CGT. The attempt of the Communists to seize power in France ended in a fiasco.

The next test of the Communist strategy took place in Italy. In 1947 the three-party ministry of Christian Democrats, Socialists, and Communists came to an end; a new ministry was formed, headed by Alcide de Gasperi, leader of the Christian Democrats. As in France, the Communists were excluded. A republic had been established by the constitution in 1947, and elections took place for the first parliament of the new regime. What political parties would emerge triumphant from these elections became the all-absorbing question before the Italian people.

Even more than in France did the situation in Italy favor the Communists. A majority of the Socialists, the left-wing group, combined with the Communists to form a Popular Front to contest the elections. The Communist party, led by Palmiro Togliatti, endeavored to mollify the fears of the electorate by making astonishing concessions to conservative opinion. In the Constituent Assembly they had voted for the inclusion of the Lateran pacts of 1929, negotiated by Mussolini and the pope, that gave special privileges to the Catholic church. They appealed for the support of the landless peasants in the south by promising to divide the large estates into peasant properties. To quiet the fears of confiscation, the Communists assured the small shopkeepers that they would respect property rights. To the workers they promised to end inflation and to give security of employment at higher wages. Along with protestations of loyal adherence to constitutional methods went a half-concealed terrorism, with threats of a general strike and violent uprisings in case the Popular Front did not get a majority at the polls.

The eyes of the world turned toward Italy during the elections of 1948. Never in modern times did national elections have such profound international significance. If the Popular Front succeeded in winning a majority, or even a near majority, Communist strategy would achieve its first success in a free election. The Western democracies awaited the outcome in Italy. It soon became evident that the vital issue in the Italian elections was that of preserving Western democracy as opposed to Eastern totalitarianism. So great was the interest in the outcome that over 90 per cent of the electorate went to the polls. The result was a victory for democracy that resounded throughout the world. The anticommunist parties received 69.3 per cent of the popular vote, and elected 392 out of the 574 members of the Chamber. For the first time in the history of United Italy, one party, the Christian Democrats, commanded a majority in Parliament. The Popular Front suffered a marked decline from the electoral strength shown by the Communists and Socialists in the elections of 1946. Poverty stricken, wracked by war, humiliated by defeat, with millions of unemployed, and their economy shattered, the Italian people yet chose the democratic way of life. Communism suffered its greatest setback in the Italian elections of 1948.

THE "COLD WAR" BETWEEN EAST AND WEST

The defeat of communism in Western Europe constituted a serious setback to the plans of Soviet Russia. Serious as it was it was only a setback; she would not—could not—give up her over-all objective of establishing a communist world order. Communism, unlike other ideologies, looks not to the past as a source of inspiration; it repudiates national traditions as fetters on its revolutionary activity. It feels uneasy in the present, knowing full well that it has not the confidence of the people, who submit unwillingly. Therefore all the fanatical energy of the Communists is directed toward the creation of a future in which they can function safely and easily. But this future must be one for all mankind; otherwise communism will continue to live dangerously, always alert for enemies that seek to encompass its ruin. As no opposition party is permitted within a communist state, no opposition nation must be permitted in a communist world. The spirit of fanaticism had passed from the body religious of Orthodox Russia to the body politic of Communist Russia.

The first bid for world revolution, in the period of the Comintern, had failed; and the party "line" had changed to Stalin's policy of "socialism in one country." It was bound to change again when the situation in the world seemed favorable to world revolution. It did change after the Second World War, when chaotic conditions in the world offered renewed opportunities to communism. The new strategy, cold revolution, resulted in a great enhancement of the power of Soviet Russia.

She was now the dominant power in Europe, protected by a belt of satellite states, constituting a *cordon sanitaire* safeguarding her from invasion by the West, and giving her a springboard from which to launch an attack on the West. Within a generation, the Soviet empire had grown to one-fifth of the world's area, extending from central Germany to the Pacific. As she grew in power, the harder became Soviet Russia's determination to make another bid for world revolution.

But how? The old method of fomenting uprisings followed by the Third International had failed. The new method of collaborating with the Socialists to get control of the parliaments in Western Europe had likewise failed. What method had succeeded, at least, in part? That followed by the cold revolution in east central Europe. Why not apply this method on a world-wide scale!

Soviet Russia's new bid for world revolution led to a strange conflict, known as the "cold war." As planned by the Russians, the cold war was to be conducted on the pattern of the cold revolution, but on an international scale. The antagonists in this "war," which still goes on, have been the communist nations, led by Soviet Russia, and the Western democracies, led by America.

The basic strategy, pursued by the Russians, was economic rather than military. They were convinced that, as Marx had foretold, the contradictions inherent in the capitalist system would inevitably bring depressions on a world-wide scale. Another depression, as great as that in 1929, was surely coming. It would begin, they asserted, in America and would spread ruin throughout the world. Popular demands in America for retrenchment would result in stopping aid to her allies in Western Europe, and without American aid these countries would be ruined. The Communists everywhere were determined to speed up what they regarded as the inevitable by preventing economic recovery in Western Europe. In time, and that soon, would come a great depression. Popular discontent would then arise, and it would be organized and directed by the local Communists into revolutionary channels. The Red army would be mobilized. Weakened, divided, distraught, terrorized, the Western nations could then easily be "taken over" by the Communists. Soviet Russia's bid for world revolution would, in this way, succeed without a world war. This was the "peaceful" strategy of the cold war.

Battles in this unique struggle, on the diplomatic stage, took the form of acrimonious disagreements over policies to prevent the settlement of urgent postwar problems. These disagreements were deliberately created by the Russians, who entered into negotiations in order to aggravate, not to mitigate, tensions; to create, not to solve, problems; and, especially, to spread propaganda for communism. Soviet Russia was determined that there be neither war nor peace in the world, but the chaos of constant and continuing indecision. She steadfastly refused to agree to the calling of a peace conference that would finally and definitely end the Second World War. She refused to join America, Britain, and France in a four-power pact to keep Germany disarmed. She paralyzed the United Nations by her frequent and irresponsible use of the veto.[4] Almost every move of Soviet Russia was calculated to create international chaos.

Creation of economic chaos within the Western nations was the other stratagem used by Soviet Russia in this war of nerves. With Western Europe flat on its economic back would come the hoped-for opportunity to seize power. In carrying out this stratagem, Soviet Russia had the powerful aid of the local Communists and their fellow travelers. Strikes and sabotage promoted by Communist-led trade-unions slowed down production, so essential to recovery. This policy of attrition was furthered by Russian threats of aggression, now in one part of the world, now in another, which forced the nations to divert

[4] See p. 398.

much of their all-too-limited resources to military purposes. Chaos and misery became instruments of Russian policy.

America intervened in the cold war as she had intervened in the two world wars—and for the same reason. The menacing shadow of dictatorship now hovered over every democratic land. Western Europe had to be put on its feet economically in order to become strong enough to resist Russian aggression. It could not do so without American aid—hence the famous Marshall Plan.[5] Originally the Plan was launched with the object of aiding every country in Europe to recover from the ravages of war. But Soviet Russia and her satellites refused to accept the Plan. On the contrary they denounced it as a blind for American "imperialism" plotting to "enslave" Europe. The Marshall Plan became the leading issue in the conflict between Soviet Russia and America.

Propaganda was used effectively in the cold war. Russian journals and radio kept up a continuous barrage of denunciations of America as a degenerate, bourgeois democracy, the center of capitalist reaction against the revolutionary working class. In reporting news from America, Russian propaganda exaggerated every evil and belittled every good in American life. It made light of the American and British contributions to the defeat of Germany; the chief credit was given to the Red army. In order to counter Russian propaganda, America established the "Voice of America," a radio broadcast, which regularly gave news, described American conditions, and explained American policies to the Eastern nations.

A dramatic incident, the Berlin blockade, highlighted the cold war in 1949. After the Second World War, Berlin had been divided into four sectors of occupation: Russian, American, British, and French. The Russians were eager to get full control of the city in order to have the prestige of being the sole power in the former capital of Germany. How could they force the

[5] See pp. 377–378.

Western powers out of Berlin without resorting to war? They resolved to use the pressure of starving the inhabitants of the Western sectors. In 1948, the Russians closed all rail, road, and water communication between the Western sectors and the rest of Germany. Over two million people faced starvation as a consequence of this blockade. To prevent such a calamity, America and Britain organized an "airlift" to supply food, fuel, and other necessities to the beleaguered Berliners. The airlift, though costly, proved to be remarkably successful, much to the chagrin of the Russians. After a siege of 328 days, the blockade of Berlin was abandoned by the Russians. The "battle" of Berlin resulted in the decisive defeat of Soviet Russia.

So bitter was the cold war that, at times, it threatened to become a "hot" one. Soviet Russia constantly made aggressive moves, now in Turkey, now in Germany, now in Iran, now in Korea. And each aggression created a crisis. A Russian army, estimated at five million and strengthened still more by the armies of the satellites, awaited the word of command. It became known that Soviet Russia possessed a large and efficient submarine fleet and a great air armada. On September 23, 1949, a reliable report made known that an atomic explosion had occurred somewhere in the Soviet Union. America no longer had a monopoly of the atomic bomb. In a dictatorship, war or peace hangs on the decision of one man. It was Mussolini who threw Italy into war against France. It was Hitler who threw Germany into a war against Russia. It was Stalin who threw Russia into a war against Japan. What if Stalin was to launch the Red army against Western Europe! There existed no force capable of checking its march to the Atlantic. A large nation like France would be just as impotent before the Red army as a small nation like Belgium. Even the combined forces of Western Europe would be no match against the Russians. Little faith remained in the power of the United Nations to maintain world peace; its effectiveness had been reduced by Russian vetoes. Some other ways had to be devised to defend the West against Russian aggression.

A new attitude toward Soviet Russia, one of deep distrust, became pronounced in the West. From bitter experience the Western statesmen had learned that it was futile to negotiate with the Russians. Their intransigeance, their unfaithfulness, and their inhumane callousness made a common settlement of any question impossible. The Americans especially revealed this changed attitude by adopting the Truman Doctrine. As the leader of the Western democracies, America was determined to oppose every move of Soviet Russia to extend her system of totalitarian dictatorship. In line with the Truman Doctrine came the Marshall Plan, the Rio de Janeiro Pact, the Western Union,[6] and the North Atlantic treaty, constituting an integrated Western policy that was inspired, formulated, and directed by America.

By far the most important regional defense system was created in 1949 by the North Atlantic treaty. It was accepted by 12 nations: the United States, Canada, Iceland, Britain, France, Belgium, the Netherlands, Luxemburg, Denmark, Norway, Italy, and Portugal. This famous pact established a new order in world diplomacy in that it was a military alliance, for the first time, of European and American states in time of peace. The treaty declared that the signatories were determined "to safeguard the freedom, common heritage and civilization of their peoples, founded on the principles of democracy, individual liberty and the rule of law." The parties agreed "to settle any international disputes in which they may be involved by peaceful means" and to refrain from using force "in any manner inconsistent with the purposes of the United Nations."

The most significant article in the treaty stated that "Parties agree that an armed attack against one or more of them in Europe or North America shall be considered an attack on all

[6] See pp. 401–403.

of them." In case of such an attack or threat of an attack, all agreed to consult on measures of defense. Each agreed to take "individually and in concert with the other Parties such action as it deems necessary, including the use of armed force, to restore and maintain the security of the North Atlantic area."

The treaty was in its every aspect a defensive alliance to establish a *Pax Atlantica*. It aimed to remove the haunting sense of insecurity felt by the Western nations as a result of the aggressive acts and threatening demands of Soviet Russia. The treaty made clear in advance the resolute determination of the West to confront a potential aggressor with the predominant power of a united front. It was universally believed that, had such a combination existed before 1939, Hitler would not have dared to plunge the world into war. Through sad experience the nations learned that dictators cannot be stopped by appeasement, or by agreements, or by international law, or by morality. Nothing but overwhelming force, ready in advance, will deter a dictator from aggression.

America played the leading part in launching the North Atlantic treaty. Now she was committed to the defense of Western Europe as a national policy. Despite all efforts of America to keep out of Europe's quarrels, she had been drawn into the two world wars, but always several years after hostilities had begun. Confidence in America's neutrality had merely served to encourage German aggression. Now she determined to make it perfectly clear that a Russian invasion of Western Europe would have to reckon with America from the very outset. Her military power, actual and potential, constituted the real force behind the North Atlantic treaty.

As might be expected, Soviet Russia and her satellites bitterly opposed the treaty. They denounced it as an aggressive move that was endangering the peace of the world. America especially was denounced as the chief "warmonger," whose aim was to make the world safe for "capitalism." Communists organized "peace" congresses in New York, Paris, and elsewhere and denounced the North Atlantic treaty as a violation of the Charter of the United Nations and as a threat to world security. But these denunciations received scant attention from any but Communists. Soviet Russia's acts had spoken louder than her words.

What has been the outcome of the cold war thus far? As neither victory nor defeat can be definitely ascertained in so strange a conflict, no answer is as yet possible. Meanwhile Western Europe, which the Russians wanted to divide, has united; its economy, which they wanted to destroy, has revived; and the Atlantic community, which they wanted to keep apart, has formed a military alliance. The appearance of Western and Eastern blocs has resulted in bisecting Europe into free and totalitarian groups of states. And the free West has to be constantly on guard against inroads from the totalitarian East. In Asia, communism has gripped China, an event of tremendous significance not only for that continent but for the entire world. Despite its setback in Europe, communism in 1950 could boast of many gains and few losses.

COMMUNISM VERSUS DEMOCRACY

Communism has become the universal issue. Never before in history have democratic ideals and methods been challenged so violently, so widely, in so many ways, and in so many aspects. Always and everywhere the Communists insist that economic security under a totalitarian dictatorship is an advance over individual liberty under democracy. They are deeply convinced that the system in Soviet Russia foreshadows all future progress. This conviction is based on the claim that communism has at last abolished class rule, by means of which all the evils of society have been perpetuated, and has established, for the first time in history, a classless society.

Class rule has been a well-known phenomenon in history. For centuries, in Europe and elsewhere, people had been ruled by "men of family," or aristocrats; and later by "men of money," or capitalists. With the advent of democracy, class rule was not entirely eliminated; men of wealth continued to have political power and social influence far beyond their numerical importance. A classless society was an ideal that democracy has been striving to realize.

Did Soviet Russia realize this democratic ideal by means of a totalitarian dictatorship? Far from it! The great innovation was not the abolition of class rule but the creation of a ruling *political* class, something unique in history. As all power is vested in the Communist party, the "men of the party" have become the rulers of the nation. It is true that the test of party membership is neither family nor wealth but devotion to party aims and loyalty to party leadership. But class rule of whatever kind, unlike democracy, inevitably develops the exclusiveness of an hereditary caste. In Soviet Russia, now for more than a generation under Communist rule, an hereditary ruling class is in the process of formation. Children of members of the Communist party find easy access to its privileged ranks. Secondary and higher education, once free, is now open only to those who can pay high fees. The military academies and schools to train civil officials are reserved, in great part, for the children of high officials.

Rule by a political class has had an unexpected effect on the social and economic order. The Communists in Russia came into power through a coup d'état, but they triumphed in the civil war that followed, because of the support they received from the workers and the peasants. The workers were promised "socialism," or the reign of economic equality, a new society which would give everyone a comfortable living and security against the economic hazards of life. What is the condition of the workers after a generation of the dictatorship of the proletariat? It is far worse than the condition of the workers in democratic England and France, not to say America. The Russian workers earn little and suffer great deprivation. It was estimated, in 1948, that the average worker in Russia has only one-tenth the living standard of the average worker in America. In Russia the average worker had to labor about 12 weeks in order to buy a wool suit, and in America only 1 week; in Russia almost 108½ hours in order to buy a pair of men's shoes, and in America only about 9½ hours; in Russia over an hour to buy a loaf of white bread, and in America only six minutes; in Russia over 2½ hours, to buy a dozen eggs, and in America only half an hour; in Russia over an hour to buy a quart of milk, and in America only 9 minutes.[7] In addition to his low standard of living, the Russian worker is subjected to all sorts of restrictions. He is obliged to have an industrial passport wherein his movements are recorded. He finds it very difficult to change his job, his place of employment, or his occupation. Under totalitarian dictatorship the worker has the choice either of subservient loyalty or starvation.

What is the condition of the Russian peasants? To win their support during the Revolution, the Communists had promised them more land, additional acres from the confiscated estates of the nobility and clergy. During the period of the New Economic Policy (1921–1928), when the cooperation of all elements in the country had still to be sought, a system of peasant proprietorship was established. At last, after so many years of struggle, the Russian peasant had realized his dream of being the proprietor of a goodly farm. But not for long! When the Five Year Plan succeeded the New Economic Policy, the peasants were obliged to give up their farms, their cattle, and their tools, and to join a "collective." The collectivization of Russian agriculture resulted in the greatest confiscation of peasant property in all modern history. Millions were deprived

[7] See *United States News,* Aug. 6, 1948.

of their holdings without compensation, and became, in theory, "owners" of the collective, in fact, state employees.

Rich and poor exist in Soviet Russia; they are called "categories," not classes. High government officials, managers of factories, professionals, especially scientists, writers, and entertainers, receive high salaries and live in comparative luxury. Their personal property, such as houses, furniture, clothes, automobiles, and savings are inherited by their children. But the great masses in town and country live in appalling poverty. Their economic security consists of steady and compulsory employment—at low wages and long hours.

Despite these unfulfilled promises in Russia, communism continues to menace democracy. And this menace comes from the fact that democratic nations have often failed to make good their profession of faith in equality. The "underprivileged," who exist in every democratic land, suffer from poverty, insecurity, neglect, and discrimination. The feeling of being disinherited in one's own fatherland and of having an inferior status under a democratic government now produces resentment that easily wells up into a repudiation of the existing order. Communists have shown remarkable astuteness in channeling resentments of all sorts into one revolutionary stream, which, they are convinced, will flood the entire world. The underprivileged constitute grist for the Communist mill. This was strikingly illustrated in the Italian elections of 1948. The Communists promised the landless peasants that, once in control of the government, they would confiscate the large estates and give farms to the peasants gratis. As already described the elections resulted in an overwhelming defeat for the Communists in the country generally. But they actually gained votes in many districts in the south by winning the support of conservative, religious peasants, many of whom hoped to become proprietors through a Communist victory.

Conservatives, as well as liberals, are now acutely aware of the necessity of government action to ameliorate the condition of the "most numerous and the most poor." As already described, the social democracy of the twentieth century [8] has raised the standard of living of the workers through higher wages and shorter hours; has guaranteed security through comprehensive social reforms; and has opened up opportunities for higher education to all, irrespective of class, race, or faith. Wherever it has been securely established, democracy has unfalteringly advanced, slowly, surely, and steadily, the progress of the nation without resorting to violence, to persecution, or to dictatorship. To win in the battle with communism, democracy must have a new vision of equality far wider and far deeper than in the past. "Equal rights to all and special privileges to none" will then become the generative principle of a new social order in which poverty and its attendant evils will have no place. Twentieth-century democracy is the best answer to the challenge of communism.

[8] See p. 103.

Chapter 10. America's Bid for World Security

TRIUMPH OF ENGLISH CULTURE IN NORTH AMERICA

America was the first child of Europe. The newly discovered world became the outpost of Western civilization as a consequence of the expansion of Europe that began in the sixteenth century. A great migration of European peoples flowed to the Americas, the world significance of which did not become fully apparent until the twentieth century. For almost three centuries after 1492, the chief importance of the New World lay in the fact that its territories constituted a stake in the game of European power politics. Whatever civilization existed in the New World was merely an echo—and a faint one—of that in Europe.

A change came with the American Revolution and the appearance of the United States. A new nation had arisen in the New World, Western in civilization and English in culture. Though small, weak, and far away, the United States made a decided impact on the Old World. From across the Atlantic Europe now heard the notes of its own civilization but arranged in a new song and pitched in a different key. It is not surprising that the United States became known as America. The new variant of Western civilization that arose in the New World received its highest expression in the United States, which was recognized as the great spokesman of all the Americas. That became evident during the nineteenth century, especially after the Civil War, when the United States, alone of all the nations in the New World, achieved the distinction of being admitted to the circle of great powers.

What was most distinctive of American civilization was its English language and culture. The original immigrants to the New World came chiefly from Spain, Portugal, France, and England, each group settling in a certain area where it established its own national language and culture. The colonists soon became deeply involved in the struggles of their mother countries for hegemony in the New World. Their cultural as well as their political fate was at stake. As a consequence of these struggles, France was eliminated from a dominant position in the culture of the New World; it was delimited to the province of Quebec, Haiti and Martinique, and French Guiana. The Iberian and English cultures divided the New World between them; the former dominated the lands south of the Rio Grande, and the latter those north of it.

The Iberian culture, however, was far less successful than the English in spreading its influence. The Spaniards and Portuguese conquered lands that were fairly well populated by semi-civilized Indians. Those who came as conquerors were not followed by large and continuous streams of immigrants from Spain and Portugal. As a consequence, the great masses of people in Latin America continued to be Indians, who spoke their native tongues and maintained their traditions, customs, and institutions. Ruling over them was a caste of Iberian or of semi-Iberian origin, living a cultural life apart from the main body of their fellow countrymen. The masses of people, south of the Rio Grande, lived merely in the shadow of Iberian culture.

Quite otherwise was the position of English culture north of the Rio Grande. The English came to what was virtually an empty continent. North America was then thinly populated by small tribes of savage Indians, who were either killed or driven off the land by the newcomers. Large and continuous streams of immigrants came from Britain to the Thirteen Colonies and to Canada. English language and culture, and English customs, traditions, and institutions became almost universal. The American Revolution cut the political but not the cultural ties that bound America to England. On the contrary, these ties were strengthened by the spread of the English language, as a result of two movements that followed the American Revolution. One was the westward movement of the Americans who carried the English language to the Pacific. The other was a new immigration from Britain and Ireland that continued beyond the middle of the nineteenth century. Being English in speech, these immigrants were easily assimilated. The first large immigration from non-English speaking lands were the Germans and Scandinavians, who constituted the bulk of American immigrants from 1850 to 1880. When they came, they found English firmly established, and were assimilated with little difficulty in the second generation. Toward the end of the nineteenth century, a new tide of immigration set in, chiefly Jews from Eastern Europe, Italians, and Poles. Assimilation now became more difficult. But the English language was by this time so deeply rooted and so widespread throughout the land that the new immigrants accepted it, slowly and with some difficulty, as generation succeeded generation. Primarily Americanization meant the acceptance of English as the language of the nation. America, however, became dubious about the capacity of the cultural "melting pot" to absorb unlimited immigration. To avoid serious problems, Chinese and Japanese were excluded. To ease the process of Americanization, new laws severely restricted immigration by admitting only a limited number from any European country. By the twentieth century, America was definitely Western in civilization and English in language and culture.

Tied to England by the intimate bonds of language and culture America became a participant in the English heritage of individual freedom and self-government. This heritage grew to be world-wide in scope as America exerted an ever greater and ever wider influence in the world.

AMERICA, PIONEER OF A NEW DEMOCRACY

Was then America destined to be merely a larger England? It was the American Revolution that precluded this, and set the new nation on the road leading to new goals in the progress of Western civilization. In breaking away from England, America embarked on a high adventure in political and social organization, inspired by a new vision of human destiny. According to H. G. Wells, the creation of the United States marked "a definite stage in the release of man from precedent and usage, and a definite step forward towards the conscious and deliberate reconstruction of his circumstances to suit his needs and aims." [1]

The United States was created a nation out of hand by a constitutional convention chosen for that very purpose. The "birth of a nation" in this manner was unprecedented. All the then existing nations of Europe, notably England and France, had not been "born." They had "grown" during the centuries, as a result of conquests, of royal marriages, and of diplomatic arrangements. The American Constitution was the first written constitution of a national state, and its essential structure has lasted to this day. It was inspired by the libertarian ideas of the eighteenth century: human equality, national rights, freedom of thought and of expression, and the separation of powers of government. A Bill of Rights, far more comprehensive than its famous predecessor, the English Bill of Rights, was incorporated in the first ten amendments of the Constitution. Among other things it guaranteed freedom of religion, of speech, of the press, and of assembly.

America was the first, large-scale, federal republic. Republics had been associated with the ancient city-states of Greece and of Rome and with the city-states of Renaissance Italy. Federal-

[1] H. G. Wells, *The Outline of History* (1921), 842.

ism had been associated with the loosely joined, tiny cantons of Switzerland. A large, highly integrated, federal state was then considered impossible. Perhaps for that very reason the right of secession was widely held in America, in the North as well as in the South. The more "perfect union," established in 1789, was destined to undergo the terrific ordeal of the Civil War, from which America emerged an "indestructible union of indestructible states."

America was the first large-scale democracy. In all the ages past, the masses of mankind had no part whatever in government; they had been ruled by military dictators, by divine-right monarchs, or by wealthy oligarchies.[2] America abolished the age-old division between rulers and ruled; hence her traditions are all democratic. As early as the Jacksonian period, American life became broadly democratic with the establishment of manhood suffrage; and the common man became the nation. The term "people" was all-inclusive in America, comprehending the entire nation. In Europe, the "people" were the lower classes, feared in France, patronized in Britain, and cajoled in Germany.

But there was a fly in the ointment of American democracy, a very ugly fly. It was slavery, which, though it was limited to the South in the nineteenth century, served to dramatize the contradiction embedded in the promise of American life. No amount of sophistry, no insistence on economic necessity, no appeal to national unity could resolve this contradiction. As generation succeeded generation, slavery became the all-absorbing issue of American life. This issue (and that of states rights) was finally settled on the battlefields of the Civil War, the outcome of which resolved this contradiction by abolishing slavery.

Another unique contribution of America to the new democratic pattern was religious freedom. By forbidding the establish-

[2] In the ancient republics of Greece and Rome the voters, rich and poor, constituted only a small percentage of the population, which consisted chiefly of slaves and foreigners.

ment of a national church and the passing of laws restricting the free exercise of religion, the Constitution established religious freedom in the full meaning of the word.[3] Separation of church and state repudiated the then existing practice of toleration extended by the state to dissenters from the established faith. In America, and only in America, was religion then a private matter, free in all ways from the power of the state to favor or to punish. The secular state, now widely accepted, owes its initial impulse to America, which solved the religious problem by not creating it.

AMERICA, PIONEER OF A NEW NATIONALISM

Like the foregoing, nationalism in America differs profoundly from that in Europe. The American past is a short one; hence the sentiment of nationality, unlike that in Europe, is based less on common traditions of the past than on common hopes for the future. Everyone now in America, excepting the few Indians, was at one time or another a "foreigner," recently or in the not-so-distant past. America, during the nineteenth century, offered the greatest opportunity possible for unrestricted immigration on a large scale. At last there was a land, vast in size, temperate in climate, rich in natural resources, where many could go to escape from the restrictions of traditional, caste-bound Europe. America became the land of escape from poverty and persecution to comfort and equality. Millions of Europeans entered the open portal of the New World, where they found opportunities on all sides—in agriculture, in commerce, and in industry. The American government freely welcomed the im-

---

[3] The states, however, continued to maintain established churches, but only for a short time. They soon followed the precedent set by the Federal Constitution, by separating church and state.

migrants into political partnership: citizenship could be easily acquired, and all public offices, except the presidency, were open to naturalized citizens. The loose social system easily absorbed those who rose from the ranks. Never before in history could masses of people of one nationality take on another so easily and so quickly.

Though the immigrants came in large national groups, they came as individuals. They were not sent en masse as colonists by governments or by companies, as had been so often the case during the colonial period. Only the Negroes came here involuntarily, as chattel slaves. The immigrants were admitted as individuals under an implied moral contract, namely, that they put their past political loyalties behind them when they became American citizens. This moral contract the immigrants, by and large, have loyally kept. The 39 million immigrants of different races, nationalities, and faiths that came to America between 1776 and 1940 never coagulated into separatisms, each living a life apart with its own language, customs, and traditions. There are no national, ethnic, or religious minorities, so common in east central Europe, in the United States. The few enclaves in America, such as the Pennsylvania "Dutch" and the Louisiana "French," are small, and in the process of disintegration. The large regions on the continent, annexed to the United States as a result of conquest or purchase, contained few white inhabitants, and these were easily assimilated.

Despite the heterogeneous origins of the American people, national unity has been maintained with little difficulty, and to a greater degree than in some of the homogeneous nations of Europe. This was strikingly illustrated during the Second World War, when the American government received the unanimous support of the people, no matter at what sacrifice in blood and treasure. Pearl Harbor sent an electric current through the nation that instantly welded into one mighty unit all Americans, even those of Japanese origin. No nation in Europe, except Britain, could boast of such unity during the greatest crisis in the history of modern times.

What made possible this extraordinary phenomenon? What are the underlying factors in American nationalism, which has so few roots in the soil of the past and yet spreads so luxuriantly throughout the broad land? First and foremost comes the unchallenged supremacy of the English language, already referred to. The mother tongue constitutes the greatest psychological factor in fashioning the national spirit and outlook; hence it receives the first consideration in all nations. The English language has been maintained in America by the public school, which has been the major factor in Americanizing the children of the immigrants. Supremacy of English is freely acknowledged by the private schools, religious and nonreligious. There are no local dialects, or patois, of any consequence in America, which actually has greater language homogeneity than an old nation like France, where ancient tongues continue to survive in certain regions. An American traveling 3,000 miles from Maine to California will hear the same language, spoken with but slight differences in accent and intonation.

Another bond of union is the English common law, which is accepted by all the states. It creates a common relationship of all individuals to the established order through its rules governing family relations, business practices, and personal conduct. Though it operates intermittently, a common legal system has a continuous effect upon the people by reaching into the intimate corners of their private lives. It is a constant reminder to them that the law which governs their private conduct is one to which they must conform in order to be part of the nation.

Another bond of union has been developed by the two-party system, which has made a contribution to American unity which has been slighted. Though both parties are basically state organizations, the necessity of choosing a candidate for president has resulted in the creation of national party conventions that adopt platforms dealing with national issues. It is through the national party that conflicting interests and views of the various sections are harmonized. Conflicts are between the elements *within* the party, and national policies are adopted by ironing out the differences among the interests and opinions of the various elements. The united front, presented by each party in national elections, comes as a result of compromise between the factions, not from the triumphant dominance of the party by one faction or by one interest. This tendency to compromise within the party makes it possible for Republicans in the agricultural Middle West to form a common front with Republicans in industrial and commercial New England, for Democrats in the agricultural South to form a common front with Democrats in the industrial and commercial North Atlantic states.

Compromise influences the attitude of each party toward the other, and of both toward national problems. They differ at times in their interpretation of the Constitution and in their methods of applying economic policies to the solution of social problems. But both parties uphold the Constitution and the fundamentals of the established social order. For this reason, America has not known, to any serious degree, reactionary and revolutionary parties that seek to overturn the existing order. Neither has it known the splinter parties of Continental Europe, each with its special ideology and with its class or religious bias, that have so frequently destroyed national unity, even in time of war. Only once in American history was compromise impossible: over the slavery issue. When that became evident, the Civil War became inevitable.

The two-party system has played an important role in assimilating the various groups of immigrants to the American political system. In their eagerness for votes the local politicians have done their utmost to familiarize the newcomers with the ways of American politics and government. Often crude, sometimes even corrupt, these activities have served to give a welcome to the immigrant. When he joins a political party he, at the same time, joins the nation with a feeling of confidence. In a truly remarkable manner has each party assimilated the new with the old population, and the various groups of immigrants with one another. In the Democratic party, the citizens of Irish and of Jewish origin in New York are joined with those of Polish and of Italian origin in Ohio; and these with the citizens of older American stock in Virginia and Massachusetts. In the Republican party, the citizens of German origin in Wisconsin and those of Scandinavian origin in Minnesota are joined with the citizens of Hungarian origin in Pennsylvania and with those of French Canadian origin in New Hampshire; and these with the citizens of older American stock in Maine and Indiana. The common practice of putting representatives of various immigrant groups on electoral tickets, bad as it often has been, yet has made for unity and harmony. In these ways the two-party system has prevented the formation in America of political parties based on race, nationality, or faith. The hyphenated Americans of the first generation of immigrants became the complete Americans of the second generation. The hope, the vision of a glorious common future for America unites all groups into a common national loyalty.

THE AMERICAN DREAM

From the days of the Founding Fathers there has existed what has been called the "American dream." Successive generations of Americans have believed that their nation, unlike all other nations, entered history "conceived in liberty, and dedicated to the proposition that all men are created equal," to use the immortal words of Lincoln. From its very birth the American nation was liberal in that it lacked a feudal aristocracy with its special privileges; an established church with its power to restrict religious freedom; a king with the prestige of divinity hedged around him; and a military caste ready to draw the sword against all who resisted tyranny. These four pillars of conservatism then existed everywhere in Europe, which made the struggle for freedom, on that continent, difficult, and victory, even if achieved, uncertain and insecure. Only America could move untrammeled along the open road of freedom in the vanguard of human progress.

The liberal American state had its counterpart in a social order, freer from class influences than that in any other country. And this arose from the fact that the population, from the beginning, consisted chiefly of elements who had been uprooted in one form or another. Almost every group that came to America was escaping from some other group in Europe: Protestants were escaping Catholic persecution; Catholics, Protestant persecution; Dissenters of all kinds, the persecution by established churches; the Irish were escaping from political and economic discrimination by the British; German liberals, from the fury of Prussian reaction; Russian Jews and Poles from the tyranny of tsarism; and Italians from the poverty of their native land. America became a land of escape even for Americans. They escaped westward looking for better opportunities than those in the settled East. Class conflicts were in this way mitigated by the "open door at home," through which passed farmers from the rocky soil of New England to the fertile prairie lands of the Middle West; adventurers seeking the gold of California; and enterprising businessmen seeking to develop untapped natural resources. There was neither time nor opportunity to solidify into classes, in which status could be inherited. No one could have "ancestors" when parents or grandparents had come into a community as immigrants or as backwoodsmen. A loosely integrated social order appeared in

America that for the first time in modern history offered a *tabula rasa* on which individuals were free to write their destiny.

CHARACTER OF AMERICAN CAPITALISM

Even the nature of the economic system differed from that in the Old World. In Europe capitalism was superimposed on a feudal economy which, though decadent, yet hindered economic development. Free enterprise was not very free, being often restricted by relics of mercantilism, and burdened with "hereditary idlers," namely, aristocrats who received handsome revenues as the lords of the land used for factories and mines. Neither was private enterprise always very private. The governments, under aristocratic influences, often intervened in business for all sorts of reasons: less so in England, more so in France, and much more so in Germany. By contrast with capitalism in Europe that in America was truly free and private. The American Revolution had completely discredited mercantilism as a policy, and the limitless natural resources of an empty continent offered full scope to private enterprise. Anyone could "go into business"; no artificial hindrances existed, such as vested aristocratic interests and the spirit of caste. Unlike the nations of Europe America was born, reared and matured in *laissez faire,* which became a national tradition.[4] In Europe it was a class policy of the *bourgeoisie;* hence it was bitterly opposed both by aristocrats and workers.

American capitalism has operated in the greatest free-trade area of modern times. When the local tariffs were abolished by the Federal Constitution, capitalism received an initial impulse

---

[4] So deep was the tradition of *laissez faire* in America that it was not until 1932 that the American Federation of Labor advocated legislation in favor of old-age pensions and unemployment insurance. See American Federation of Labor, *Report of Proceedings,* Vol. 52 (1932), 169.

of which it took full advantage. As the country grew in population and in territory, and as the standard of living rose from generation to generation, the domestic market became ever greater. The real secret of the success of American capitalism lies in the existence of this immense outlet. Largely for this reason it had no need of the international division of labor, so vital to the success of British capitalism, whose free-trade policies were predicated on the other nations remaining producers of food and raw materials. Nor did American capitalism have need of imperial and foreign markets to dispose of surplus manufactures. The British manufacturer of cotton goods planned to produce one shirt for a Briton, one for an Indian, and one for a Chinese. The American manufacturers planned to produce three shirts, all for the American, whose wages were high enough to buy them.

A balanced economy was developed in America such as existed in no other land. France, it is true, also had a balanced economy: a backward agriculture was balanced by a backward industry. Not so in America where the most advanced agriculture was balanced by the most advanced industry. Until the twentieth century, America absorbed virtually all her manufactures; her exports consisted chiefly of food and raw materials. As the agricultural population decreased because of the rise of industry, agricultural production in America actually increased because of the application of machinery and science to farming. The balanced economy continued on a still higher level of production of both agriculture and industry. Within America, capitalism had succeeded in creating a unified, almost self-contained economic world.

This unique economic system was not established without many conflicts, the most serious of which was that over slavery. The Civil War was not a struggle between landed and capitalist interests, such as took place in England during the first half of the nineteenth century. The landed interest of the South was based on cotton, a product that was essential to the manufacturing interest of the North. Not a few of the Northern manufacturers sympathized with the Southern slaveholders, who assured them a large and steady supply of this essential raw material. But the free economy of American capitalism, whether in agriculture, commerce, or industry, was seriously hampered by the one-crop system in the South, which made of that region a kind of economic colony. Because of great profit to a few plantation owners, slavery presented an insuperable obstacle to the economic progress of the South, and therefore of the nation as a whole. Neither a highly developed agriculture could flourish, despite its fertile soil, nor industry develop, despite its great natural resources in coal and iron. The victory of the North over the South in the Civil War united the nation not only politically but also economically. The South was finally integrated into America's free economic system, when its natural resources were opened to capitalistic enterprise. It is well to remember that the great industrial development of America, now the marvel of the world, began after the Civil War.

THE DYNAMIC SOCIAL ORDER

The anomalous class structure in the South, reminiscent of feudalism with its landed aristocracy and servile peasantry, disappeared with the abolition of slavery.[5] The unique social order

[5] The European aristocratic system was transplanted to America during the colonial era. As in Europe it was based on large estates, primogeniture, and entail. During the American Revolution this system was undermined when many estates of the Tories were confiscated by the state legislatures, broken up into small parcels, and sold to farmers. After the Revolution, the great estates in the Hudson River Valley and the vast properties of the Penn family in Pennsylvania were broken up and sold in a similar manner. Primogeniture and entail were abolished in nearly all the states. See J. Franklin Jameson, *The American Revolution Considered as a Social Movement* (1940).

that developed in America now stood in clear relief. America, according to Jeffersonian democracy, was to create a classless society by giving everyone property, or at least the opportunity to acquire it. Property made the free citizen; hence the diffusion, not the abolition, of property was the Jeffersonian ideal of a classless society.

Ever since the founding of the American commonwealth two powerful currents have flowed in American life: business enterprise and political democracy, or property and liberty. Sometimes they flowed side by side; sometimes, they intermingled; and, latterly, they have flowed in opposite directions. The philosophy that underlay the Constitution came chiefly from John Locke, whose fundamental political idea was that government had been instituted to protect men in their natural rights of life, liberty, and property. As property made men secure and free, the first duty of the state was to protect property rights. The American Constitution applied Locke's idea in two ways. In the first place, it gave special protection to property rights through the Fifth Amendment, which forbade the government to deprive a man of his property "without due process of law." In the second place, it placed limitations on the power of the government, and gave to the judiciary the task of maintaining these limitations. The Founding Fathers feared that property rights might be undermined, either by the survivals of mercantilistic monopoly or by the nascent radicalism of political democracy.

During most of the nineteenth century, the social order in America was in harmony with the political order established by the Constitution. There were few if any conflicts between property and liberty. Property then consisted chiefly of land, which was cheap and plentiful. Anyone could acquire a farm almost for the asking. By the time of the Civil War, ownership of land by the free men who tilled it had become well-nigh universal in America. And American farmers did not harden into a class of "peasant proprietors" as in Europe, where the same family worked the same farm from generation to generation. The American social rhythm prevented the establishment of a peasantry rooted in the soil. The farmer was always selling his farm to buy a better one, or seeking opportunities to go into business, or to moving West where cheap, fertile land awaited the ploughman. In truth the American farmer was more of a real-estate speculator than a tiller of the soil. As the population of America before the Civil War was overwhelmingly agricultural, the Jeffersonian ideal of a free America consisting of free citizens, all actual or potential property owners, was realized to a remarkable degree.

No stratified working class, or "proletariat," developed in America. The native factory workers who appeared early in the nineteenth century were pushed out of the factories and up into the middle class by the tide of Irish and German immigrants that flowed to America during the forties and fifties of the nineteenth century. Later in the century, these in turn were pushed out and up by the new tide of immigrants: Italians, Russian Jews, and Poles, who now became the working class in America. Immigrants, coming as peasants and proletarians, soon joined the American procession to the middle class of landowning farmers, businessmen, professional men, officials, and white-collar employees. It was the exception rather than the rule to find an American son of an immigrant father in the same economic class. America was all middle class, actually or potentially, the workers being a middle class in transition.

Nor did a capitalist class as such appear in America, as it had in Europe. The European capitalists had hardened into a class analogous to the landed aristocrats; son succeeded father as head of a business, as son succeeded father as lord of a manor. But, as in the cases of farmers and workers, the rhythm of American economic life made difficult the coagulation of the capitalists into a class. A vast industrial vacuum existed into which crowded all kinds of individual enterprisers, coming from anywhere, who moved freely in and out of the American world of free private enterprise. Not infrequently those with unusual ability and initiative or ruthless ambition—a grocery clerk like John D. Rockefeller, a mechanic like Henry Ford, an immigrant like Andrew Carnegie—climbed the highest rung of the capitalist ladder. And there was a constant movement up and down this ladder. The business of America was business; hence capitalism was a popular system and received almost universal support. As long as the opportunity to rise existed, the worker felt that he had a business card in his jeans. That at least was the situation during the nineteenth century.

Were there then no class divisions in America? There were: those in the middle class and those striving to enter it. The American middle class was not a replica of the European *bourgeoisie,* with its definite status in the social hierarchy. Within the American middle class all was in flux; some were going up, and others, down; some were coming in, and others, going out. As a result of its dynamic nature, American economy was constantly shifting its base and changing its direction. The flow of mechanical inventions, creating new products and new methods of production, destroyed old markets and created new ones. Those operating in the old were eliminated for the benefit of those in the new. The periodic depressions wiped out one wealthy group and prepared the way for another, consisting of those who were shrewd enough to get in on the ground floor when the turn to prosperity began. "Three generations from shirtsleeves to shirtsleeves" was almost the law of succession of families in the American middle class.

What greatly aided this social mobility was the educational system. For the first time in history a system of schooling was established open to all, free, public, and secular. Each grade in this unique system prepared the student for that above, so that it constituted an open educational corridor, from the kindergarten through the university. Anyone could prepare himself to rise in the social scale by taking advantage of the educational corridor. Many did. The college-bred son of a poor worker seldom followed the calling of his father. Early in the nineteenth century "schools for all" had become an American ideal; most of the states had made elementary education compulsory and had established free public schools. Later in the century free higher education was created by the state universities for all who qualified. Hitherto education, especially higher education, had been a privilege of the wealthy classes. In the golden ages of the European nations—the Italy of the Renaissance, the England of Elizabeth, and the France of Louis XIV—fewer than a quarter of the people were educated; the rest were illiterate. In other words a few were highly civilized, and the mass of people, semicivilized and even barbaric. America proclaimed the ideal of civilization for all classes, and, at great cost, created an educational system designed to raise the cultural level of every group in the nation.

There was one exception to this social and cultural mobility, namely, the Negro. He alone in America had the fixed status of caste; while all about him was movement, the Negro remained stationary. On the land he was a "peasant," whether tenant, sharecropper, or proprietor. In the factory he was a "proletarian," relegated to the lowest paid labor. Limited to menial occupations, generally barred from the professions and from white-collar jobs, "last to be hired and first to be fired," the Negro became the economic helot of American life. The low economic position of the Negro was matched by his inferior cultural, political, and social status. Educationally he was generally limited to elementary schooling; and, in some sections of the South, he did not receive even this. Politically he was, in the South, a second-class citizen, deprived of the vote, and only too frequently of his civil rights. Socially he was segregated: in the schools, in living quarters, in travel, in amusements, and in social life generally. Segregation in the South was legal as decreed by the notorious "Jim Crow" laws; elsewhere in America it was widely practiced. Emancipation had freed the Negro from legal subjection but had not given him the American elixir of equality to enable him to rise into the all-embracing middle class. The position of the Negro, as a caste of outcasts, constituted a dramatic violation of the promise of American life. This violation began to awaken the American conscience when the twentieth century opened.

Early in the nineteenth century, America attracted little attention in the world. Europeans, generally, regarded the new nation as isolated, rather primitive in its life and backward in its culture. That America had established herself as a democracy was known, but the significance of that fact was not realized. However, twice during the nineteenth century, the attention of Europe was called to the importance of America as a world phenomenon. In both instances it was by a book, each of which created a literary sensation when it appeared. The first was by the Frenchman, Alexis de Tocqueville, whose *Democracy in America* appeared in 1835. De Tocqueville could be truly described as a literary Columbus, who discovered the new democratic world of America. In that distant land he beheld, not an isolated phenomenon, but the unique pattern of democracy for all mankind. With prophetic insight de Tocqueville visualized the great role that America was destined to play in the future of mankind. The second book was *The American Commonwealth,* by the Briton James Bryce, which appeared in 1888. It was an authoritative study of the American political system in its full maturity after the Civil War. The value of Bryce's work lay in its judicious appraisal of American democracy, now united, strong, and rapidly becoming a great world power. It acquainted Europeans—and even Americans—with the orientation of a new force in history that was destined to become dominant in the twentieth century.

AMERICA'S ADVANTAGES, NATURAL
AND ACQUIRED

To both nature and man may be ascribed the rise of America
to preeminence. At the very outset it is important to note that,
geographically, America is a continental nation with an inter-
oceanic location, bordering on both the Atlantic and the Pacific.
Having access to all the ports of the world, she is in the center
of world trade routes. Another important geographic advantage
lies in the fact that, except for Alaska and Hawaii, the territory
of the United States is contiguous. It is crossed and crisscrossed
by great navigable rivers; and for a considerable stretch along
the northern border lies the chain of oceanlike Great Lakes,
all of which make for easy water transportation throughout the
vast land. Again, because of its central location in North
America, the United States has easy water and land transportation with the vast hinterlands, Canada to the north and Latin
America to the south, with which trade can be easily developed.

America possesses a concentration of natural resources,
greater than that of any area of similar size in the world. It
lies in the temperate zone, but has a variety of climate and rain-
fall that make possible the cultivation of all sorts of plants and
animals. From the great plains come cattle; from the great
forests, lumber; and from the fertile lands, cotton and foodstuffs of all kinds. Some regions are suited for the transplanta-
tion of plant and animal life from other parts of the world.
America is now a large producer of soya beans, transplanted
from China; of figs, from Smyrna; and reindeer from Lapland.
America also possesses immense resources essential to modern
industry, especially coal, iron, and oil. From 1900 to 1939 her
average annual production of coal was about 40 per cent of
that of the world; of iron ore, about 33 per cent; and of oil,

more than 50 per cent. America's water-power resources are practically unlimited.

Nature has made America practically invulnerable to invasion by sea. Two ocean moats, the Atlantic and the Pacific, protect her from hostile fleets launched from Europe or from Asia. This natural advantage was greatly enhanced by the Panama Canal, which, by making North America a continental island, gave the United States the double military advantage of vastness of territory and of island position. A fair-sized navy, with bases in the Caribbean, could now protect the country from attacks coming across the Atlantic; and by easy transit through the Panama Canal it could quickly come to the aid of the West coast in case of attacks coming across the Pacific. America was also fairly secure from invasion by land. Unlike the great powers in Europe she had no powerful, hostile neighbors. Because of her impregnable position America could with impunity send armies and fleets to Europe and to Asia without fear of attacks at home. No other great nation in modern history was so favorably situated. America, therefore, felt free to develop her great natural resources, to stabilize and to strengthen her democratic political system, and, above all, to establish a new society that would carry out the "promise of American life."

Man with his arts supplemented nature with her gifts. From the very beginning America has been peopled by the most adventurous and the most energetic elements in the Old World, who have had the hardihood to start life anew in a faraway land. Having free opportunity and plenty of elbow room, the Americans have used the arts and sciences, which they had brought with them from Europe, with far greater ingenuity than could the Europeans. Moreover the lack, in the early days, of a sufficient labor supply to exploit the tremendous resources of the new land was the necessity that became the mother of mechanical invention on an unprecedented scale. From the revolutionary cotton gin to the convenient gadget, the continuous stream of American inventions culminated in mass production, which made America a pioneer of the new Industrial Revolution in the latter part of the nineteenth century.

America was, therefore, first in the economy of the twentieth century. The god of the machine created a horn of plenty out of which poured immense quantities of goods in a steady and increasing stream. The surplus economy, visualized at the dawn of the Industrial Revolution in the eighteenth century, became an actuality in twentieth-century America. A nation having less than 7 per cent of the world's population and living on less than 7 per cent of the world's area, produced and consumed, in 1948, over 33 per cent of the world's output of goods and services. Even in 1928, America had produced more goods than had Britain, Germany, and France combined. Machine power was the secret of America's high productivity. By extensively utilizing automatic, power-driven machinery the output per man-hour in America was far greater than that elsewhere. It was estimated, in 1949, that the American worker had six times more machine power behind his pair of hands than had his British counterpart. In America, in 1850, animals had provided 79 per cent of the energy used for work; men, 15 per cent; and machines, only 6 per cent. But, in 1930, animals provided 12 per cent; men, 4 per cent; and machines, 84 per cent.[6] It is estimated that at this rate of progress, machines will, in 1960, supply 96 per cent of all the energy used in America. In about a century, from 1850 to 1944, the total output of goods and services increased 29 times, though the man-hours of labor increased only 5½ times.[7] National annual production rose from about 50 billion dollars in 1900, in terms of prices of today,

[6] T. R. Carskadon and R. Modley, *U.S.A.: Measure of a Nation* (1949). The capital investment per worker increased from $2,115 in 1879 to $4,051 in 1946. See *Report of Council of Economic Advisors,* December, 1947.

[7] J. F. Dewhurst, "America's Horn of Plenty," *New Leader,* Apr. 24, 1948; see also J. F. Dewhurst, *America's Needs and Resources* (1947).

to the staggering figure in 1950, of 255 billion dollars.[8] Steel production, everywhere the barometer of industrial efficiency and progress, was, in 1948, greater in America than in all the rest of the world combined.

Agriculture, too, showed marked increases in productivity, despite the rapid decline of the agricultural population. Of all persons gainfully employed in America the proportion of farmers declined from 77.5 per cent in 1847 to less than 24 per cent in 1947.[9] Agricultural production, however, increased enormously during this period. It is estimated that, in 1847, the American farmer produced a crop to meet the needs of himself and three others; in 1947, of himself and twenty others. From 1929 to 1947, agricultural production increased by as much as 45 per cent.[10]

The First World War revealed America's astonishing productivity. But that during the Second World War constituted the most stupendous feat in economic history. During the war years, America miraculously doubled her already great output of goods and services. She not only provided her own military machine with munitions, food, shelter, and clothing, but, in addition, sent abundant military and civilian supplies to her allies, and yet maintained her civil population at a higher standard of living than ever before. America's production of ships, naval and merchant, exceeded the combined tonnage of the rest of the world. The navy that America built during the war dwarfed her not inconsiderable prewar navy. Airplane production was the greatest up to that time, and far exceeded all estimates and expectations. As the war progressed, it clearly became a battle of production between the Allies and the Axis. And America, the "arsenal of democracy," tipped the scales of victory to the side of the Allies.

[8] *The President's Message to Congress,* Jan. 5, 1950.
[9] John Ise, *Economics* (1946), 516–517.
[10] *The President's Message to Congress,* Jan. 5, 1948.

Peace found America at the very pinnacle of economic power. Unlike the other great belligerents, she had not been invaded or bombarded, and her industrial plant had suffered no such destruction as had been visited on the industries of Germany, Britain, Russia, and Italy. Her economic machine was not only intact but on a higher level of production than ever before. Commercially, America led all other nations both in domestic and foreign trade. Until 1914 America had been a debtor nation importing large amounts of capital, chiefly from Britain, to finance her growing industries. A financial shift took place after the First World War that resulted in America becoming a great creditor nation.[11] New York displaced London as the financial capital of the world.[12] It is estimated that America's foreign investments, from 1914 to 1930, equaled that of Britain all during the nineteenth century.[13] After the Second World War, America's financial power pervaded the entire world. She became the only source of capital needed for reconstructing bombed-out cities, for repairing damaged factories, and for supplying relief to war-torn populations. America was virtually the sole creditor country in the world.

It would hardly be an exaggeration to say that America, in the mid-twentieth century, became the central pillar sustaining world economy. Nothing of economic importance could take place in any part of the world without reference to America; she alone had complete freedom of action in the field of international economic policy. Any shift in economic policy, any uncertainty in her financial structure, immediately had reverberations throughout the world. Far more than in the case of

[11] In 1914 America was a debtor to the extent of 3 billion dollars; in 1922 she was a creditor to the extent of 19 billion. See Lewis L. Lorwin, *Economic Consequences of the Second World War* (1941), 433.

[12] In 1930 America exported 547 million dollars, and Britain, 190 million dollars. J. S. Roucek (ed.), *Contemporary Europe* (1947), 110.

[13] Lorwin, *op. cit.,* 439.

Britain during the nineteenth century did the economic life of the world now pivot on America.

Leadership of Western civilization was passing from Europe to America. In contrast to weak, divided, and impoverished Europe, stood America, strong, united, and rich. History records no rise to power like that made by America in so short a time. The 6,000,000 people of 1800, living under semiprimitive conditions in isolation on a strip of territory bordering on the Atlantic, became the 150,000,000 of 1950, living in the highly developed continent-nation, whose influence reached every corner of the world. What was the price of this extraordinary progress? What was the effect of America's impact on the world? How was the promise of American life kept? These questions Americans had to answer to themselves, to the world, and to history.

PROPERTY RIGHTS VERSUS HUMAN RIGHTS

Let it be recalled that American ideas of equality and liberty have been associated with opportunity to acquire property through private enterprise. And this opportunity, open to all, existed during the nineteenth century. As a consequence, the national wealth grew apace as production increased by leaps and bounds. This great upswing, however, had unexpected results: it led to a concentration of industry into monopolistic or semimonopolistic corporations that eliminated many small business enterprises. During the period 1935–1944, four of the largest firms in iron and steel did about two-thirds of the business; five in petroleum refining, about three-fifths; four, in meat packing, about one-half; four, in radio manufacturing, about one-half; and one firm alone in tin-can manufacturing, over one-half.[14]

[14] S. H. Slichter, *The American Economy* (1948), 16. See also *United States News,* Dec. 16, 1949.

It was estimated that, in 1948, 455 corporations controlled 51 per cent of all business assets in America.[15] Sometimes slowly, sometimes quickly the small property owner was disappearing. Very striking was the fact that the independent American farmer was passing, as tenant farming was rapidly increasing. In 1930 it was estimated that 17 out of 20 Americans were propertyless. Those who had an independent source of livelihood as farmers, businessmen, and professional men constituted only 14 per cent of all persons gainfully employed.[16] The Jeffersonian dream of equality through property had turned to ashes.

Sharp class divisions appeared in American society at the beginning of the twentieth century. At one end was a small group of capitalists, "multimillionaires," whose wealth far outranked that of the richest classes of Europe; and, at the other end was, in the words of Franklin D. Roosevelt, "one-third of a nation ill-housed, ill-clad, ill-nourished," living precariously in the midst of the plenty produced by the economic system. The contradictions in American life resulted in a new conflict, that between property rights and human rights, traditionally one and inseparable. This conflict constituted the leitmotif of American social history during the first half of the twentieth century.

The first battles in the war between "wealth and commonwealth" were efforts to recapture the Jeffersonian dream of a nation of small property owners. It led to the enactment of two famous laws: the Interstate Commerce Act of 1887, which, among other measures, prohibited the railways from giving rebates and other advantages to large shippers; and the Sherman Antitrust Act of 1890, which prohibited combinations in restraint of trade. Both laws aimed to bolster up the small farmer and small businessman in their competitive struggle with Big Business.

[15] Chester Bowles, *New Leader,* June 5, 1948. See also C. A. Hickman, *World Economic Problems* (1947), 167.

[16] Lewis Corey, *The Unfinished Task* (1942), 56–57.

In the era of "trust busting" that followed, new popular statesmen appeared: William Jennings Bryan, Robert La Follette,
Theodore Roosevelt, and Woodrow Wilson. They led the radical movement against Big Business, represented by the capitalists John D. Rockefeller, J. Pierpont Morgan, Andrew
Carnegie, and Edward H. Harriman. Denunciation of Wall
Street, the financial center of Big Business, resounded throughout the land. Essentially, "trust busting" was an intraclass struggle between the big and little capitalists, with the workers on
the side lines cheering the latter. Despite antitrust laws and
decisions of the Supreme Court, Big Business won out. There
was little place for the small enterpriser in the new economic
era demanding large outlays of capital, mass production, and
scientific management.

Did the triumph of Big Business mean that the promise of
American life was to remain unfulfilled? During the first half
of the twentieth century the struggle between property rights
and human rights continued, in different forms and under
different circumstances. It was the over-all issue in every presidential election during that period. The farmer and the small
businessman continued the strife, but in addition a new and
powerful protagonist of human rights entered the field, namely,
organized labor. Trade-unionism had appeared early in the
nineteenth century, but it had played little part in economic life.
After the Civil War, with the upswing of industry, large national federations of trade-unions appeared, such as the Knights
of Labor, organized in 1869, and the American Federation of
Labor, organized in 1886, to coordinate the demands of labor.
Occasionally, great strikes in key industries rocked the nation,
notably the Homestead strike against the Carnegie Steel Company (1892), the Pullman strike against the railway companies
(1894), and the coal strike in Pennsylvania (1902). However,
the trade-unions failed to enroll a significant proportion of the
American workers, largely because the latter continued to be

a class in constant state of dissolution. Unlike the European trade-unionists, who became socialists, the American trade-unionists frankly accepted capitalism. What they demanded, in the words of the famous labor leader, Samuel Gompers, was "more, more, now."

With the advent of the twentieth century, organized labor became more powerful, better organized, and more militant. Every year saw great conflicts between capital and labor, often on a nation-wide scale. As years went on, industrial unions appeared, especially in the heavy industries, that enrolled hundreds of thousands of workers in one big national union. A new force in American trade-unionism arose with the organization, in 1938, of the Congress of Industrial Organizations (CIO). This new federation made a special point of organizing the workers in the new mass-production industries, such as automobiles and rubber. It became more militant in spirit and more radical in policy than was its rival, the conservative AFL. Both, however, united in upholding the traditional policy of American trade-unionism of demanding "more, more, now" from the capitalist horn of plenty.

The Great Depression after the First World War broke the spell of laissez-faire capitalism in America. The widespread misery that it caused affected nearly all classes. The nonpropertied elements, having little to fall back upon, suffered most; it was estimated that about 15 million workers were unemployed. But the propertied elements also suffered; millions of farmers and small businessmen were reduced to destitution. The Depression threw a lurid light on the failure of capitalism to give security through ownership of property. What a "boom" gave, a "bust" took away. Least affected by the Depression were the great corporations that continued intact, even becoming stronger by absorbing the business of those who were ruined. Many stockholders in the great corporations were wiped out, but their places were soon taken by new ones. As a consequence of this economic tornado, the conflict between "wealth and commonwealth" in America became vividly concrete in the life of the individual citizen.

FALL OF LAISSEZ FAIRE AND RISE OF THE WELFARE STATE

The Great Depression was the great divide in American life. It was followed by social and economic changes that ushered in a new era, signalized by the spectacular triumphs of the Democrat, Franklin D. Roosevelt, in the four presidential elections from 1932 to 1944. The great political tradition of limiting a president to two consecutive terms was repudiated by the upsurge of social discontent that found expression in the radical policies of Roosevelt. What helps to explain his electoral success was the almost solid support that he received from the workers, especially from trade-unionists. The New Deal, inaugurated by Roosevelt, clearly and definitely repudiated *laissez faire,* so long accepted as an economic gospel in America. It proclaimed the doctrine of state intervention through government supervision and regulation of economic life in order to raise the standard of living of the "one-third of a nation ill-housed, ill-clad, ill-nourished." Roosevelt urged that the power of the government was now to be used to give economic security to the average citizen, whether worker, farmer, or businessman, as he could no longer by himself buffet the economic storms of capitalist enterprise.

Important laws carried out the promise of the New Deal. The Securities and Exchange Commission (SEC) protected the investor by supervising the financial activities of corporations and by regulating practices on the stock market and the issuing of securities. The farmers were given government subsidies to guarantee them a fair price for agricultural products. Most radical of all the New Deal measures were those affecting labor. The Wages and Hours law put a "floor" on wages and a "ceiling" on hours of labor. The social security laws established old-age pensions and unemployment insurance for workers. The National Labor Relations law (Wagner act) guaranteed to the trade-unions the right of collective bargaining. As a consequence of the law, trade-union membership increased enormously; in 1935, when the law was passed, it was about 3,650,000, which rose to about 15,000,000 by 1948. These much-needed reforms gave a new directive to American economy and government, and did much to abate the contradictions that had arisen between property rights and human rights. Democracy was now in the saddle, and it was the democracy of the twentieth century with its solicitous regard for the economic welfare of the masses, as well as for the traditional political and civil liberties, so deeply ingrained in American life and thought.

Trade-unionism and social reform could and did raise the standard of living of the working masses. But concentration in commerce and industry provided ever fewer opportunities for a man with little capital to go into business. Was then America going the way of Europe in establishing a class-bound society, even though on a more equitable foundation? American traditions of equality to a chance in life were all against permanent class divisions. In what other way could the door of opportunity be kept open? America's answer was the popularization of higher education.

Higher education, under modern conditions, is no longer the appanage of a cultural elite as it had been in the past. Modern economic life, to function at all, requires scientific knowledge and technical training on the part of those who direct its activities. And more and more has education been geared to this requirement. Moreover the growth of population and the higher standard of living, especially in the cities, enormously increased the demand for the services of doctors, teachers, lawyers, journalists, and government officials. New professionals appeared, such as social workers, psychologists, and radio commentators and entertainers. Business itself became a profession, because of the special knowledge required by its new technique. America led the way to the new opportunities by opening wide the doors of schools, colleges, and universities that devoted themselves to preparing their students to earn a living in the new society. Chiefly by means of knowledge could a man now climb the economic ladder. A great stimulus to higher education in America was given by the G.I. "Bill of Rights." Those veterans of the Second World War, who were qualified to pursue advanced studies, were given generous aid from funds voted by Congress. Thousands of young Americans took advantage of this aid and flocked to the colleges and universities. The progress of higher education in America has been truly astonishing. In 1900 only 238,000 students, about 4 per cent of the youth between 18 and 21, were enrolled in colleges and universities; in 1949 the enrollment was 2,500,000, over 16 per cent of the youth of the nation. Secondary education became almost universal; in 1949 over 70 per cent of those from 14 to 18 were in high school. The beneficiaries of secondary and higher education, no matter how poor, were in a position to command entrance into the higher ranks of business and government and into rapidly expanding professions, old and new. Education kept the door of opportunity open for many in America.

During the twentieth century, America attained the highest standard of living recorded in the annals of history. That only increased production makes possible a rising standard of living is an axiom of all economic thinking. Until the advent of the Industrial Revolution, great wealth for the fortunate few and dire poverty for the unfortunate many had been the universal rule. This condition was not materially changed for some time after the coming of modern industry, except in one important respect: a fairly large middle class in comfortable circumstances

appeared. The great masses in town and country continued to
live in dire poverty, as they still do in backward China and
India, where the wealthy few live in superabundant luxury.
America led the way in showing the possibility of general well-
being in an economy based on high production. An unprecedented increase in national income took place, when it almost
tripled from 1929 to 1948. In terms of purchasing power, from
1929 to 1947, the average income of Americans, after taxes which
continued on the high war level, rose 39 per cent.[17] The per
capita income, at 1929 prices, rose from $300 in 1879 to $1,100
in 1949.

How was the increase in national income distributed among
the various classes? The farmers made the greatest advance
during the decade 1939–1948, their personal incomes having
increased 335 per cent; then came the business and professional
men with an increase of 270 per cent; and finally came the wage
and salary earners with an increase of 184 per cent.[18]

Although profits rose higher and faster, wages rose sufficiently
to mark a notable advance in the condition of labor. High wages,
rather than high profits, now constitute the acid test of national
prosperity. What was the share of labor in the total income
from business? What was the extent of employment? The
progress of American labor was truly phenomenal. The average real wages of workers, in terms of 1949 prices, increased
threefold from 1900 to 1950.[19] Of the total personal income,
in 1929, 51 per cent went to salaries, wages, and other labor
income; and, in 1948, 63 per cent.[20] About 13,400,000 non-
farming families, in 1948, had a median annual income from
wages or salaries of about $3,500.[21] The policy of American

[17] Speech of President Truman, *The New York Times,* Nov. 18, 1947.
[18] *The United States News,* Apr. 23, 1945.
[19] *The New York Times,* June 15, 1950.
[20] *The Midyear Economic Report of the President to Congress,* July, 1949, 89.
[21] *The Gift of Freedom,* U.S. Department of Labor, 1949, 29, 32.

labor of getting "more, more, now" proved phenomenally successful.

As wages rose, hours of labor fell. In 1850 the average American laborer worked 70 hours a week; in 1900, 60 hours; and, in 1948, only 40 hours. Yet the industrial worker produced five times as much in 1948 as he had in 1850. This seeming contradiction can be explained by the widespread use of machinery in industry.[22] Despite technological unemployment in many instances, employment generally increased. In 1933 about 39,000,000 were gainfully employed; in 1949 the number reached the stupendous total of about 59,000,000.

By comparison with other nations, America, in the mid-twentieth century, was vastly better fed, better housed, and better clothed than any other community in history. This well-being was strikingly shown by the lengthening of the average life span during the first half of the twentieth century. In 1900 the average length of life in America was 49.2 years; in 1948 it rose to 67.2 years.[23] Such general well-being had been visualized by European revolutionists only as a result of the abolition of capitalism and the establishment of socialism. But in America it had been achieved through free, private enterprise. The secret of America's extraordinary success was high production, without which no economic system, capitalist or socialist, can hope to promote general prosperity. The low, very low standard of living in Soviet Russia dashed the hopes of those who had fervently believed that the economic good life would come automatically with the abolition of capitalism. To achieve high production has now become the universal desideratum in every country, whatever its form of government.

[22] During 1924–1925, the value of the output per worker in America was $2,666; in Britain, only $944. But the annual wage of the American worker was two and a half times that of the British worker. See C. R. Noyes, *America's Destiny* (1935), 78.

[23] *The New York Times,* Feb. 16, 1950.

However bright the American picture—and it is bright— there is a dark side to it. Not everyone is prosperous; many even live in a state of dire poverty. In 1948 it was estimated that about 8 million families and individuals received incomes of less than $1,000 a year, a sum hardly sufficient to maintain a decent standard of living. Poverty is an anachronism in a land of plenty, and America has dedicated herself to the task of abolishing destructively low incomes that wreck homes, impair health, and deprive children of their opportunities in life.

Of all the elements in America the Negro profited least from the upswing of prosperity. Primarily, this was the result of his inferior status in American society, which limited his power as a citizen and as a worker. America became acutely conscious of the evil of discrimination, practiced not only against the Negro but also against other elements. After the Second World War, the movement to abolish racial inequalities of all kinds in America made notable progress during the short period from 1945 to 1950. Many Negroes became enfranchised in the South, after the Supreme Court had banned all-white primaries and as a result of some of the states' abolishing the poll tax. Another gain for the Negro, in theory at least, was a decision of the Supreme Court compelling Oklahoma to provide a Negro student, denied admission to the state's law school, immediate and equal educational facilities. Another decision of the Supreme Court declared that racial restrictions of whatever kind in housing covenants were not enforceable in law. Still another decision favorable to Negroes barred racial segregation in dining cars in interstate railways. A California court invalidated the law aimed at the Japanese, which prohibited the ownership of agricultural land by persons ineligible for citizenship, on the ground that such a law violated the Charter of the United Nations. Congress repealed the law denying citizenship to Asiatics living in the United States; these aliens to whom the right of citizenship had been denied because of race were now permitted to seek naturalization. Even more comprehensive were the laws passed by some of the states that forbade, under penalties, employers, employment agencies, and trade-unions to discriminate against workers because of race, color, creed, or national origin. Such discrimination was condemned as a violation of civil rights that sapped the very foundations of a free, democratic nation. These measures are hopeful signs pointing the way to the elimination of discriminatory practices, thereby giving all elements of the population equal opportunities to share in America's horn of plenty.

END OF AMERICAN ISOLATION

America entered the twentieth century bursting with stored-up energy. The extraordinary economic development and the abounding spirit of self-confidence engendered among the people augured ill for the continuance of traditional isolationism. So great a center of power could not for long be isolated from world affairs. Once launched on a world career, would America be a threat or a promise? Would she, like the great European powers, embark on an imperialist policy and extend her dominion "over palm and pine"? Would she become a "bad neighbor" and pursue aggressive policies in the Western Hemisphere? These were the questions that came to the minds of many as America rose to world hegemony during the first half of the twentieth century.

The Spanish-American war, at the end of the nineteenth century, marked the end of America's historic policy of isolation. During most of the nineteenth century, isolationism had been a necessary policy for America, whose energies were absorbed in subduing a continent and in perfecting her political unity. Moreover she was then militarily weak and uncertain of her unity. Isolationism really meant permanent neutrality, of which the Monroe Doctrine was the international expression. It may be said that nearly all of America's foreign policy during the nineteenth century consisted of the Monroe Doctrine.

As a result of her victory over Spain, in 1898, America unwittingly yet inevitably entered the path of imperialist expansion. In the Caribbean she acquired Puerto Rico and what amounted to a protectorate over Cuba; and in the Pacific, the Philippines and Guam. In effect the Caribbean became an American "lake" when, during 1914–1916, Haiti and Nicaragua were occupied by American troops. An uprising against Colombia, in 1903, fomented by Americans, resulted in the establishment of the Republic of Panama. Promptly, only too promptly, Panama ceded the Canal Zone in perpetuity to the United States. Soon thereafter the latter built the Panama Canal. These acts received sanction from the "Roosevelt Corollary" of the Monroe Doctrine proclaimed by President Theodore Roosevelt. According to the President's interpretation of the Monroe Doctrine, the United States herself had the only right to intervene in Latin America, in order to forestall intervention by European powers. The Roosevelt Corollary gave the official seal to American imperialism.

That America, whose very existence was the outcome of a revolt against imperialism, should herself join in the imperialist game was astonishing, to say the least. A sharp division over imperialism rose among the American people, and became an issue in presidential elections. Many sympathized with the resentment felt by Latin Americans against "Yankee imperialism," and against the Monroe Doctrine, which was now derided by the latter as a mask for aggression by the "Colossus of the North." Many Americans, however, were convinced that expansion was America's "manifest destiny," a sentiment forcefully expounded by Theodore Roosevelt. "We have no choice, we the people of the United States," he declared, "as to whether or not we shall play a great part in the world. That has been determined for us by fate, by the march of events. We have to play that part. All that we can decide is whether we shall play it well or ill." [24]

What were the causes of this momentous change in America's fundamental policies? Was "manifest destiny" a blind fate that drove America to forsake her historic role? In truth it was a great change in the world situation that was chiefly responsible for American imperialism. This great change was brought about by the rise of Imperial Germany. As described elsewhere, Germany beheld in Britain her supreme antagonist on the diplomatic chessboard, her great competitor in world markets, her chief obstacle to world dominion. Britain's main strength lay in her control of the seas, which could be wrested from her only by a navy more powerful than her own. At the beginning of the twentieth century, a mighty German navy made its appearance, the first challenge to British sea power since Trafalgar, in 1805. A naval rivalry began between Germany and Britain that raged fast and furious.

How did America fit into this European scene? She now became acutely aware of something that she had long known but had not fully appreciated, namely, that all during the nineteenth century the British fleet had been the power behind the Monroe Doctrine. The American navy was then too weak to withstand an attack by European powers bent on aggression in Latin America. America could therefore bask in her isolation as long as the British fleet patrolled the Atlantic.

In case of a conflict between Germany and Britain resulting in the triumph of the former, British sea power would be destroyed. The German fleet would then be in control of the Atlantic. This prospect caused a vast and growing uneasiness among Americans, now for the first time deeply concerned about national security. Britain was consistently a liberal nation, pacifically inclined. Germany was a semiautocratic nation

[24] A. C. Coolidge, *The United States as a World Power* (1927), 374.

and very militaristic. British interests in the New World generally harmonized with those of America. Moreover, Britain had, in Canada, a large stake in the maintenance of friendly relations with America. Germany with her strident egotism, with her ruthless will to power, with her overweening colonial ambitions would, if triumphant, make swift, aggressive moves everywhere in the world. Especially would her ambition veer toward South America, where German trade and investments were growing rapidly. Would America then feel safe and secure behind the Monroe Doctrine, which Germany was bound to challenge?

It now became clear that American ventures in the Caribbean were inspired by fear for the security of the Monroe Doctrine. The extensions of American authority in this region aimed to establish an American defense system, with bases on the islands, in order to protect the mainland and that most vital artery, the Panama Canal, which made possible swift and easy passage of American fleets from one ocean to the other. The acquisition of the Philippines and of Hawaii, likewise, had a defensive motive. They were to serve as outlying, far-flung defenses of America's West coast in case of an attack from across the Pacific.

How was America's traditional isolationism affected by this change in the world situation? It continued in a contradictory sort of way, with intervention in Latin America and in the Far East and with strict isolation in respect to Europe. This contradiction was aggravated by the still more irritating one of a democratic nation pursuing an imperialist policy, for whatever reason. The territories acquired from Spain did not and could not find a legitimate place in the American constitutional system; hence their status remained undefined. They were ruled more or less autocratically by American officials appointed by the President. These contradictions were to be resolved in a most resolute manner by the two world wars.

As the twentieth century neared August 4, 1914, it became evident that only a world war could end the tension created by the international situation. Crisis succeeded crisis, each more serious than the preceding one. Should war break out, it would not be confined to Europe because the great issue of German militarism had world-wide implications. What would be the attitude of America if her hallowed tradition of isolationism were confronted with the stark reality of world conflict? Would she stoutly assert her neutrality and enforce it with her now powerful navy? Or would she promptly join Britain and France "to make the world safe for democracy" and declare war on Germany?

AMERICA IN THE TWO WORLD WARS

When the First World War broke out, America unhesitatingly did neither. She proclaimed her neutrality, but both people and government were neutral neither in thought nor in deed. An overwhelming majority of the American people openly voiced their sympathy for the Allies, and especially for Britain to whom Americans were now closely drawn for the first time in their history. President Wilson, for all his insistence on America's cherished doctrine of "freedom of the seas," maintained it firmly as against Germany and indulgently as against Britain. His attitude may be explained by the long-range view that America now had of her security and of her determination to continue her democratic way of life undisturbed. This broke through the technicalities and the logic surrounding her neutrality in the world-wide conflict. As German armies passed from victory to victory, Germany's bid for world dominion became clearer and sharper. The Allies at bay turned to America as the one hope of making the world "safe for democracy." This appeal did not fall on deaf ears. America felt within herself the stirrings of her future mission as the world champion of democracy, foretold by de Tocqueville, and she thrust aside her tradition of isolationism. Germany's sinking of the "Lusitania" and her unlimited submarine warfare touched off something more in America than resentment against these ruthless acts. America entered the war on the side of the Allies with no commitments whatever, except to make every effort to establish a new world order, based on freedom and security as formulated by President Wilson's Fourteen Points. For the first time in history, American soldiers fought on the battlefields of Europe.

With the defeat of Germany, America's hopes of a new world order rose high. But they were soon dashed to the ground. As so often happened in Europe, the treaty of Versailles, like many former treaties, established a peace that contained the seeds of another war. The terms were such that the defeated would seek revenge and the victorious would make every effort to solidify their gains. America's disappointment with the treaty was deepened by the resentment that she felt when the Allies refused to pay their war debts. To the dismay of Europe, America returned to her traditional isolation. She refused to make any agreement to uphold the treaty of Versailles or to join the League of Nations to create a new world order. In disgust with Europe's shortsightedness and ingratitude, America determined that she would not again be drawn into European conflicts. The Neutrality law of 1937 abandoned America's doctrine of the freedom of the seas by making it unlawful for American citizens to travel on a belligerent ship or to sell or transport munitions to belligerents. America's return to isolation was due not only to her disgust with Europe but also to her newly found security. Germany's fleet was at the bottom of the sea.

But the old spell of isolationism had been broken by America's massive intervention during the First World War. Try as she would she could not recreate the mood of her historic policy. A new spell had been woven, when America had appeared as the world's mighty champion of democracy. Reading the history of the period between the two world wars the impression is left that while America was consciously and deliberately striving to return to isolation she was, at the same time, pervaded by feelings of uneasiness in doing so. No longer, as in former times, did America have the easy confidence in her self-sufficiency, in her self-righteousness, in her self-defense. Would the "world be safe for democracy" if she succeeded in returning to her ancient moorings?

A new enemy of democracy, totalitarian dictatorship, had suddenly and unexpectedly appeared. And it soon became apparent that the new enemy was far more powerful, far more uncompromising, and far more ruthless than had been the Germany of the Kaiser. Openly and defiantly, the totalitarian states —Communist Russia, Fascist Italy, and Nazi Germany— proclaimed world revolution against what they termed "decadent pluto-democracy." Even more ominous was the fact that they were joining forces against the democracies. In 1936 Mussolini and Hitler formed the Axis; and in 1939 a pact was entered into by Hitler and Stalin. Totalitarian dictatorship cast its long shadow over Asia. Japan fell under the complete control of the militarists, who actively set about to carry out their long-matured plan of making Japan the "lord of the Far East." In order to present a united front throughout the world against the democracies, the European dictatorships allied themselves with Japan. During 1939–1940 Soviet Russia entered into a neutrality pact, and the Axis powers, into a military alliance with Japan. Fear and dismay spread throughout the democratic world.

What about America? With growing uneasiness America began to realize that the world was now less safe for democracy than when Imperial Germany had been the only threat. Far-sighted American statesmen, such as the Democrat, Franklin D. Roosevelt, and the Republican, Henry L. Stimson, came to the unshakable conclusion that American isolationism encouraged the totalitarian dictators in their ambitions for world domination. If the democratic nations of Europe were destroyed, "one by one," America would then indeed find herself in isolation, confronting the victorious dictators all by herself. President Roosevelt became the outstanding and eloquent spokesman of America's duty, even necessity, to do all in her power to "quarantine" the aggressive dictators. What confused the situation were the contradictions in America's policy: (1) that between intervention in respect to Latin America and the Far East and isolation in respect to Europe and (2) that between imperialist policies and democratic professions. America had to resolve these contradictions before she could again appear as the defender of world freedom.

And resolve them she did. The Roosevelt administration inaugurated the "good neighbor" policy toward Latin America by withdrawing American troops from Haiti and Nicaragua, by repealing the Platt amendment which had made Cuba a protectorate of the United States, and by granting self-government to Puerto Rico. Even more important was the adoption of a new version of the Monroe Doctrine. The Roosevelt Corollary (advanced by Theodore Roosevelt) was repudiated; henceforth the Doctrine was no longer to be enforced unilaterally by the United States but multilaterally by Pan-America, including the Latin-American states and the United States united to prevent aggression from within or from without the New World. A far more striking repudiation of imperialism was America's promise of independence to the Philippines, a promise she later faithfully kept, when on July 4, 1946, the Philippines became an independent republic. Cleared of the taint of imperialism America could now appear as the democratic pillar of fire in the night of totalitarian dictatorship that was spreading throughout the world.

When the Second World War broke out, America's attitude

was firm and clear. Though officially neutral, she was determined to aid the European democracies, which were fighting for their very lives, frankly and openly, in every way short of war. Isolationist sentiment was still strong, but even stronger was the feeling of America's responsibility for the fate of democracy. American intervention in Europe took place on an immense scale, resolving the contradiction that had existed in her foreign policy. The neutrality law of 1937 was repealed, and America sent supplies of all kinds, including arms and warships, to the beleaguered democracies. Armed American merchant ships crossed the ocean bound for belligerent ports. America became the "arsenal of democracy" through lend-lease, which gave immense aid to all nations fighting the fascist Axis. Outstanding as the unflinching champion of democracy against fascism was Franklin D. Roosevelt, who, in the words of Winston Churchill, "changed decisively and permanently the moral axis of mankind by involving the New World inexorably and irrevocably with the fortunes of the Old." Japan's treacherous attack on Pearl Harbor sounded the death knell of American isolation. With practical unanimity, America entered the Second World War. In no other war in American history were the people so firmly and so completely united behind their government.

America's entrance into the war sealed the fate of the Axis powers. Far more than even during the First World War was her power now felt in aiding her allies: in the production of supplies, in the transportation of goods, on the field of battle, and in maintaining the morale of her Allies. The many victories won, and the many lands conquered by the Axis powers served, in the end, only to exhaust them. The Allies could bear their losses, no matter how heavy, being certain of prompt and abundant aid from inexhaustible America. At the end of six long years of desperate fighting, the Axis powers, one after another, collapsed in total defeat.

AMERICA CONFRONTS SOVIET RUSSIA

The victory of the Allies over the Axis powers was won at a terrific cost. Europe was bled white, and the Continent, that for so long had dominated the world, sank into impotence. The great nations—England, France, Germany, and Italy—that had created Western civilization were impoverished, weakened, and, in the case of Germany, completely ruined. Even their grip upon themselves was failing because of loss of nerve. That, however, was not the temper of Soviet Russia. Though devastated and impoverished, Soviet Russia, alone of the European Allies, emerged from the war strong and aggressive. The Communist party succeeded in accomplishing in one decade what the tsars had failed to accomplish in centuries of effort, namely the control of Russia's western borderlands and of most of the Balkans. And Soviet Russia suffered no failure of nerve. Quite the contrary! She was energized to prodigious efforts by the driving power of her mission to spread the gospel of communism throughout the world.

America, as already described, emerged from the Second World War the richest and most powerful nation in the world. Would she, as after the First World War, slump back into isolationism now that democracy was safe from fascist dictatorship? Quite the contrary was the case. America took a leading part in organizing the United Nations of which she became the most influential and most consistent supporter. American troops occupied ex-enemy countries: Germany, Japan, Trieste, and Austria. An historic statement was made on September 6, 1946, by Secretary of State James F. Byrnes, when he declared that as long as "an occupation force is required for Germany the army of the United States will be a part of that occupation force." This statement of policy quieted the fears of Europe lest America again return to isolation. There was no turning back; America now was definitely committed to play an active role in the world affairs.

What was to be the nature of this role? It soon became evident that it was to be as the defender of Western civilization against its greatest enemy, Soviet Russia. America is the oldest child of Western Europe and most completely resembles it. Born in the age of enlightenment, when Western ideals were boldly and triumphantly proclaimed, she, more than any other nation, has had a clear call to defend them. And she has answered this call promptly and readily.

During the war America had shown marked friendliness for Soviet Russia as a doughty ally, and had tolerated communism as an "opinion," to be accepted or rejected like any other opinion on politics or economics. Americans, especially President Roosevelt, were convinced that the Russians would, when peace came, cooperate with the democracies in reconstructing ruined Europe and in building new roads to world peace and security. After the war, Soviet Russia's many violations of solemn treaty obligations, her frequent use of the veto to paralyze the United Nations, her truculence in diplomatic negotiations, her hand in the overthrow of democratic governments in Central Europe caused first, confusion, then resentment, and finally, understanding. American statesmen had to undergo a process of re-education in regard to communism in general and to Soviet Russia in particular.

America now clearly realized that Soviet Russia was relentlessly pursuing her over-all aim to establish world communism. The first and most essential step would be to conquer Western Europe. Would the Red army stop at the water's edge when it reached the Atlantic? Or would a Communist Europe become the basis for attacks on America? The latter now realized that the oceans no longer constituted moats around her bastions and that she had become the heart and center of a world foreshortened by the airplane. Measured in flying time, America was no more distant from the European Continent than Britain had been before the airplane had annihilated distances. America's security now depended, like that of Britain in the past, on preventing the domination of the Continent by one great power.

The reduction of the number of great powers to two, America and Russia, created an unprecedented situation in international relations. These two superpowers, completely opposed to each other in their ideologies, in their policies, in their ways of life, soon became rallying centers for the other nations that aligned themselves either on the side of democratic America or on that of Communist Russia. Russia was dedicated to world revolution, aiming to establish, by any and all means, a universal totalitarian dictatorship. America, repudiating her carefree, isolationist past, now realized that democracy, once a national ideal, had become an international responsibility. Every democracy looked to America as the one power able and willing to defend it against the onslaughts of communism, from within and from without. And with good reason. America gave every evidence of her sincere desire for peace by virtually disarming after the end of the Second World War and by offering to surrender her monopoly of the atomic bomb.[25]

But Soviet Russia talked peace and prepared for war. She did not demobilize, to any extent, after the Second World War. Her armies and those of her satellites constituted the greatest military force in the world. Moreover, she was rapidly building large numbers of submarines and war planes. Russian scientists and technicians were working feverishly to produce atomic bombs. If they succeeded, the military situation would change markedly to the disadvantage of America; the latter, instead of Western Europe, might become the first object of Russian aggression. A sudden, swift air raid across the North Pole against

[25] See p. 399.

American industrial centers by Russian planes carrying atomic bombs might destroy America's power to retaliate. A Russian Pearl Harbor could then be successful.

In a most extraordinary manner America set about to meet her new international responsibilities. Immediate was the need to revive and to strengthen Western Europe, America's first line of defense against Russian aggression. President Truman became the leading champion of democracy against communist dictatorship as, before him, President Roosevelt had been its champion against fascist dictatorship. During the Truman administration, America adopted far-reaching policies to aid Western Europe economically, militarily, and politically. She promptly took up the European man's burden with a willingness that astonished the world.

The first and most essential aid to be given by America had to be economic. Such aid would give assurance that Europe's factories and mines would be set going, that its trade would be revived, and that business confidence would be restored. America, the lone solvent nation in an insolvent world, offered to create an economic plasma bank for the stricken nations of Europe by proposing the now famous Marshall Plan.

In 1947 Secretary of State George C. Marshall, speaking for the American government, delivered an address that resounded throughout the world. He declared that America stood ready to extend generous aid to the European nations, provided they showed a willingness to help themselves by reorganizing their economies to increase production. American aid was to provide "a cure rather than a palliative" in order "to permit the emergence of political and social conditions in which free institutions can exist." Secretary Marshall urged the adoption by the European nations of common policies to supplement one another's economy in order to carry out his idea of joint self-help. In order to implement what became known as the Marshall Plan, a conference of all the nations in Europe was called to devise a general plan of rehabilitation and to assess the amount of American aid that each nation would need.

This conference met in Paris, and consisted of representatives of sixteen European nations: Britain, France, Italy, the German Federal Republic, the Netherlands, Belgium, Luxemburg, Denmark, Norway, Sweden, Ireland, Iceland, Austria, Switzerland, Portugal, Turkey, and Greece. Soviet Russia refused to attend, and compelled her satellite nations to abstain from attending the conference as well. And the reason was obvious. European recovery would allay discontent, thereby effectively stemming the tide of communism, which always rises when living standards fall. Communism has been quick to take advantage of unstable economic conditions, on the theory that "the worse the better." Soviet Russia, her satellites, and Communists in every land loudly and bitterly denounced the Marshall Plan as a scheme of American "imperialism" to dominate Europe.

The conference drew up a detailed plan of rehabilitation and gave estimates of the amount of American aid needed by each of the sixteen nations that had accepted the Marshall Plan. Part of this aid was to consist of outright gifts in the form of food, fuel, and fertilizers; part, of loans for industrial equipment; and part, of shipments of raw materials and machinery, which would be sold to individuals in each country, the proceeds of which would be used by America to purchase goods in that country. The Marshall Plan was to run for a period of four years; its cost was estimated to be from 16 to 20 billion dollars for these years.

America's prime objectives in giving this generous aid was to establish political and social stability in Western Europe and to promote the economic integration of that region. Nevertheless, uneasiness spread among many Europeans lest this aid be given at the price of a country's independence, especially in matters social and economic. America, in the main, was committed to private enterprise; she had abandoned *laissez faire* but not capitalism. But nearly all of the European democracies had chosen socialist or semisocialist governments that were embarking on extensive schemes of nationalization. Would capitalist America insist that a nation, to be a beneficiary of the Marshall Plan, renounce its policy of nationalization? America promptly quieted these fears by declaring that she would in no way dictate to the nations who accepted the Plan; they were to be free to follow any economic policy, socialist or capitalist, that best suited their interests.

In 1948, Congress created the European Recovery Program (ERP), with authority to supervise the working of the Marshall Plan. The ERP has been instrumental in devising ways and means for eliminating restrictions on trade between the sixteen countries, and between them as a unit and the rest of the world. After two years the economic revival of the Marshall Plan countries became notable. Anxiety turned into hope, and hope into confidence as Western Europe rose slowly to its feet.

Of all the countries in Western Europe, Britain was the greatest beneficiary of American aid. And the reason was that America regarded Britain as the most powerful, the most stable, and the most reliable of all the European democracies. Britain had shown her mettle in fighting all by herself, for a time, the united power of Nazi Europe, aided by Soviet Russia. In case of another world war, Britain might become a base of operation for America against Soviet Russia, as she had been against Germany during the Second World War. Therefore it was all-important to prevent Britain from collapsing economically. America came to the conclusion that she must do her utmost to bolster British economy, and what she did in this regard constitutes an astonishing record of generosity and foresight. About $25,000,000,000, the sum owed to America by Britain in lend-lease transactions, was wiped out. On top of this, America, for several years, sent to Britain large quantities of goods in the form of relief, under the United Nations Relief and Rehabilitation Administration (UNRRA). Then, in 1946, America granted a loan of $3,750,000,000 on exceedingly favorable terms. And when this sum was used up, a new form of American aid was given, under the Marshall Plan. During the period, 1945–1950, America loaned or gave to Britain the immense sum of $7,000,000,000. The daughter, who, in 1776, left her mother's house slamming the door, now returned a friend, rich, powerful, and generous.

The political stability and the economic integration of Western Europe, the immediate objectives of the Marshall Plan, were likewise to serve as a basis for the revival of military power. Would Soviet Russia, however, stand idly by and watch Western Europe rise to its feet? Might she not suddenly decide to turn the "cold" war into a "hot" one? Should that occur, Western Europe would again become a battlefield, bringing untold havoc, ruin, and suffering. Liberation again might come through American intervention, but sad experience had taught Europeans the terrors and costs of being liberated and ruined at the same time.

What could be done to prevent a third world war? The answer was, only the overwhelming power of an alliance between America and Western Europe. After being forced to intervene during the two world wars, America came to the conclusion that the prevention of a third world war would be better—and cheaper—than victory. This change of attitude led America to make her great bid for world security by proposing the North Atlantic treaty.[26] In 1949, America and eleven nations of Western Europe formed the now famous pact, which became a hard-and-fast military alliance, with a unified system of defense, supported in part by generous contributions from America. The hard core of this alliance consisted of America, Britain, and Canada, whose association became exceedingly close, even

[26] See pp. 324–325.

intimate. The cooperation of their armed forces, established during the war, has continued intact. They cooperated in the development of the atomic bomb. After the war, American air forces were stationed in Britain. When the latter, by herself, could no longer bear the burden of guarding the Mediterranean, America promptly sent naval forces into that strategic sea.

The North Atlantic treaty was the most important international decision made by America since the promulgation of the Monroe Doctrine. For the first time in history, America entered into a military alliance with European powers in time of peace. Neutrality, the capstone of isolationism, was now definitely abandoned. America's policy of neutrality had merely served to encourage the aggressions of Wilhelm II and of Hitler by giving them assurance that America would stay out of European conflicts. Now, by entering the North Atlantic Pact, America has made it perfectly clear that, should Stalin launch an invasion of Western Europe, she would be in the war from the outset. American military power, actual and potential, constitutes the real force behind the pact.

Whatever was left of American isolationism quickly vanished when confronted by the Russian menace. America determined not to be again caught napping, as at Pearl Harbor. In Congress, Republicans united with Democrats in backing the foreign policies and defense measures urged by the Truman administration. The Republican leader, Senator Arthur H. Vandenberg, was in the intimate confidence of President Truman. America determined to create a system of defense so powerful that it would deter any aggressor from embarking on war. In 1948, Congress, as a beginning, voted over 3 billion dollars for a top air force, a sum larger than that requested by President Truman. A law followed establishing conscription, which, though not immediately applied, was unprecedented in American history in time of peace. In 1949, Congress appropriated 15 billion dollars for defense, a record peacetime outlay. An almost universal conviction existed, namely, that, whatever the cost, America must be able to retaliate, swiftly and effectively, in case of war. No price was too high to pay for national security.

Never before in history did any nation play the role that America now plays in the world. With her tremendous military power she refuses to conquer other nations. On the contrary, she extends to them protection against aggression. With her great economic power she refuses to compel the impoverished nations to become her dependents by subordinating their economy to hers. On the contrary, she helps them to reconstruct their shattered resources so that they may become independent of her aid. From June, 1945, to January, 1949, America extended foreign aid in the form of grants and credits totaling $24,802,-000,000. "Many nations have risen to the summit of human affairs," declared Winston Churchill, "but here is a great example where new-won supremacy has not been used for self-aggrandizement but only for further sacrifice." [27]

THE AMERICAN WORLD REVOLUTION

America's bid for world security had, as its prime objective, the promotion of peace and prosperity everywhere. The American dream of earlier days had sought to establish a democratic social and political order at home. In a sense it was the ideological by-product of isolationism. When, however, isolationism vanished in the twentieth century, American idealism took a new direction, that of seeking the way to establish a new and better world order. What has been the unique and outstanding economic achievement of America? It is her wonderful technological system of production, which, if applied universally, could greatly mitigate the condition of the starved and semistarved

[27] *The New York Times,* Apr. 1, 1949.

millions everywhere. Poverty has been the great evil that so frequently has facilitated the stride of communism to power.

America, like Soviet Russia, is the center of a world revolution. But the American plan of world reorganization is diametrically opposed to that of Soviet Russia. In the first place, America aims to make universal the democratic way of life, based upon self-government and civil liberty, in contrast to the irresponsible dictatorship of the Russian police state. "American democracy is based upon a fundamental distrust of any irresponsible elite, and is committed to mass control, in the last analysis; to the principle that the gains of civilization are essentially mass gains, and should be distributed throughout the mass without delay; to the principle that human happiness may best be promoted by advancing the common man to a continually higher level." [28] In the second place, America favors the creation of a world organization, based on the free association of free nations, that would respect and defend democratic liberties by an international bill of rights. Soviet Russia, on the contrary, aims to establish a world organization on totalitarian principles, dominated by herself, in which all the other nations would be her satellites. In the third place, America aims to abolish poverty and to establish security, but not by the Russian method of social revolution. The American plan calls, first and foremost, for high productivity as the only method by which poverty can be abolished. As a pioneer of the system of mass production, America has become the economic model for all nations. She has proclaimed her willingness to share her industrial and scientific know-how with the rest of the world to help in the war "against poverty." In his famous Point Four, President Truman offered to make America's "imponderable resources in technical knowledge" available to peace-loving peoples in their efforts to realize their aspirations for a better life.

[28] Charles E. Merriam, *Civic Education in the United States* (1934), 42.

Whenever and wherever nations have been free to choose between the American and Russian plans of world revolution they have always chosen the former. Judged by results the American methods of abolishing poverty and of giving economic security have been far more successful than have been the Russian methods to achieve these aims by confiscation of property and by regimentation of labor. Soviet Russia exports revolutionary ideology, whereas America exports advanced technology. Wherever the Russian plan of world revolution triumphed, as in east central Europe, it was followed by poverty, suppression, and terrorism. Wherever the American plan triumphed, as in Western Europe, it was followed by economic recuperation, by social reform, and by the strengthening of democratic liberties. The cold war now being waged between America and Soviet Russia is really the struggle between the two rival world revolutions. What the outcome of this strange and unprecedented struggle will be, no one, in 1950, could accurately foretell.

Chapter 11. Toward a United World

WAR, AN UNSOLVED PROBLEM

Past events and developments, particularly those of the last fifty years, have clearly indicated that the world was drawing closer together. Improved transportation and communication and growing economic interdependence were all working to create a united world. Despite these notable advances, wars, national and international, were constantly breaking out to halt the progress toward international comity. The great problem facing the present generation is how to solve national conflicts, arising in an interdependent world without resorting to the most terrible of all calamities, namely, war.

As described in previous chapters, great progress has taken place in many fields. Democracy, both political and social, has been extended; popular education in the lower and higher grades has become widespread; the standard of living of the masses has been raised; and subject peoples have been freed. But no such progress can be shown in establishing a united world free from the ravages of war. It is a melancholy reflection that if anything wars have become more widespread, more destructive, and more barbarous as century succeeded century. Science, which is responsible for creating the surplus economy that makes possible the abolition of poverty, is, at the same time, responsible for creating weapons of fearful destructive power. From the invention of gunpowder to that of the atomic bomb the history of warfare has been the history of ever-increasing destructiveness. All attempts to limit or to prevent the use of these weapons have, on the whole, failed. The first world effort to make at least a beginning in the direction of limiting arma-

385

ments took place at the Hague Peace Conference, in 1899. Not
only did the conference fail to accomplish this objective, but
the very opposite policy was subsequently pursued by the great
powers. An armament race began that resulted in two world
wars in one generation, something unprecedented in modern
history. Never before had humanity suffered a calamity so vast
in scale and so deep in misery as the Second World War. The
losses in life and property were so tremendous that it is impossible to compute them. The fearful torture of prisoners and
the wholesale massacre of noncombatants, systematically organized and coldly executed by the Germans and the Japanese,
have no precedent in the history of man's inhumanity to man.
War lost all chivalry, all humanity, all rules of conduct, and
became a death struggle between nations like that between
beasts in the jungle.

What is the nature of the international order—or disorder—
that has made possible this greatest of all tragedies in the history
of mankind? What is the nature of man that war on an ever-
increasing scale and with ever-greater brutality throws its dark
shadow on human progress? Can it be, as pessimists claim, that
war arises from the "rooted bellicosity of human nature"? Is
then mankind doomed to pass from war to war until all civilization is wiped out by some all-destructive weapon? The causes
of war are many and they have been systematically studied by
scholars in all lands.[1] There is a general agreement among them,
stated or implied, that the root cause of war is not man's evil
nature but his incapacity thus far to understand and to master
the forces in the modern world that make for war. Extraordi-
narily gifted and boldly adventurous in the arts of political and
social invention, man has succeeded in creating new and better
systems of government and of society. And yet, at the same time,
he has shown poverty and timidity in the art of creating a stable
and peaceful international order. But the prospect of wholesale

[1] See especially Quincey Wright, *A Study of War,* 2 vols. (1942).

destruction held out by atomic and biologic warfare, in case
of a third world war, has created a movement in every land
seeking to devise ways of establishing a united world in place
of the system of international anarchy that has plagued mankind from the dawn of modern times to the present. In the
field of international relations, as in that of the domestic arts,
necessity may prove to be the mother of invention.

INTERNATIONAL RELATIONS AND
WORLD PEACE

Invention in the realm of ideas, like that in the realm of science,
comes through knowledge. Until the First World War, diplomacy had been a sealed book to the average man. It had become the exclusive sphere of professional diplomats, ministers
of foreign affairs, and heads of governments, who conducted
international relations, unchecked by parliaments and with little
responsibility to public opinion. Unlike domestic affairs, foreign
affairs were cloaked in secrecy, and matters of great import,
often affecting the very existence of nations, were decided by
a few insiders, and remained unknown to the public until revealed during a serious crisis, and sometimes not even then.
Secret diplomacy was accepted in democratic England and
France as in semiautocratic Germany and in wholly autocratic
Russia. Again, unlike domestic affairs, foreign affairs were non-
partisan. All parties, whether those of the government or those
of the opposition, acquiesced to a situation which put the minister of foreign affairs in the privileged position of not having to
render an account of his activities to parliament. It was deemed
of vital importance that the foreign policy of a nation be continuous, whatever the party or parties in power. When the
British Liberals swept into power in 1906, they reversed the
Conservative domestic policies. But the Liberal foreign minister,

Sir Edward Grey, continued the policies of his Conservative predecessor, Lord Landsdowne. Even more striking was the case of Théophile Delcassé, in France. He became foreign minister in 1898, and remained continuously in office, despite the ups and downs of French ministries, until 1905, when he was compelled to resign during the great Moroccan crisis. However, Delcassé's anti-German policy was resumed by his successors, and continued unchanged until 1914.

The old, secret diplomacy did, in a way, seek to prevent war through the method of the balance of power.[2] But this method failed tragically. The first half of the twentieth century witnessed no less than 12 wars involving European nations, not counting civil and colonial wars.[3] The two world wars were so calamitous that the world has come to regard peace not merely as a dream of prophets and philosophers but as a *sine qua non* for mankind's survival. International relations have ceased to be the concern only of diplomats and have become matters of vital interest to the general public. In almost every land, books, journals, motion pictures, and the radio have set themselves the task of educating the public in international relations. Organizations and schools have appeared to promote the study of the subject. College courses, popular forums, and institutes have spread knowledge of international affairs, past and present. Political parties, almost for the first time, have committed themselves to specific foreign policies. An intense, almost feverish, interest in international relations has swept America, although prior to 1914 she had evinced little interest in such matters. Isolationism had been not only a national policy but even more a prevailing mental attitude. But despite her traditions, her inclinations, and her desires, America had been forced into two

[2] See pp. 130–132.

[3] These were the Boer, the Russo-Japanese, the Italian-Turkish, the first Balkan, the second Balkan, the First World War, the Polish-Russian, the Greco-Turkish, the Italian-Ethiopian, the Italian-Albanian, the Second World War, and the Russo-Finnish War.

world wars by international crises not of her own making. Isolationism vanished, and the problem of world peace became one of great concern to the American people.

The drive for world peace was further intensified by the realization of the fearful suffering visited upon mankind as a consequence of the revolutionary changes in the art of war. For the first time war became "total," in that it was waged not only by armed forces but by all the people in every belligerent nation. Behind the lines during the two world wars the civil population was organized politically, economically, socially, educationally, and psychologically to further the war effort. Total war virtually abolished the traditional differences between civil and military, between combatants and noncombatants, and between fortified and unfortified places. The factory and railway became targets no less than the fortress and munitions works. The new weapons used in the First World War—poison gas, the airplane, and the submarine—were as deadly to the nonfighter as to the fighter. In the Second World War, when air power was in the ascendant, bombing planes laid waste great cities, killing indiscriminately men, women, and children. The most terrifying event in the history of warfare took place when, on August 5, 1945, one atomic bomb, dropped by an American airplane, destroyed the Japanese city of Hiroshima, killing 70,000 people, injuring many more, and destroying everything within a radius of a mile and a half. The average noncombatant was no longer safe behind armies and fleets. Death was at his very doorstep.

Modern methods of warfare have resulted in weakening the defense and in strengthening the attack, thereby giving new advantages to the aggressor. The greatly enhanced striking power of mechanized weapons, such as tanks, rockets, and bombing planes, have encouraged aggression on the part of militarist nations. For long, preparation for defense had counted heavily on powerful fortifications and on natural barriers. The two world wars demonstrated that fortifications, however powerful, no longer give efficient protection against attack. That was proved when the most powerful line of fortifications in history, the Maginot line, was easily breached by German tanks and bombers. The effectiveness of natural barriers has likewise vanished with the bombing plane that easily and swiftly crosses mountains, rivers, channels, seas, and even oceans. Barriers of distance have been abolished by the airplane, causing the world to shrink immeasurably. The latest type of airplane, traveling faster than sound, can get to any place from any place in an incredibly short time. No place in the world is now more than 60 hours from any airport. As Britain realized during the Second World War that she was no longer an "island," America is now becoming acutely aware of the fact that she is no longer safe in the embrace of two oceans. Swift airplanes or flying missiles carrying atomic bombs, launched from Europe or from Asia, have the power to deliver devastating attacks on American industrial centers. The outlook for Britain is even worse. It is estimated that one atomic attack on this highly concentrated industrial country would put it *hors de combat.*

Whether a nation is defeated or victorious, recovery becomes a difficult problem under modern conditions. Before the advent of total war, destructiveness was largely limited to the battlefield. Defeat meant humiliation through loss of territory and payment of an indemnity. However severe the terms of a treaty of peace, there generally remained a basis of recovery for the defeated nation. Even the exceedingly harsh terms of the treaty of Frankfort, imposed on France by Germany after the Franco-Prussian war, did not prevent France's rapid recovery. But total war, with its wholesale destruction of economic life, brings ruin to the belligerent nations. When peace comes, there is no longer a basis for recovery. After the Second World War, defeated Germany, once wealthy and powerful, became a heap of rubble amidst which a nation of beggars struggled to keep alive. Victorious Britain, once the "workshop of the world," was compelled to adopt a spartan regime of "austerity" for the entire population in order just to keep going. Defeated Japan was reduced from great wealth to the dire poverty of the Orient. America, alone among the belligerents, emerged wealthy and intact, chiefly because she was unscathed. But this good fortune may not attend her in another world war, as distance no longer lends the enchantment of security.

Only highly industrialized nations can now wage war effectively. Because of mechanized warfare, battles are fought between machines rather than between men. To manufacture the costly, complicated war machines requires the technological skill and the natural resources of a highly industrialized nation. These machines have a short life. They are quickly outmoded by new inventions, and are quickly destroyed in battle. Replacement, both in quality and in quantity, then becomes a matter of life or death, and the expense can be borne only by the few, rich, industrial nations. The small, poor nations inevitably sink into a state of helplessness, and are reduced to the position of satellites of the few powerful, aggressive nations. This was well illustrated in the case of the small nations in east central Europe. They quickly yielded to Germany after the First World War, and as quickly to Soviet Russia after the Second World War.

At all times war has been expensive, but never before as ruinously expensive as today. Preparedness lays a heavy burden on even the richest nations, because of the great cost of maintaining huge armed forces on land, on sea, and in the air. As much as 85 per cent of the 1949 budget of America was devoted to paying the cost of the two world wars and of armed preparedness against future war. To bear the enormous expense, governments borrow all they can from foreigners and from their own citizens, tax the latter to the point of confiscation, and liquidate their foreign holdings. Formerly, when armaments were fairly simple and cheap, the size of the population determined national power; the larger the population, the larger the army. Today, with mechanized warfare, what counts even more than a large population is a highly developed industry, based on abundant natural resources. The high cost of war in life, in property, and in morale, coupled with the knowledge that no defense is adequate, has at last convinced mankind that world peace can be realized only through a world organization.

THE LEAGUE OF NATIONS

As anarchy was incompatible with domestic peace, so was international anarchy incompatible with a peaceful world order. Every other method of attaining security, international as well as national, had failed: isolationism, preparedness, alliances, and balance of power. As long as each nation depended on itself for its own defense, there was little hope in the world for substantial progress toward world peace. Each nation, or combination of nations, seeking its own security brought insecurity to all nations, including itself. Treaties of peace that followed the victory of one nation over another or of one combination of nations over another have generally contained the seeds of another war. Notable instances were the treaty of Vienna (1815) that ended the Napoleonic Wars and prepared the way for the nationalist wars; the treaty of Paris (1856) that ended the Crimean war and prepared the way for the Russo-Turkish war; the treaty of Frankfort (1871) that ended the Franco-Prussian war and prepared the way for the First World War; and, most important of all, the treaty of Versailles (1919) that ended the First and prepared the way for the Second World War. Defeated nations do not accept defeat, and victorious nations are not sure of their victory; the consequence is that both prepare to renew the struggle by renewing their strength through greater armament. Only too frequently has war resulted in one victor and two losers.

All efforts to "humanize" warfare have been of little avail. The codes of international law, the rules of the Red Cross, the decisions of the Hague conferences have been more honored in the breach than in the observance. Victory would bring forgiveness, or at least forgetfulness, of ruthless conduct during the war. So believed the nation guilty of violating the codes of war. Agreements of nations to limit armaments have, like those to humanize warfare, been of little avail. The famous Washington Conference (1921-1922) that agreed to limit the size of the navies of Britain, the United States, France, Japan, and Italy, came to naught, as did the treaty between Britain and Germany (1935) to limit the size of the German navy.

The First World War revealed the system of "international anarchy" in all its weakness and in all its futility. Everything pertaining to it—national sovereignty, military alliances, and balance of power—had resulted in the greatest war in all modern history up to that time. The great power game was played out; the balance of power had brought not peace but a sword. At last world opinion swerved toward collective security through a world organization, which was uppermost in the minds of the delegates to the Peace Conference that met in Paris, in 1919. President Wilson became the greatest and most ardent champion of a world order in which the aggression of one nation against another would promptly become the vital concern of all nations. The "Covenant," adopted by the Conference as part of the treaty of Versailles, created the League of Nations. Now it can be said that the importance of this body lay only in the fact that such a body at last came into being. For the first time in history, a permanent, continuous world organization appeared dedicated to the maintenance of world peace and security. Secret diplomacy was to be abolished by the requirement that all treaties be made public and registered with the League. Armaments were to be limited through collective agreements. Most important of all, war as an "instrument of national policy" was to be curbed by economic and military sanctions, to be applied by the members of the League against an aggressive nation. Unity of power was now to succeed the balance of power that had failed so signally in preserving the peace of the world. Hope ran high, and many came to believe that, in time, the League would become a "parliament of man" that would solve the age-old problem of war.

During the period from 1924 to 1930, the high noon of the League, that body seemed to be fulfilling its promise. Under the auspices of the League, international agencies of all kinds were created to investigate evil practices in all parts of the world and to suggest ways and means of remedying them. In a number of instances, it succeeded in settling disputes between small nations. In one notable instance, the League took action against a great power. In 1935, when Italy attacked Ethiopia, it acted promptly by ordering economic sanctions against the aggressor.

However, the League contained a number of weaknesses, any one of which could seriously hamper its effectiveness. Together, they constituted a constant threat to its very existence. In the first place, the League lacked "teeth"; no international force of any kind was provided by the Covenant to enforce its decision. The League could only *request* the members to take military or economic action against an offending nation; and each member had the right to refuse to do so. Furthermore an important decision required a unanimous vote of the Council, the important body of the League; and no member was obliged to bow to such decision. In the second place, America steadfastly refused to join the world organization that she herself had been most instrumental in founding. America's repudiation of the League gave a great blow to that body under which it staggered throughout its entire existence. In the third place, the greatest weakness of the League lay in the very nature of its organization. It contained an irreconcilable, hence fatal, contradiction in that it was a world organization of national, sovereign states. Its foundation, being weak, the superstructure of the League soon began toppling. Every nation-member, large or small, stood ready to defy the League whenever its national ambitions conflicted with that body's decisions. Both the old and the new nations were jealous of their sovereignty: the old, because of pride in their great traditions; and the new because of exuberance in their new found independence. National sovereignty paralyzed international action in the many conferences on disarmament and in the efforts to uphold treaty obligations. In defiance of the League, Poland flouted the treaty in regard to minorities, and Japan refused to restore Manchuria to China. The one limitation that the Covenant placed on sovereignty, the right to make war, was flouted by Italy when she invaded Ethiopia. The League's order to boycott Italy was accepted by the members, but it was enforced by them halfheartedly, hence ineffectively. That world organization was now a sword without an edge. And the result was the triumph of Italy over the League, as well as over Ethiopia. As in the past, the members of the League continued to be national, sovereign states, and even more intensely national and more insistently sovereign than ever before.

Because of these weaknesses, the League became a center of inertia. It feared to exert authority lest such exertion end in collapse. More and more did the League shift its responsibilities, either by refusing to take up serious disputes or by evading them through all sorts of subterfuges. As it was then said, the League "touched nothing that it did not adjourn." Before long the balance of power diplomacy reappeared with all its ancient evils: secret treaties, competitive armaments, international intrigues, and rival coalitions. The League shriveled into nothing-

ness when Germany, Italy, and Japan withdrew their membership. No barrier now existed to bar the aggressive designs of
the Axis powers. The outcome was the Second World War.

THE UNITED NATIONS

The League of Nations was dead but it left behind it the precedent for a "more perfect union" of the nations. Even before the
Second World War had ended, a "world constitutional convention" met in San Francisco with the object of creating a new
international order. On June 26, 1945, it adopted a "Charter,"
establishing the United Nations. Sober realism, instead of the
romantic internationalism of the League period, characterized
the mood of the delegates to this famous convention. They
clearly realized that a world organization stronger than the
League was necessary to save mankind from the even greater
catastrophe of a third world war.

How was the Charter of the United Nations an improvement
on the Covenant of the League of Nations that had failed so
tragically in the hour of need? Would the nations be willing
to surrender their sovereignty and form a world government
having supreme power over them? Clearly, not. Would they
be willing to surrender their sovereignty in the right to make
war? Probably. A world organization would have no reason
for existence unless it could prevent war. The United Nations,
like the League of Nations, was an association of nations each
of which retained its sovereignty, but in several respects it appeared to be far stronger than the League. In the first place,
nearly all the nations of the world were members, including
the United States. And the adherence of the greatest power in
the world gave immense prestige to the newly born world
order. The chief organs, the Assembly and the Security Council,
were—or appeared to be—stronger than those of the League.

Like the Assembly of the League, the Assembly of the United Nations, representing all its member-nations, each having one vote, was mainly a world forum, with the right to discuss and to make recommendations. But real power to act lay with the Security Council, consisting of eleven members: five permanent ones, the Big Five, namely, America, Britain, Soviet Russia, France, and China; and six, representing the other members of the United Nations, elected for a term of two years by a two-thirds vote of the Assembly. But there was an important difference between the Council of the League and the Security Council of the United Nations. Action by the former in important matters required the unanimous consent of its fifteen members; but similar action by the Security Council required only an affirmative vote of seven of its eleven members. There was, however, a fly in the ointment. This was the famous veto, according to which any one of the Big Five could block action by the Security Council on any matter that it considered important, by interposing a "veto."

Unlike the Covenant, the Charter provided for "teeth." An international general staff was to be organized by the Big Five, with power to make available armed forces, to be supplied by the members of the United Nations. In case of a breach of the peace, the general staff, acting on a decision of the Security Council, would take prompt action against an aggressor. Military power, ready for action, was to be placed behind the new world organization.

If the absence of America was the weakness of the League of Nations the presence of Russia was the weakness of the United Nations. The attitude of the Western democracies toward the United Nations was clearly and definitely favorable. At last a world organization had been set up, far from perfect, it is true, but nevertheless sufficiently strong to initiate a world movement against war. Because of the dread of a third world catastrophe, all the nations, it was firmly believed, would be willing to compromise their differences in order to strengthen the United Nations. In time, its authority would be universally recognized, so that even the most powerful nation would not dare defy it. The veto would wither away through disuse. What was all-essential was the loyal cooperation of every member, especially of the Big Five, in the attainment of this goal.

Very different was the attitude of Soviet Russia toward the United Nations. It is a fundamental principle of Marxism that no world peace and security is possible as long as capitalism exists. Hence there can not be cooperation between capitalist and communist nations; war between them is inevitable, sooner or later. Any world organization, not completely under communist control, is, therefore, useless and worthless at best, and, at worst, a scheme by which capitalism entrenches itself in preparation for the coming conflict.

In conformity with this theory, Soviet Russia made every effort to weaken the United Nations. By making frequent use of the veto, she all but paralyzed the Security Council, which became veto-bound into inaction.[4] This was an unexpected turn of affairs, as it had been assumed by the creators of the Charter that the veto would be used sparingly, and only to prevent military action against any of the Big Five. Another method adopted by Soviet Russia to weaken the United Nations was to boycott most of the specialized agencies and commissions created by that body to deal with the many concrete problems that arose to threaten the peace of the world. Instead of cooperating with the others, Russia did everything in her power to prevent the United Nations from acting in disturbed areas. In 1948, Soviet Russia was twice cited before the bar of the United Nations on charges of threatening international security, and both times these charges were sustained by overwhelming majorities. Fearing that the other members of the United Na-

---

[4] By the end of 1949 the veto was used, in all, 43 times. Of these, Soviet Russia was responsible for 41 and France for 2.

tions might do something drastic without her, Soviet Russia promptly joined the commission to organize military forces to enforce the decisions of the Security Council. The reason for her changed attitude soon became evident. Every plan proposed by the other members of the commission, every effort for a compromise plan, was blocked by the Russian members, whose real purpose in joining was to prevent the United Nations from enforcing its decisions. As a consequence, the "teeth" provided by the Charter never grew.

A striking illustration of Russian intransigeance involved the proposed plan to control atomic energy. Having the great advantage of a monopoly of the atomic bomb, America, nevertheless, submitted a plan designed to internationalize it. This plan, known as the Baruch Plan, proposed to establish an international agency in which would be vested exclusive ownership and management of all basic materials needed for nuclear fission. It would have the power to regulate and to control all atomic manufacture. Though an agency of the Security Council it would not be subject to the veto. International inspection was to be instituted to prevent any nation from secretly manufacturing atomic bombs. America agreed to give up all her atomic bombs to this international body, once the plan was working effectively. No heavier sacrifice could be made by any nation than that which America voluntarily offered to make for world security. Soviet Russia opposed the Baruch Plan, and submitted one of her own. It required that, at the very outset, America destroy her stockpile of atomic bombs, dismantle the plants for manufacturing them, and make public her atomic secrets. It favored the creation of an international atomic commission, but insisted on the retention of the veto on acts of this body. The Russian plan likewise opposed international inspection as an infringement of national sovereignty. The Security Council accepted the American plan and rejected the Russian substitute for it. In 1948 the Assembly endorsed the American plan by an overwhelming vote; the six dissenting votes were cast by Soviet Russia and her satellites. It was plain that the Russians aimed to make ineffective all efforts to internationalize the control of nuclear energy.

Were Soviet Russia's tactics designed to wreck the United Nations? Not at all! She continually and vociferously asserted her loyalty to that body, and tenaciously clung to her membership. Soviet Russia favored the maintenance of the United Nations, but in a state of animated paralysis. Its existence provided a point of contact between herself and the rest of the world, which she could use to gauge the orientation of her fellow members, together and separately. Moreover, the Assembly and the Security Council provided unrivaled rostra for communist propaganda, of which the Russian members took full advantage. For Soviet Russia to withdraw would automatically convert the United Nations into an anti-Soviet world organization, which would become a strong collective security organization, with its own armed forces ready to oppose aggression in any part of the world. This was the very last thing that Soviet Russia wanted.

Russian tactics succeeded in discrediting the United Nations as a potent international force. The world was in a quandary. It was not possible to amend the Charter because Soviet Russia, as one of the Big Five, had the power to veto any amendment. For the noncommunist nations to withdraw from the United Nations and form a rival international organization would split the world into communist and noncommunist combinations. A third world war would thereby be hastened. Russian obstruction reduced to nullity the advantages that the United Nations had over the League of Nations. Because of its weakness, the former, like the latter, became active in creating international agencies which issued numerous reports on international problems. The member nations "indulged in an incredible multiplication of the instruments for insuring peace, but on the other hand they have consistently rejected all responsibility for employing these instruments where their own interests were not advantaged."

SYSTEMS OF REGIONAL DEFENSE

The impasse into which the United Nations had fallen created consternation. Resentment against Soviet Russia, who was held chiefly responsible for this situation, mounted high in all democratic countries. A new determination now arose: to work with Russia if possible, without her if not possible. In order to avoid the veto, the United Nations was by-passed when prompt action became necessary to prevent catastrophe in any part of the world. For this reason, the Marshall Plan was initiated and put into practice outside the United Nations. And, for the same reason, the Truman Doctrine was proclaimed, and American aid was given to Greece and Turkey without invoking the authority of the United Nations.[5] Far more important was the movement for regional defense. As the Charter recognized the inherent right of self-defense, it authorized the formation of mutual defense pacts, within the framework of the United Nations, by nations in the same region. If peace could not be realized on a world basis, the next best thing was to endeavor to protect certain areas from aggression. Regional pacts would, to some degree, remove the haunting sense of insecurity felt by the Western nations because of the aggressive acts and threatening demands of Soviet Russia.

The first regional pact appeared in the Western Hemisphere. A conference, representing the Latin-American states and the United States, was held in Rio de Janeiro, in 1947, and adopted a treaty of mutual defense. This treaty upheld the community of interests of nations in the Western Hemisphere by asserting

[5] See p. 312.

that an attack on one of them was an attack on all, whether by a nation outside the Americas or by one American nation against another. In the event of an attack, the signers of the treaty agreed to consult together to take action. Each nation reserved the right of decision in respect to implementing its obligation. If war was decided upon, only those who had so voted were bound by the decision.

The next regional pact to be formed was the Western Union in Europe. What could prevent Stalin from following Hitler's method of taking on one country at a time? What if in a mood of revolutionary exaltation Soviet Russia was to decide to push westward toward the Atlantic? No single nation would be able to defend itself against an onslaught of the combined armies of Soviet Russia and her satellites.

Another serious problem confronting Western Europe was the need for economic rehabilitation. In these days of mass production requiring a huge market, individual nations, each competing with the other, can hardly hope to succeed. None would be able to rise to its feet, even with the lavish aid of the Marshall Plan, because mass production requires a larger unit than the individual nation of Western Europe; its absence in that region accounts for much of the economic ills before and after the war. But a united Western Europe would create the large economic unit essential to economic recovery. That is the reason why the Marshall Plan was predicated on a united effort of its beneficiaries to second American aid by economic cooperation. Europe, or at least the Western "fringe," must unite or perish from poverty and from military weakness. Its 300,000,000 highly industrialized, highly skilled people, having immense natural resources, would then be more than a match for backward Russia. For these reasons the utopia of yesterday, a united Western Europe, became the necessity of today and the salvation of tomorrow.

In 1948, Britain, France, and the Benelux countries (Belgium,

Netherlands, and Luxemburg) entered into a pact called the Western Union. It was something startlingly new, nothing less than the first practical step to realize the dream of establishing a United States of Europe. These five nations agreed (1) to "fortify and preserve the principles of democracy, personal freedom and political liberty, the constitutional traditions and the rule of law which are their common heritage"; (2) to coordinate their policies in commerce, industry, and finance; (3) to arbitrate all conflicts that may arise between them; (4) to cooperate in foreign affairs by forbidding any member of the Union to join any coalition directed against any other member; and (5) to organize for common defense by coordinating their armed forces against an attack from any quarter. Europe was now bisected into Eastern and Western blocs. In 1949, the Western Union was merged with the North Atlantic Pact,[6] thereby bringing America into the regional defense system of Western Europe.

Both the democratic West and the totalitarian East have resorted to the system of regional pacts. The balance of power is no more, and one world is not yet; hence the regional pact is accepted by the New World in the Rio treaty, and by the Old World in the North Atlantic treaty and in the Eastern bloc of Soviet Russia and her satellites. This system, novel in the history of diplomacy, has been devised to prevent the outbreak of a third world war by organizing powerful defense systems. If successful, regional defense will mark the intermediate step between the international anarchy of the balance of power and a truly authoritative United Nations to establish universal peace. The abolition of war remains the unfinished business of the mid-twentieth century.

[6] See pp. 380–381.

Chapter 12. The Unfinished Task

During the first half of the twentieth century, problems that had long existed were posed before mankind in the highly dramatic manner of world wars and world revolutions. These problems, dealing chiefly with the abolition of poverty, of imperialism, and of wars, were world problems. They now demand world solutions, both immediate and drastic, or at least definite plans for a new and better world order. Otherwise, the existing system will undergo continual convulsion, and the world will slump into a new "dark ages." With the solution of these problems would go the fears that have haunted the life of man from the beginning of history: fear of starvation for lack of a means of livelihood; fear of the foreigner coming to rule and to exploit; and fear of the sword hanging by a thread over each nation.

At all times the march of civilization has been characterized by extending the limits of the possible. The impossible has continually receded with the advance of science and technology and with the spread of political and social democracy. Yet what has been called the "cultural lag," or the disproportion between the progress of science and technology, on the one hand, and that of social and political organization, on the other, has continued. This disproportion can be diminished, and even abolished, by a new and better social and political order that would use the physical power now at hand to advance the greatest good of the greatest number. So widespread is this view that there now exists a far greater consensus of opinion regarding the need of solving world problems than ever before in history. Because of the spread of revolutionary discontent, mankind cannot wait for the long-term trends of history to evolve solutions, but has to proceed with conscious purpose to create the "great society" of the future.

In some favored lands, notably America, Britain, and France, changes have taken place that anticipate the world of tomorrow. These industrially advanced nations aim to solve the problems of poverty by increasing production and by distributing the national wealth more equitably. And they have adopted comprehensive, far-reaching systems of social services with the object of giving security to the workers against the economic hazards of life. Truly remarkable is the great productivity and the high standard of living in America. If any nation can be said to have abolished poverty, at least in its abject form, that nation is America. Equally remarkable is the British system of social services that gives to the individual the highest degree of security in the world. Long class-bound socially and economically, Britain is now further along the road toward economic equality than any other country. France has followed Britain's lead, but cautiously and hesitatingly. Her productive capacity is smaller, and her system of social services more modest than that of Britain.

Regarding the problem of colonial imperialism, America, Britain, the Netherlands, and France have devised methods of solving it peacefully. America set a notable example when, freely and of her own accord, she granted independence to the Philippines. And when India, the largest and most important of all colonies, became virtually an independent nation, the structure of colonial imperialism everywhere slumped on its very foundations. This great reform was accomplished as a result of free and friendly negotiations between British and Indians. The Netherlands, following the example of Britain, took a great step when they granted self-government to Indonesia. France has devised, in the French Union, a similar method of substituting cooperation for domination in relation to her colonies. As a consequence of these reforms by the democratic nations, colonial imperialism has virtually disappeared from Asia and the East

Indies. It persists only in the backward parts of Africa, and even there it has been considerably modified in the interest of the natives.

Regarding the problem of war, most important of all problems confronting mankind in the mid-twentieth century, the attitude of America, Britain, and France is entirely clear. All three have given full and complete evidence of their willingness to do everything in their power to promote the peace of the world. Soon after the Second World War, they virtually disbanded their armies, and drastically reduced their naval and air forces. They proposed the formation, with Soviet Russia, of a four-power pact to prevent future German aggression. They gave full support to the United Nations and showed a willingness to curb the veto power of the permanent members of the Security Council. They proposed plans for the general reduction of armaments and for the internationalization of atomic energy. Their good faith in making these proposals was evidenced by their readiness to implement them.

However, no one nation and no combination of nations, no matter how powerful, can solve these problems. They can be solved only by the cooperative efforts of all the nations in the world. For over a century, marked tendencies toward a unified world order have appeared. Commerce and industry have created bonds of economic interdependence between nations. Democracy, both political and social, has advanced the idea and the practice of universal freedom. The League of Nations and the United Nations have endeavored to lay the foundations of world security. The decline of colonial imperialism has diminished in many regions the inequalities that had existed between races and nations. The benefits of the great advances in science and technology, made by the Western nations, can now be used to quicken the pace of progress of backward peoples. The great savings that would come from a reduction in the cost of armaments could be turned into channels of social and economic betterment if wars were eliminated and a united world established. And the prospects seemed bright after the Second World War when Germany and Japan were eliminated as powers to be reckoned with in world affairs. These militarist nations were dedicated to war, which they regarded both as a supreme good in itself and as the chief instrument of national policy. As long as Germany and Japan played leading roles in international affairs, their influence always made for war. With their complete defeat, peace efforts would no longer encounter the opposition of powerful nations ever-ready to draw the sword.

But the one world, visualized after the Second World War, has vanished. And it is Soviet Russia that bears the chief responsibility for dashing to the ground all hopes for world unity. True to their Marxist-Leninist faith the Russians are profoundly convinced that communism and capitalism cannot live in the same world; sooner or later these two must grapple to the very death. For this reason, Soviet Russia has effectively nullified all efforts of the Western democracies to bring about world unity. Their proposals to form a four-power pact against Germany, to strengthen the United Nations, to reduce armaments, and to internationalize atomic energy came to naught. On the contrary, Soviet Russia has made every effort to prepare for what she considers an inevitable conflict. She has set the pace of rearmament which the Western democracies have been obliged to follow in order to safeguard their very existence. An armament race of the most portentous kind is now proceeding fast and furiously, heightened by the dread of atomic warfare.

The cold war between Soviet Russia and the Western democracies, ironically enough, is fought most bitterly on the field dedicated to a peaceful one world. The United Nations has become the daily scene of battles between the two worlds. That body, instead of solving international problems, has been used by the Russians as a means of intensifying them. Never before has the world been divided so sharply into two hostile camps.

This was dramatically shown in the crisis created by the Russian satellite, North Korea. Suddenly, on June 25, 1950, an army of North Koreans invaded South Korea, determined to conquer that democratic country for communism. This armed invasion was a direct violation of the Charter of the United Nations outlawing aggression. To meet this challenge the Security Council demanded a cessation of hostilities and the withdrawal by North Korea of her armed forces. North Korea refused.

The United Nations was now galvanized into prompt and vigorous action. Acting under a mandate from the Security Council, President Truman, supported by an almost unanimous Congress, ordered American armed forces to give aid to South Korea. He further ordered these forces to prevent any attack by Communist China on Formosa, which he declared would threaten the security of the Pacific area. Britain promptly placed her Pacific fleet under American command. The Security Council then voted a resolution condemning the government of North Korea for its refusal to obey the order to withdraw its armed forces and recommended to the members of the United Nations that they furnish "such assistance to the Republic of Korea as may be necessary to repel the armed attack." Another resolution of the Security Council requested the member nations to place their armed forces at the disposal of a unified command. America was requested to designate the commander of this new United Nations army. General MacArthur was so designated. This army was to fly the United Nations flag along with the flags of the participating nations. For the first time in history an international army appeared acting under a world authority. Soviet Russia openly supported North Korea, boycotted the Security Council, and denounced the latter's action and that of the United States.

With the ever-present threat to their democratic way of life, the Western powers must be ever ready to defend it, backed by a united people. For this reason they are making strenuous efforts to solve for themselves the problems of poverty, of discrimination, and of colonialism. For if ever they are called to undergo the trial of battle it must be with a clear conscience. Otherwise they will enter the conflict weakened by the divided loyalties of their people.

An old world is dying and a new world is struggling to be born. That is the vital meaning of the wars and revolutions of the first half of the twentieth century. It is, therefore, of the greatest importance for the present generation not to expend any effort in defending what is already dying. It should, however, exert all possible effort to maintain intact those values bequeathed by the past that continue the "chain of being" of Western civilization. Of these values the most precious are individual freedom and self-government, won as a result of wars and revolutions in the past. Any violation of these values is bound to vitiate all the freedoms and all the securities thus far attained. Only on the rock of democracy can a free one world be built.

Bibliography

GENERAL: J. C. Roucek (ed.), *Contemporary Europe* (1947); Walter C. Langsam, *The World since 1914* (1940); F. Lee Benns, *Europe since 1914* (1949); Geoffrey Bruun, *The World in the Twentieth Century* (1950); Robert Ergang, *Europe in Our Time: 1914 to the Present* (1948); G. D. H. Cole, *The Intelligent Man's Guide to the Post-War World* (1947); E. P. Hanson, *New Worlds Emerging* (1949); E. H. Carr, *The Twenty Years Crisis* (1939); C. L. Becker, *How New Will the Better World Be?* (1944); Kurt London, *Backgrounds of Conflict* (1945); J. A. Schumpeter, *Capitalism, Socialism, and Democracy* (1947); A. C. Ewing, *The Individual, the State and World Government* (1947); Eric Fischer, *The Passing of the European Age* (1948); Feliks Gross (ed.), *European Ideologies* (1948); and Hans Kohn, *The Twentieth Century* (1949).

CHAPTER 2

CAPITALISM AND THE TRANSITION FROM A LIBERAL TO A PLANNED ECONOMY: John A. Hobson, *Evolution of Modern Capitalism* (1926); A. A. Berle and G. C. Means, *The Modern Corporation and Private Property* (1933); W. L. Thorp (ed.), *Economic Problems in a Changing World* (1939); R. A. Brady, *Business as a System of Power* (1943); W. Loucks and J. W. Hart, *Comparative Economic Systems* (1943); L. Baudin, *Free Trade and Peace* (1939); H. C. Simons, *Economic Policy for a Free Society* (1948); L. von Mises, *Human Action: A Treatise on Economics* (1949); C. E. Ayres, *The Theory of Economic Progress* (1944) and *The Divine Right of Capital* (1946); James Burnham, *The Managerial Revolution* (1941); Lewis Corey, *The Crisis of the Middle Class* (1935); Emil Lederer, *The Middle Class* (1937); Harold G. Moulton, *Controlling Fac-*

tors in Economic Development (1949); Arthur R. Burns, *The Decline of Competition* (1936); A. F. Lucas, *Industrial Reconstruction and the Control of Competition* (1937); R. Liefman, *Cartels, Concerns, and Trusts* (1932); David Lynch, *The Concentration of Economic Power* (1946); G. W. Stocking and M. W. Watkins, *Cartels or Competition* (1948); R. A. Brady, *The Rationalization Movement in German Industry* (1933); D. Warriner, *Combines and Rationalization in Germany* (1931); H. W. Laidler, *Concentration of Control in American Industry* (1931); H. W. Macrosty, *The Trust Movement in British Industry* (1907); L. S. Lyon *et al., Government and Economic Life,* 2 vols. (1939–1940); Arthur Salter, *Recovery* (1932); A. H. Hansen, *Economic Stabilization in an Unbalanced World* (1932); Eugene Staley, *World Economy in Transition* (1939); J. B. Condliffe, *The Reconstruction of World Trade* (1940) and *The Commerce of Nations* (1950); F. Delaisi, *Political Myths and Economic Realities* (1927); Herbert Feis, *The Changing Pattern of International Economic Affairs* (1940); W. F. Bruck, *Social and Economic History of Germany from William II to Hitler, 1888–1938* (1938); A. E. Kahn, *Great Britain in the World Economy* (1946); Lewis L. Lorwin, *Economic Consequences of the Second World War* (1941) and *Time for Planning* (1945); N. S. Buchanan and F. A. Lutz, *Rebuilding the World Economy: America's Role in Foreign Trade and Investment* (1947); C. A. Hickman *et al., World Economic Problems* (1947); Geoffrey Crother, *The Economic Reconstruction of Europe* (1948); Barbara Ward, *The West at Bay* (1948); Lionel Robbins, *Economic Planning and International Order* (1937); T. H. O'Brien, *British Experiments in Public Ownership and Control* (1938); Lincoln Gordon, *The Public Corporation in Britain* (1938); Seymour E. Harris (ed.), *The New Economics* (1947); Seymour E. Harris, *Economic Planning* (1949); E. F. M. Durbin, *Problems of Economic Planning* (1949); F. A. Hayek, *The Road to Serfdom* (1944); L. R. Klein, *The Keynesian Revolution* (1947); and G. E. Hoover (ed.), *Twentieth Century Economic Thought* (1949).

CHAPTER 3

PROGRESS OF POLITICAL DEMOCRACY: A. F. Hattersley, *A Short History of Democracy* (1930); C. D. Burns, *Democracy* (1929); R. H. Tawney, *Equality* (1931); H. J. Laski, *Democracy in Crisis* (1933); C. N. Callender (ed.), "The Crisis of Democracy," *Annals of the American Academy of Political and Social Science* (1933); John A. Hobson, *Democracy and a Changing Civilization* (1934); R. Bassett, *The Essentials of Parliamentary Democracy* (1935); J. S. Fulton and C. L. Morris, *In Defense of Democracy* (1935); M. Ascoli and F. Lehmann (eds.), *Political and Economic Democracy* (1937); H. F. Armstrong, *We or They* (1937); C. E. Merriam, *The New Democracy and the New Despotism* (1939); Ernest Barker, *Reflections on Government* (1942); D. Bryn-Jones, *Toward a Democratic New Order* (1945); A. D. Lindsay, *The Modern Democratic State* (1947); H. Lauterpacht, *An International Bill of Rights of Man* (1945); "To Secure These Rights," *Report of the President's Committee on Civil Rights* (1947); A. N. Holcombe, *Human Rights in the Modern World* (1948); L. Stapleton, *The Design of Democracy* (1949); and *Human Rights. Comments and Interpretations, a* symposium edited by UNESCO, with an introduction by Jacques Maritain.

CHAPTER 4

PROGRESS OF SOCIAL DEMOCRACY: Sidney and Beatrice Webb, *Industrial Democracy* (1920); Gilbert Slater, *Poverty and the State* (1930); H. U. Faulkner, *The Quest for Social Justice* (1931); C. W. Pipkin, *Social Politics and Modern Democracies,* 2 vols. (1931); Norman J. Ware, *Labor in Modern Industrial Society* (1935); Lewis Corey, *The Unfinished Task: Economic Reconstruction for Democracy* (1942); William H. Beveridge, *Full Employment in a Free Society* (1945); David McC. Wright,

Democracy and Progress (1948); "The Gift of Freedom," *United States Department of Labor* (1949); L. G. Chiozza-Money, *Insurance Against Poverty* (1912); Carlton J. H. Hayes (ed.), *British Social Politics* (1913); William H. Beveridge, *Unemployment* (1930) and *Social Insurance and Allied Services* (1942); R. H. Tawney, *The British Labor Movement* (1925); Helen F. Hohman, *The Development of Social Insurance and Minimum Wage Legislation in Great Britain* (1933); J. H. Richardson, *Industrial Relations in Great Britain* (1938); G. D. H. Cole, *A Short History of the British Working-class Movement, 1789–1937*, 3 vols. (1938); Francis Williams, *Socialist Britain* (1949); D. J. Saposs, *The Labor Movement in Post-war France* (1930); Lewis L. Lorwin, *Syndicalism in France* (1914); Henry W. Ehrmann, *French Labor from Popular Front to Liberation* (1947); W. Oualid, "National Insurance in France," *Journal of Political Economy* (June, 1934); W. H. Dawson, *Social Insurance in Germany* (1912); C. W. Guillebaud, *The Works Council* (1928); N. Reich, *Labor Relations in Republican Germany* (1938); H. A. Millis and R. E. Montgomery, *Organized Labor* (1945); F. R. Dulles, *Labor in America* (1949); and David Lasser, "Labor and World Affairs," *Foreign Policy Association Reports* (November, 1949).

CHAPTER 5

NATIONALISM: PAST, PRESENT, AND FUTURE: Carlton J. H. Hayes, *Essays on Nationalism* (1926) and *The Historical Evolution of Modern Nationalism* (1931); Hans Kohn, *The Idea of Nationalism* (1944); "Nationalism," *A Report by a Study Group of Members of the Royal Institute of International Affairs* (1939); F. Hertz, *Nationality in History and Politics* (1944); E. Barker, *National Character and the Factors in Its Formation* (1948); Feliks Gross (ed.), *European Ideologies* (1948); R. Rocker, *Nationalism and Its Relation to Culture* (1937); "The World Trend toward Nationalism," *American Academy of Political and Social Science Supplement* (1934); A. Cobban, *National Self-determination* (1948); W. Friedman, *The Crisis of the*

National State (1943); J. Braunthal, *The Paradox of Nationalism* (1946); Otto Bauer, *Die Nationalitätenfrage und die Sozialde-mokratie* (1924); Hans Kohn, *Nationalism in the Soviet Union* (1933) and *A History of Nationalism in the East* (1929); W. C. Buthman, *The Rise of Integral Nationalism in France* (1939); J. S. Roucek, *The Workings of the Minorities System under the League of Nations* (1929); Oscar Janowsky, *Nationalities and National Minorities* (1945); J. B. Schechtman, *European Popu-lation Transfers, 1939–1945* (1946); and E. M. Kulischer, *Europe on the Move* (1948).

CHAPTER 6

COLONIAL IMPERIALISM: ITS DECLINE AND FALL: Mary E. Townsend and Cyrus H. Peake, *European Colonial Expansion* (1941); Parker T. Moon, *Imperialism and World Politics* (1926); *The Colonial Problem,* Royal Institute of International Affairs (1937); John A. Hobson, *Imperialism* (1949); Nathaniel Peffer, *The White Man's Dilemma* (1927); L. Woolf, *Imperialism and Civilization* (1928); V. I. Lenin, *Imperialism, the Highest Stage of Capitalism* (1933); Vernon McKay, "Empires in Transition," *Foreign Policy Association Reports* (May, 1947); E. M. Winslow, *The Pattern of Imperialism* (1948); A. Viallate, *Economic Im-perialism and International Relations* (1923); A. K. Weinberg, *Manifest Destiny* (1935); Grover Clark, *The Balance Sheets of Imperialism* (1936) and *A Place in the Sun* (1936); Brooks Emeny, *The Strategy of Raw Materials* (1934); Eugene Staley, *Raw Materials in Peace and War* (1937); *Raw Materials and Colonies,* Royal Institute of International Affairs (1936); Lord Hailey, *Future of Colonial Peoples* (1944); and Owen Latti-more, *The Situation in Asia* (1949).

CHAPTER 7

TOTALITARIANISM, A REVOUTIONARY REPUDIATION OF DEMOCRACY. Communism: M. Eastman (ed.), *Capital, the Communist Manifesto and other Writings by Karl Marx*

(1932); G. D. H. Cole, *What Marx Really Meant* (1934); S. F. Markham, *A History of Socialism* (1931); A. Rosenberg, *A History of Bolshevism,* translated from the German, by I. F. D. Morrow (1934); Harold J. Laski, *Communism* (1927); Joseph Stalin, *Leninism,* 2 vols. (1933); J. Strachey, *The Theory and Practice of Communism* (1936); J. Somerville, *Soviet Philosophy* (1946); R. N. C. Hunt, *The Theory and Practice of Communism* (1950); and S. N. Harper and R. Thompson, *The Government of the Soviet Union* (1950).

Fascism: A. Cobban, *Dictatorship* (1939); Feliks Gross (ed.), *European Ideologies* (1948); Benito Mussolini, "The Political and Social Doctrine of Fascism," *International Conciliation* (January, 1935); H. Finer, *Mussolini's Italy* (1935); G. Salvemini, *Under the Axe of Fascism* (1936); W. G. Welk, *Fascist Economic Policy* (1938); M. Ascoli and A. Feiler, *Fascism for Whom?* (1938); F. L. Schuman, *The Nazi Dictatorship* (1936); Louis L. Snyder, *Race: A History of Modern Ethnic Theories* (1939); C. W. Guillebaud, *The Social Policy of Nazi Germany* (1941); Rohan Butler, *The Roots of National Socialism* (1942); F. L. Neumann, *Behemoth* (1942); and Otto Nathan and Milton Fried, *The Nazi Economic System* (1944).

CHAPTER 8

GERMANY'S BID FOR WORLD DOMINION: THE TWO WORLD WARS: W. H. Dawson, *The Evolution of Modern Germany* (1919); T. Veblen, *Imperial Germany and the Industrial Revolution* (1915); W. Ebenstein, *The German Record* (1945); Louis L. Snyder, *From Bismarck to Hitler* (1935); W. M. McGovern, *From Luther to Hitler* (1941); H. Quigley and R. T. Clark, *Republican Germany* (1928); R. T. Clark, *The Fall of the German Republic* (1935); S. H. Roberts, *The House That Hitler Built* (1937); F. W. Foerster, *Europe and the German Question* (1940); Konrad Heiden, *Der Fuehrer: Hitler's Rise to Power* (1944); and E. Röpke, *The Solution of the German Problem,* translated from the German by E. W. Dickes (1947).

CHAPTER 9

RUSSIA'S BID FOR WORLD REVOLUTION: W. H. Chamberlin, *The Russian Revolution,* 2 vols. (1935); John Maynard, *Russia in Flux* (1948); B. D. Wolfe, *Three Who Made a Revolution: Lenin, Trotsky, Stalin* (1948); David Shub, *Lenin* (1948); I. Deutscher, *Stalin* (1949); Michael Florinsky, *World Revolution and the U.S.S.R.* (1933), and *Toward an Understanding of the U.S.S.R.* (1939); W. H. Chamberlin, *Russia's Iron Age* (1934); L. E. Hubbard, *The Economics of Soviet Russia* (1939); A. Baykov, *The Development of the Soviet Economic System* (1947); David J. Dallin, *The Real Soviet Russia* (1945); Julian Towster, *Political Power in the U.S.S.R., 1917–1947* (1948); F. L. Schuman, *Soviet Politics at Home and Abroad* (1946); Martin Ebon, *World Communism Today* (1948); E. H. Carr, *The Soviet Impact on the Western World* (1946); David J. Dallin, *Russia and Post-war Europe* (1943); Vera M. Dean, *Russia: Menace or Promise* (1947); Max Beloff, *The Foreign Policy of Soviet Russia, 1929–1941,* 2 vols. (1947–1949); Historicus, "Stalin on Revolution," *Foreign Affairs* (January, 1949); Angelo Rossi, *A Communist Party in Action,* translated from the French by W. Kendall (1949); Walter Bedell Smith, *My Three Years in Moscow* (1949); and S. N. Harper and R. Thompson, *The Government of the Soviet Union* (1950).

CHAPTER 10

AMERICA'S BID FOR WORLD SECURITY: J. B. Rae and T. H. D. Mahoney, *The United States in World History* (1949); O. T. Barck Jr. and N. M. Blake, *Since 1900: A History of the United States in Our Times* (1947); L. M. Hacker, *American Problems Today* (1938); C. L. Becker, *The United States: An Experiment in Democracy* (1920); Harold J. Laski, *The American Democracy: A Commentary and an Interpretation* (1948); Gerald W. Johnson, *Our English Heritage* (1949); Herbert Croly, *The*

Promise of American Life (1909); T. V. Smith, *The American Philosophy of Equality* (1926) and *The Democratic Tradition in America* (1941); J. U. Nef, *The United States and Civilization* (1942); Ernest M. Patterson (ed.), "The United States and the Future," *Annals of the American Academy of Political and Social Science* (1943); Gunnar Myrdal, *An American Dilemma,* 2 vols. (1944); H. Finer, *America's Destiny* (1947); Henry B. Parkes, *The American Experience. An Interpetation of the History and Civilization of the American People* (1947); F. L. Paxon, *History of the American Frontier* (1924); G. M. Stephenson, *A History of American Immigration, 1820–1924* (1926); Norman J. Ware, *The Labor Movement in the United States, 1860–1895* (1929); F. R. Dulles, *Labor in America* (1949); Thomas C. Cochran, *The Age of Enterprise* (1942); J. T. Adams, *Our Business Civilization* (1929); "Recent Economic Changes in the United States," *Report of the Committee on Recent Economic Changes of the President's Conference on Unemployment,* 2 vols. (1929); Lewis Corey, *The Decline of American Capitalism* (1934); Stuart Chase, *The Economy of Abundance* (1934); *Big Business: Its Growth and Its Place,* Twentieth Century Fund (1937); A. H. Hansen, *America's Role in World Economy* (1945); George Soule, *Prosperity Decade* (1947); Broadus Mitchell, *Depression Decade* (1947); J. F. Dewhurst *et al., America's Needs and Resources* (1947); S. H. Slichter, *The American Economy* (1948); T. R. Carskadon and R. Modley, *U.S.A. Measure of a Nation* (1949); James A. Barnes, *Wealth of the American People: A History of Their Economic Life* (1949); A. N. Holcombe, *The Middle Class in American Politics* (1940); "Higher Education for American Democracy," *Report of the President's Commission on Higher Education* (1947); Dexter Perkins, *Hands Off: A History of the Monroe Doctrine* (1941); Walter Lippman, *U.S. Foreign Policy; Shield of the Republic* (1943); W. H. Chamberlin, *America: Partner in World Rule* (1945); J. C. Vincent *et al., America's Future in the Pacific* (1947); Vera M. Dean, *The United States and Russia* (1947); James F. Byrnes, *Speaking Frankly* (1947); J. S. Campbell, *The*

United States in World Affairs (1948); and Elmer Plischke, *Conduct of American Diplomacy* (1950).

CHAPTER 11

TOWARD A UNITED WORLD: A. Vagts, *The History of Militarism* (1937); Hans Speier and Alfred Kähler (eds.), *War in Our Time* (1939); Quincey Wright, *A Study of War,* 2 vols. (1942); L. L. Bernard, *War and Its Causes* (1944); B. Brodie (ed.), *The Atomic Weapon: Atomic Power and World Order* (1946); W. T. R. Fox, *The Super-powers* (1944); Robert Strausz-Hupé, *The Balance of Tomorrow* (1945); Emery Reeves, *Anatomy of Peace* (1945); Erno Whittmann, *History: A Guide to Peace* (1948); Vera M. Dean, *The Four Corner-stones of Peace* (1946); Harold Butler, *Peace or Power* (1947); Feliks Gross, *European Ideologies* (1948); Richard N. Coudenhove-Kalergi, *Pan-Europe* (1926); Albert Guérard, *Europe Free and United* (1945); Felix Morley, *The Society of Nations* (1932); Ely Culbertson, *The World Federation Plan* (1942); S. J. Hemleben, *Plans for World Peace through Six Centuries* (1943); A. Boyed (ed.), *United Nation's Handbook* (1946); L. M. Goodrich and C. Hambro, *The Charter of the United Nations* (1947); Crane Brinton, *From Many One* (1948); Herbert V. Evatt, *The United Nations* (1948); Ernest M. Patterson (ed.), "World Government," *Annals of the American Academy of Political and Social Science* (1949); and Vannevar Bush, *Modern Arms and Free Men* (1949).

Index